EQ5 SIMPLIFIED

An Easy Learning Guide By Fran Iverson Gonzalez

The Electric Quilt Company
419 Gould Street, Suite 2
Bowling Green, OH 43402

The Electric Quilt Company
419 Gould Street, Suite 2
Bowling Green, OH 43402-3047
419-352-1134
E-mail: sales@electricquilt.com
Web site: www.electricquilt.com

Credits

Editors:	Monica Vay, Jill Badenhop, Angie Maidment
Cover Design:	Jill Badenhop
Book Design:	Pam Brossia
Technical Help:	Ann Rutter

Quilt design shown on front cover designed by Fran Iverson Gonzalez.

Acknowledgements

My sincere thanks to:

Larry Gonzalez for his strong support, perfect logic, and endless patience.

Karen Gonzalez for her artistic sense, business sense, and sense of the ridiculous.

Betsy and **Sarah Meyer** for their delight in this art form and my contribution to it.

Carol and **Roger Miller** at Quilt University for their vision, flexibility, and professionalism.

The students at **Quilt University** for their friendship, determination, and insatiable desire to learn.

Craig Hamer at Hewlett-Packard for his generosity in sharing HP's excellent products.

Ethel Mecklem and **Jean Folkes** for their excitement, enthusiasm, and thorough testing of this tutorial. Any mistakes that remain are mine alone!

The entire **Electric Quilt Company 'crewe'** who knows how to start a parade and let the good times roll. Thank you, **Ann Rutter**, **Monica Vay**, **Pam Brossia**, **Angie Maidment**, and **Jill Badenhop** for your skillful editing and typesetting, and for being so very easy to please!

Introduction

Electric Quilt 5 (EQ5) is a very powerful, highly versatile computer program for creating, editing, coloring, saving, and printing original and traditional quilt patterns. With EQ5's wide range of flexible features and convenient tools, you can experiment easily with the unlimited possibilities of color and design.

In a perfect world, you could approach every quilt project without restrictions. In reality, however, there are practical limitations that you must consider when designing your quilts. These can include factors such as size, color, construction techniques, or fabric yardage.

EQ5 is the perfect tool for an imperfect world because you can use it to generate the full range of design possibilities, from quilts that satisfy your wildest creative desires to those that stay within your practical limits.

This tutorial presents many practical applications of EQ5's powerful design features. Working through these exercises will teach you how to use the program's tools to create your own uniquely personal quilt designs. There are also suggestions throughout the book that will simplify quilt construction and finishing.

EQ5 Simplified is divided into two parts and should be used in conjunction with the EQ5 manuals: *Getting Started* and the *EQ5 Design Cookbook*. **Part I** serves as an introduction to EQ5, while **Part II** assumes a working knowledge of EQ5's basic features, as reviewed in Part I.

Both sections are project-oriented and consist of a series of graduated exercises that should be completed in the order in which they are presented. The quilts in this book are original patterns that were developed specifically for use in this tutorial. They are designed to expand and strengthen your EQ skills.

There are many ways to accomplish specific tasks in EQ5, so experiment freely without limiting your approach to just those found here. With just a little practice, you will gain enough confidence to develop your own unique, innovative approach to computerized quilt design!

The Mouse

Throughout this tutorial, you will be instructed to click on various items with your mouse. Except where specified otherwise, you will always click with your *primary* mouse button.

- The *primary mouse button* on a right-handed mouse is the **left** button.
- The *primary mouse button* on a left-handed mouse is the **right** button. (A left-handed mouse must be selected in the Windows Control Panel.)
- The remaining button on either type mouse is the **secondary** button.

Table of Contents

Part I

Part II

EQ5

SIMPLIFIED PART I QUILTS

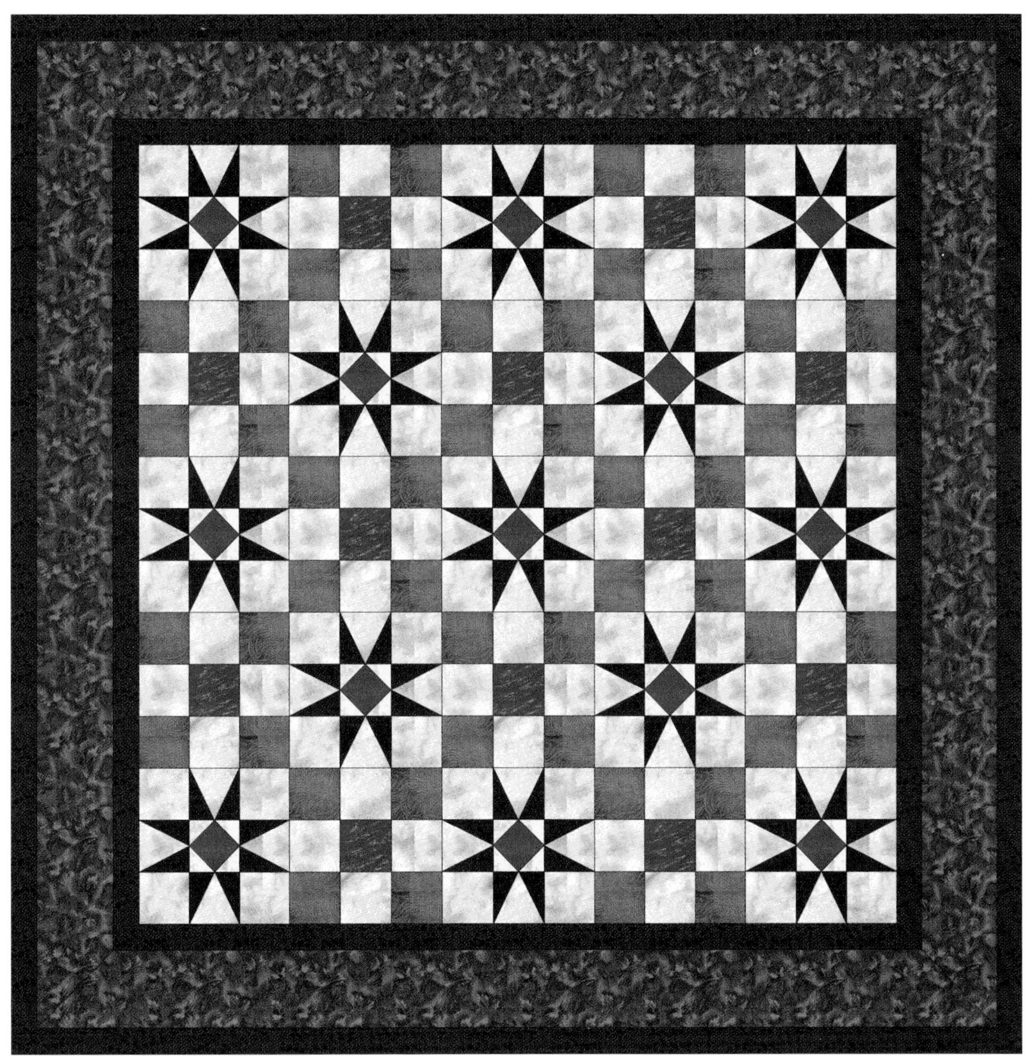

LESSON 1

NINE PATCH STAR

LESSON 2 STARS SQUARED

LESSON 3 TWO STEPPING STARS

LESSON 4 STAR-GAZING

Fabric Tips

Choosing Colors for Your Quilts

In my years of teaching, I have noticed that the fabric selection process is the one area that causes the greatest anxiety in quilters. Everyone has a sense of color, but relatively few trust their instincts when selecting fabrics for a quilt.

As you work through the lessons in this book, you will discover that EQ5 can simplify the fabric selection process considerably. The secret to success is a little confidence and a few simple guidelines. You can apply these important principles of color, value, and scale when selecting fabrics in a quilt shop or in EQ5:

- Choose one main color, a group of colors, or a particular fabric that contains colors that you like. If you select a group of colors, decide which color you will use as the main color in your quilt. If you choose a multi-colored fabric, determine which color in the print "reads" as the dominant color. If you prefer a structured approach to combining colors, refer to a Color Wheel for inspiration.

- Choose coordinating fabrics based on this main color, group of colors, or special fabric. These fabrics must vary noticeably in their relative lightness and darkness to each other. Generally, fabrics can be categorized in relation to each other: dark, dark/medium, medium, medium/light, and light. You can choose degrees of variation in between these distinctions, depending upon the number of fabrics that you need to incorporate into your particular quilt design.

- The fabrics that you choose for your quilt should contain prints of different scales and styles. For example, you can combine a small pin-stripe, a medium polka dot, a large floral, and a solid color or a tone-on-tone print that reads as a solid color.

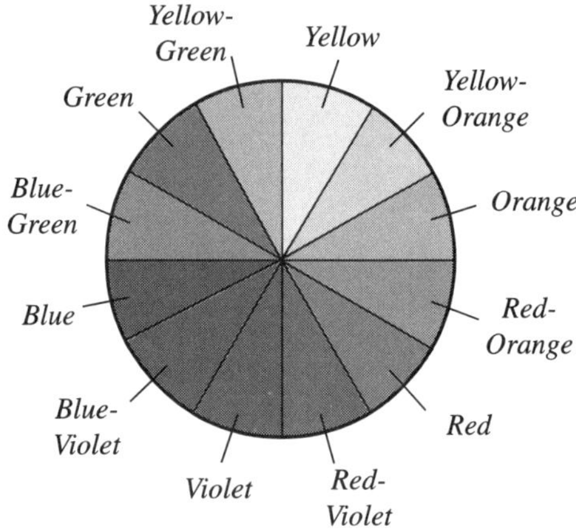

A Color Wheel with typical color location. Complementary colors are across from one another on the wheel (example: Yellow and Violet). Using these colors together will make both colors appear at their greatest intensity.

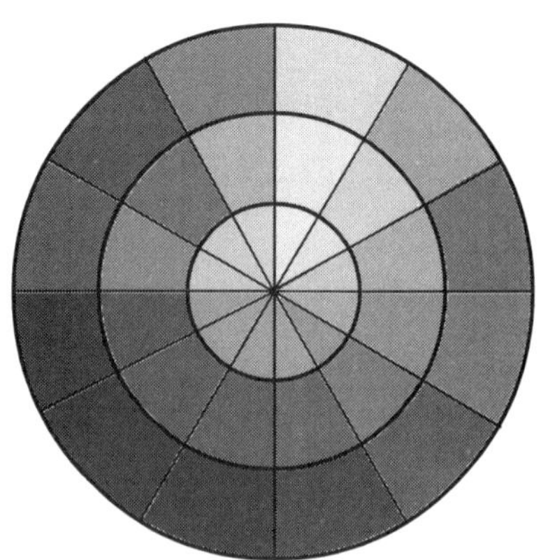

Color Wheel with light values (innermost ring), medium values (middle ring), and dark values (outermost ring). Actual color placement is same as the above illustration.

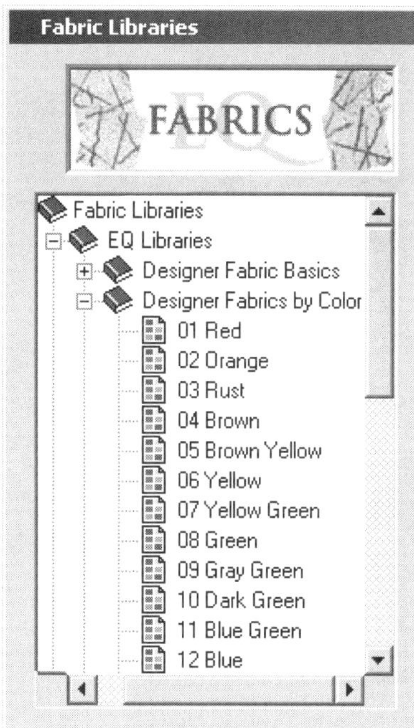

EQ5's Fabric Library allows you to view and copy different fabrics of the same colors. This is just one example of the many features offered in EQ5.

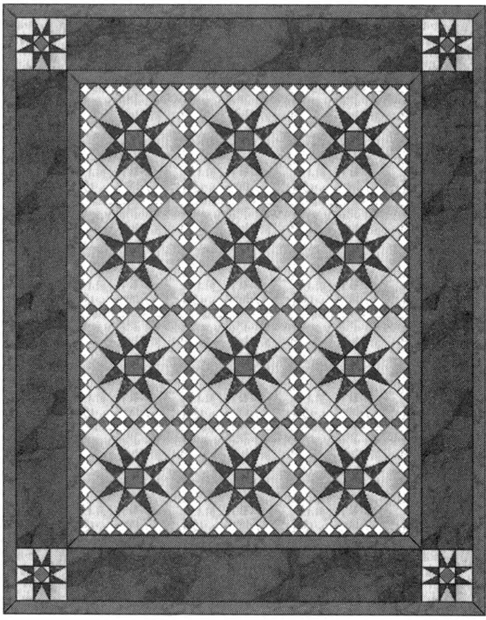

Stars Squared Quilt from Lesson 2

In EQ5, you can begin with a palette that you like and add more palettes and fabrics from the vast EQ libraries. You can also incorporate fabrics from EQ's add-on collections in STASH, your own scanned fabrics, or fabric swatches that you have downloaded from the Internet.

Color placement is another very important consideration when planning a quilt. Here are my general guidelines:

- Identify the most dominant design element in the quilt and create the highest contrast with these patches. In the Stars Squared quilt in Lesson Two, for example, the star points are the dominant design element. These points should show the highest contrast with the medium/light background fabric, so I used the fabric with the darkest value in these patches.

- Determine the next dominant design element in the layout and use a dark/ medium value in these patches. In Stars Squared, this is the chain that is formed by the placement of the Double Nine Patch blocks.

- Assign values of decreasing contrast to the remaining design elements. In Stars Squared, for example, I placed medium and medium/light fabrics in the center of the Star blocks. This contrast highlights the star without detracting from it.

I assigned the lightest value to the patches on either side of the chain that is formed by the Double Nine Patch blocks. The resulting contrast adds depth and emphasizes the chain, without competing with the Star blocks.

The background fabric is a medium/light value that adds an excellent contrast to the overall design.

• Border fabrics should frame and enhance, but not compete with, the pieced area of the quilt. You can see how I applied this principle in the Stars Squared borders.

You will discover other, more subtle, considerations for fabric placement as you create more complex quilt designs. For now, however, these simple guidelines will help to build your confidence with color placement.

When you are comfortable with these basic concepts, start experimenting on your own. In the Stars Squared quilt, for example, reverse the values and assign the lightest value to the star points and the darkest value to the background. The resulting contrast will have a different effect, but the impact will be the same. The star points will still dominate!

As you work through this tutorial, practice these fabric selection and color placement techniques. Sharpen your color sense by exploring the infinite possibilities that EQ5 gives you. Soon you will be very confident in your ability to achieve the effect that you want in your quilt designs!

Example of Stars Squared Quilt with values reversed.

Planning an EasyDraw™ Quilt

Lesson 1

Lesson 1 – Planning an EasyDraw™ Quilt

In this lesson, you will learn to use the basic tools of EQ5 by designing a Nine Patch Star quilt. You will learn to:

- *Start a new project*
- *Find Help*
- *Set up the Drawing Board*
- *Draw a block with the Grid tool*
- *Save your work*
- *Undo your last action*
- *Color a block*
- *Draw a block with the Line tool*
- *Delete a line in EasyDraw™*
- *Select a Horizontal layout*
- *Select the borders*
- *Set blocks into a Horizontal layout*
- *Color the borders*
- *View the Sketchbook*
- *Complete Notecards*
- *Print a quilt design*
- *Exit EQ5*

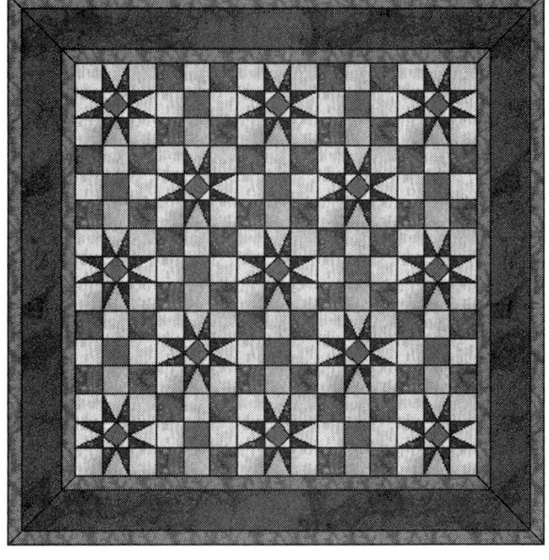

Nine Patch Star Quilt

Starting a New Project

When you run Electric Quilt 5, the opening screen will appear. There are two tabs on this opening screen: *Create a New Project* and *Open an Existing Project*.

Click on the Create a New Project tab and then type *Nine Patch* in the file name box.

Click on OK. Your project will now be identified by the name Nine Patch.

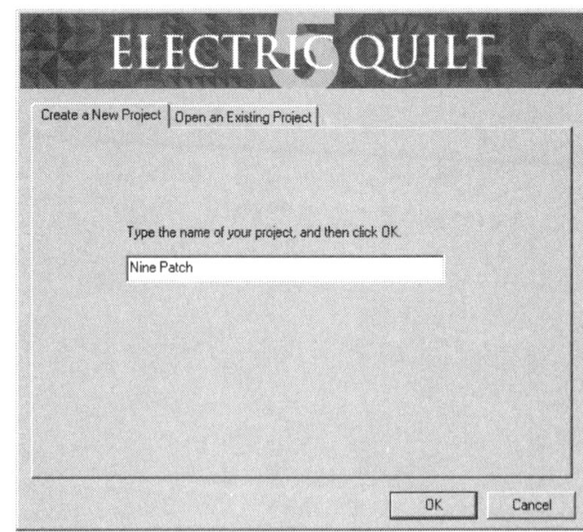

EQ5 Opening Screen

Tip

- **EQ5, like any Windows program, allows long file names that can include spaces. There are nine symbols that are invalid, however, and should never be used: / \ : * ? " < > |**

EQ5 will open to either the Quilt Worktable or the Block Worktable. Your screen may look different than the following figure, depending upon which worktable is open. Notice that the Nine Patch project file name is displayed in the upper-left corner of the screen.

Project File Name

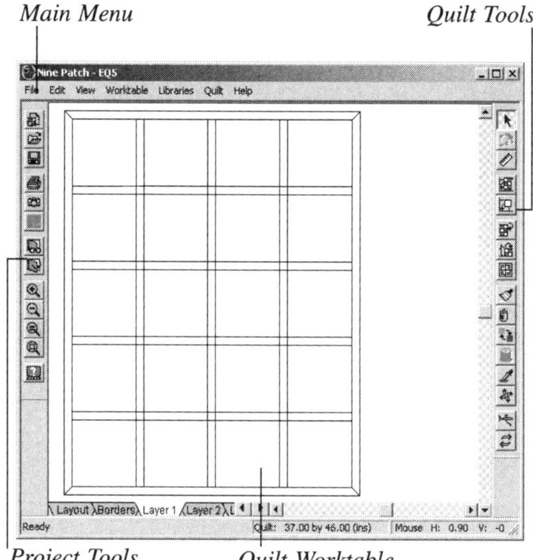

The main menu is across the upper-left portion of the screen, just below the EQ5 logo and your project file name. The Project Tools are displayed on the left side of the screen and one of the following is displayed on the right side of the screen: the *EasyDraw™ Tools*, the *PatchDraw Tools*, or the *Quilt Tools*.

To identify a tool in a toolbar, place the cursor over that button. EQ5 will display the tool name in a tooltip and describe its function on the lower-left of the screen.

Tooltip

Finding Help

Help is the last item in the main menu and is one of the most valuable resources for EQ5. Click on Help and then click on EQ Help in the Help menu. The EQ5 Help screen will open and you will be able to find information on any feature or function in EQ5. Click on the X in the upper-right corner of the screen to close Help.

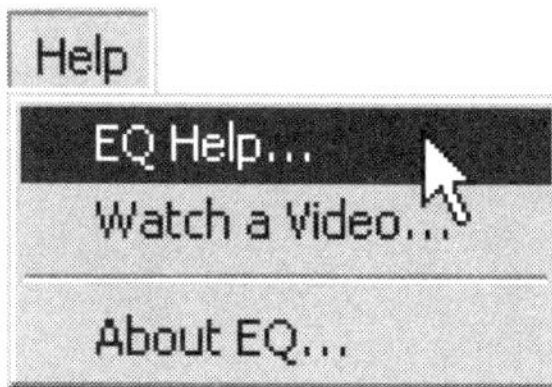

Click on Help and then click on EQ Help

Get into the habit of referring to the Help file whenever you have questions about EQ5! This is a very thorough Help file and it will answer most, if not all, of your questions.

Help Video Button

Tip

- **There are many wonderful resources that will support your use of EQ5! You have already discovered the EQ5 manuals and the Help file. There are also videos within the program that illustrate EQ5's basic design functions. The Help Video Button is the last tool on the main toolbar.**
- **The Electric Quilt Company maintains a dynamic website that offers valuable information, instructive projects, free downloads, excellent products, and continuous, interactive technical support. You can find the EQ website here: www.electricquilt.com**
- **There are many individual websites that support EQ products. Many of these websites are listed on the EQ site, including a very active mailing list for EQ users that is hosted by Planet Patchwork. Go here to enroll: www.planetpatchwork.com/Mailinglists.htm**
- **You will find a full range of EQ classes taught online by experienced faculty at Quilt University. www.quiltuniversity.com**

1

Drawing with the Grid Tool

Now you are ready to start designing the Nine Patch Star quilt! Your first task in designing any quilt is to collect or draw the blocks that you will use in the layout. Shown at the right is the Nine Patch block, the first design that you will draw for your Nine Patch Star quilt.

Nine Patch Block

As with any drawing procedure, you must first prepare the drawing board for the specific design that you want to draw. This is true even when you use a pencil and graph paper!

1 Click on Worktable in the main menu and then click on Work on Block.

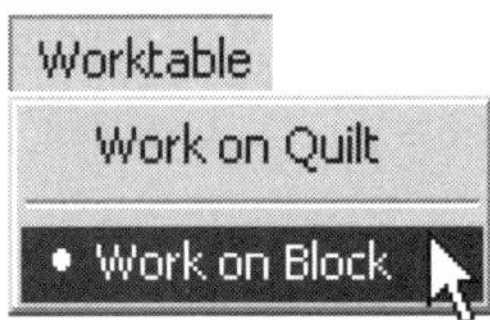

Step 1

2 Click on Block in the main menu and then move your cursor to New Block. In the menu that extends from New Block, click on EasyDraw™.

Step 2

Tip

- **You are choosing EasyDraw™ because it is the appropriate worktable for drawing pieced designs.**
- **PatchDraw is the appropriate worktable for drawing appliqué designs.**
- **The Overlaid worktable allows you to combine EasyDraw™ and PatchDraw designs together in one block. You will learn more about the PatchDraw and Overlaid worktables later in this tutorial.**

3 When the EasyDraw™ worktable opens, the Line tool will be activated automatically. A blank block will appear on your screen, together with the EasyDraw™ Tools, which will be displayed on the right of the worktable. There may be graph paper lines on your block.

4 Click on Block again and then click on Drawing Board Setup in the Block menu.

Step 4

5 Click on the General tab of the Drawing Board Setup dialog box and use the arrows to set the horizontal and vertical Snap to Grid Points to 18. Set the horizontal and vertical Block Size to 6. Click on OK.

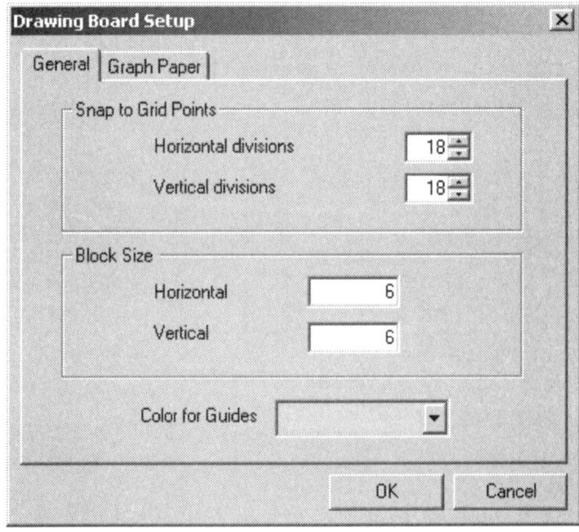

Step 5

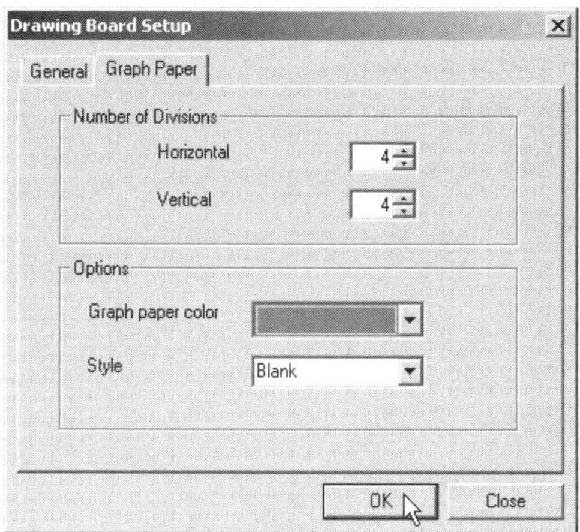

Step 6

Step 7 – Grid Tool and Grid Cursor

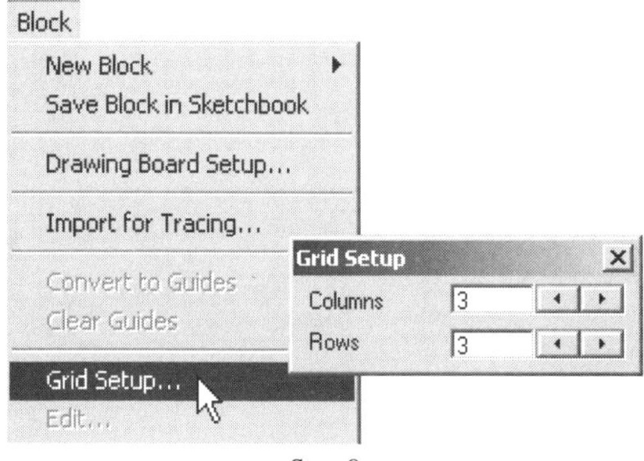

Step 8

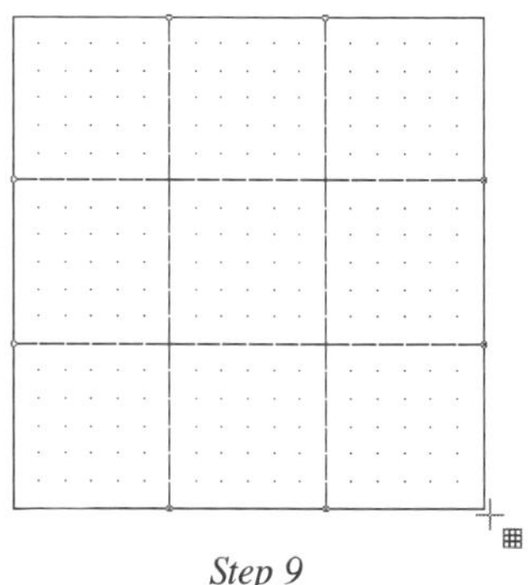

Step 9

Tip

- **The Snap to Grid Points establish a network of evenly-spaced dots on the block background. These dots help you to draw the design accurately because the lines that you draw will snap to these points. The Snap to Grid Points must be evenly divisible by the number of grid divisions in the block. To draw this Nine Patch, for example, you will use a 3 x 3 grid. Notice that the 18 x 18 Snap to Grid Points specified for this block can be divided evenly by 3.**
- **The Block Size dimensions that you designate here determine only the shape of the block, that is, whether the block displays on the worktable as a square or as a rectangle. You can print the block any size, no matter what size you specify in this dialog box.**
- **See the EQ5 manuals and the Help file for more information on the Drawing Board Setup.**

6 Click on the Graph Paper tab, and then under Options, click on the arrow next to Style. Click on Blank. Since you are not using Graph Paper, you can disregard the Number of Divisions. Click on OK.

7 Click on the Grid tool in the EasyDraw™ Tools. Notice that the cursor has changed to crosshairs with a small grid design.

8 Click on Block in the main menu and then click on Grid Setup in the Block menu. A small dialog box will appear in which you can designate the grid properties. Use the arrows in the Grid Setup box to set the Columns and Rows to 3. Click on the X to close the Grid Setup box.

Tip

- **You can also open the Grid Setup box by clicking on the small black square on the corner of the Grid tool.**

9 Position the center of the crosshairs cursor in any corner of the block outline. Click and, holding down the mouse button, drag the cursor diagonally across the block, releasing the button on the block outline in the opposite corner. This will create a Nine Patch design (3 x 3) on the worktable.

If you click and release the mouse button when the crosshairs are too far from the corner of the block, the grid will not extend to the edges of the block. If this happens, refer to the next section, "Undoing Your Last Action." After you undo the previous grid, redraw it, being careful to start and end on the corners of the block outline.

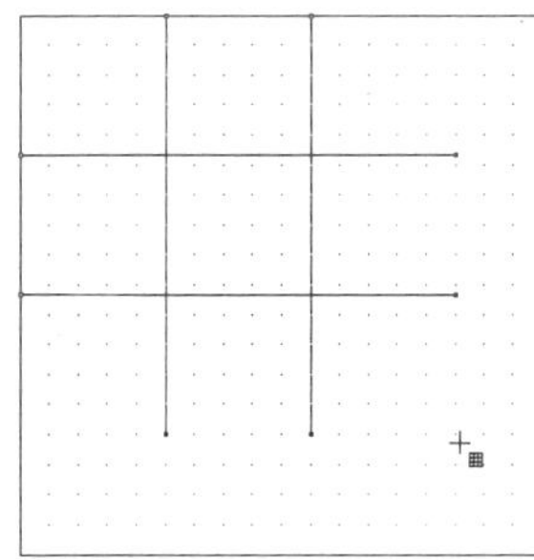

When the crosshairs are too far from the edge of the block, the grid will not extend all the way to the edge.

10 When you have successfully drawn the Nine Patch block, click on the Save in Sketchbook button in the Project Tools. This action saves the Nine Patch block in the project Sketchbook.

Step 10 – Save in Sketchbook

Tip

- **With the default settings, EQ5 will automatically save the project file any time the Sketchbook is changed.**
- **You can also save a block by clicking on Block in the main menu and then clicking on Save Block in Sketchbook in the Block menu. This action will save the block in the Sketchbook and in the project file.**
- **After drawing a design, you must save it to the Sketchbook before you can use it in a quilt layout.**
- **You cannot save when the Sketchbook is open.**
- **EQ5's one-step save is different from the two-step saving procedure required in EQ4. If you prefer to use the two-step save, uncheck the option in File, Preferences to automatically save project file when the Sketchbook changes. With this unchecked, you must Save in Sketchbook and then Save to store your designs permanently in the project file.**
- **By default, EQ5 will automatically back up your project every three minutes. This option can be changed in Preferences.**

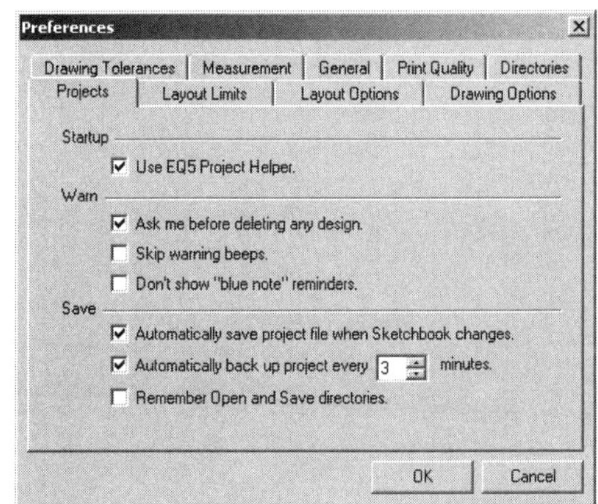

Advanced users can set saving options in the File menu under Preferences.

Undoing Your Last Action

In many cases, you can undo your last action in EQ5 by clicking on Edit in the main menu and then clicking on Undo in the Edit menu. You can also use the shortcut Ctrl+Z to undo. Some actions, such as a save, cannot be undone.

Depending upon the particular actions, you can sometimes undo several actions in reverse sequence by repeatedly using Edit / Undo or the shortcut Ctrl+Z.

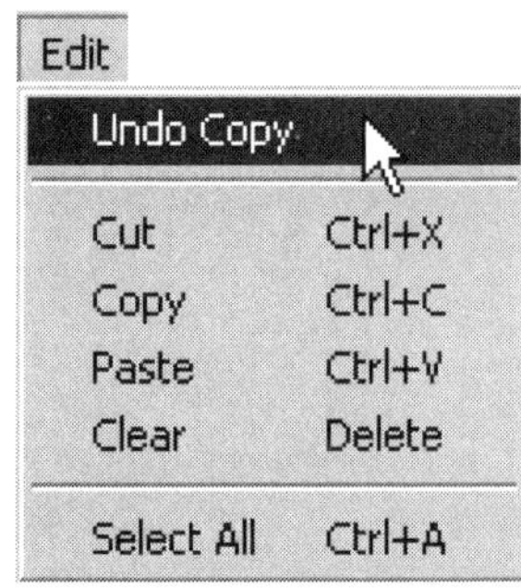

Undo your last action through the main menu.

Coloring a Block

Now that you have drawn and saved your Nine Patch block, you are ready to color your design! You will notice that there are folder-type tabs on the lower-left side of the EasyDraw™ worktable. One is labeled *EasyDraw™* and the other is labeled *Color*.

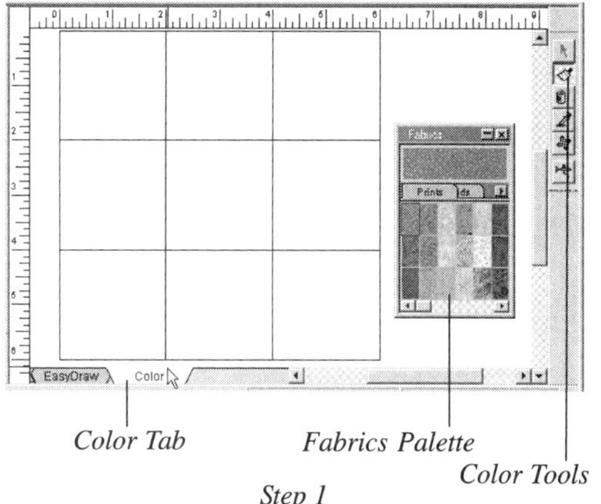

Step 1

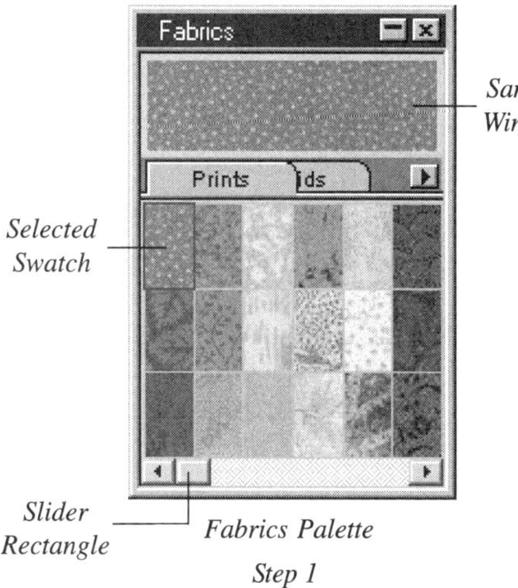

Step 1

1 Click on the Color tab on the lower-left side of the EasyDraw™ Worktable. The Fabrics palette will appear next to the Nine Patch block. Notice that the EasyDraw™ Tools have been replaced with the Color Tools. The Paintbrush tool is automatically engaged.

For this block, you will choose three different values: one for the four corner patches, one for the center patch, and another for the remaining patches.

The Fabrics palette contains a Prints tab, a Solids tab, and a sample window. The selected swatch on the open tab is framed in the sample window. The slider bar is below the swatches. Click and drag the slider rectangle to view all of the swatches on the displayed tab.

Tip

- **You can resize the Fabrics palette by positioning the cursor on the edge of the box. The cursor will change to arrows that you can then use to stretch the box in any direction. You can also move the Fabrics palette by clicking on the blue bar at the top of the palette and dragging it to a new location on the worktable.**

2 On either the Prints or the Solids tab, click on the swatch that you have chosen for the corner patches. This fabric will appear in the sample window. Click on the corner patches in the block to set the color.

3 Now choose a fabric for the center patch by clicking on a swatch in the palette. Click on the center of the Nine Patch to set the color.

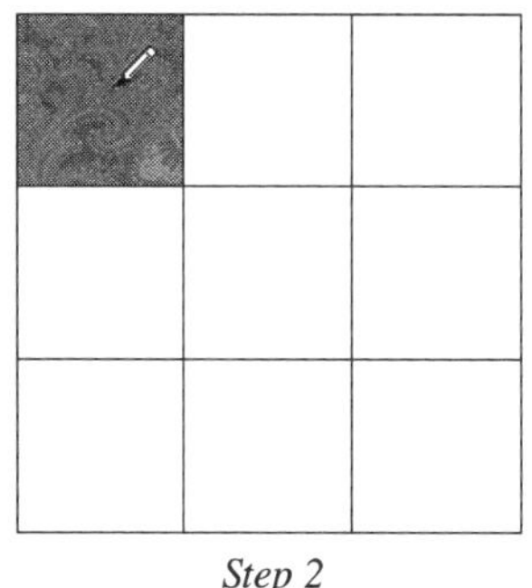

Step 2

1

4 Following the same procedure, color the four remaining patches. Color all patches, even if you use the color white.

Tip

- **To change the colors in a block, simply click on a new swatch in the palette and then click on the patches that you want to recolor. The new fabric will replace the previous fabric.**

5 Click on the Save in Sketchbook button to save the colored block in the Sketchbook and in the project file.

Step 4

Step 5 – Save in Sketchbook

Drawing with the Line Tool

Now you are ready for something a little more adventurous! You are going to use the Line tool to create a new block design called the Eight-Pointed Star.

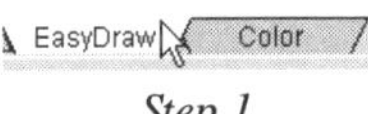

Step 1

Line Tool – This is automatically selected when you click on the EasyDraw™ Tab.

1 With the Nine Patch block still on the worktable, click on the EasyDraw™ tab to return to the drawing mode. The Line tool will be engaged automatically.

Tip

- **You might find it helpful to use the Rulers when you are drawing blocks. To put the Rulers on the worktable, click on View in the main menu and then click on Rulers so that it is checked. The Block Size that you specified in the Drawing Board Setup will determine the length of the rulers on the worktable.**

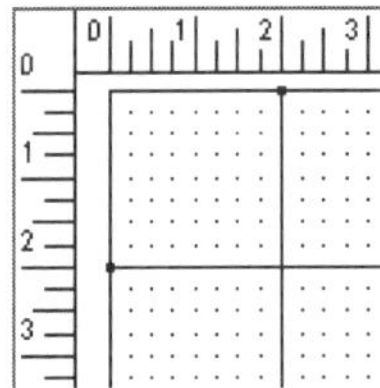

Rulers on the Worktable

2 Using the Line tool, add the star points to the Nine Patch block, as shown. Draw the lines by clicking on the point at which you want the line to begin, dragging the cursor to the end point of the line, and releasing the mouse button. If you want to delete a line, see the next section "Deleting a line in EasyDraw™."

3 Draw lines to form the center diamond in the Eight-Pointed Star design.

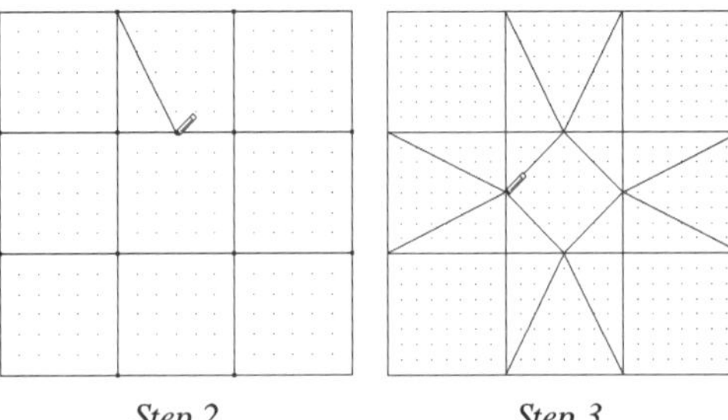

Step 2 *Step 3*

4 Click on the Color tab. With the Paintbrush tool, select a fabric in the palette for the center of the star and click on it to color.

Step 4

Paintbrush Tool – This is automatically selected when you click on the Color Tab.

5 Select a fabric for the star points and click on them to color.

Eight-Pointed Star Block

Step 8 – Save in Sketchbook

6 Select a fabric for the center triangles and click on them to color.

7 Select a fabric for the remaining patches and click on them to color.

8 Click on the Save in Sketchbook button to save the colored block in the Sketchbook and in the project file.

Deleting a Line in EasyDraw™

To delete a single line in a block drawing: Click on the Select tool and then click on the line to be deleted. The line will be marked with a break and surrounded by nodes. Press the Delete key on the keyboard to eliminate the line.

To delete several lines in a block simultaneously: Click on the Select tool and, holding down the Shift key, click on all unwanted lines. Press the Delete key to eliminate the lines.

To delete all the lines in a block: Click on Edit in the main menu and then click on Select All in the Edit menu. The entire drawing will be highlighted. Press the Delete key to erase all of the lines in the drawing.

Select Tool

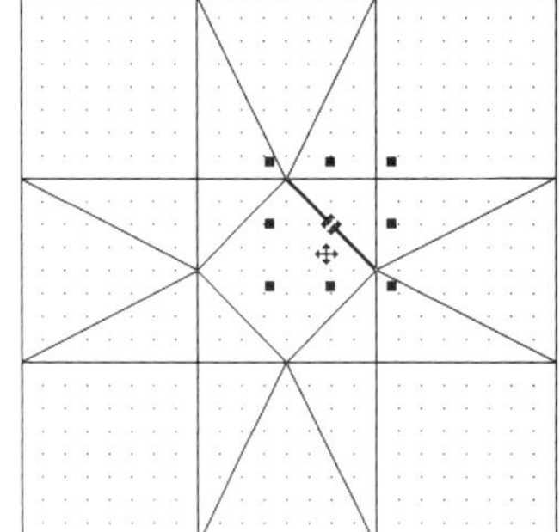

Deleting a Single Line

Tip

- **You can also use Cut or Clear in the Edit menu to delete selected lines in EQ5.**

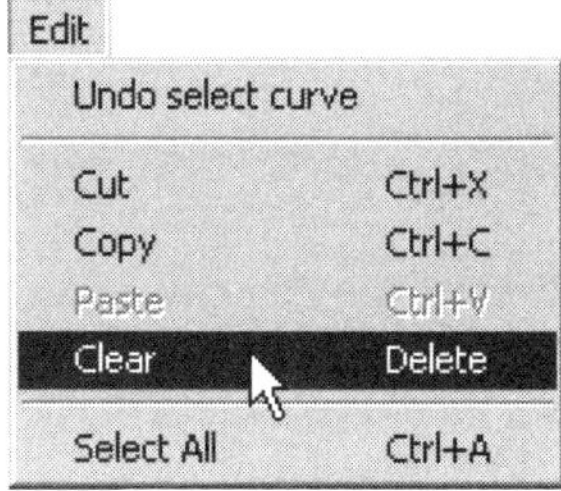

Tip – Deleting a Line

Selecting a Horizontal Layout

Your blocks are completed, so you can now establish the layout for your Nine Patch Star quilt!

1 Click on Worktable in the main menu and then click on Work on Quilt. The Quilt Worktable is now open. Notice that your right toolbar changed automatically when you selected Work on Quilt. These are the Quilt Tools.

Tip

- **Notice that the word *Quilt* replaced the word *Block* in the main menu. These two main menu items will change, depending upon whether you are working on a quilt design or a block design.**

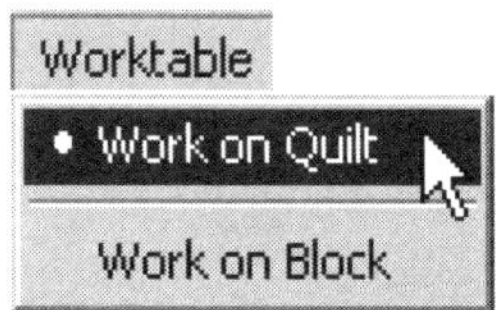

Step 1

1

2 Click on Quilt in the main menu and then click on New Quilt. A box will appear that lists the various quilt layouts that are available to you in EQ5. Click on Horizontal.

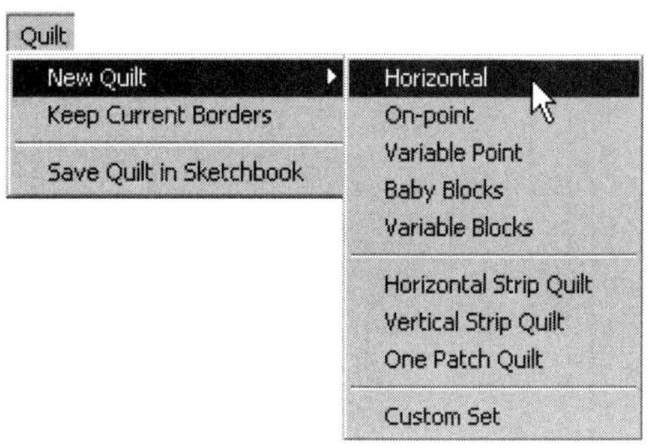

Step 2

3 Click on the Layout tab at the lower-left of the screen. Use the arrows and slider rectangles to set the following values in the Horizontal layout box:

Number of blocks:	Horizontal – 5 Vertical – 5
Size of blocks:	Width – 6.00 Height – 6.00
Sashing:	Width – 0.00 Height – 0.00
Sash border:	unchecked

Notice that the Quilt Tools and Save in Sketchbook are grayed out and not available to you when you are on the Layout tab.

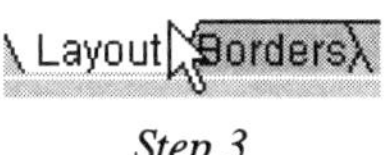

Step 3

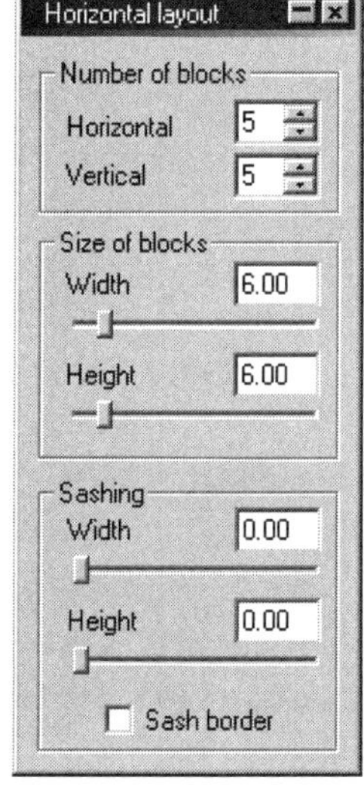

Step 3

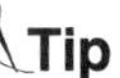**Tip**

- **To change the values by .25" increments, click to the left or to the right of the slider rectangles to decrease or increase the measurement.**
- **You can also click on the slider bar to select it and then use the keyboard arrow keys to adjust the values by .25" increments.**
- **You can change the nudge settings of these palette sliders under Layout Options in the Preferences dialog box. Please see the EQ5 manuals or the EQ Help file for more information.**

Selecting the Borders

Your blocks are drawn and your quilt layout is established. It's time to choose the border styles and sizes for your Nine Patch Star quilt!

1 Click on the Borders tab at the lower-left of the screen. A Borders box will appear. By default, every new quilt layout has one, one-inch mitered border that you can keep, modify, or remove.

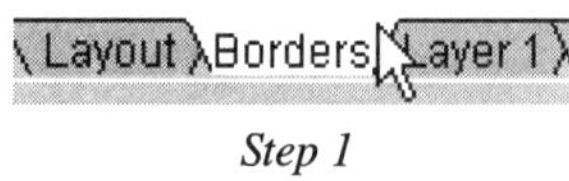

Step 1

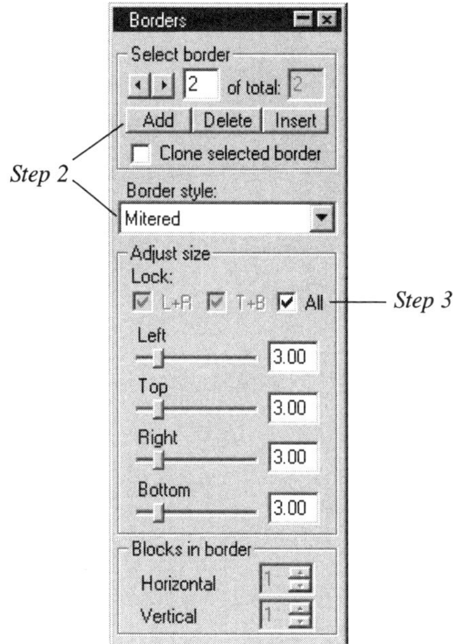

Borders Box

This first border is automatically selected when you click on the Borders tab. For the Nine Patch Star quilt that you are designing in this lesson, no changes are necessary to this default border.

2 Click on the Add button in the Borders box to add a second border. Click on the arrow below Border style to view the many border style options available to you in EQ5. Click on Mitered to select it.

3 Under Adjust size, choose Lock: All. This convenient feature ensures that all borders will be sized simultaneously. You can also lock together the top and bottom or left and right borders for resizing.

With all sides still locked, click and drag one of the slider rectangles to set all sides of this second border to 3.00. You can also highlight the current number on one border side and type in the new value. If you type in the value for one side with all borders locked, click on the slider rectangle for this side and the other border sides will adjust to the size of this one.

Tip

- **In EQ5, the quilt borders are always numbered from the center of the quilt on outward. The innermost border is border number one.**
- **To change the border measurements by .25" increments, click to the left or to the right of the slider rectangles to decrease or increase the measurement.**
- **You can also click on the slider bar to select it and then use the keyboard arrow keys to adjust the values by .25" increments.**
- **You can change the nudge settings of these box sliders under Layout Options in the Preferences dialog box. Please see the EQ5 manuals or the EQ Help file for more information.**
- **You can create a borderless quilt by setting all sides of the single default border to 0.00. You can also remove all borders by using the Delete button in the Borders box.**

4 Click on the Add button to add a third border. No changes are necessary because this border style is the default setting which is a one-inch, mitered border.

Notice that the Quilt Tools and Save in Sketchbook are grayed out and not available to you when you are on the Borders tab.

5 Click on the Layer 1 tab and Save in Sketchbook. The Quilt Tools are activated and your quilt size is displayed on the lower-right of the screen.

Tip

- **It's easy to adjust a border even after you have set designs into the quilt layout. With the quilt on the worktable, simply click on the Border tab and then click on the border that you want to change.**

  This border will be shaded and the box for that border will open. Change the values in the Borders box. Click on the Layer 1 tab and Save in Sketchbook.

Setting Blocks into a Horizontal Layout

You will now discover how the block designs will interact in the layout!

1 Click on the Set tool in the Quilt Tools. The Blocks palette will open on the worktable. Click on the Eight-Pointed Star block to select it. If you saved more than one coloring of the this block, use the arrows at the bottom of the Blocks palette to display the coloring that you want to set into the quilt layout.

Tip

- **The Blocks palette is the box on the Quilt Worktable that contains all of the designs and colorings that you saved in your Block Sketchbook.**
- **There are several tabs in the Blocks palette that you will explore later in this tutorial. These tabs are for storing blocks, motifs, stencils, embroidery designs, and pictures.**
- **Use the slider bar to view all of the designs in the Block palette.**

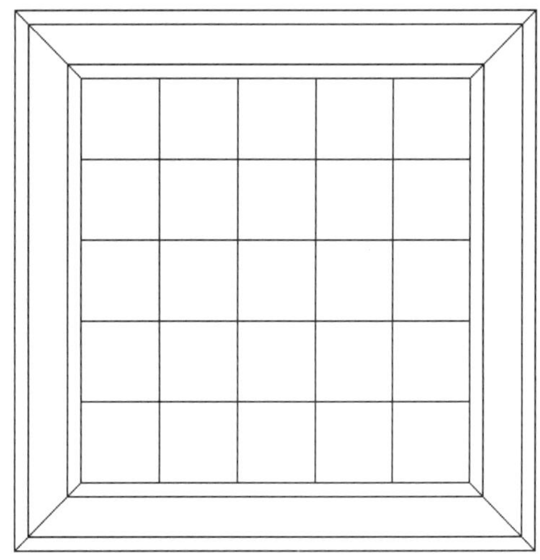

Your quilt layout should now look like this.

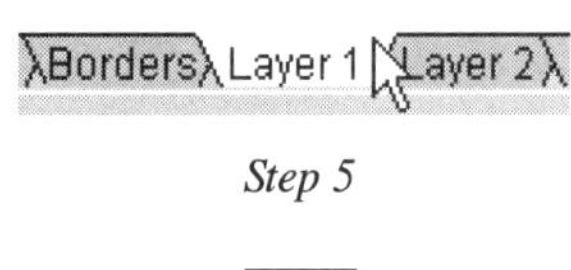

Step 5

Step 5 – Save in Sketchbook

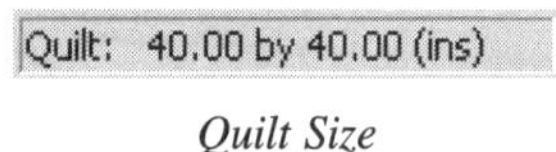

Quilt Size

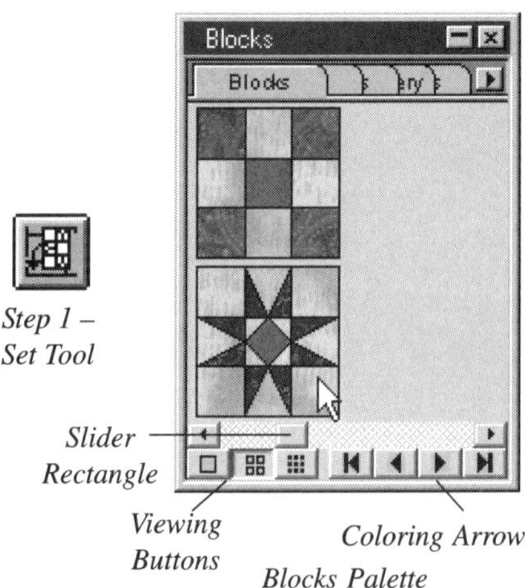

Blocks Palette

Step 1

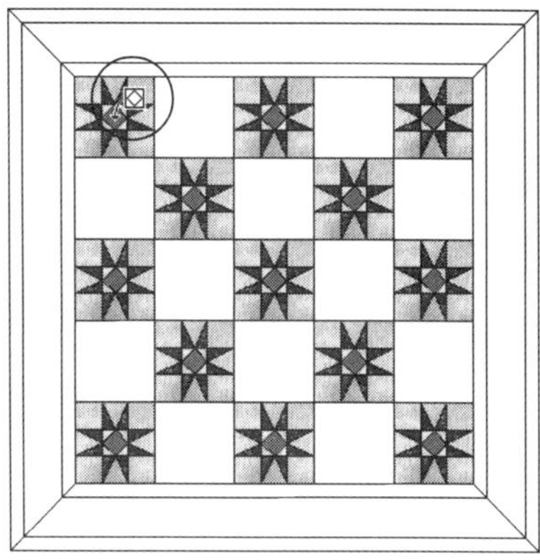

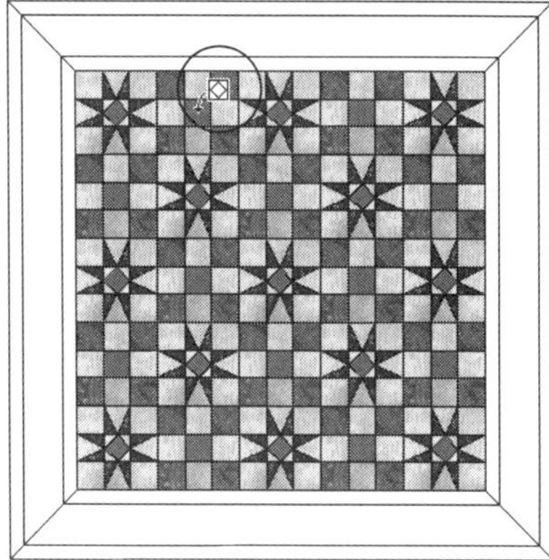

Step 2 & 3

Step 1 – Plain Block Tool

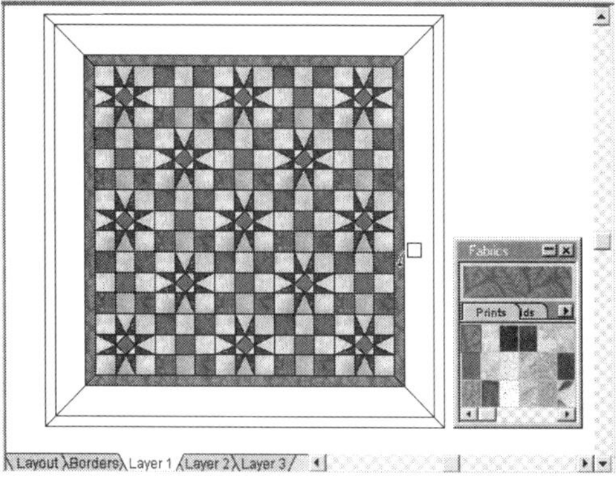

Step 1

- **The three viewing buttons along the bottom of the Blocks palette allow you to display one, four, or nine blocks simultaneously.**
- **If you saved more than one coloring of a design, select the design and then use the arrow keys at the bottom of the Blocks palette to view the various colorings.**
- **You can resize the Blocks palette by positioning the cursor on the edge of the box. The cursor will change to arrows that you can then use to stretch the box in any direction.**
- **You can also move the palette by clicking on the blue bar at the top of the palette and dragging it to a new location on the worktable.**

2 With the Eight-Pointed Star Block selected, position the cursor on the first block space in the upper-left corner of the quilt layout. Hold down the Alt key while you click on this space with your primary mouse button. Alternate spaces in your quilt layout will fill with the Eight-Pointed Star block.

3 Click on the Nine Patch in the Blocks palette. Position the cursor on any empty block space in the quilt layout. Alt+click to set this block in the remaining spaces.

Tip

- **Click on a space in the quilt layout to fill just that single space with a block.**
- **Use Alt+click to fill alternate spaces in the layout or Ctrl+click to fill all spaces in the layout.**

Coloring the Borders

This is the last step in completing your Nine Patch Star quilt design!

1 Click on the Plain Block tool in the Quilt tools. The Fabrics palette will open. Click on a swatch in the Fabrics palette and then Ctrl+click to color the entire first border.

To change your fabric selection, simply choose a new swatch in the palette and Ctrl+click on the border that you want to recolor. The new color will replace the previous color.

1

Tip

- **You can use either the Plain Block tool or the Paintbrush tool to color plain quilt borders. You can color each side of a border separately by clicking individually on each segment.**

2 Select a fabric in the palette for each of the remaining borders and then Ctrl+click to color all sides of the border. Save in Sketchbook.

**Tip**

- **You can save a quilt in the Sketchbook by clicking on Quilt in the main menu and then clicking on Save Quilt in Sketchbook.**

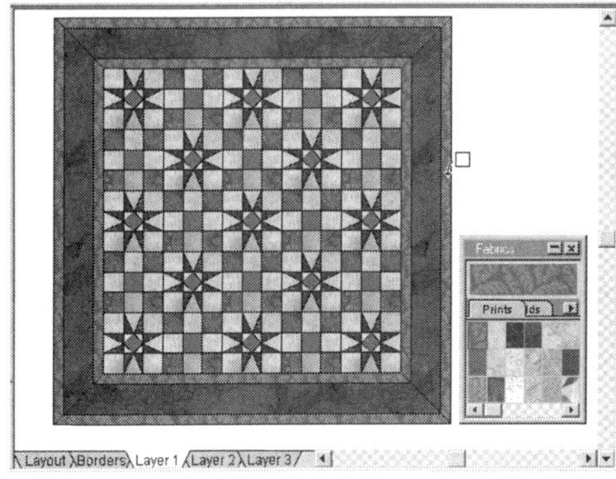

Step 2

Step 2 – Save in Sketchbook

Viewing the Sketchbook

Now you can view all of your new designs in the Sketchbook!

Each EQ5 file contains a Sketchbook that stores the pieced and appliqué designs, the quilts, and the fabrics that you saved with that particular project. The Sketchbook is the heart of each project and you can easily **view, retrieve, document,** or **delete** anything that you have saved there. You will learn more about the Sketchbook in Lesson 2.

Step 1 – View Sketchbook

1 Click on the View Sketchbook button to open the Sketchbook. This button is in the Project Tools on the left side of the worktable.

2 The Sketchbook will open on the worktable, displaying four side tabs: *Quilts, Blocks, Fabrics, and Colors.*

3 Click on the Quilts tab to open the Quilt Sketchbook. Here you will see your Nine Patch Star quilt.

4 Click on the Blocks tab to open the Block Sketchbook. Notice that there are five tabs at the top of the Block Sketchbook: *Blocks, Motifs, Stencils, Embroidery, and Pictures*. Click on the Blocks tab. The other tabs will be empty because you have not saved any designs of these types in this project.

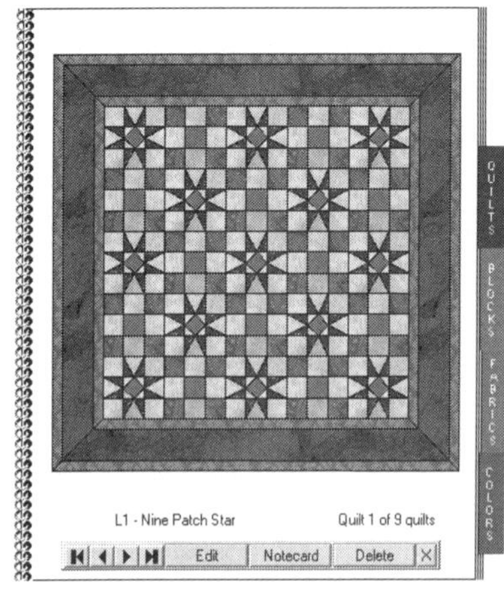

Step 2 & 3

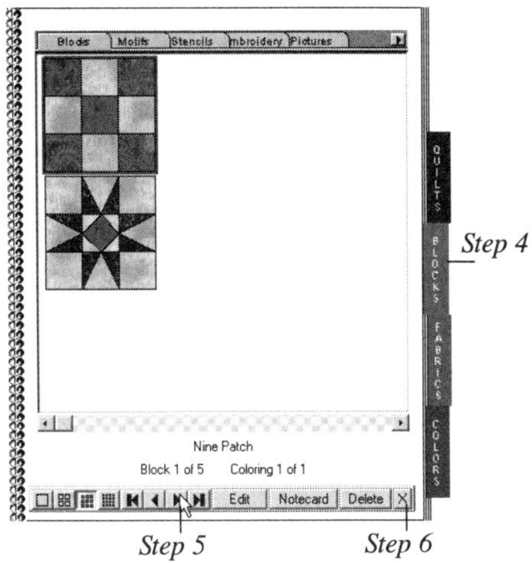

5 You will see your Nine Patch and Eight-Pointed Star block designs in the Block Sketchbook. The Nine Patch block is automatically selected because it is the first block saved in the Sketchbook.

Click on a block and then use the four arrows at the bottom of the Sketchbook to display the line drawing and all saved colorings of this selected block.

6 Click on the X in the lower-right corner of the Sketchbook to close it.

Tip

- **You can also use the keyboard shortcut F8 to open the Sketchbook or you can click on View in the main menu and then click on Sketchbook.**

Completing Notecards

The Notecard feature is a convenient tool that makes it easy for you to store text with your Sketchbook designs.

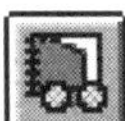

Step 1 – View Sketchbook

Step 1

1 Click on the View Sketchbook button to open the Sketchbook or use the shortcut F8. Click on the Blocks tab. Click on the Nine Patch block and then click on the Notecard button at the bottom of the Sketchbook. A notecard will appear on top of the Sketchbook with the cursor positioned on the first line.

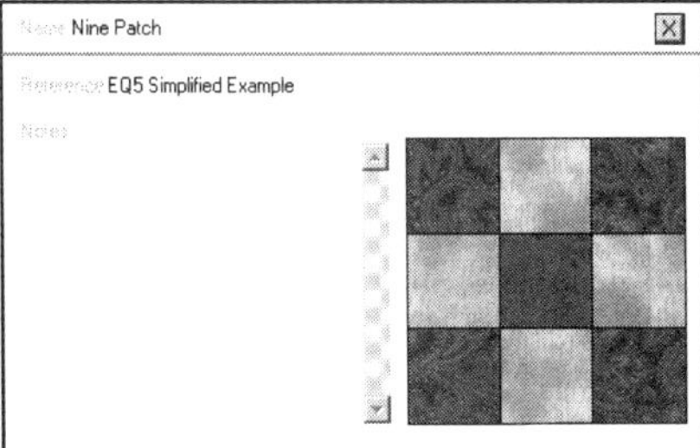

Step 2 & 3

2 Type Nine Patch in this space. Press the Tab key to move the cursor to the Reference line and type in any information that you want here such as a reference or source for the block design.

3 Press the Tab key to move to the Notes line. Any notations about the block such as construction hints, size preferences, or fabric choices can be made under the Notes area. Click on the X in the upper-right corner of the card to close it.

4 Click on the Nine Patch in the Sketchbook. You will notice that the block name is displayed below the slider bar, together with the total number of blocks in the Sketchbook and the number of saved colorings of this particular block.

Place the cursor in the center of the Nine Patch block and a tooltip will appear that displays the block's name.

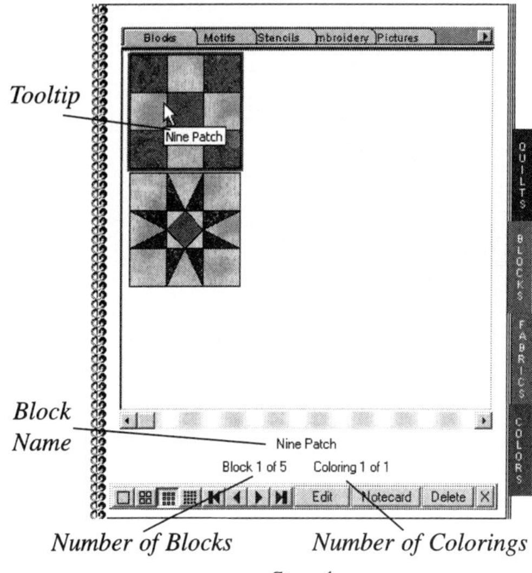

Step 4

Tip

- **Designs copied from the EQ5 Libraries or other EQ software are already named. This information is transferred automatically onto EQ5 Notecards when these designs are copied into a project Sketchbook.**
- **You can rename any block on its Notecard and this will change the name that is displayed in the Sketchbook.**

5 Following the same procedure that you used in Steps 1-3, create a Notecard for the Eight-Pointed Star design.

Name Eight-Pointed Star
Reference EQ5 Simplified Example
Notes

Step 5

6 Click on the Quilts tab to display the Nine Patch Star quilt. Click on the Notecard button and then type in Nine Patch Star. Make any other notations in the References and Notes sections.

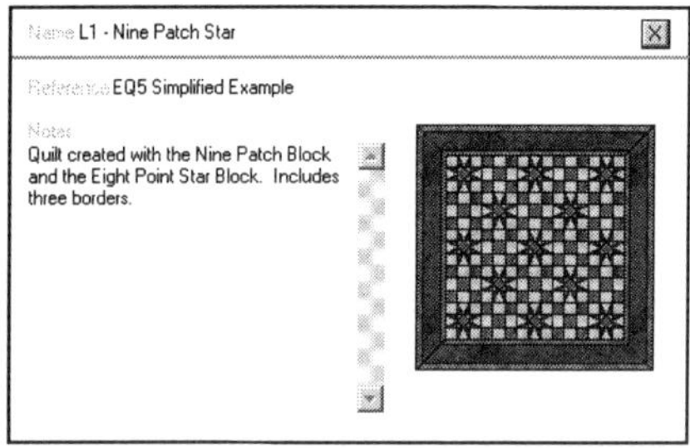

Step 6

7 Click on the X in the upper-right corner to close the Notecard. If you created more than one quilt, use the arrow keys on the Quilt tab to view the other quilt designs. Click on the X in the lower-right corner to close the Sketchbook.

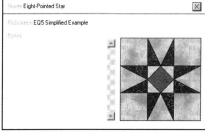

Save Button – After adding information to a Notecard, you must save before exiting EQ5.

Tip

- **After adding information to a Notecard, you must click on the Save button before exiting EQ5. The Save button is the third tool in the Project Tools and is represented by a floppy disk icon.**
- **When copying a block, appliqué, or quilt design into EQ5, be sure to note the source and any other pertinent information about the design on the Notecard. If you are copying a design from a magazine, for example, you should record the designer, the publication, the date, and the page number for future reference.**

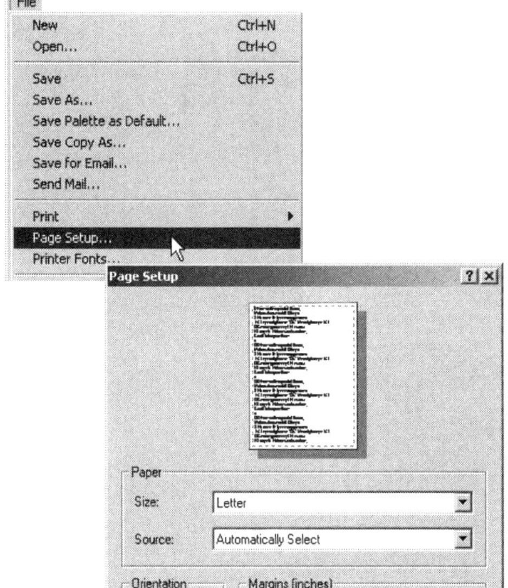

Step 1

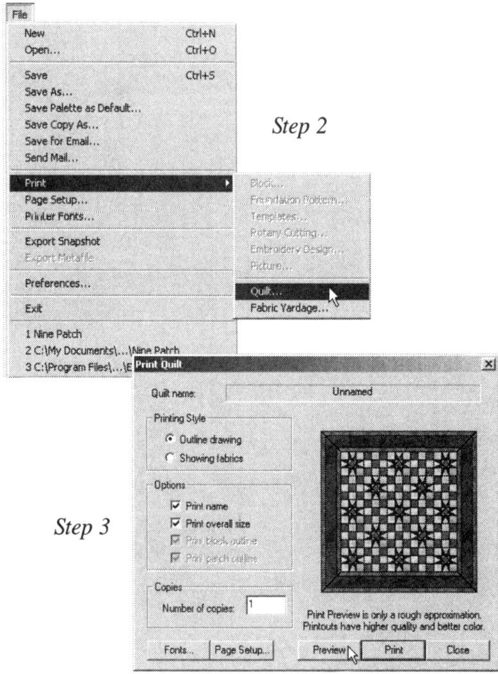

Step 2

Step 3

Printing a Quilt Design

EQ5 offers you a wide variety of printing options that you will explore as you work your way through this tutorial. In this lesson, you will exercise the selections for printing a quilt.

1 Click on File in the main menu and then click on Page Setup in the File menu. The Page Setup dialog box will open and you can choose paper characteristics, print orientation, and page margins. If you click on Printer, you can access printer information and properties. Click on OK, Cancel, or click on the X at the upper-right corner to close the Page Setup dialog box.

2 With your Nine Patch Star quilt on the worktable, click on File in the main menu and then click on Print in the File menu. Click on Quilt in the extended menu. A Print Quilt box will open.

3 Under Printing style, click on Outline drawing. Under Options, click on Print Name so that it is checked. Click on Print overall size so that it is checked. Notice that the Print overall size is available to you only when Print name is checked. Click on Preview.

4 To magnify the print preview, click on the Zoom In button. Position the cursor in a corner of the area that you want to magnify. Click, and holding down the mouse button, drag the cursor diagonally to the opposite corner of this area. Release the mouse button. You will now see a magnified view of the selected area.

Click on the Zoom Out to return to the previous view or click on Fit to Screen button to return to normal viewing. Click on Print to print the quilt outline.

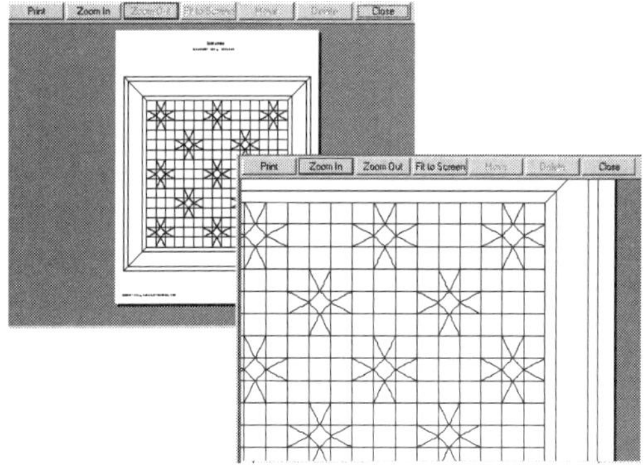

Step 4

After printing, EQ5 will return to the Quilt Worktable. Now you will print your quilt showing fabrics.

5 Click on File in the main menu and then click on Print in the File menu. Click on Quilt in the extended menu (As shown in Step 2). A Print Quilt box will open.

6 Under Printing style, click on Showing fabrics. Under Options, click on Print block outline and Print patch outline so that they are checked. These options are available to you only when you have selected Showing fabrics. Click on Preview and Print.

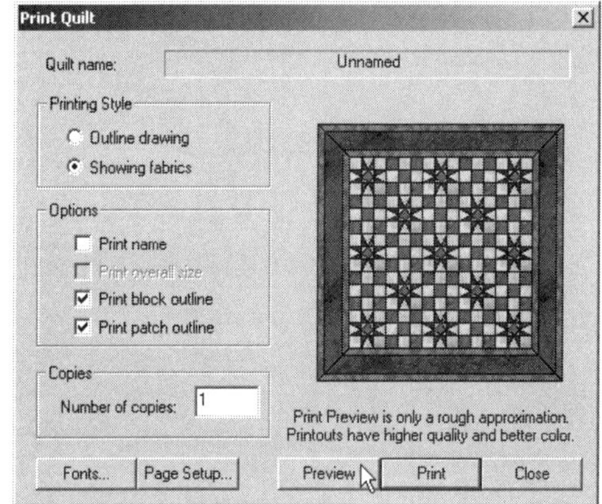

Step 6

EQ5 will print your quilt in the fabrics that you have chosen, with patch and block outlines visible.

7 After printing, EQ5 will return to the Quilt Worktable. Click on File in the main menu and then click on Print in the File menu. Click on Quilt in the extended menu (As shown in Step 2).

8 Under Printing style, click on Showing fabrics. Under Options in the Print Quilt box, click on Print Block outline and Print patch outline so that they are unchecked. Click on Preview and Print.

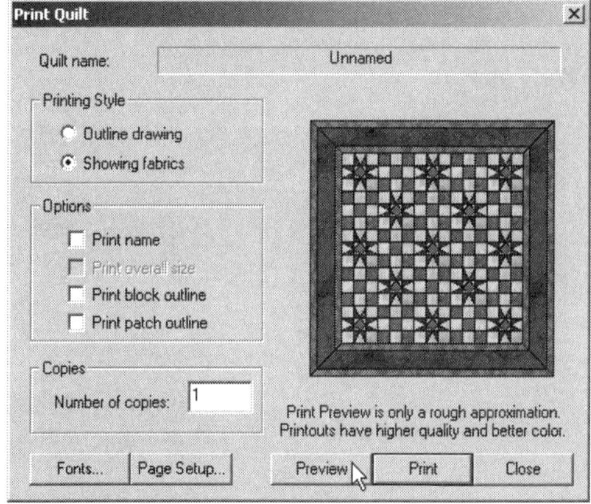

Step 8

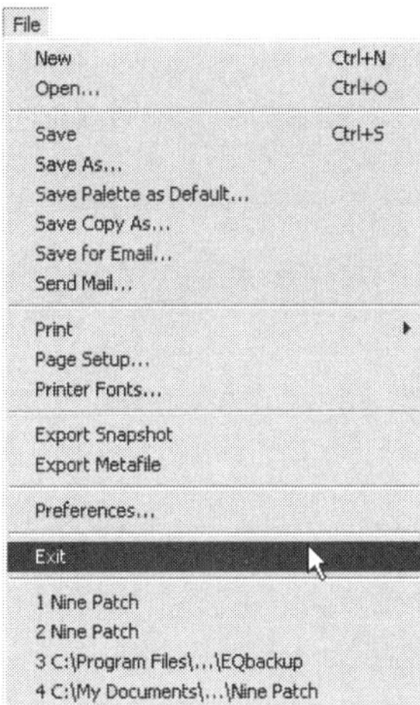

Exiting EQ5

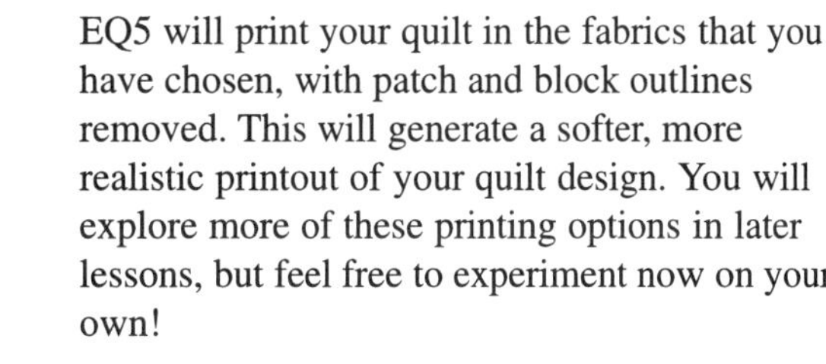

EQ5 will print your quilt in the fabrics that you have chosen, with patch and block outlines removed. This will generate a softer, more realistic printout of your quilt design. You will explore more of these printing options in later lessons, but feel free to experiment now on your own!

Exiting EQ5

Click on File in the main menu and then click on Exit. Your project will close automatically when you exit the program.

CONGRATULATIONS! You have completed Lesson 1 and have learned the basic skills needed to design, document, and print a quilt in EQ5.

Here is the finished quilt!

Changing an EasyDraw™ Quilt

Lesson 2

Lesson 2 – Changing an EasyDraw™ Quilt

In Lesson 2, you will create a new quilt by modifying the Nine Patch Star that you designed in Lesson 1. This new quilt design is called Stars Squared. The blocks are set on the diagonal in this layout. You will review certain basic skills (denoted by *) and you also learn to:

- *Retrieve a project*
- *Retrieve a block from the Sketchbook*
- *Modify a block*
- *Draw with the Grid tool**
- *Color a block**
- *Use the Eyedropper tool*
- *Complete Notecards**
- *Retrieve a quilt from the Sketchbook*
- *Keep current borders*
- *Select an On-point layout*
- *Change the borders*
- *Set blocks into an On-point layout*
- *Color the borders**
- *Set blocks into a border*
- *Use the Tape Measure tool*
- *Explore the Sketchbook*
- *Print blocks*
- *Exit EQ5**

Stars Squared Quilt

Retrieving a Project

Run EQ5. You will see two tabs on the opening screen: *Create a New Project* and *Open an Existing Project.*

1 Click on the Open an Existing Project tab. You will notice that there is a list of your most recently used project files, as well as a list of existing EQ5 projects. When the list is too long to fit within a window, EQ5 will provide a vertical slider bar for viewing the entire list. Notice that Electric Quilt 5 automatically added a .PJ5 extension to your project when it was saved in Lesson 1.

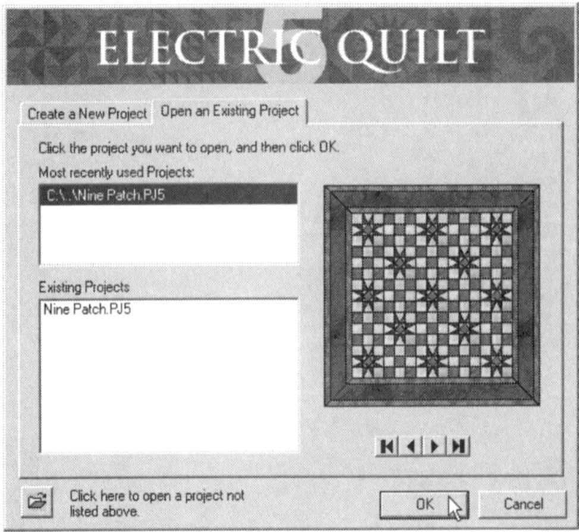

Step 1 & 2

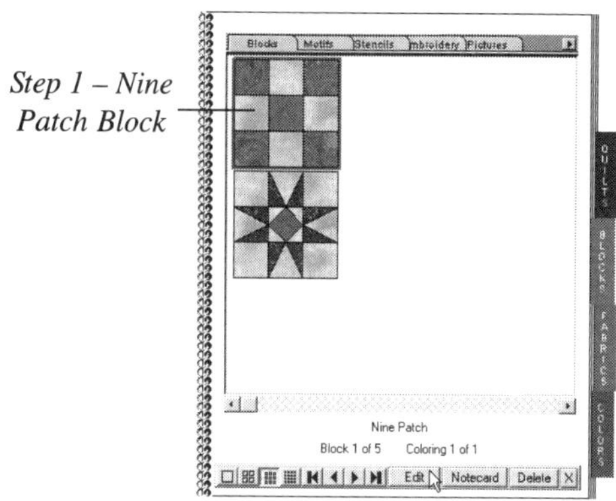

Step 1 & 2 – Retrieving a Block

2 Click on the Nine Patch.PJ5 in either list. When you click on a project file, EQ5 will display the first quilt in that project's Sketchbook. You can view the other quilts in this previewed project file by using the arrow buttons under the displayed quilt. Click on OK to open the project file or press the Enter key.

3 The project will open to the Sketchbook and to the last worktable that you had open before you exited the program.

2

Retrieving a Block from the Sketchbook

The new block that you will create for this Stars Squared quilt is the Double Nine Patch. It is based on the Nine Patch block that you saved in your Sketchbook in Lesson 1. You will use the Grid tool to draw this new block.

1 Click on the Blocks tab in the Sketchbook. Click on the Nine Patch block to select it.

2 Click on the Edit button at the bottom of the Sketchbook.

The EasyDraw™ Worktable will open, together with the EasyDraw™ Tools. The Nine Patch block design will be displayed on the worktable, ready for editing. The Line tool will be engaged automatically.

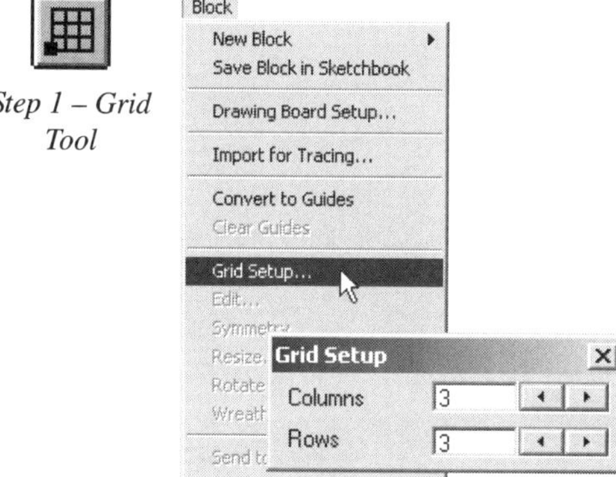

Step 1– Modifying a Block

Modifying a Block

1 Click on the Grid tool in the EasyDraw™ Tools. This is the tool that you used in Lesson 1 to draw the Nine Patch block. Click on Block in the main menu and then click on Grid Setup. In the Grid Setup box, set the Columns and Rows to 3.

2 Draw a small Nine Patch within the upper-left patch of the Nine Patch block. Use the same click, drag, and release technique that you used to draw the Nine Patch grid in Lesson 1.

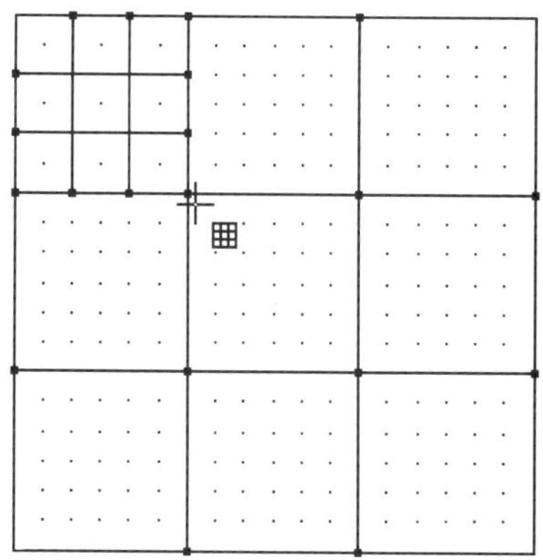
Step 2 – Modifying a Block

3 Draw additional Nine Patch grids in the center patch and in the remaining corner patches of the Nine Patch block.

4 Click on the Save in Sketchbook button.

Here is your Double Nine Patch block, ready to be colored!

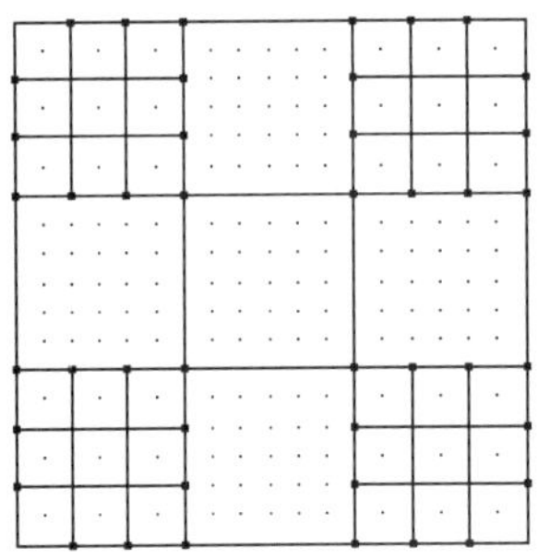

Step 3

Step 4 – Save in Sketchbook

5 Click on the Color tab at the lower-left of the screen. The Color Tools will now be available to you with the Paintbrush tool already engaged. The Fabrics palette will also open.

Step 5

6 For this block, you will choose four different fabrics. Click on the fabric swatch in Prints or Solids that you have chosen for the background patches. This fabric will appear in the sample window. Click on the appropriate background patches in the Double Nine Patch block to color them with this selected fabric.

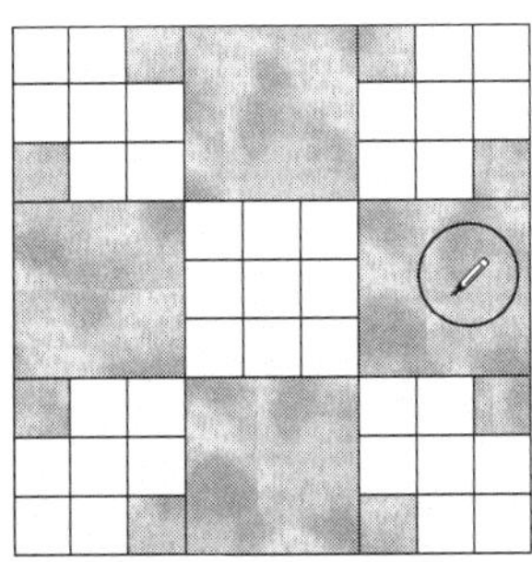

Step 6

Tip

- **You can use the Eyedropper tool to locate a specific fabric that you have used in a previously-colored design. With the design on the worktable and the Eyedropper engaged, click on the patch that is colored with the fabric that you want to find in the palette. This fabric will be displayed in the sample window of the Fabrics palette.**

  As soon as you click on the patch with the Eyedropper and the color is identified, the cursor will revert to the last paint tool that you used. You will need the Paintbrush tool to color the patches in this block. Click on a patch to color it with this fabric. Save in Sketchbook.

- **If you want to find more than one color in the palette:**

  Retrieve the original block again, find the next color using the Eyedropper and then retrieve the partially colored second block. Color the patches with the selected swatch. Save your block after each addition of color. You can always delete the partial colorings when you are finished.

- **The Eyedropper tool is available to you on all of the drawing worktables and on the quilt worktable. See the EQ manuals and the Help file for more information.**

Eyedropper Tool and Eyedropper Cursor

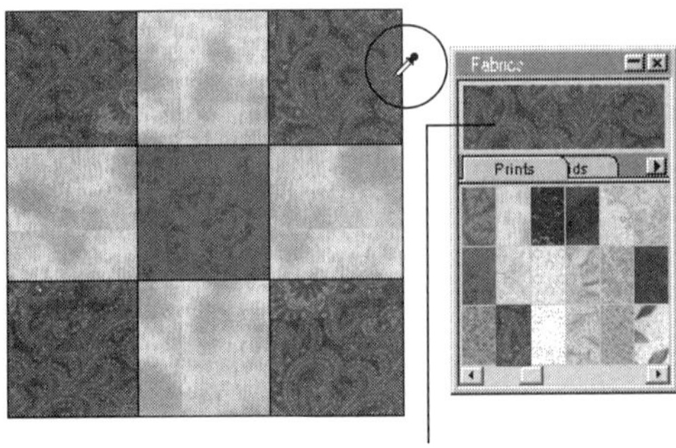

Fabric selected with the Eyedropper Tool appears in the Sample Window of the Fabrics Palette

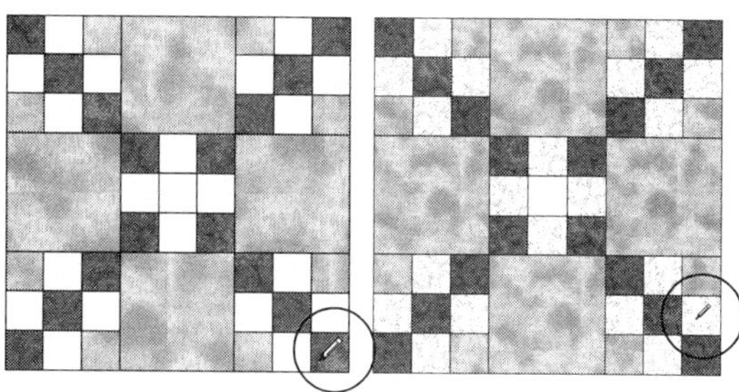

Step 7 *Step 8*

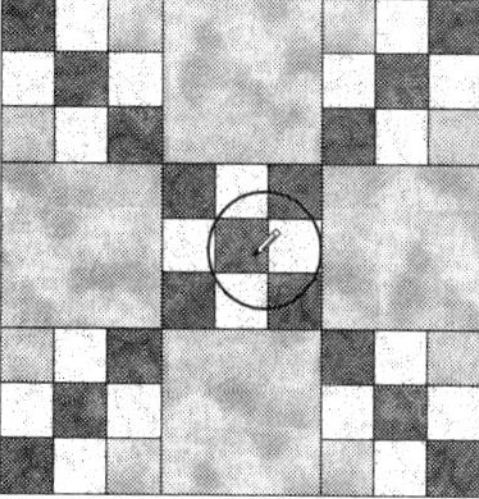

Step 9

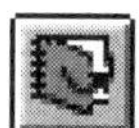

Step 10 – Save in Sketchbook

7 Choose a fabric for the patches that form the chain in the block design. Click on the appropriate patches to color them with this fabric.

8 Choose a fabric and color the patches that are on either side of the chain patches, as shown.

9 Choose the final fabric for the center patch of the block. Click on this patch to color.

10 Click on the Save in Sketchbook button to save the colored block in the Sketchbook and in the project file.

You have completed your new block and it is ready for a Notecard!

Completing Notecards

Step 1 – View Sketchbook

Step 2

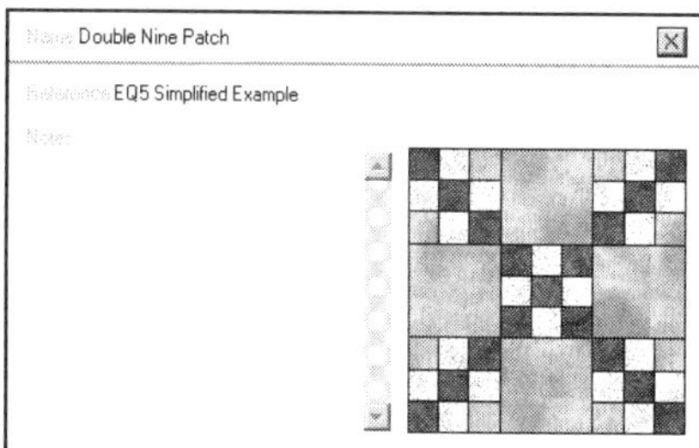

Step 3

Step 5 – Save

1 Click on the View Sketchbook button or use F8 to open the Sketchbook.

2 Click on the Double Nine Patch block and then click on the Notecard button.

3 The cursor is in position on the Name line. Type Double Nine Patch on this line. Use the Tab button on your keyboard to move the cursor to the Reference and Notes sections. Add any information that you want to save with this block design. Click on the X in the upper-right corner to close the Notecard.

Tip

- **If you added text only in the Name or Reference section, you can close the Notecard by pressing the Enter key.**
- **If you added text in the Notes section, you must use the X to close the Notecard.**

4 Following Steps 2 and 3, complete Notecards for each of the blocks in your Block Sketchbook. Close the Sketchbook.

5 Click on the Save button to save this information with your project file.

Now you are ready to establish the new layout and borders!

Retrieving a Quilt from the Sketchbook

Step 1 – View Sketchbook

1 Click on the View Sketchbook button or open the Sketchbook with the F8 shortcut. Click on the Quilts tab. If you have more than one quilt in the Quilt Sketchbook, use the arrow keys at the bottom of the Sketchbook to display the final Nine Patch Star quilt.

2 Click on the Edit button at the bottom of the Sketchbook to place this quilt on the worktable.

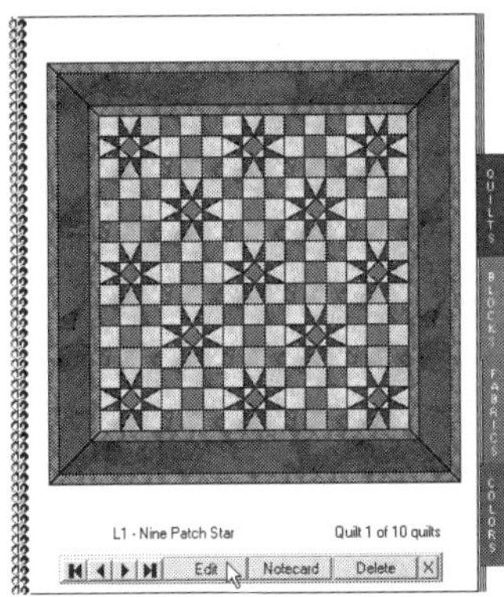

Step 2

Tip

- **You can toggle easily between the block and quilt worktables through the main menu. If you are on a block worktable and you want to open the quilt worktable, click on Worktable and then click on Work on Quilt.**
- **If you are on the quilt worktable and you want to open a block worktable, click on Worktable and then click on Work on Block.**

Selecting an On-Point Layout

As you learned in the beginning of this lesson, the blocks in this quilt will be set on the diagonal. Although this will require that you establish a new layout, EQ5 makes it easy for you to retain the border arrangement from a previous quilt!

1 Click on Quilt in the main menu. Click on Keep Current Borders in the drop-down menu so that it is checked.

Step 1

2 Click on Quilt again and then click on New Quilt. Click on On-point in the extended menu.

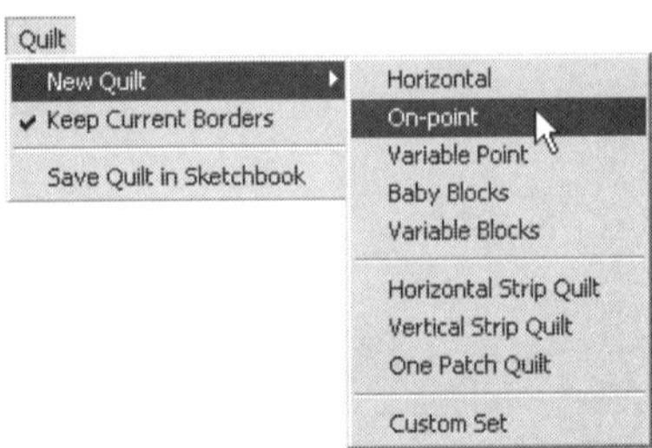

Step 2

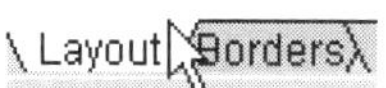

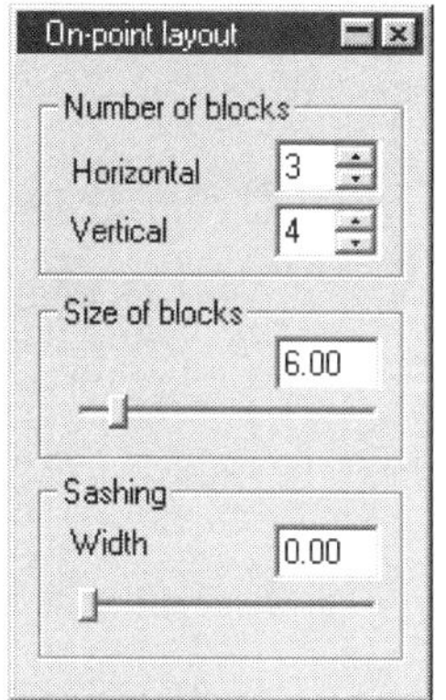

Step 3

On-point Quilt

3 Click on the Layout tab at the lower-left of the screen. Use the arrows and slider bars to set the following values:

Number of blocks:	Horizontal – 3 Vertical – 4
Size of blocks:	6.00
Sashing Width:	0.00

Your screen should look like the On-point example in Step 3 to the left.

Changing the Borders

You kept the border setup from your Nine Patch Star quilt, but you will modify these specifications slightly for this new layout.

Step 1

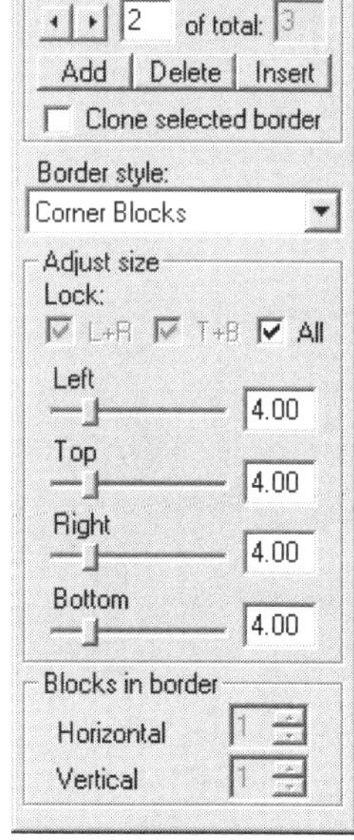

Step 2

Step 3

1 Click on the Borders tab in the lower-left of the Quilt Worktable. The Borders box will appear. Click on the second border in the layout to select it.

2 Click on the down arrow under Border style in the Borders box. Click on Corner Blocks. Set the border size at 4.00.

3 Click on the Layer 1 tab.

Tip

- **Notice that your quilt's size is displayed in the lower-right side of the screen.**
- **To display EQ5's measurements in centimeters, click on File and then click on Preferences. Click on the Measurement tab in the Preferences dialog box. Under Measurement Units, click on Centimeters, and then click on OK.**

You are ready to set the blocks into the On-point layout!

Setting Blocks into an On-Point Layout

Step 1 – Set Tool

1 Click on the Set tool in the Quilt Tools. The Blocks palette will appear on the worktable.

2 Click on the Eight-Pointed Star and use the arrow keys below the block to find the coloring that you want to use in the layout. Position the cursor on the first whole block in the upper-left corner of the quilt layout. Ctrl+click to set this block into the layout.

3 Click on the Double Nine Patch block and use the arrow keys to select the coloring that you want to use. Position the cursor on any remaining empty block space in the quilt layout. Ctrl+click and the Double Nine Patch will fill the remaining spaces.

Tip

- **Because row formation is different for the horizontal and the diagonal layouts, the Ctrl+click and Alt+click actions function differently.**
- **Experiment with the Lesson 1 and Lesson 2 quilt to learn how to use Ctrl+click and Alt+click in each of these layout styles.**

Coloring the Borders

1 Click on the Paintbrush tool and the Fabrics palette will appear. Click on the color that you have selected for your first border and position the cursor on any one of these border segments. Ctrl+click to fill the first border with this color.

2 Choose a fabric for the second border and position the cursor on any one of these border segments. Ctrl+click to fill the second border with this color.

3 Click on the Set tool and then click on the Eight-Pointed Star block in the Block palette. Be sure that you are displaying the coloring that you want to set into the quilt layout. Ctrl+click to set this block in all four corners of this border simultaneously.

4 Click on the Paintbrush tool and choose a fabric for the third border. Ctrl+click to color this border.

5 Click on the Save in Sketchbook button to save your work.

Paintbrush Tool *Set Tool*

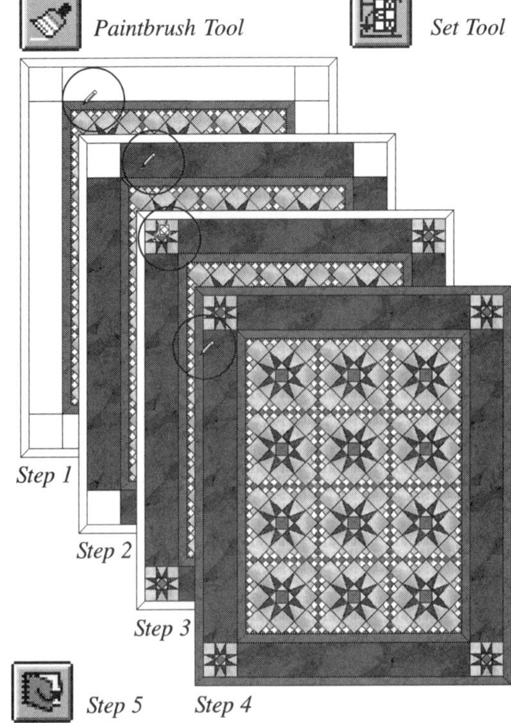

Step 1 – Tape Measure Tool

Step 2

Step 1 – View Sketchbook

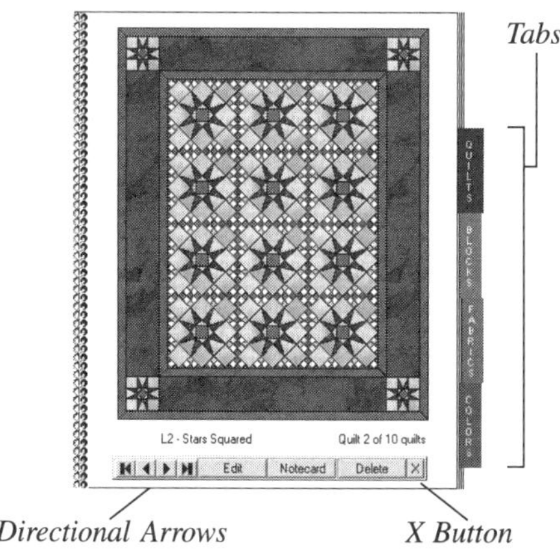

Step 2

Using the Tape Measure Tool

The Tape Measure tool is a very convenient, easy-to-use feature that can be used on all Layers and tabs of the Quilt Worktable. With this tool, you can accurately measure between any two points on the Quilt Worktable.

1 With the quilt on the worktable, click on the Tape Measure tool.

2 Position the cursor on the point at which you want to begin measuring. Holding down the mouse button, drag the cursor to the point at which you want to end the measurement. The measurement will display on the screen until you release the mouse button.

Exploring the Sketchbook

Now that you have saved several designs, this is an excellent time to explore the Sketchbook's features!

1 Click the View Sketchbook button to open the Sketchbook or use the shortcut F8.

2 Click on the Quilts tab.

The four **directional arrows** allow you to display the quilts that you have saved in this Nine Patch project file.

The **Edit** button places the displayed quilt on the Quilt Worktable.

The **Notecard** button opens the Notecard for the displayed quilt.

The **Delete** button removes the displayed quilt from the Sketchbook.

The **X** closes the Sketchbook.

Tip

- **You can also press the Enter key to close the Sketchbook.**

2

3 Click on the Blocks tab.

The five tabs along the top of the Block Sketchbook are: *Blocks, Motifs, Stencils, Embroidery,* and *Pictures*.

The first four buttons at the lower-left corner of the Sketchbook are **display options**. You can choose to *display one, four, nine,* or *sixteen* designs simultaneously.

The four **coloring arrows** allow you to *view the line drawing and all colorings* that you have saved of a selected design.

The **Edit** button places the selected design on the appropriate worktable.

The **Notecard** button opens the Notecard for the selected design.

The **Delete** button removes the selected coloring from the Sketchbook. This button will also remove the selected design and all colorings if you delete while displaying the line drawing.

The **X** closes the Sketchbook.

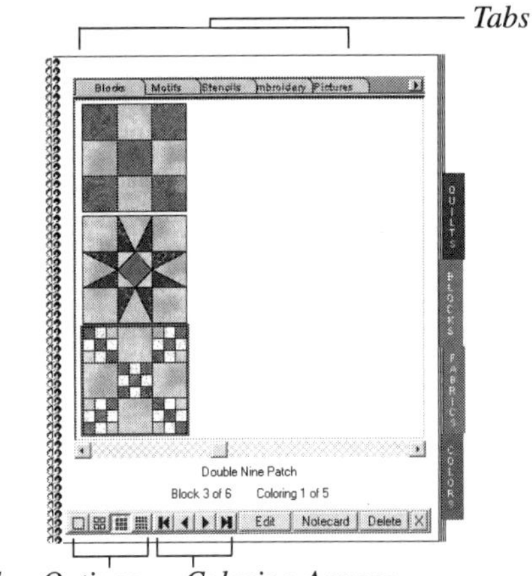

Step 3

4 Click on the Fabrics tab to view the fabric palette for this project.

The four buttons at the lower-left corner of the Sketchbook are **display options**. You can choose to *display four, nine, sixteen, or twenty-five* blocks simultaneously.

The **Notecard** button opens the Notecard for the selected fabric.

The **Delete** button removes the selected fabric from the Sketchbook.

The **Clear** button removes all fabrics from the Sketchbook.

The **X** closes the Sketchbook.

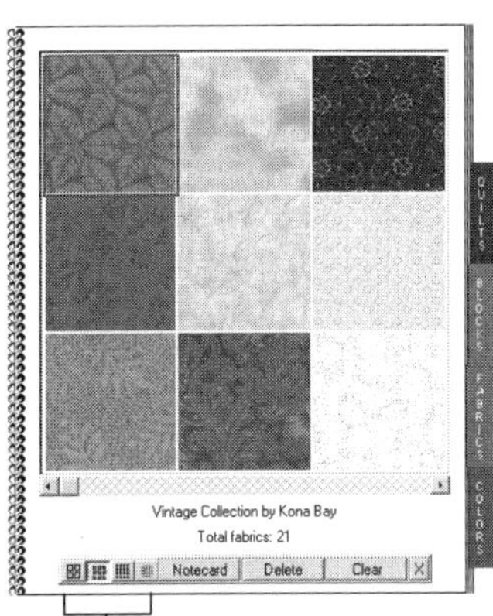

Step 4

5 Click on the Colors tab to view the solid colors that comprise the fabrics in this project.

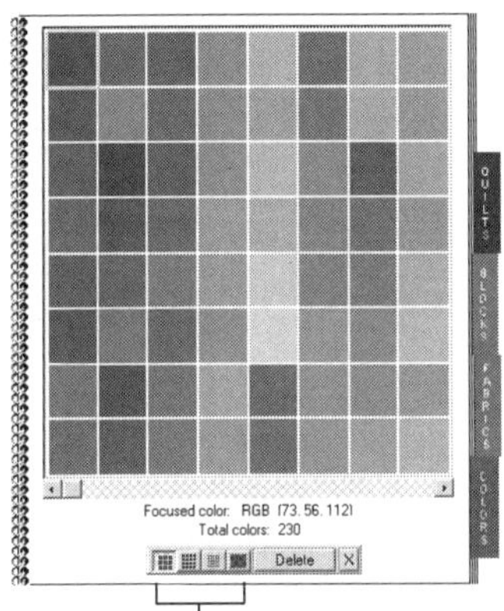

Step 5

Step 1 – Edit Quilt

Step 1 – Select Tool

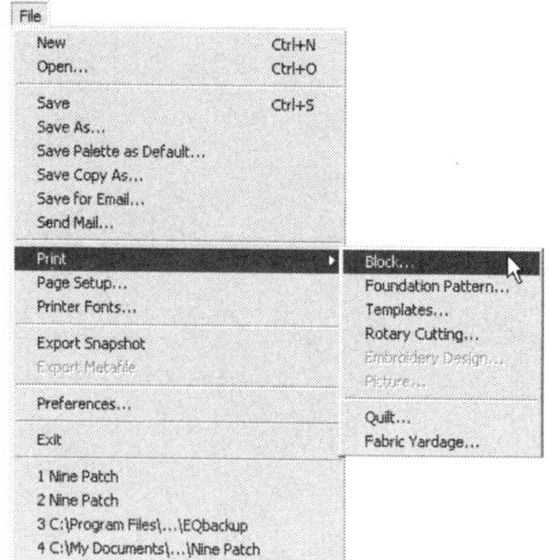

Step 2

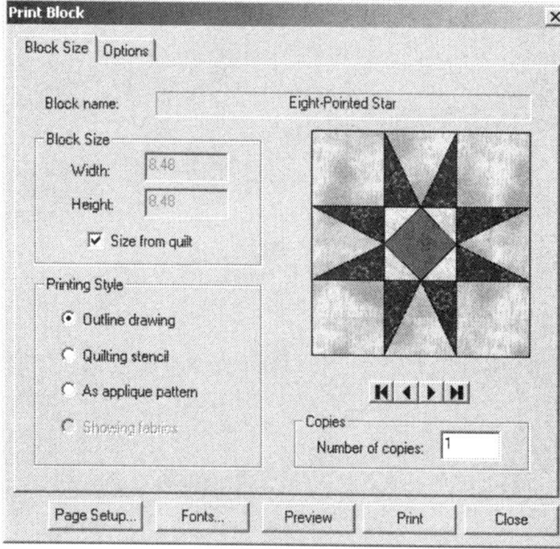

Step 3 & 4

The four buttons at the lower-left corner of the Sketchbook give you several **display options** for *viewing color swatches.*

The **Delete** button removes the selected color from the Sketchbook.

The **X** closes the Sketchbook.

Tip

- **Complete a Quilt Notecard for this Lesson 2 quilt, called Stars Squared. Click on the Save button in the Project toolbar after closing the Sketchbook. This will ensure that the Notecard information will be saved in the project file.**

2

Printing Blocks

You are going to experiment with some of EQ5's block printing options. You will first print from the Quilt Worktable and then you will print from the EasyDraw™ Worktable.

1 With the Sketchbook open, click on the Quilts tab. Click on your Stars Squared quilt and then click on Edit to place it on the worktable. Click on the Select tool and then click on one of the on-point Eight-Pointed Star blocks in the layout.

2 Click File, click Print, and then click Block. A Print Block box will appear that contains two tabs: *Block Size* and *Options*. Click on the Block Size tab. The selected block is displayed here and there are options for *block size, printing style,* and the *number of copies* you want to print.

3 Click on Size from quilt so that it is checked. EQ5 will print the actual size of the block, as it is used in your quilt. Because this particular block is on-point in the quilt layout, the size that is displayed here is the diagonal measurement of the design.

4 Under Printing Style, click on Outline drawing. Click Preview and then click Print. You will notice that EQ5 will tile the printout onto another piece of paper if you have your page setup for standard 8.5" x 11" paper. Check the EQ5 Help file or the manuals for information on how to change the page setup.

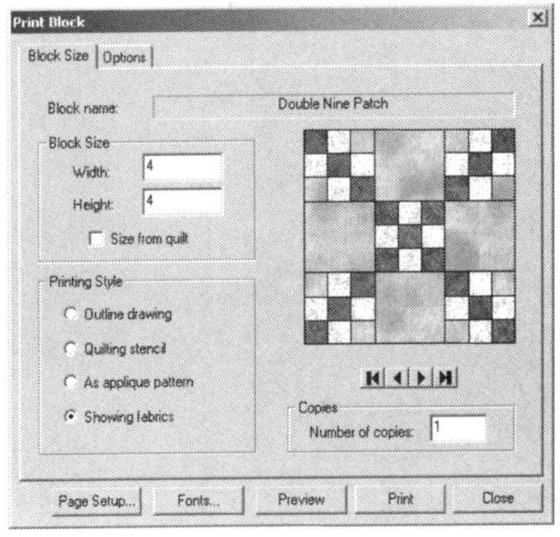

Step 5

5 After printing, EQ5 will return to the Quilt Worktable. Click on one of the whole Double Nine Patch blocks in the layout. Click on File, click on Print, and then click on Block.

Under Block Size, click on Size from quilt so that it is unchecked. Type in 4 for block width and height. Use the coloring arrows below the design to display the colored version of the block. Under Printing Style, click on Showing fabrics.

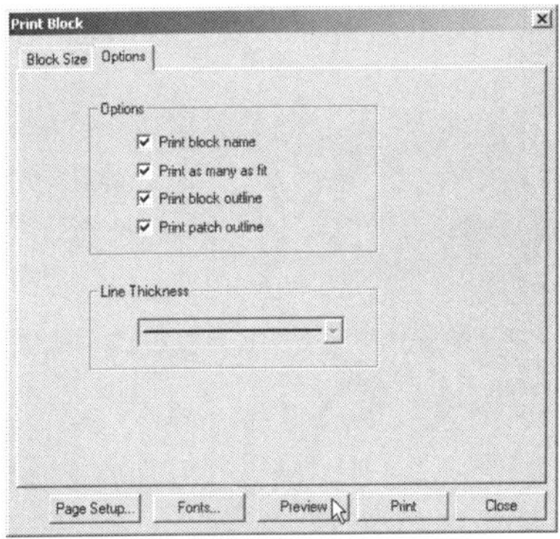

Step 6

Tip

- **Notice that in the Print Block box, Showing fabrics is available to you only when a colored version of the block is displayed.**

6 Click on the Options tab. There are more options available to you here: *block name display, maximum number of designs on a page, patch and block outline,* and *line thickness*. Click on all options so that they are checked. Preview and Print.

7 To print from the EasyDraw™ Worktable, open the Sketchbook (F8). Click on the Blocks tab and then click on the Nine Patch block. Click on Edit to place this block on the worktable. Click on File, click on Print, and then click on Block.

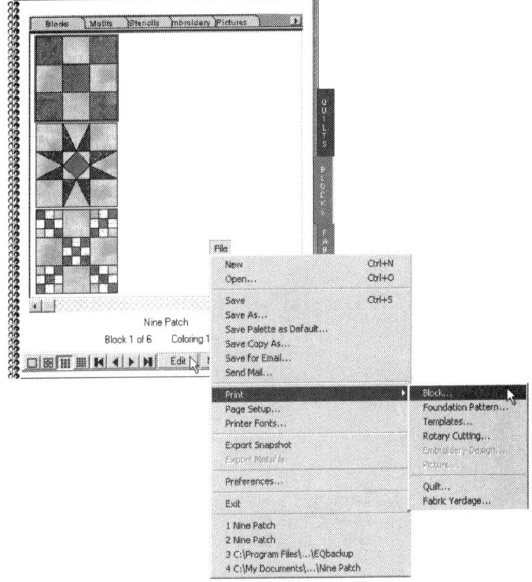

Step 7

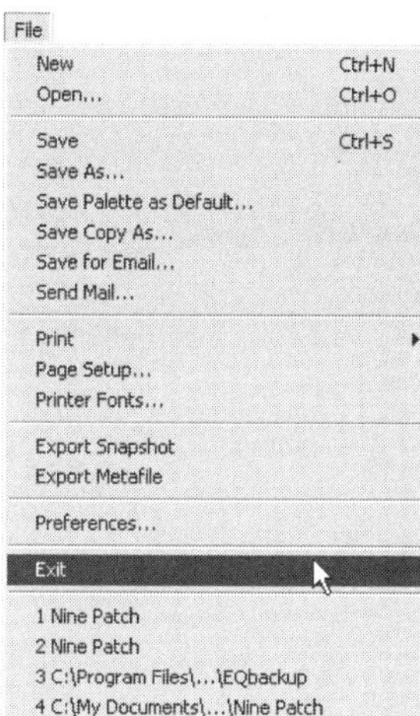

Exiting EQ5

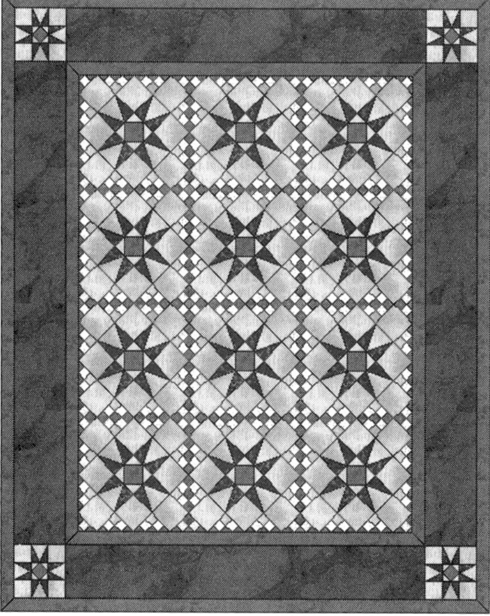

Here is the finished quilt!

8 The Print Block box will open with the same options that you have when you print from the Quilt Worktable. On a drawing worktable, however, you cannot select Size from quilt because the design is not in a quilt layout. You must specify a block size on this worktable. As you have learned, you can size from quilt or specify the block size when printing from the quilt worktable.

Make your selections and then Preview and Print. You will experiment with more printing options in the following lessons.

Exiting EQ5

Click on File and then click on Exit.

CONGRATULATIONS! You have completed Lesson 2 and have acquired many new skills. You will learn even more in Lesson 3!

Expanding the Quilt Design

Lesson 3

Lesson 3 – Expanding the Quilt Design

In Lesson 3, you will modify the Stars Squared quilt that you designed in Lesson 2 to create a design called Two-Stepping Stars. In addition to reviewing several tasks from the previous lessons (denoted by *), you will learn to:

- *Retrieve a project**
- *Retrieve a quilt from the Sketchbook**
- *Add sashing*
- *Change the borders**
- *Color sashing, sashing blocks, and borders*
- *Set blocks into a border**
- *Complete Notecards**
- *Delete designs from the Sketchbook*
- *Print foundation patterns*
- *Print templates*
- *Generate Rotary Cutting instructions*
- *Calculate fabric yardage*
- *Export a snapshot: quilts and blocks*
- *Exit EQ5**

Two-Stepping Stars Quilt

Retrieving a Project

Run EQ5. On EQ5's opening screen, click on the Open an Existing Project tab and then click on Nine Patch.PJ5. As you learned in Lesson 2, EQ5 will preview your Nine Patch project quilts in the display area of this dialog box. Click OK.

Your project will open to the Sketchbook and to the last worktable that you had opened before you exited the program.

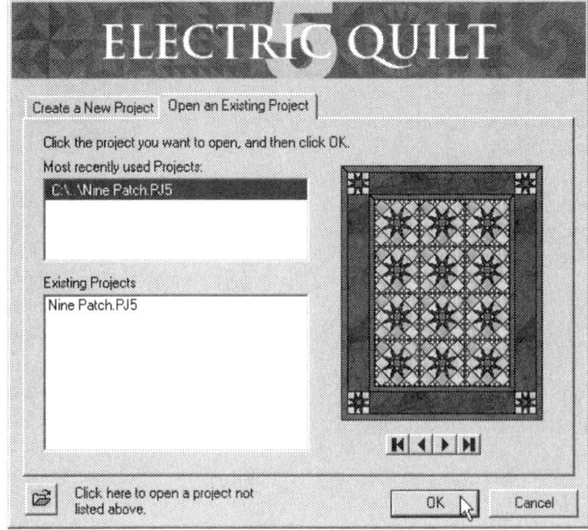

Retrieving a Project

Retrieving a Quilt from the Sketchbook

Open the Sketchbook and click on the Quilts tab. Use the arrows to display Stars Squared, the Lesson 2 quilt. Click on Edit in the Quilt Sketchbook to place Stars Squared on the worktable.

The On-point palette will appear when the Layout Tab is clicked.

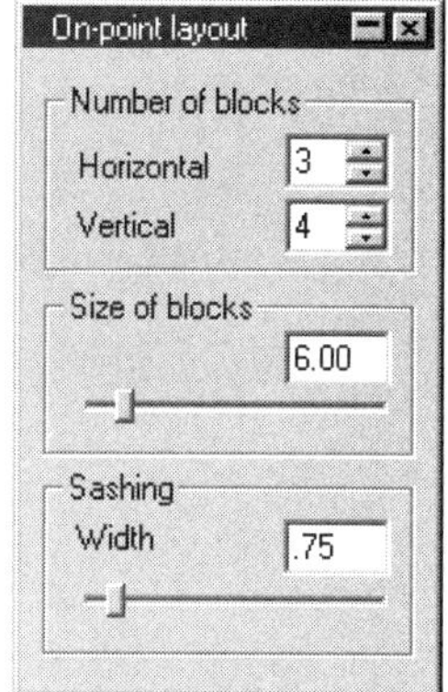

On-point layout palette

Step 1

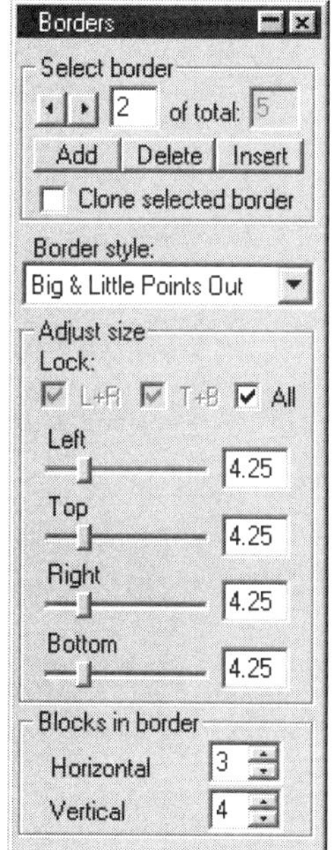

Step 2 – Border 2

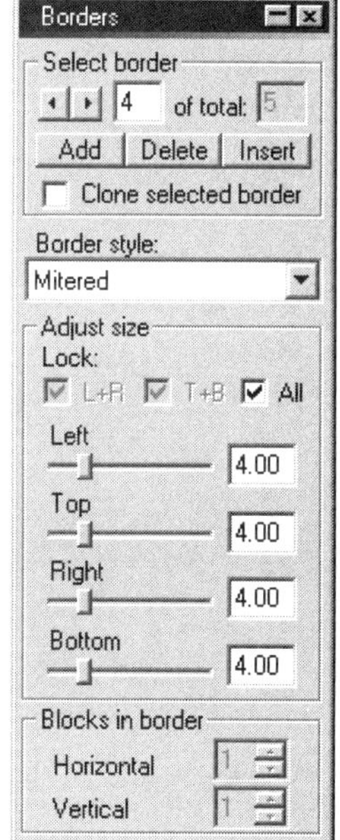

Step 4 – Border 4

Tip

- **It will not be necessary to designate New Quilt in the Worktable menu because you will not be changing the block orientation of your quilt in this lesson. You will be adding sashing and changing borders.**

Adding Sashing

With your Stars Squared quilt on the worktable, click on the Layout tab and the On-point palette will appear. You will change only the sashing width value in this dialog box. The new value is .75. All other layout values for your new Lesson 3 quilt will remain unchanged.

Changing the Borders

1 Click on the Borders tab and the Borders box will appear.

2 Click on the Add button twice to increase the number of borders to five. Make no changes to the first border. Click on the second border in the quilt layout and make these selections:

Border style:	Big & Little Points Out
Adjust size:	4.25 (Lock: All)
Blocks in border:	Horizontal – 3 Vertical – 4

Tip

- **To open the Borders box for a particular border, you can click directly on that border in the quilt layout. You can also use the arrows under Select border in the Borders box to choose a border. The border will darken when selected.**

3 No changes are necessary for the third border.

4 Click on the fourth border and make these selections:

Border style:	Mitered
Adjust size:	4.00 (Lock: All)

5 The fifth border will remain at the default settings for a one-inch mitered border.

Notice that your new quilt size is displayed at the lower-right of the screen.

6 Click on the Layer 1 tab. Click Save in Sketchbook. The Double Nine Patch and Eight-Pointed Star blocks will refill the quilt layout automatically. You are now ready to color the new sashing and modified borders.

Quilt Layout on Borders Tab

New Quilt Size

Step 6 – Layer 1 Tab

Step 6 – Save in Sketchbook

Coloring Sashing, Sashing Squares, and Borders

You can use either the Plain Block tool or the Paintbrush tool to color sashings, sashing squares, and borders. In this lesson, you will use the Paintbrush tool.

Step 1 – Paintbrush tool

1 Click on the Paintbrush tool and the Fabrics palette will open. Click on the color that you have selected for the sashing and position the cursor on one sashing segment. Ctrl+click. Some, but not all, of the sashings will fill with color. Position the cursor on any remaining uncolored sashing segment. Ctrl+click to finish coloring.

2 Click on the selected color for the sashing squares. Ctrl+click on any sashing square. Some, but not all, of the sashing squares will fill with color. Ctrl+click on any remaining uncolored sashing square to complete the coloring process on all sashing squares. Save in Sketchbook.

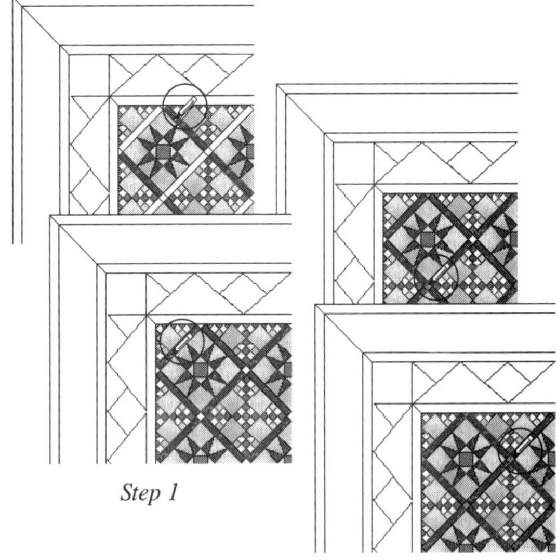

Step 1

Step 2

3 Click on the selected color for the first border. Ctrl+click on this border and it will fill with color.

4 Click on the second border and then click on the Set tool. Click on the Eight-Pointed Star block in the Blocks palette. Ctrl+click on one of the corner blocks to set this design in all corners. Position the cursor in one of the Big Points Out. Ctrl+click to set the design in these large border triangles.

Step 4 – Set Tool

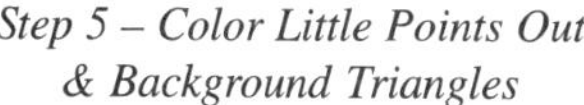

Step 5 – Color Little Points Out & Background Triangles

Step 5 – Save in Sketchbook

Step 6 – Color remaining borders

Save

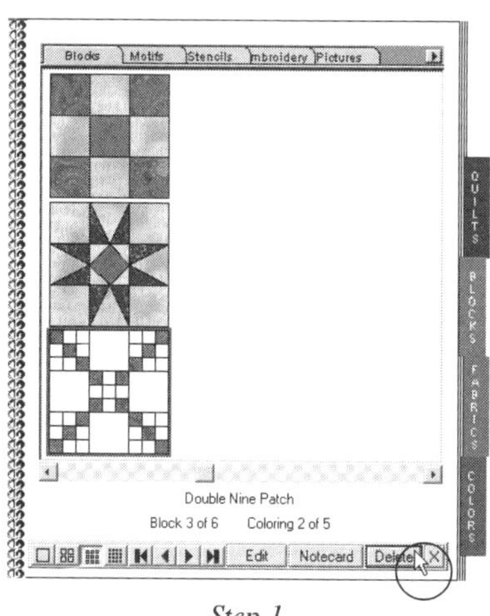

Step 1

5 Click on the Paintbrush tool and then select a fabric for the Little Points Out in this border. Ctrl+click to set this color. Select a fabric for the background triangles and Ctrl+click to set this fabric. Save in Sketchbook.

6 Select colors for the remaining borders and, following the same procedure, color these borders. Save in Sketchbook.

Your Two-Stepping Stars quilt is finished! Complete a Quilt Notecard for this design in the Sketchbook. Refer to the Completing Notecards section in Lesson 1 for full instructions. Remember to click on the Save button after adding information to the Notecard. Now that your quilt is completed, it is a good idea at this point to clean up your Sketchbook. In the next section, you will remove the designs that you saved as you were developing your quilt.

Deleting Designs from the Sketchbook

If you followed the instructions in this lesson, you saved often and now have several unfinished quilts in your Sketchbook. It should be easy to identify your final designs because you completed Notecards for these quilts. The names will display with the quilts in the Sketchbook. Be careful that you save these named quilts and delete only the unfinished designs!

You can delete designs from any of the Sketchbook tabs.

1 To delete a design from the Block Sketchbook, open the Sketchbook and click on the Blocks tab. Click on the tab that contains the design that you want to delete. Select the design that you want to delete and then click on the Delete button at the bottom of the Sketchbook. If you delete the line drawing first, all of the colorings of the design are deleted with it.

2 To delete a quilt, open the Sketchbook and click on the Quilts tab. Use the arrows on the Sketchbook page to display the quilt that you want to delete. Click on the Delete button at the bottom of the Sketchbook.

3 To delete a fabric or color sample, select the sample and then click on the Delete button at the bottom of the Sketchbook.

4 When EQ5 asks you if you want to delete the object and/or its coloring, answer Yes and the design will be eliminated from your Sketchbook. EQ5 will warn you if the design you are attempting to delete is used in a block or quilt design.

5 You must save Sketchbook changes to your disk drive to make them permanent. Click on Save after closing the Sketchbook.

Tip

- **It is wise to Save in Sketchbook often while working on a project! Unwanted items can be discarded easily by deleting them from the Sketchbook.**

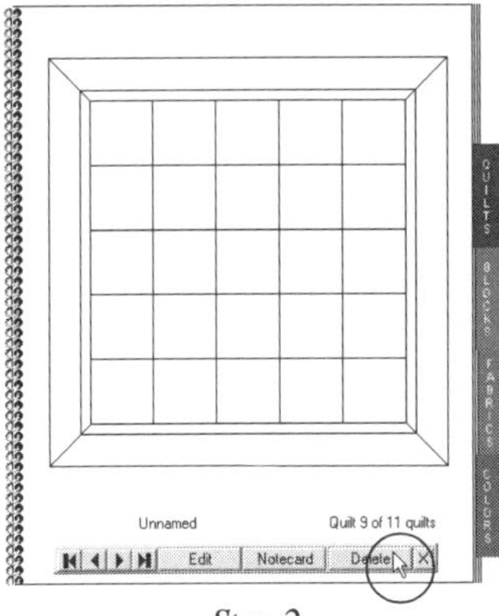

Step 2

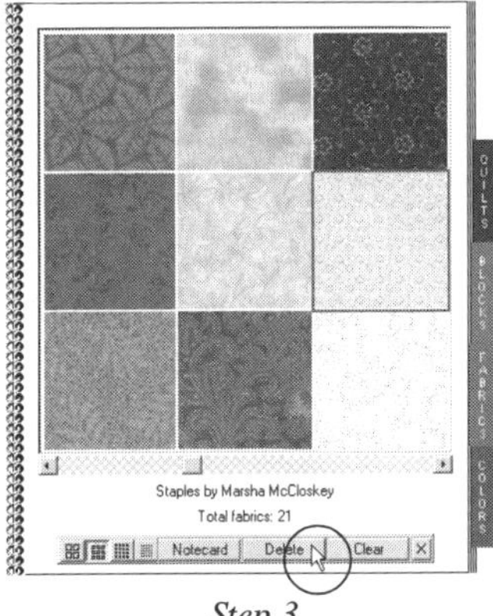

Step 3

Step 5 – Save Button

Printing Foundation Patterns

It's easy to print out foundation patterns in EQ5, even if the designs are complex!

1 With your Two-Stepping Stars quilt on the worktable, click on the Select tool. Click on one of the whole Eight-Pointed Star blocks in the quilt layout. Click on File, click on Print, and then click on Foundation Pattern in the extended menu.

Tip

- **You will learn how to generate printouts for triangular blocks in Lesson 6. The triangular blocks in this quilt are the partial blocks in the border and those along the edge of the pieced area in the layout.**

2 In the Print Foundation Pattern box you will see three tabs: *Sections, Numbering,* and *Options*. Click on the Sections tab. EQ5 automatically divides a foundation pattern into sections in preparation for construction.

Select Tool

Step 1

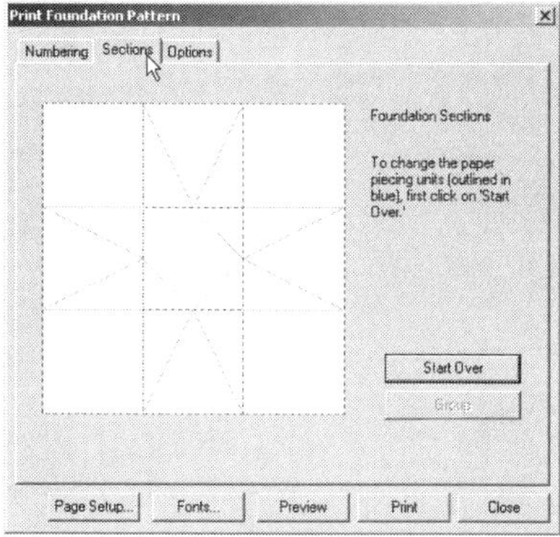

Step 2

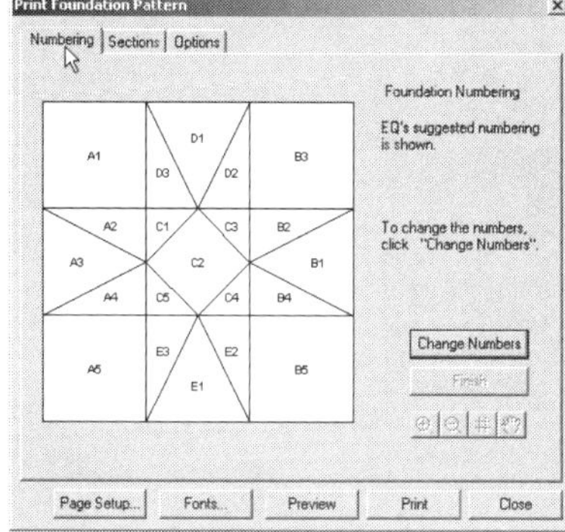

Step 3

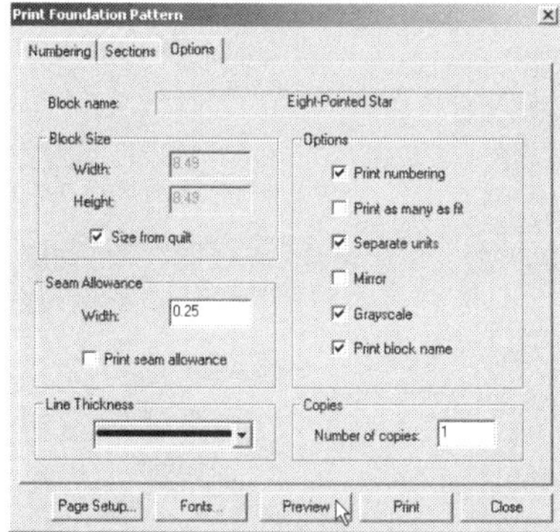

Step 4

You can change this sectioning, however, and divide a block into the construction units that you prefer. Please see the EQ5 manual or the Help file for more information. For this Lesson, you will use the sectioning recommended by EQ5.

3 Click on the Numbering tab. EQ5 automatically numbers the construction sequence for a foundation pattern. You can change the numbering sequence on this tab by clicking on Change Numbers and then clicking on the patches in the sequence that you prefer. Please see the EQ5 manual or the Help file for more information. For this Lesson, you will use the numbering recommended by EQ5.

4 Click on the Options tab. As you can see, there are many choices here. For this Eight-Pointed Star foundation pattern, select the following options:

Block Size
- Size from quilt: checked

Seam Allowance
- Print seam allowance: unchecked

Line thickness
- The last option in the drop down menu

Options (checked)
- Print numbering
- Separate units
- Grayscale
- Print block name

5 Click on Preview and Print.

6 You can also move or delete foundation pattern sections in EQ5. With the Eight-Pointed Star block still selected in the layout, click on File, click on Print, and then click on Foundation Pattern. Use the same settings as in Step 4, except uncheck Print block name. This will give you more room on the page. Click on Preview.

3

7 In the Print Preview, click on the Move button and then click on one of the foundation pattern sections. This section will highlight in red. Holding down the mouse button, drag this section to another part of the page. Now, click on the Delete button at the top of the page and then click on one of the sections. This section will highlight in red. Press the Delete key on the keyboard to eliminate this section.

Move Tool Cursor

Delete Tool Cursor

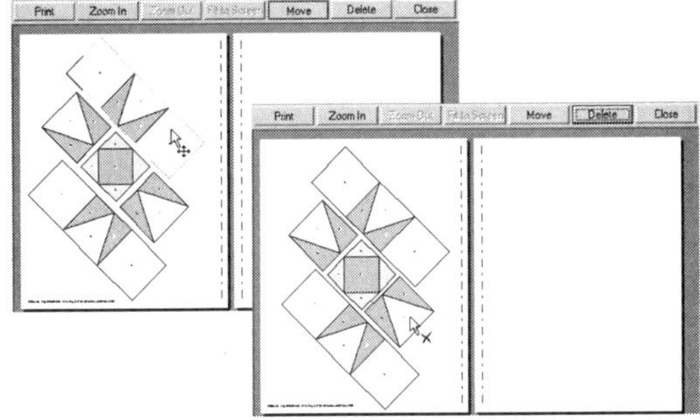

Step 7

These Move and Delete functions make it easy to conserve paper when printing in EQ5!

Be sure to check the EQ5 manuals or the Help file for more information about EQ5's printing features.

Printing Templates

It is also very easy to print out templates in EQ5!

1 With your Two-Stepping Stars quilt on the worktable, click on the Select tool. Click on one of the whole Eight-Pointed Star blocks in the quilt layout. Click on File, click on Print, and then click on Templates in the extended menu.

Step 1 – Select Tool

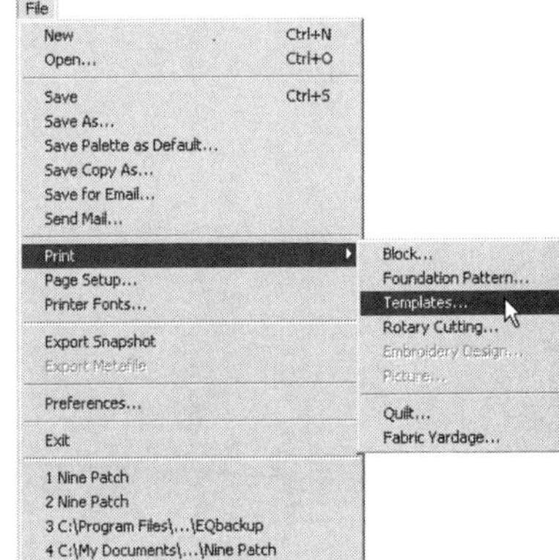

Step 1

Tip

- **You will learn how to generate templates for triangular blocks in Lesson 6.**

2 The Print Templates box will open. In the previous section, you generated a foundation pattern printout that was sized from the quilt layout. For this template printout, you will set the size of the block and change the seam allowance. Set these values in the Print Templates box:

Block size:	Width – 9 Height – 9
Seam allowance:	.5
Print seam allowance:	checked
Print key block:	checked
Line thickness:	select one

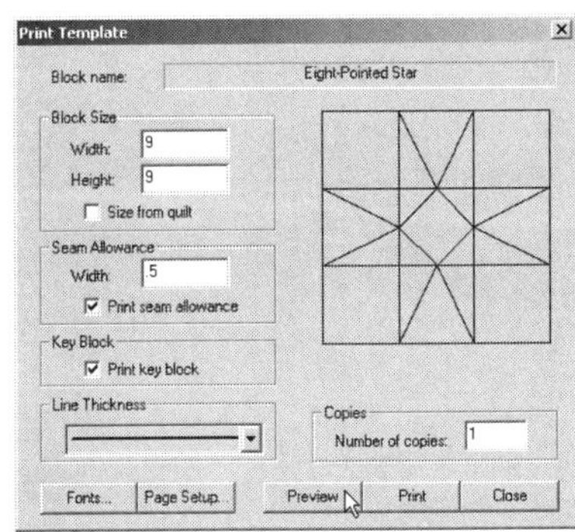

Step 2

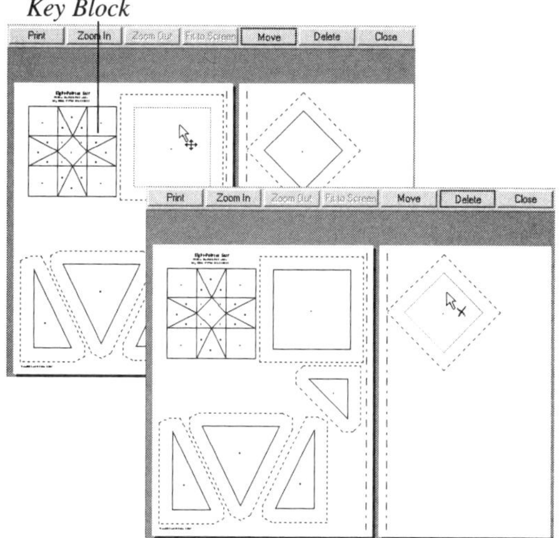

Step 3

Click on the Preview button. The Key block is the small drawing of the design that appears in the upper-left corner of this window and also then on the printout. The template letters are marked here and serve to identify the corresponding template pieces in the block design. You can turn off this feature in your printout by removing the check for this option.

3 On the Print Preview page, click on Move and then, holding down the mouse button, click and drag one of the templates to another location on the page. Click on the Delete button on the Print Preview page and then click on a template. Press the Delete key on the keyboard to remove this template from the printout. Print.

Tip

- **Notice that EQ5 has already trimmed the corners on the triangle templates.**

Generating Rotary Cutting Instructions

EQ5 will create rotary cutting instructions for a block design that can be constructed with this method.

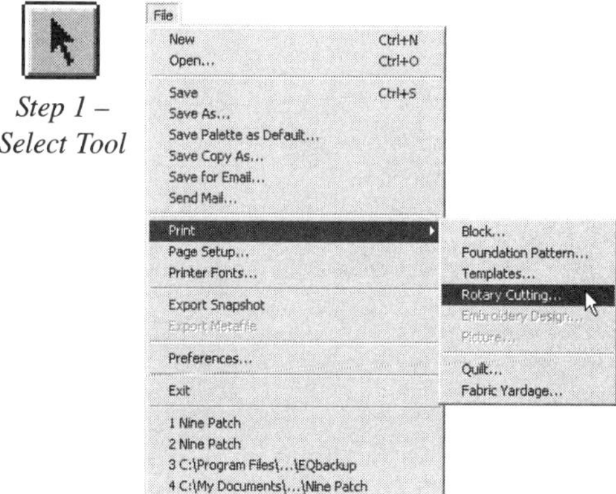

Step 1

1 With the Two-Stepping Stars on the worktable, click on the Eight-Pointed Star block with the Select tool. Click on File, click on Print, and then click on Rotary Cutting.

2 A Print Rotary Cutting Chart box will open. Choose the following settings:

Block Size:	Size from quilt
Seam Allowance:	.25
Round to Nearest:	1/16

Click on Preview. EQ5 will give you the patch count of each piece in the block that can be rotary cut. You will also find the patch dimensions, including the height of the strip and the width and angle of the individual patches to be cut.

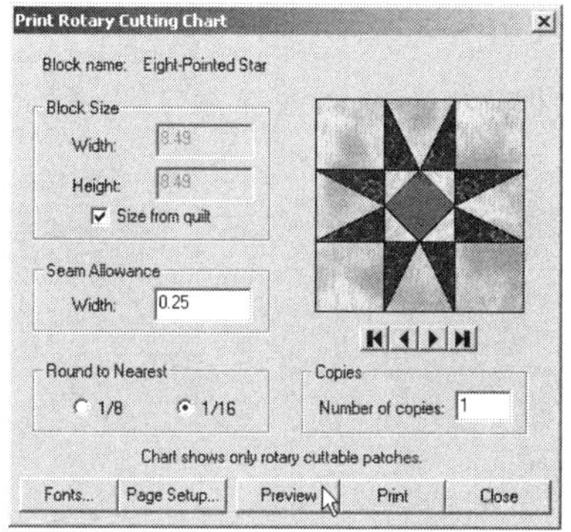

Step 2

Tip

- **Be sure to check the EQ5 Help file for more information on rotary cutting! Open the Help file and then type in rotary cutting on the Search tab. Click on List Topics and then double-click on Printing Blocks. Scroll down to *Printing a Rotary Cutting Chart* and *Special Notes about Rotary Cutting.***

Calculating Fabric Yardage

EQ5 will also calculate the amount of fabric that you need for a quilt design!

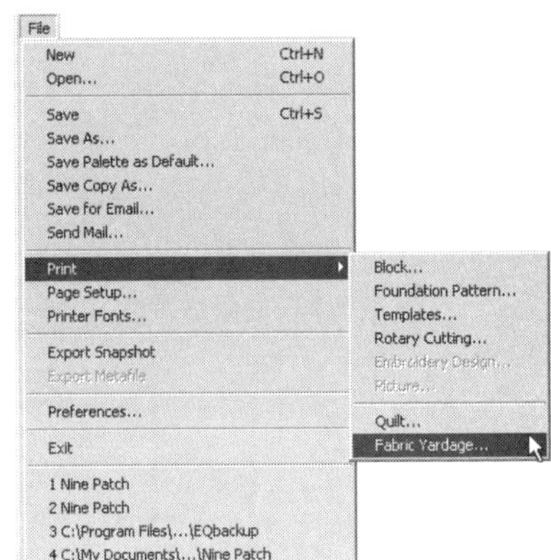

Step 1

1 With your Two-Stepping Stars quilt on the worktable, click on File in the main menu. Click on Print and then click on Fabric Yardage.

2 The Print Fabric Yardage box will open. Click on the arrow under Fabric Width to display the available options and then click on the width that you want to select.

3 Under Seam Allowance, type in the desired width and then click on Preview. EQ5 will show you the number of patches and the required yardage for each fabric in your quilt, based on the fabric width and seam allowance that you have specified. Print.

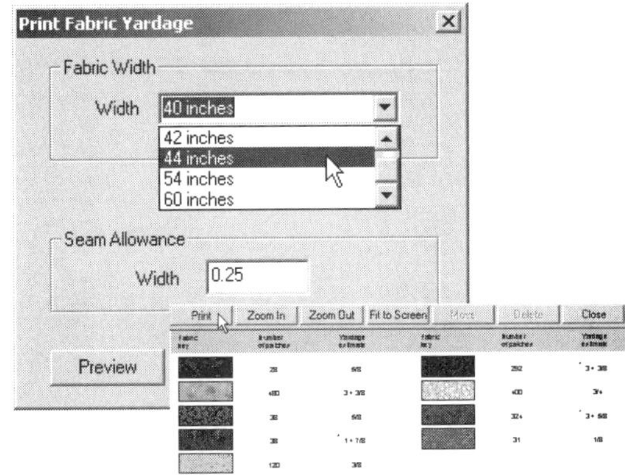

Step 2 & 3

Tip

- **Be sure to read the information in the Help file about how EQ5 calculates fabric yardage! Open the Help file and type in yardage on the Search tab. Click on List Topics. Double-click on Printing a Quilt and then scroll down to *About the Yardage Estimate.***

Export Snapshot Tool

Export Snapshot Cursor

Exporting a Snapshot: Quilts and Blocks

The Export Snapshot tool allows you to capture a portion of your screen to save as a graphic image. You can save this image to a file, copy it to the Windows clipboard to use in another Windows program, or send it to your printer. You will now use the Export Snapshot tool to capture your quilt design.

Step 1 & 2

3

Step 3

File
New Ctrl+N
Open... Ctrl+O
Save Ctrl+S
Save As...
Save Palette as Default...
Save Copy As...
Save for Email...
Send Mail...
Print
Page Setup...
Printer Fonts...
Export Snapshot
Export Metafile
Preferences...
Exit
1 Nine Patch
2 Nine Patch
3 C:\Program Files\...\EQbackup
4 C:\My Documents\...\Nine Patch

Exiting EQ5

Here is the finished quilt!

1 With the quilt on the worktable, click on the Export Snapshot tool. The cursor will look like a magnifying glass with cross hairs.

2 Click in one corner of the design and, holding down the mouse button, drag the cursor diagonally across the quilt until it is completely framed. When you release the mouse button, the Export Snapshot dialog box will open.

3 From the three options here, you can choose how you will use the graphic image that you generated. You can save it as a bitmap file, paste it into another Windows application, or send it to the printer. For this lesson, click on the Print button to print the snapshot of your quilt design.

4 Open the Sketchbook (F8) and then click on the Blocks tab. Select any block and then click on Edit to place it on the worktable.

5 Use the Export Snapshot tool to generate a snapshot of this block. Choose Print in the Export Snapshot box.

Be sure to check the EQ5 manual and the Help file for more information about exporting snapshots.

Exiting EQ5

Click on File and then click on Exit.

CONGRATULATIONS! You are gaining confidence and experience in EQ5, and can now significantly alter a quilt layout and generate a variety of printouts, including rotary cutting instructions and fabric yardage requirements.

Completing the Quilt Design

Lesson 4

Lesson 4 – Completing the Quilt Design

In Lesson 4 you will use the Graph Pad, EQ5's versatile layering feature, to superimpose quilting stencils on your quilt design. The quilt that you will create in this lesson is called Star Gazing. In addition to reviewing several tasks from the previous lessons (denoted by *), you will learn to:

Star Gazing Quilt

- *Retrieve a project**
- *Copy designs from the Libraries*
- *Draw a block with Guides*
- *Clear Guides*
- *Complete Block Notecards**
- *Modify a layout and borders**
- *Clone a border*
- *Set blocks into the layout**
- *Set & edit designs on Layers:*
    - *Block stencils*
    - *Border stencils*
- *Complete a Quilt Notecard**
- *Print appliqué templates and quilting stencils*
- *Exit EQ5**

Retrieving a Project

Run EQ5. In the opening screen, click on the Open an Existing Project tab and then click on Nine Patch.PJ5. Click on OK.

The project will open to the Sketchbook and to the last worktable that you had open. Press the Enter key or click on the X in the lower-right corner of the Sketchbook to close it.

Retrieving a Project

As always, your first task is to gather the designs that you will use in the quilt. You will now copy two designs from the EQ Libraries. You will use one as an appliqué block and the other as a quilting stencil in your new Star Gazing quilt. You will also draw a new stencil based on a block design from your Sketchbook.

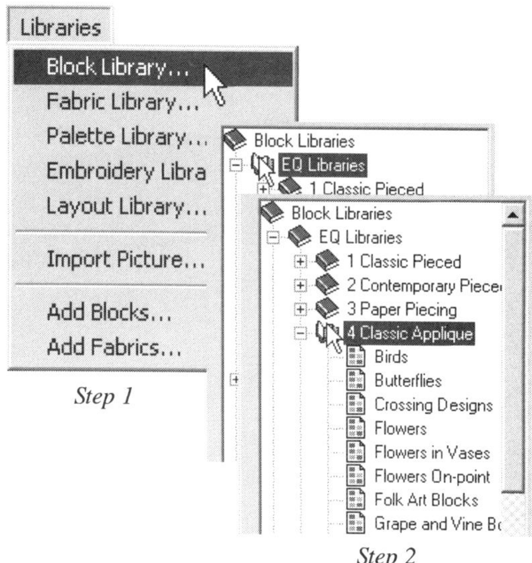

Step 1

Step 2

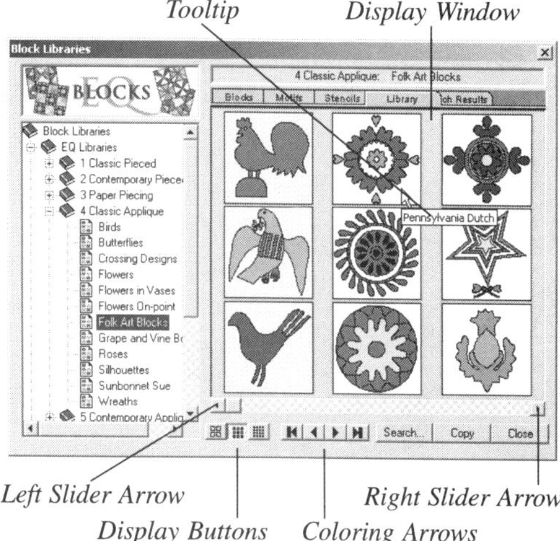

Step 3

Step 4 – Pennsylvania Dutch block

Copying Designs from the Libraries

1 Click on Libraries in the main menu and then click on Block Library in the Libraries menu. A Block Libraries box will open.

2 Click on EQ Libraries to open the list. Click on 4Classic Appliqué. The block styles within this library will appear in a list below the library name.

3 Click on Folk Art Blocks in the 4Classic Appliqué library. The designs within that style will appear in the display window. Click and hold down the right slider arrow to view all of the designs in the style. Use the left slider arrow to return to the front of the style library. Place the cursor, without clicking, over any design and a tooltip will appear that displays the design's name.

There are five tabs along the top of the Block Libraries box. The *Blocks, Motifs,* and *Stencils* tabs display the designs that are in your current project Sketchbook. The *Library* tab displays the designs that you are viewing in the open block style library. The name of this library style appears above the Library tab. The *Search Results* tab displays the designs for which you have conducted a search in the EQ5 Libraries.

Notice that you have several viewing options in the Block Libraries box. You can view four, nine, or sixteen blocks simultaneously, depending upon which display button you have selected.

The arrow buttons below the displayed blocks allow you to view the line drawing, grayscale, and colored versions of the selected block.

4 Use the slider rectangle or the slider arrow to find the Pennsylvania Dutch block. Click on this design and then click on the Copy button at the bottom of the Block Libraries box. The block will disappear temporarily, but will reappear the next time this block style library is opened.

5 Scroll down the EQ Libraries list and click on 7Quilting Stencils. The block styles within this library will appear in a list below the library name.

6 Click on the Border Stencils style in the 7Quilting Stencils library. The designs within this style will appear in the display window. Click on the Continuous Line Ovals and then click on the Copy button to copy it to the Sketchbook. Click on Close to close the Block Libraries box.

Tip

- **There are no colored versions of the designs in the 7Quilting Stencils library.**

7 Open the Block Sketchbook (F8) and click on the Pennsylvania Dutch block. Click Edit to place the block on the Block Worktable. Click on the Color tab and color this design. Save in Sketchbook.

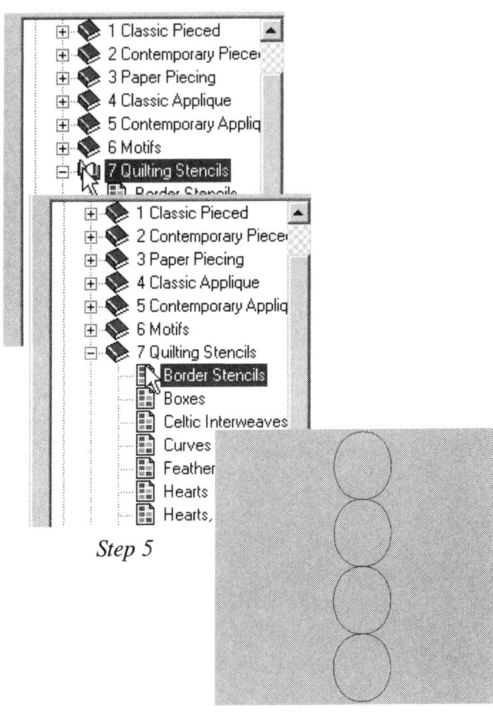

Step 5

Step 6 – Continuous Line Ovals

Step 7 – Color and Save in Sketchbook

Drawing a Block with Guides

It is often helpful to base the drawing of a new block on the structure of a previously drawn block, that is, one that is already in your Sketchbook or in the EQ Libraries. Using this technique, you will now draw a Snowball block to use as a quilting stencil on your Star Gazing quilt.

1 Click on the View Sketchbook button or use F8 to open the Sketchbook. Click on the Blocks tab and then click on the Eight-Pointed Star block. Click on Edit to place it on the worktable.

2 Click on Block in the main menu and then click on Convert to Guides in the Block menu. The lines forming the Eight-Pointed Star block are no longer displayed as solid lines, but as dashed lines. These guides will help you to draw the new stencil, but they will not appear in the finished design.

3 The Line tool is already engaged. Draw diagonal lines in the four corner patches as illustrated. Save in Sketchbook.

Step 2

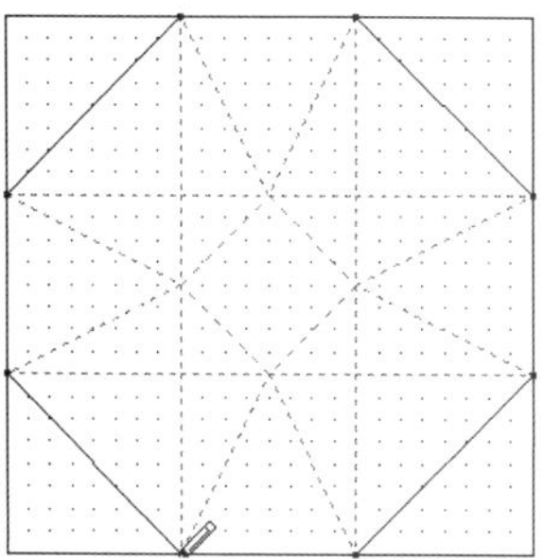

Step 3 – Draw lines and Save in Sketchbook

Tip

- **Remember that you can delete lines using the Select tool and the Delete key. For detailed instructions, see "Deleting a line in EasyDraw™" in Lesson 1.**

4 To erase the guides, click on Block in the main menu and then click on Clear Guides. The guides will disappear and the drawn block will remain. Click the Refresh button.

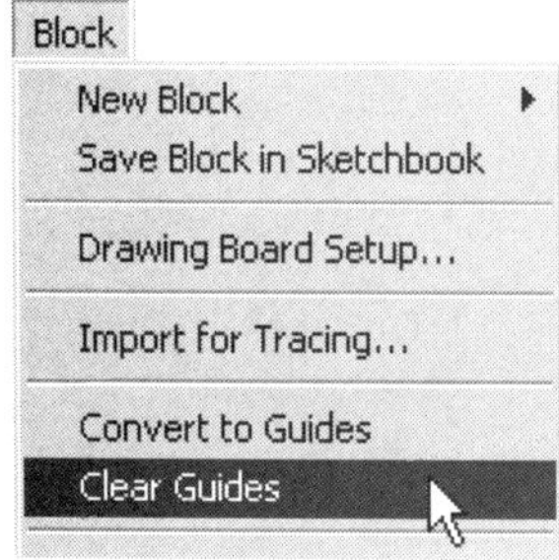

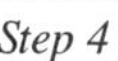

Step 4

Step 4 – Refresh Button

Tip

- **There is an EasyDraw™ Worktable Context Menu that provides a shortcut to these functions. Click anywhere on the worktable with the secondary mouse button. The menu that appears allows you to Convert to Guides and Clear Guides.**

5 Open the Sketchbook (F8) and complete a Block Notecard for this design. Name this stencil Snowball. Refer to the "Completing Notecards" section in Lesson 1 for full instructions.

Notice that the Pennsylvania Dutch block is already named. This design was copied from the EQ Libraries and its Notecard information was transferred with the design. Notice that the Continuous Line Ovals design is on the Stencils tab and is also already named because it, too, was copied from the EQ Libraries.

Remember to click on the Save button after closing the Sketchbook.

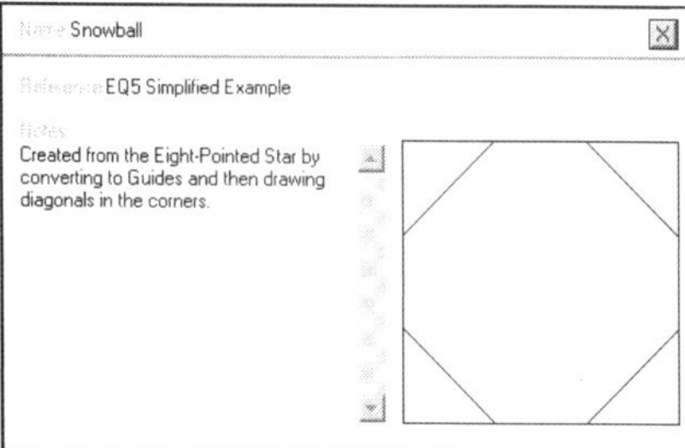

Step 5 – Create Notecard & Save

Modifying a Layout and Borders

1 Open your Sketchbook and click on the Quilts tab. Use the arrows to display the Nine Patch Star quilt from Lesson 1. Click on Edit to place it on the worktable.

Step 1

2 You will not change any values on the Layout tab. Click on the Borders tab and the first border will be selected automatically. Make the following change in the first border:

Adjust size: .75 (Lock: All)

3 Click on the second border and make the following changes:

Border style:	Spaced Squares
Adjust size:	2.5 (Lock: All)
Blocks in border:	Horizontal – 1 Vertical – 1

4 Make the following change in the third border:

Adjust size:	.75 (Lock: All)

5 You are going to create a clone for the next border! Click on the third border and then, in the Borders box, click on Clone selected border so that it is checked. Click on the Add button. This will add a new border to the outside edge of the quilt. This new border will be a clone of the third border.

6 Now you are going to insert a new border into the sequence. This Insert feature allows you to add a border before the selected border. With the last border still selected, uncheck the Clone selected border. Click on the Insert button. A new border will be added before the last border, for a total of five borders. Click on the fourth border and make the following change:

Adjust size:	2.50 (Lock: All)

7 Click on the Layer 1 tab. Save in Sketchbook. Your Star Gazing quilt layout is now established and ready to be filled with designs!

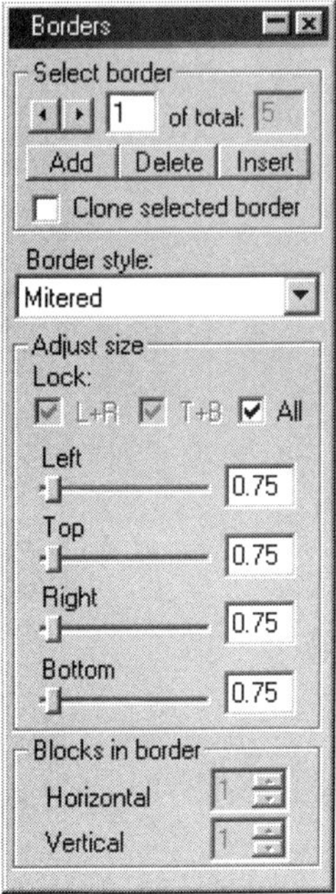

Step 2 – Border 1

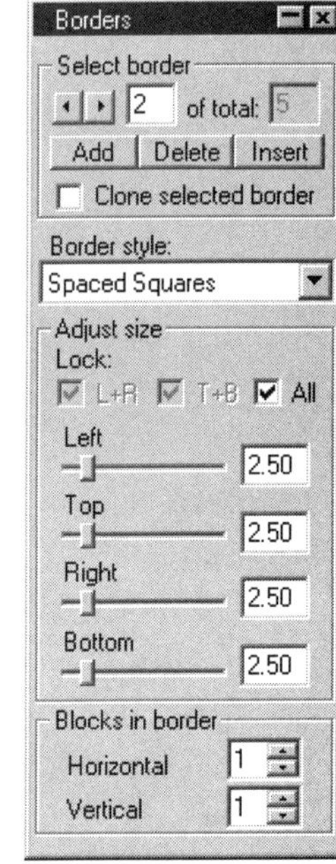

Step 3 – Border 2

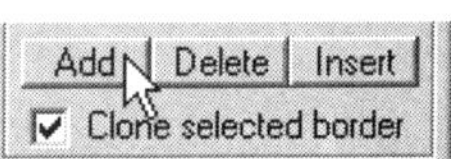

Step 5 – Clone Border 3

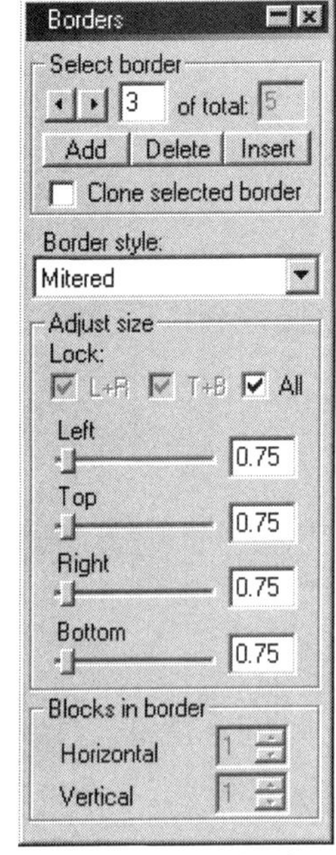

Step 4 – Border 3

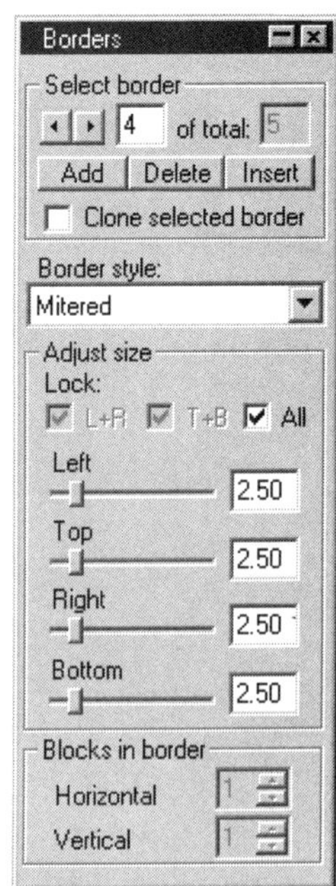

Step 6 – Border 4

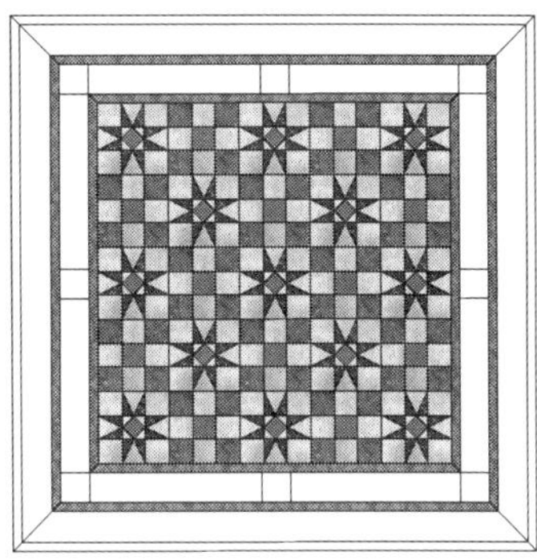

Step 7 – Here is the current quilt. In the next section you will be replacing these blocks with new designs.

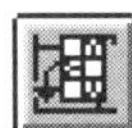

Step 1 – Set Tool

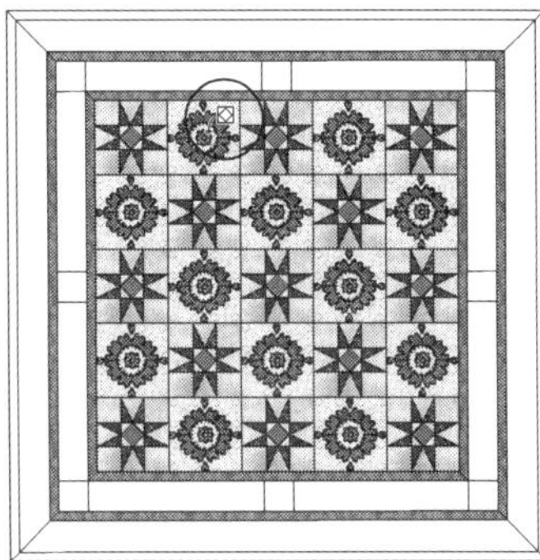

Step 2

Step 3 – Use Paintbrush Tool or Plain Block Tool

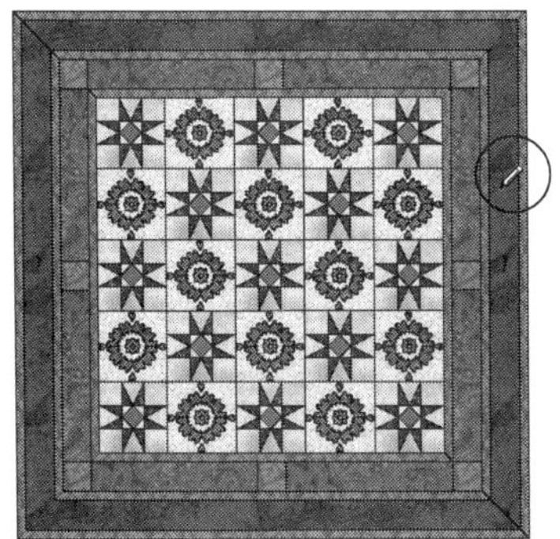

Step 3 – Color Borders & Save in Sketchbook

Setting Blocks into the Layout

1 Click on the Set tool and the Blocks palette will open on the worktable. The Eight-Pointed Star blocks will remain in the same spaces in the layout.

Tip

- **At this point, you can replace this coloring of the Eight-Pointed Star block with another from the Sketchbook. Simply click on the Eight-Pointed Star in the Blocks palette and then click on the arrow keys at the bottom of the palette to display the new coloring that you want to use. Alt+click on one of the Eight-Pointed Star blocks in the quilt layout to replace all of these blocks with the new coloring.**

2 Click on the Pennsylvania Dutch appliqué block and position the cursor on any Nine Patch block in the quilt layout. Alt+click to fill these block spaces with this design.

3 Click on the Paintbrush tool or the Plain Block tool to color the borders in your quilt. Color the spaced squares and the corner squares in the second border with Ctrl+click. Color all segments of a border simultaneously with Ctrl+click. Save in Sketchbook.

Setting and Editing Designs on Layers

The Layers feature in Electric Quilt 5 defines three distinct layers in your quilt:

Layer 1 is the basic design layer of the quilt layout and is composed of pieced blocks and/or appliqué blocks and borders. Layer 1 also includes the Custom Set layout.

Layer 2 consists of appliqué motifs that are placed over the basic design layer. An appliqué motif is an appliqué design that has no background square and "floats" on Layer 2 of the quilt layout.

Layer 3 contains quilting stencils that are superimposed on Layers 1 and 2. Any design can be used as a stencil because Layer 3 will display only the outline of a block.

You learned in Lesson 1 that multiple blocks can be set simultaneously on Layer 1, the basic design layer. Designs on Layer 1 (Custom Set), Layer 2 (appliqué), and Layer 3 (quilting stencils) must be set individually. However, EQ5 does provide several tools that make this process fast, efficient, and precise.

Layer 1 Layer 2 Layer 3

Layer Tabs

As you work on Layers in this lesson, you will use a variety of tools: *the Set tool, the Graph Pad, the Adjust tool, the Zoom tools*, and *the Thread Color tool.* You are already familiar with the Set tool from Lessons 1, 2, and 3. You will exercise the Thread Color tool toward the end of this lesson.

The Graph Pad

The Graph Pad is a powerful EQ5 feature that allows you to accurately size and place individual designs on Layers. This feature contains advanced tools for block placement, block rotation, block size, layering order, border constraint, and multiple design alignment and sizing.

Click to Place the Graph Pad on the worktable

To place the Graph Pad on the worktable, click on View in the main menu. Click on Graph Pad in the View menu if this item is not already marked with a check.

Adjust Tool

The Graph Pad is activated only when a design
4 has been selected with the Adjust tool.

When designs are selected, the Graph Pad looks like the figures to the right.

Position *Rotation* *Size*

Selected Block 12.000 24.000 0 6.000 6.000

This is the left side of the graph pad.

This is what you will see on the right side of your graph pad when only one design is selected.

This is what you will see on the right side of your graph pad when multiple designs are selected. The left side of the graph pad will be grayed out.

In this lesson, you will use these Graph Pad tools: *Block Size, Same Size, Align,* and *Rotation.*

The Adjust Tool

The Adjust tool is the primary editing tool for placing designs on Layers. With this tool, you can move, resize, and delete designs on Layer 1 (Custom Set), Layer 2 (appliqué), and Layer 3 (quilting stencils). You will learn more about the Adjust tool in the next sections as you set designs on Layers.

Zoom In Tool

Zoom Out Tool

Refresh Screen Tool

Fit to Window Tool

Click and hold cursor in circle.
Still holding down the mouse button, drag cursor to the second circle and then release.
Here is the view on the worktable after zooming in.

This same process can be performed on whatever is currently on your worktable.

Tip

- **The Quilt Tools perform the same functions on Layers 2 and 3 that they do on Layer 1, the basic design layer. You can select, measure, set, color, rotate, and flip designs on Layers 2 and 3, just as you can on the basic quilt layout.**
- **For example, you can replace a design on Layers 2 and 3 with the same method that you replace a block design on Layer 1 in the basic quilt layout. Click on the Set tool, select the replacement design in the Blocks palette, and then click in the center of the design that you want to replace. The new design will replace the old design in the quilt layout.**

The Zoom Tools

The Zoom tools are especially helpful for accurate placement of designs on Layers.

To Zoom In:
Click on the Zoom In tool. Click on the quilt worktable and, holding down the mouse button, drag the cursor diagonally to frame the area that you want to enlarge. The screen will fill with selected area.

To Zoom Out:
Click on the Zoom Out tool and the screen will return to the previous viewing.

To refresh the screen:
Click on the Refresh Screen tool and the screen will be redrawn. This action is especially helpful in clearing your screen of debris.

To fit the design to the maximum viewing size (normal viewing):
Click on the Fit to Window tool.

Setting Block Stencils on Layers

Now it's time to add the quilting stencils to your layout! This process might seem complicated, but it is actually very easy. After establishing the first two rows of stencils, you will copy and paste to create identical rows in the layout.

Step 1

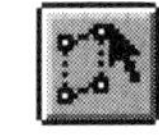

Adjust Tool

1 If the Graph Pad is not at the bottom of the worktable, click on View and then click on Graph Pad in the View menu so that it is checked. The Graph Pad will appear at the bottom of the worktable, but it will not be activated until you select a design with the Adjust tool.

Tip

- **Any design in EQ can be used as a stencil on Layer 3. It doesn't matter if you select black and white or colored blocks from the Blocks palette. EQ5 automatically superimposes only the outline of the block design on Layer 3 of your quilt layout. Any design on Layer 3 will display as quilting stitches, that is, as dashed lines.**
- **If you prefer the quilting stencils to appear as solid lines, set the designs on Layer 2. To set a design as a stencil on Layer 2, you must display the line drawing of the design in the Blocks palette. Click on the design and use the arrows in the Blocks palette to display the line drawing. The quilting stencils that are illustrated in this lesson were set on Layer 2.**
- **Experiment by setting one stencil on each Layer and deciding which effect you prefer. To delete a stencil on Layers, click on the Adjust tool, click on the stencil, and then press the Delete key.**

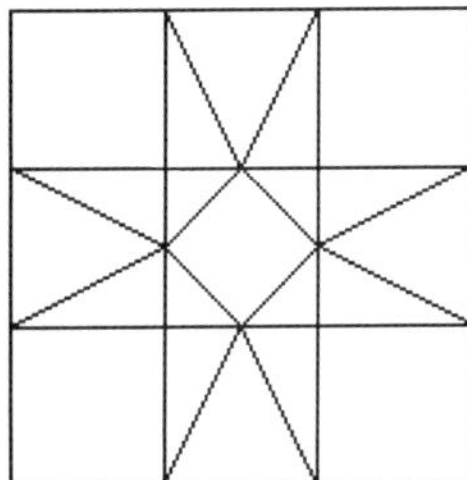

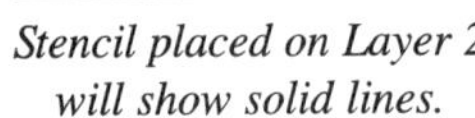

Stencil placed on Layer 2 will show solid lines.

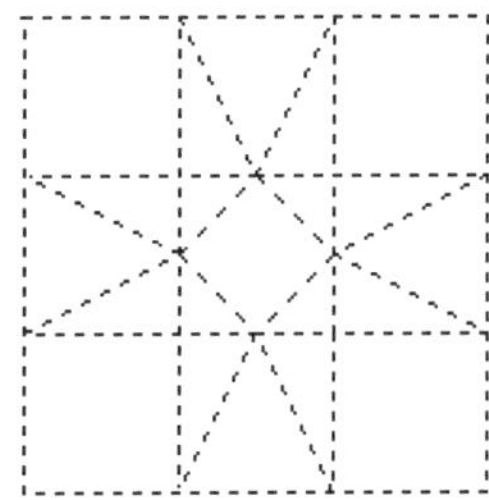

Stencil placed on Layer 3 will show dashed lines.

2 Click on the Layer on which you will place your stencils. Click on the Set tool. The Blocks palette will open on the worktable. Click on the Block tab in the Block palette and then click on the Eight-Pointed Star block.

If you are setting this design on Layer 2, be sure to select the line drawing!

If you are setting this design on Layer 3, it will be transparent automatically.

Step 2 – Set Tool

You are now going to place stencils in the first row of this quilt layout.

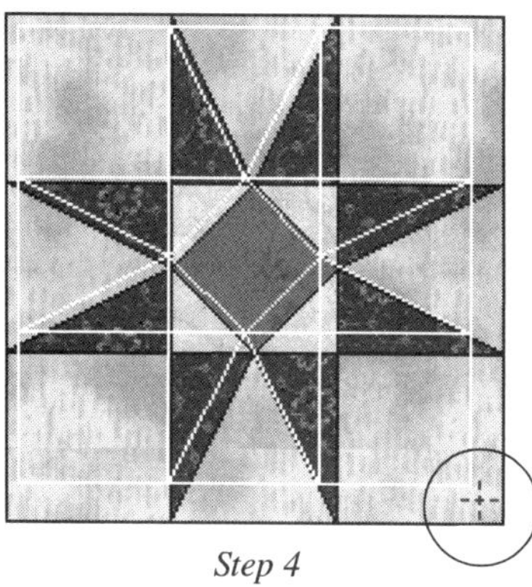

Step 4

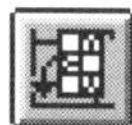

Step 5 – Set Tool

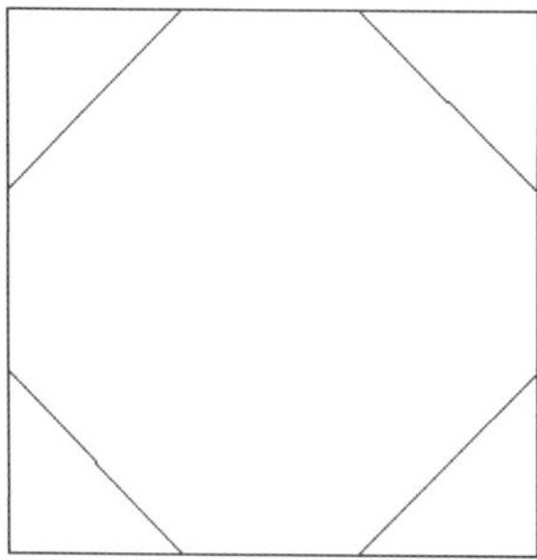

Step 6 – Snowball Stencil

Step 6

3 Magnify the first row of the quilt by clicking on the Zoom In tool and dragging the cursor diagonally across this area of the layout. This section of the quilt will be magnified on the screen and the cursor will revert back to the Set tool.

4 Position the cursor in a corner of one of the Eight-Pointed Star blocks in the layout. Hold down the Shift key and the cursor will change to crosshairs. Click and drag diagonally to form a frame over the Eight-Pointed Star block. You can release the Shift key once you have started to draw.

When you release the mouse button, an Eight-Pointed Star stencil will appear in the frame. Don't worry about accurate size or placement at this point. You will adjust the size and placement of the stencils in the next steps.

Tip

- **Remember to use Edit/Undo or Ctrl+Z to undo an action.**

5 Click on the Set tool and, holding down the Shift key, place Eight-Pointed Star stencils over the two remaining Eight-Pointed Star blocks in the first horizontal row.

6 Click on the Snowball stencil in the Block palette. Hold down the Shift key and place this design over the first Pennsylvania Dutch block in the layout. Place another Snowball stencil over the second Pennsylvania Dutch block in this row. Each block in the first horizontal row now has a quilting stencil positioned over it.

You will now establish one of these stencils as your "reference," which you will then use to accurately size and place the other stencils in the layout.

7 Click on the Adjust tool and then click on one of the Eight-Pointed Star stencils. The Graph Pad will be activated and the Block Size tool will display the design dimensions. The Block Size tool is the third Graph Pad tool from the left. Use the arrow keys on the Block Size tool to set the size to 6.00 x 6.00. The design is now accurately sized.

Block Size

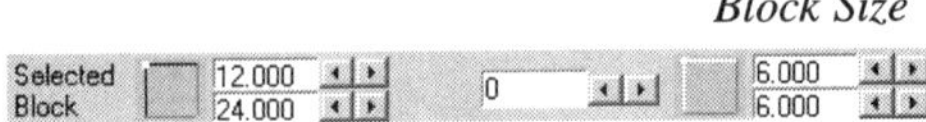

This is the left side of the graph pad.

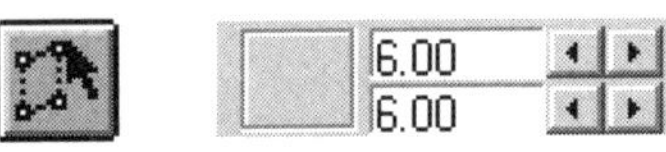

Step 7 – Adjust Tool and Stencil Size

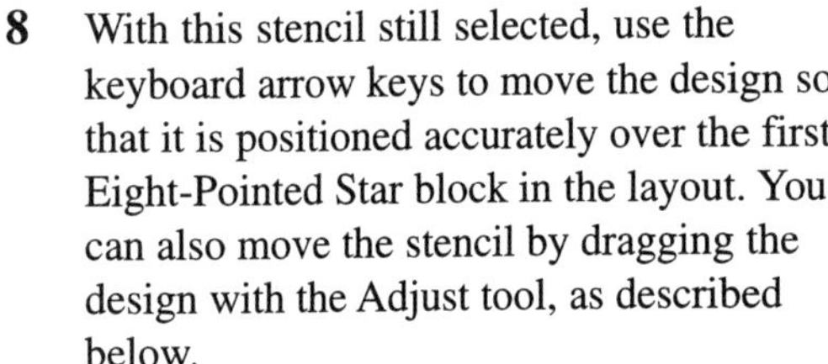

8 With this stencil still selected, use the keyboard arrow keys to move the design so that it is positioned accurately over the first Eight-Pointed Star block in the layout. You can also move the stencil by dragging the design with the Adjust tool, as described below.

This first stencil is now correctly sized and positioned on the quilt layout. You will use this as your "reference" design to size and place the other stencils in the layout.

Step 8

To move a design on Layers:
Click on the design with the Adjust tool, then click on it again, holding down the mouse button. Directional arrows will appear in the center of the block, indicating that the design is in moving mode. You can now drag the block to the desired position. You can also click on the design with the Adjust tool and then use the keyboard arrow keys to move the design.

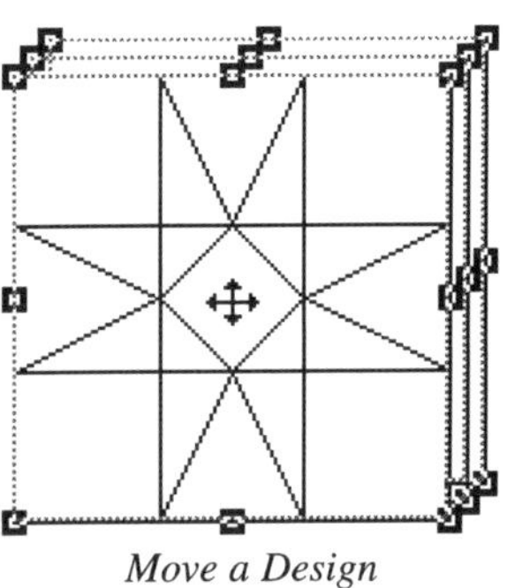

Move a Design

To resize a design on Layers:
Click on the design with the Adjust tool, and then resize, pulling the nodes that surround the image. You can also use Shift + a keyboard arrow to change the size of a selected design by increments. The top and left keyboard arrows will shrink a design. The bottom and right keyboard arrows will enlarge a design.

To delete a design on Layers:
Click on the design with the Adjust tool and then press the Delete key.

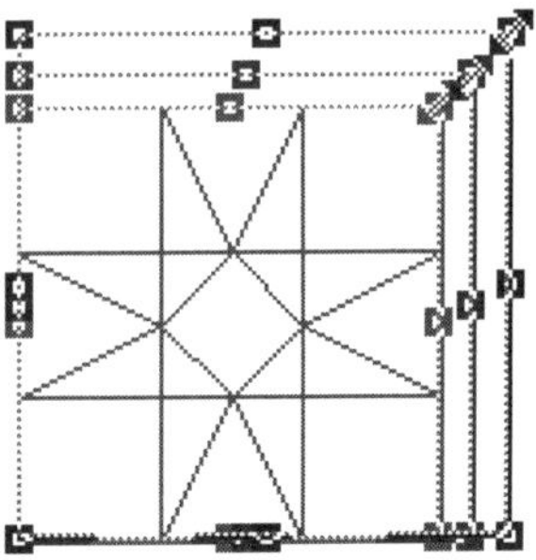

Resize a Design

Step 9 – Same Width Same Height Tool

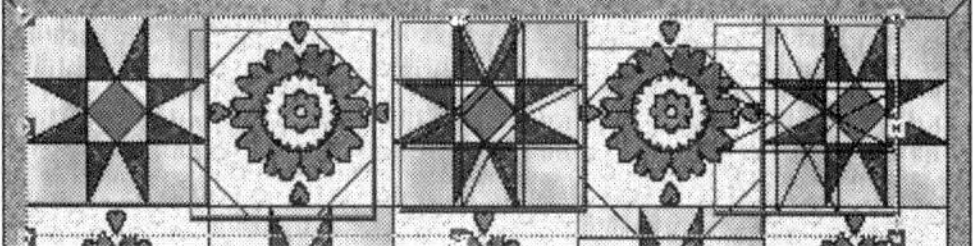

Same Width Same Height Tool applied to first row of stencils

Align Tools

Step 10 – Align Top Tool

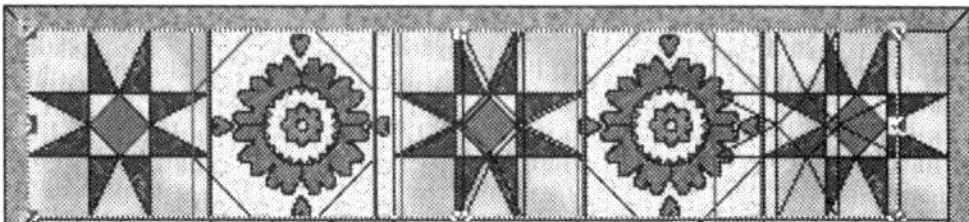

Align Top Tool applied to first row of stencils

Step 11 – Adjust Tool & Save in Sketchbook

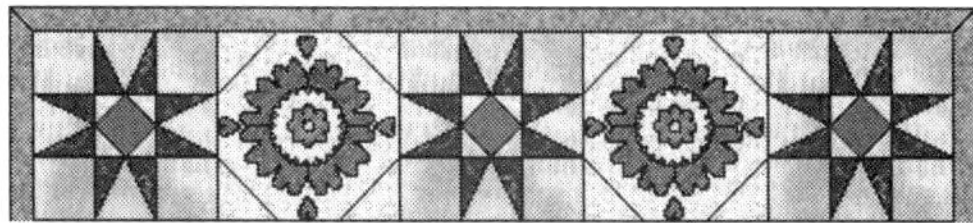

First row of stencils properly positioned

To select all designs on a Layer:
Click on the Adjust tool, hold down the Ctrl key and click on any design on that Layer. All of the designs on that Layer will be selected and highlighted. This is especially helpful when you want to find a design on a busy worktable.

9 With the first, correctly-sized stencil selected with the Adjust tool, hold down the Shift key and click on all of the new stencils that you set in the first horizontal row. With all of the stencils selected, click on the Same Width Same Height tool on the Graph Pad. All of the stencils will adjust automatically to the size of the first, or reference, stencil.

There are tools on the Graph Pad that will help you to align your designs on Layers: *Align Left, Align Right, Align Top,* and *Align Bottom.*

10 Your stencils are still selected with your first stencil as a reference. Remember that you already positioned the reference stencil accurately on the layout. Click on the Align Top tool to line up the other stencils to the top edge of the reference block. Click outside of the selection box.

Tip

- **It doesn't matter which design you choose as your reference in a quilt layout, as long as it is correctly sized and/or positioned and you select it first with the Adjust tool.**
- **You can easily replace a design on Layers. Click on the Set tool, select the replacement design in the Blocks palette, and then click on the design to be replaced in the layout.**

11 Your stencils are now aligned horizontally. To adjust the vertical position of each stencil in this row, click on each individually with the Adjust tool and use the left or right arrow keys on the keyboard to nudge the stencil into position over the pieced block. You should use the Zoom tools to help you to do this accurately. Click off of a stencil when it is properly positioned. Save in Sketchbook.

Tip

- **You can change the nudge settings of the Graph Pad under Layout Options in the Preferences dialog box. Please see the EQ5 manuals or the EQ Help file for more information.**

Black is the default color for quilting stencils in EQ5. On a dark quilt, however, it can be impossible to see black stencils. To make stencils more easily visible on your particular quilt color combination, you can change the quilting thread color with the Thread Color tool.

Use the Thread Color tool to change color for quilting stencils.

12 Click on the Thread Color tool and then click on a solid color in the Fabrics palette that will contrast well with the fabrics in your quilt. The cursor will look like a threaded needle. Ctrl+click to recolor all of the stencils simultaneously. Save in Sketchbook.

Step 12– Thread Color Cursor

Tip

- **If you have placed stencils on Layer 2 in a quilt layout that also has appliqué designs on that Layer, you must click on the quilting stencils individually to recolor them. If you use Ctrl+click in this situation, the outlines of the appliqué motif will also recolor.**

Now that this first horizontal row of quilting stencils is correctly sized and positioned, you can use it to create identical rows of stencils!

13 Click on the Adjust tool and, holding down the Shift key, click on each stencil in this first row. When the entire row is selected, Ctrl+C to copy and then Ctrl+V to paste another row of stencils on the worktable.

Step 13 – Adjust Tool

Tip

- **Use the Zoom Out or the Fit to Window buttons in the Zoom tools to return to normal viewing.**

14 Position the cursor over the new stencil row. Directional arrows appear that indicate the cursor is in the moving mode. Click and drag this new row of stencils into position over the third horizontal row of blocks. With the row still selected, Ctrl+C and then Ctrl+V. Position this new row of stencils over the fifth row of blocks. Save in Sketchbook.

Step 14 – Complete row 3 & 5, Save in Sketchbook

Step 15 – Save in Sketchbook

15 Click on the Adjust tool and then click on one of the Snowball stencils in the first row. Ctrl+C to copy and then Ctrl+V to paste another copy of this design on the worktable. Position this stencil over one of the Pennsylvania Dutch blocks in the second row. Copy an Eight-Pointed Star stencil from the first row and paste it on the worktable. Move this stencil over an Eight-Pointed Star design in the second row. Continue to copy and paste Snowball and Eight-Pointed Star stencils until all of the blocks in the second row have quilting stencils superimposed on them. Save in Sketchbook.

Step 16

16 Click on the first stencil in the second row and use the keyboard arrow keys to position it accurately over the Pennsylvania Dutch block in this horizontal row. This stencil is now correctly sized, positioned and can be used as a reference for the other stencils in this row! Save in Sketchbook.

Step 17 – Align Top Tool

17 With the first stencil in the second row still selected, hold down the Shift key and click on the remaining stencils in that row. Click on the Align Top tool and all of the stencils in the second row will align properly. Click outside of the selection box.

Step 18 – Save in Sketchbook

18 Click on each stencil in this row individually and adjust the vertical position, if necessary. The second row of stencils is now correctly sized and positioned. Save in Sketchbook. You can use this row to create identical rows of stencils!

19 Holding down the Shift key, click on each stencils in the second row. Ctrl+C to copy and then Ctrl+V to paste another row of stencils on the worktable.

20 Position the new row of stencils over the fourth horizontal row. Save in Sketchbook.

Step 20 – Complete row 4 & Save in Sketchbook

Setting Border Stencils on Layers

Now you will place quilting stencils on the borders! You can use the same copy and paste technique that you used to set stencils on the rows of blocks.

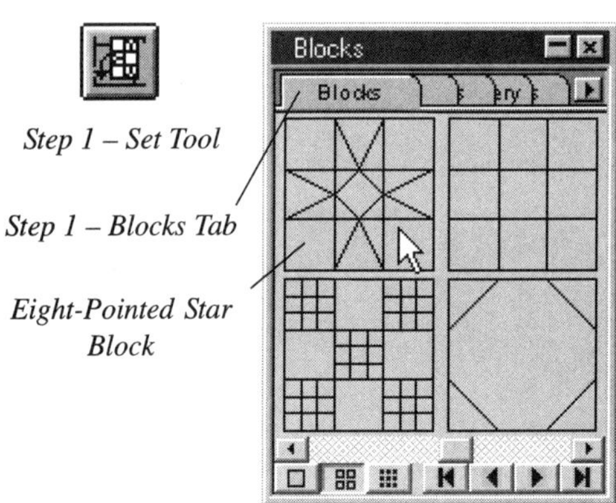

Step 1 – Set Tool

Step 1 – Blocks Tab

Eight-Pointed Star Block

1 Click on Layer 2 (for solid quilting lines) or Layer 3 (for dashed quilting lines). Click on the Set tool and then click on the Block tab in the Blocks palette.

2 Click on the Eight-Pointed Star block. Remember to select the line drawing if you are placing the stencil on Layer 2.

Holding down the Shift key, click and drag to set this stencil on one of the small squares in the second border. Click on the square with the Adjust tool and set the block size on the Graph Pad to 2.500 x 2.500. Adjust the position of this stencil so that it is placed accurately over the square. This is your reference stencil. Save in Sketchbook.

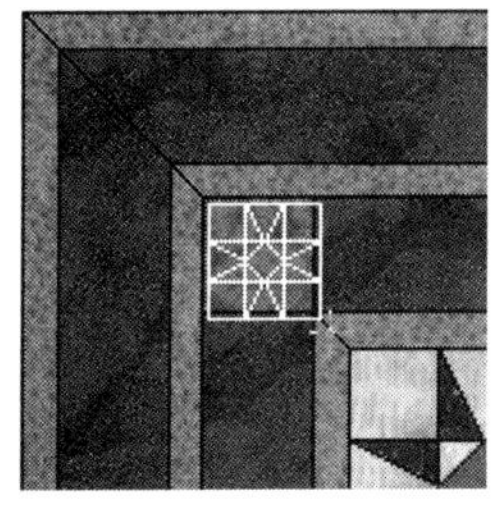

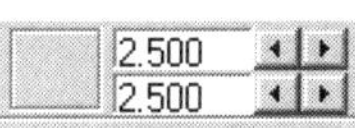

Stencil Size

Save in Sketchbook

Step 2

3 Click on the Adjust tool and then click on the Eight-Pointed Star stencil. Ctrl+C to copy. Ctrl+V seven times to paste seven Eight-Pointed Star stencils on the worktable.

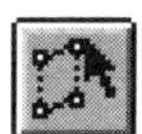

Step 3 – Adjust Tool

4

Tip

- **Change the color of the quilting stencil, if necessary, with the Thread Color tool.**

4 Click on one of the seven Eight-Pointed Star stencils to select it. Click and drag the stencil over one of the spaced squares in the second border. Drag each of the seven stencils individually to their approximate location on the quilt as shown to the right. Now you are ready to align them with the reference stencil.

Step 4 & 5

Tape Measure Tool

Step 6 – Tape Measure

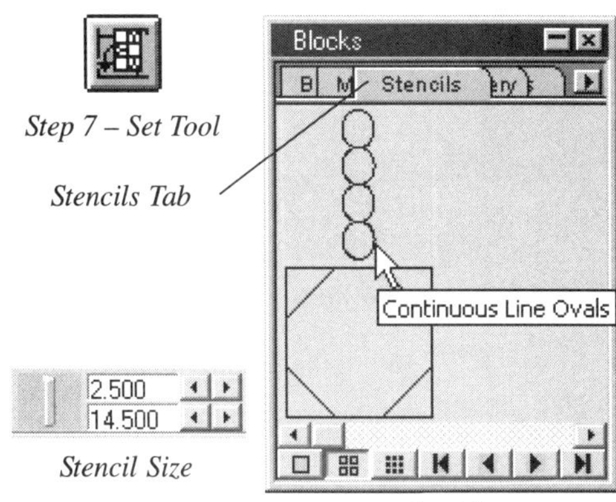

Step 7 – Set Tool

Stencils Tab

Stencil Size

Step 7

Step 9 – Align Left or Align Right

Step 10 – Second border is now filled with stencils on the left and right sides.

5 Click on the reference stencil again. Use the appropriate Align tool to line up star stencils in the squares on the same side of the border as the reference stencil. Align each side of the border separately, using the corner stencil in the previously aligned segment as a reference. Save in Sketchbook. Refer to pages 66 and 67 for more help regarding aligning stencils.

6 Click on the Tape Measure tool and measure between two of the spaced squares in the second border. Zoom in, if necessary. The length of this space is 14.500.

7 Click on the Set tool and then click on the Stencils tab in the Blocks palette. Click on the Continuous Line Ovals stencil and, holding down the Shift key, draw this design on the worktable. Click on the stencil with the Adjust tool and set the size on the Graph Pad to 2.500 x 14.500.

8 With the design still selected, move it to one of the vertical sides of the second border. You can use the Adjust tool or the keyboard arrow keys to position it accurately. Ctrl+C and then Ctrl+V to copy and paste the design. Move the copy into position to fill the rest of this vertical border.

9 Using the first stencil as a reference, hold down the shift key and align the two stencils either to the left or to the right.

10 With the two stencils still selected, Ctrl+C to copy and Ctrl+V to paste another copy of this stencil set on the worktable. Move this new stencil set to the opposite vertical border, using the arrow keys or the Adjust tool. Save in Sketchbook.

11 Now you will rotate this design to create quilting stencils for the horizontal sides of this border. Click on only one of the border stencils with the Adjust tool. Ctrl+C and Ctrl+V to place another copy on the worktable. With the new stencil selected, use the arrows on the Graph Pad Rotation tool to set the angle at 90°. Move the stencil into position on one of the horizontal sides of the border, using the keyboard arrow keys or the Adjust tool.

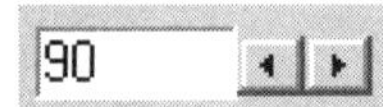

Step 11 – Graph Pad Rotation Tool

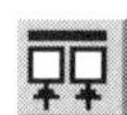

Step 12 – Align Top or Align Bottom

12 Ctrl+C and Ctrl+V to create another copy of the stencil. Move the copy into position to fill the rest of this horizontal border. Using the first border stencil as a reference, align the two stencils either to the top or to the bottom.

Step 13 – Second border is now filled entirely with stencils.

13 With the two stencils still selected, create a copy of this stencil set on the worktable. Move this new stencil set to the opposite horizontal border, using the arrow keys or the Adjust tool. The second border is now complete! Save in Sketchbook.

Tip

- **Remember to use the Thread Color tool to change quilting stencil color. Remember to use the Zoom tools when you are working on Layers!**

4

14 Click on the Tape Measure tool and measure the length of the fourth border. Be sure to measure down the center of the border, from mitered seam to mitered seam. This measurement is 40.50. You will need two Continuous Line Oval stencils that measure 20.25 each to fill each side of this border.

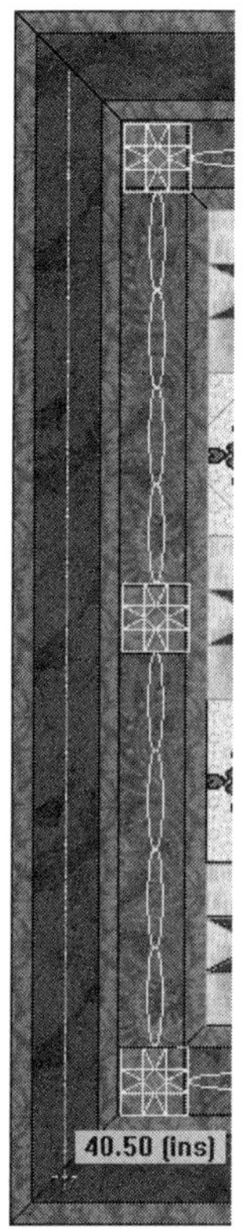

Step 14

15 Click on the Set tool and then click on the Stencil tab. Click on the Continuous Line Oval stencil and, holding down the Shift key, place this design on the worktable. Click on it with the Adjust tool and set the size to 2.500 x 20.250. Move the stencil into position, filling half of one vertical side of the fourth border.

Set Tool

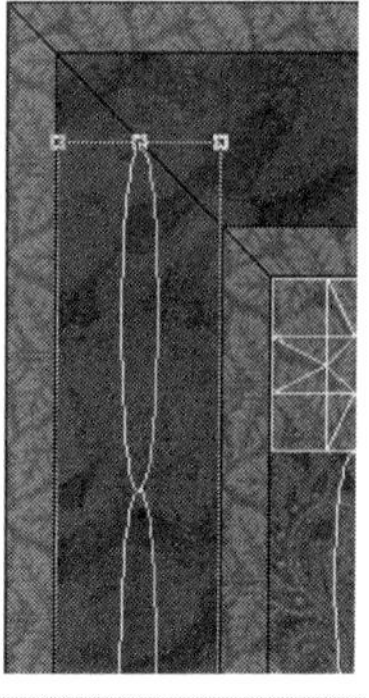

Step 15

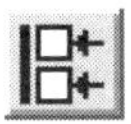

Step 16 – Align Left or Align Right

16 Ctrl+C and Ctrl+V to copy and paste another stencil on the worktable. Position the new copy carefully to fill the rest of this vertical border. Using the first stencil as a reference, align the two stencils either to the left or to the right.

Step 17 – Fourth border is now filled with stencils on the left and right sides.

17 With the two stencils still selected, Ctrl+C to copy and Ctrl+V to paste another copy of this stencil set on the worktable. Move this new stencil set to the opposite vertical border, using the arrow keys or the Adjust tool. Use the Align tools so that these new stencils are level with the stencils on the opposite of the quilt. Save in Sketchbook.

Step 18

18 With the Adjust tool, click on one of the stencils in the fourth border. Ctrl+C and Ctrl+V to place another copy on the worktable. With the new stencil selected, use the arrows on the Graph Pad Rotation tool to set the angle at 90°. Move the stencil into position on one of the horizontal sides of the fourth border, using the keyboard arrow keys or the Adjust tool.

Step 19 – Align Top or Align Bottom

19 Ctrl+C and Ctrl+V to place another copy of the design on the worktable. Move the copy into position to fill the rest of this horizontal border. Using the first border stencil as a reference, align the two stencils either to the top or the bottom.

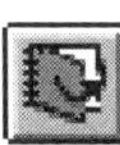

Step 20 – Complete Border & Save in Sketchbook

20 With the two stencils still selected, Ctrl+C to copy and Ctrl+V to paste another copy of this stencil set on the worktable. Move this new stencil set to the opposite horizontal border, using the arrow keys or the Adjust tool. Save in Sketchbook.

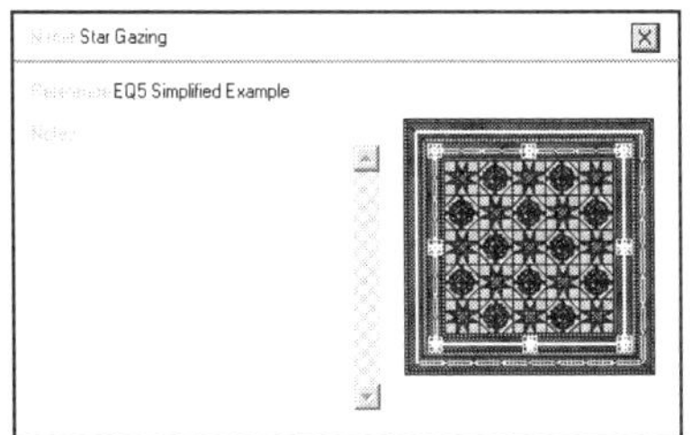

Step 21 – Create Notecard & Save

21 Open the Sketchbook (F8) and then click on the Quilts tab. Use the arrows to display the final copy of your new quilt. Click on the Notecard button and type in *Star Gazing* as your quilt name. Close the Notecard. Delete any unfinished designs in the Quilt Sketchbook. Close the Sketchbook and Save.

Tip

- **You can make size changes on Layer 1 even after you have added Layers 2 and 3. EQ5 will automatically resize any designs on Layers, but you may have to adjust their placement. This feature is available to you under the Layout Options in the Preferences dialog box. Please see the EQ5 manuals or the Help file for more information.**

Printing Appliqué Templates and Quilting Stencils

The printing functions for templates and stencils are similar to those for blocks and foundation patterns.

Step 1 – Select Tool

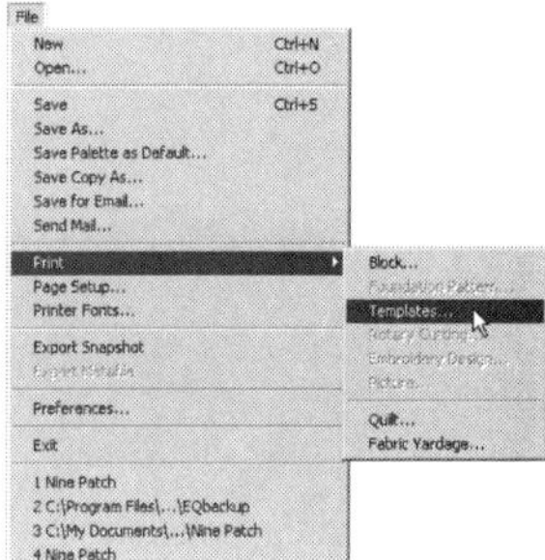

Step 1

1 With your stenciled Star Gazing quilt on the worktable, click on the Layer 1 tab. Click on the Select tool and then click on one of the appliqué blocks in the layout. Click on File, click on Print, and then click on Templates. The Print Templates box will open.

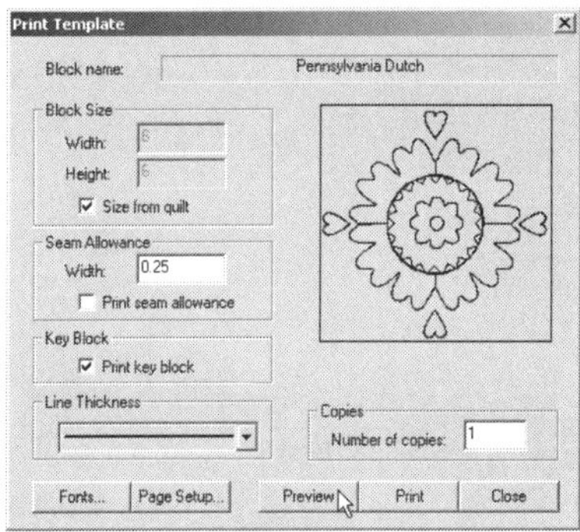

Step 2

2 Click on Size from quilt under Block Size in the Print Templates box. Uncheck Print seam allowance. Check Print key block. Click on Preview.

3 Click on the Move button on the Print Preview page and then click on one of the templates to select it. Drag the template to another location on the page.

4

4 Click on the Delete button and then click on one of the templates. Press the Delete key on the keyboard to eliminate this template pattern. Click on Print.

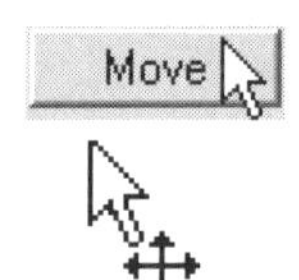

Step 3 – Move button & Cursor

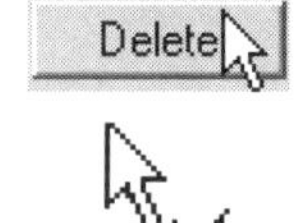

Step 4 – Delete button & Cursor

Now you will print quilting stencils.

5 Click on the Layer on which you placed your quilt stencils. Click on the Select tool and then click on one of the Eight-Pointed Star stencils. Click on File, click on Print, and then click on Block. The Print Block box will open.

Step 5 – Select Tool

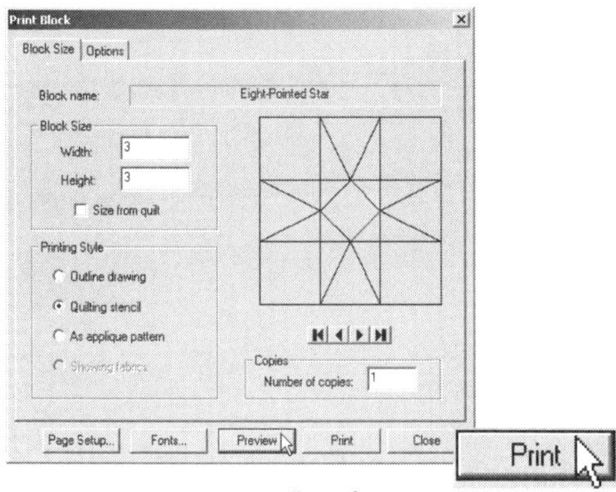

Step 6

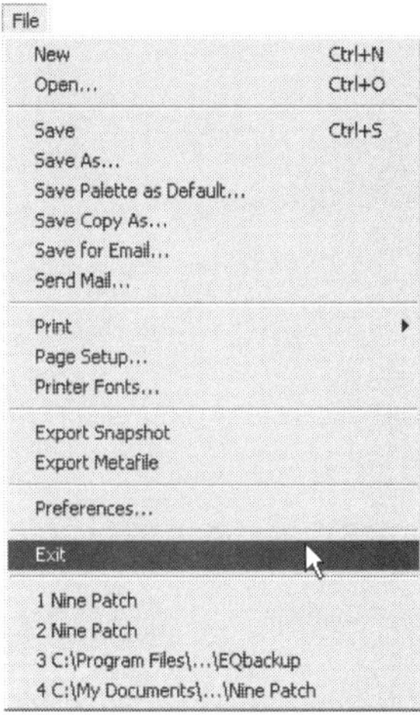

Exiting EQ5

Here is the finished quilt!

6 Click on the Options tab and then check Print block name and Print as many as fit. Click on the Block Size tab and then uncheck Size from quilt. Type in 3 for the Width and Height. Under Printing Style, check Quilting stencil. Click on Preview and Print.

Exiting EQ5

Click on File and then click on Exit.

CONGRATULATIONS! You have exercised the full array of EQ5's basic quilt design functions. You are now an experienced EQ5 user and can design, color, edit, save, and print your own quilt designs!

Now that you have completed Part I, you will find it very helpful to practice your new EQ5 skills. Enter several of your own previously completed quilt designs into the program, using Part I as your guide. Compare various factors such as your actual finished quilt sizes and your actual yardage requirements with the quilt sizes and the yardage estimates that you generate in EQ5. Experiment further by adjusting the quilt layouts and modifying your original designs. Add quilting stencils. Generate a variety of printouts that illustrate the printing options. You will become more proficient with each new quilt design that you create in EQ5!

After you have mastered the basic EQ5 design procedures featured in Part I, you will be ready to explore the more advanced concepts and techniques that are presented in Part II of this tutorial. Part II will help you to develop your EQ5 proficiency by focusing on the program's more sophisticated capabilities.

Remember that this tutorial is intended to serve as a guide to EQ5. There are a variety of ways to accomplish specific tasks in the program, so you should not limit your approach to just those found here.

EQ5

SIMPLIFIED PART II QUILTS

LESSON 5 ANTIQUE ROSE

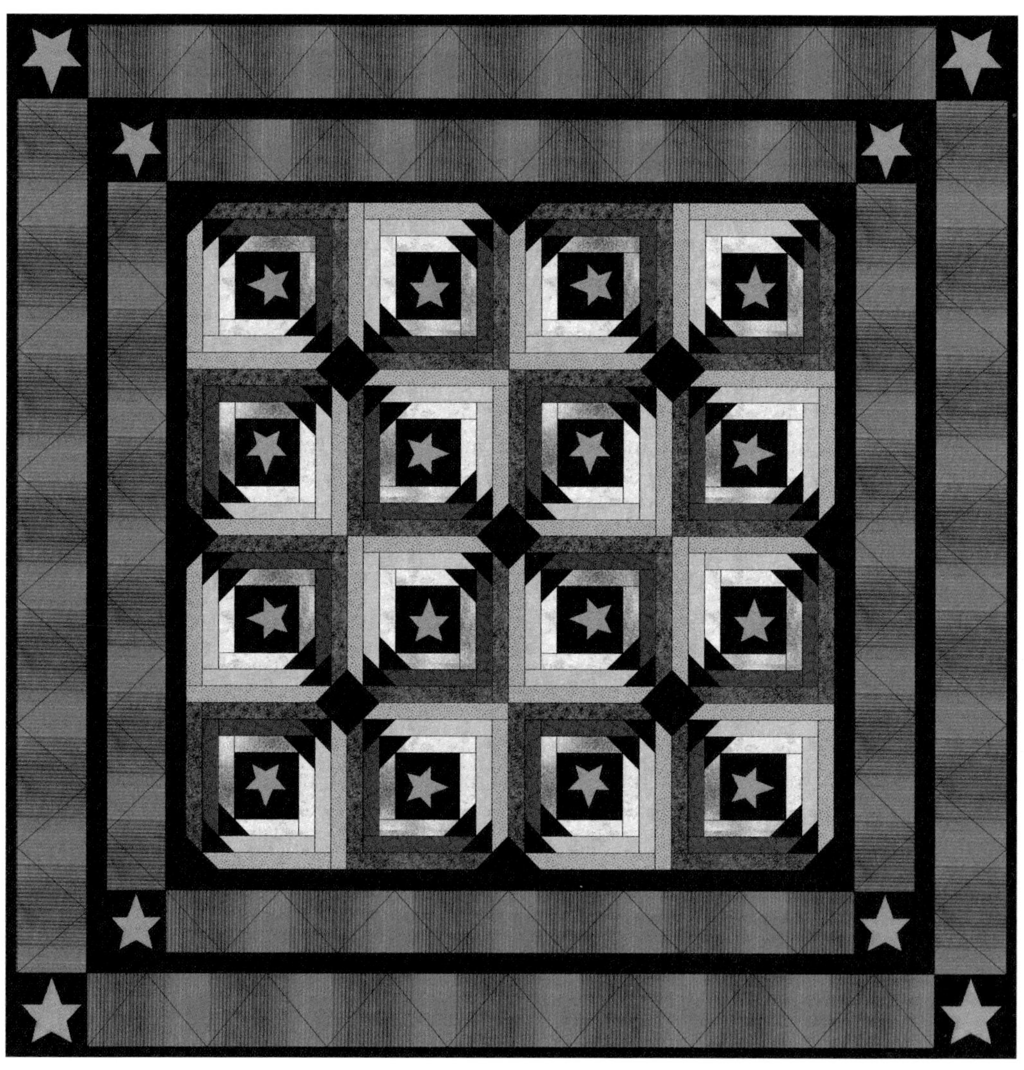

LESSON 6 SYMMETRY SERIES I

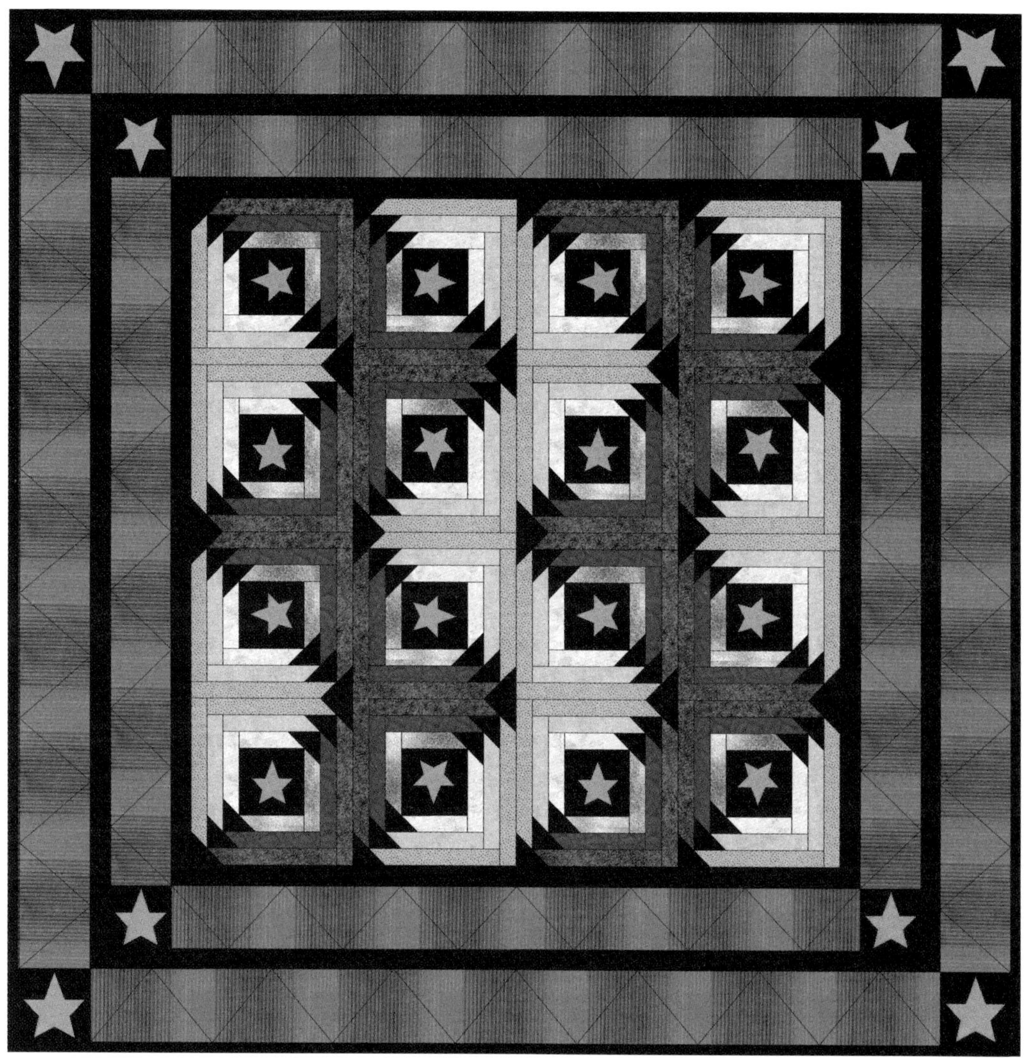

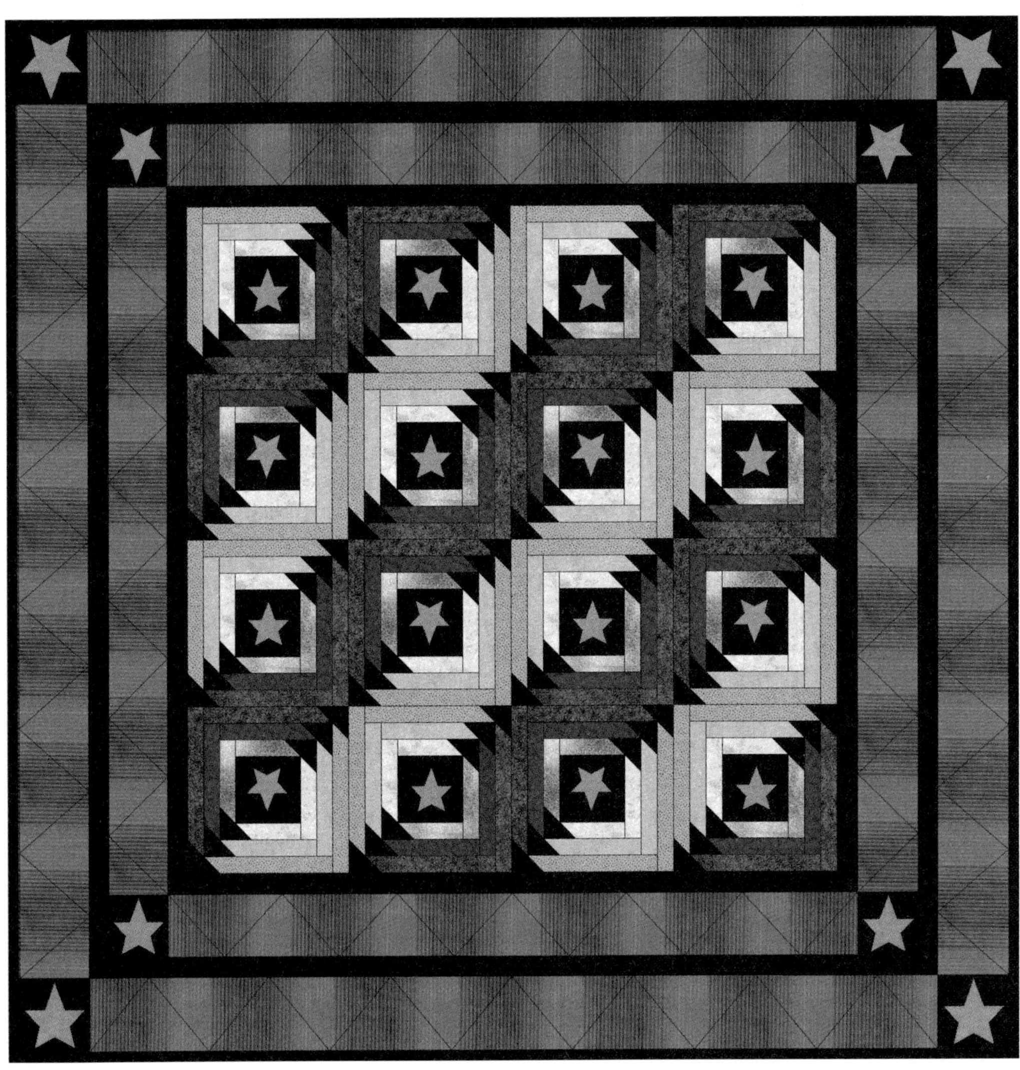

LESSON 6 SYMMETRY SERIES III

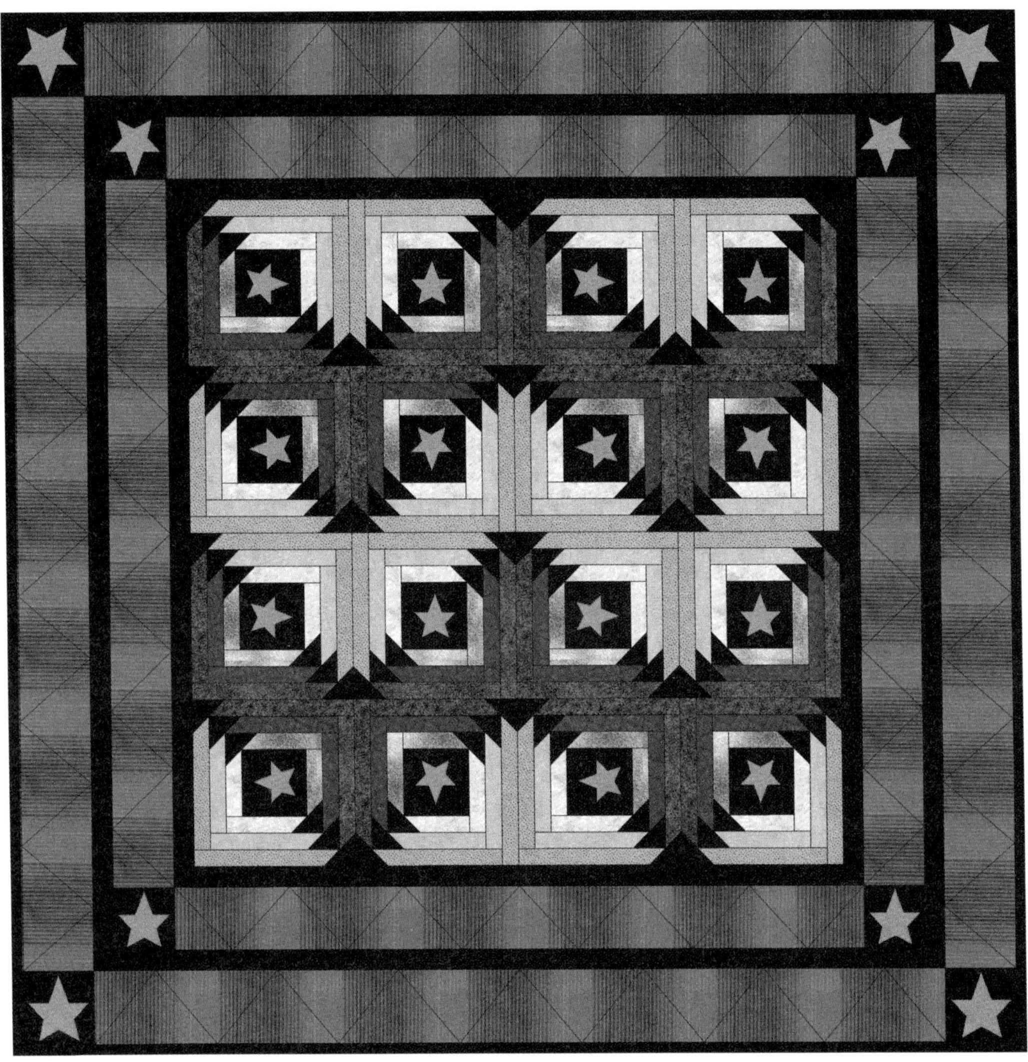

LESSON 6 SYMMETRY SERIES IV

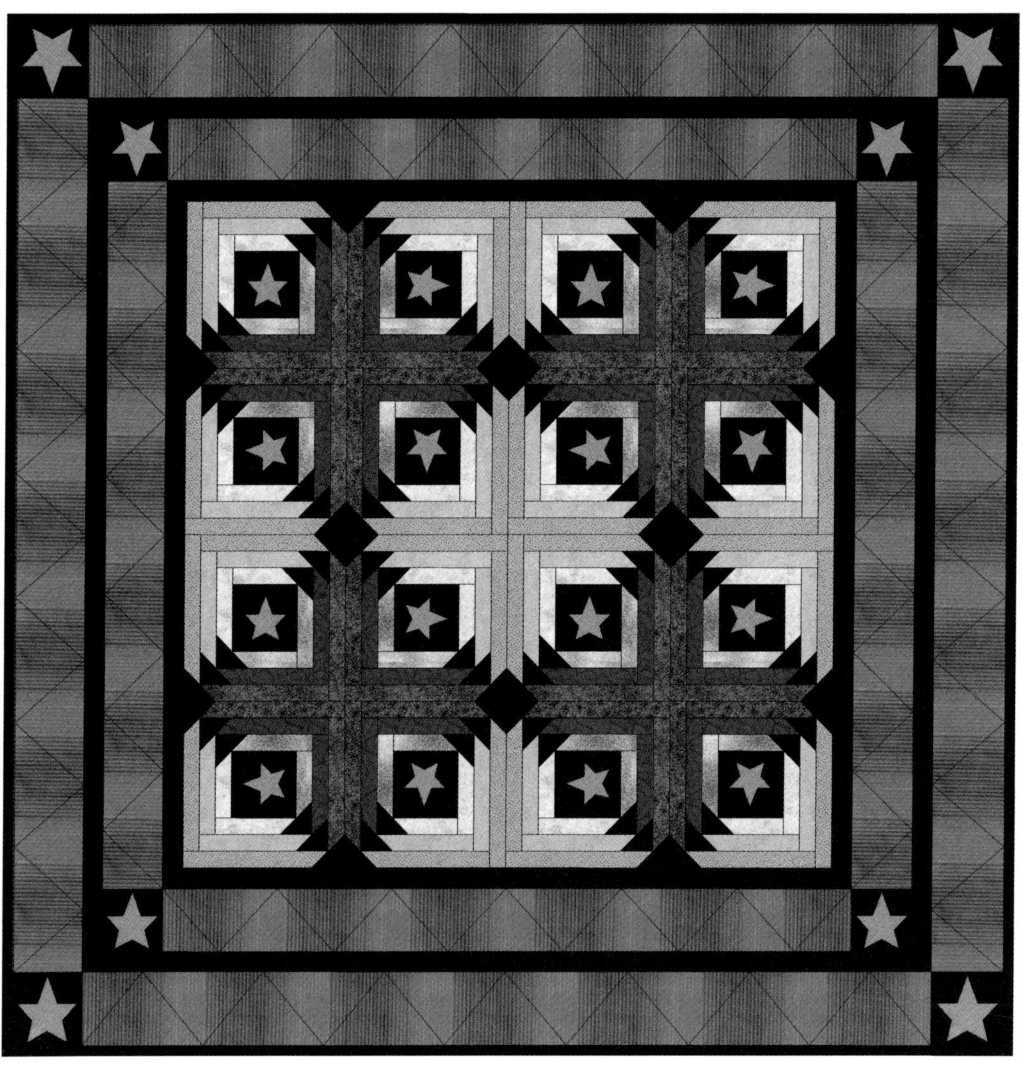

LESSON 6 SYMMETRY SERIES V

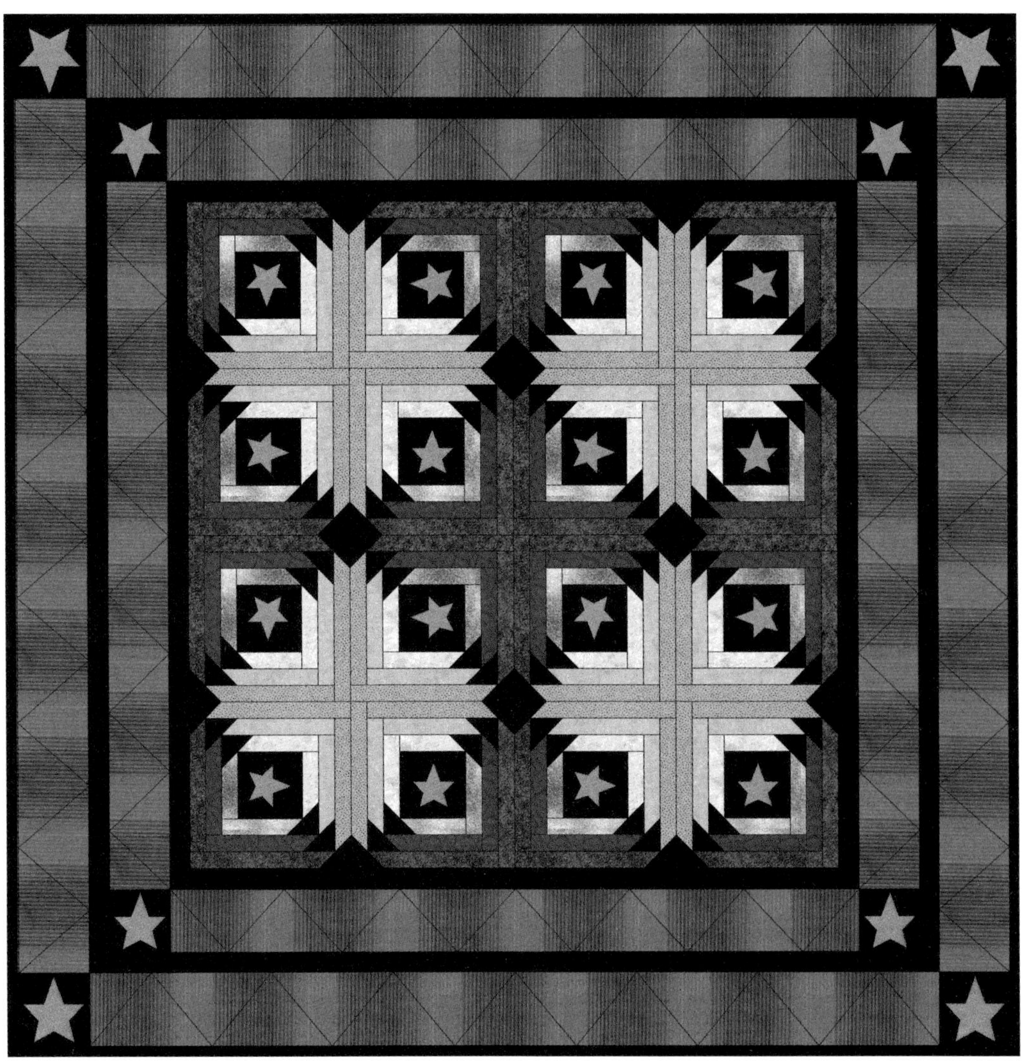

LESSON 6 SYMMETRY SERIES VI

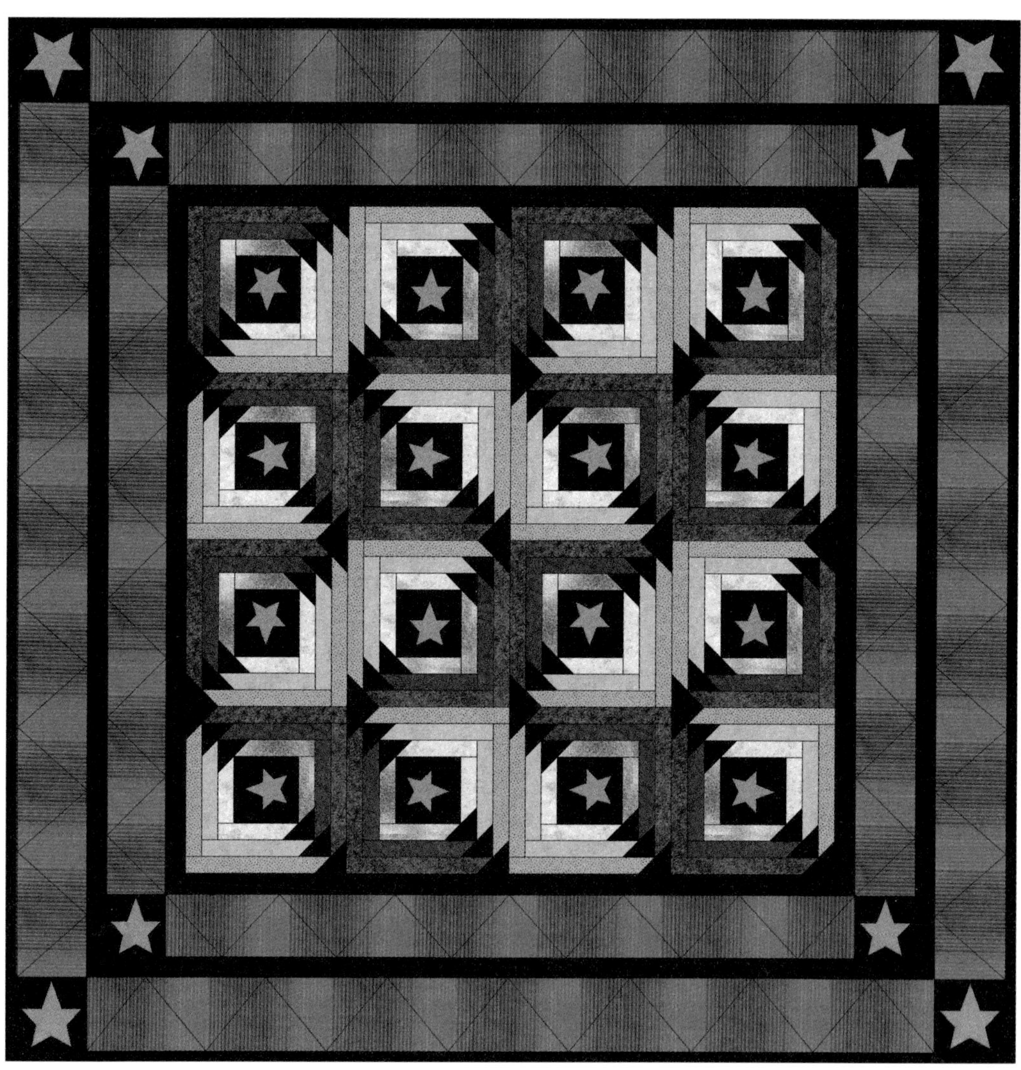

LESSON 6 SYMMETRY SERIES VII

LESSON 7 TIC-TAC-ROSE

LESSON 8
SPARKLERS

LESSON 10 PATCHWORK PATIO

Planning a PatchDraw Quilt

Lesson 5

Lesson 5 – Planning a PatchDraw Quilt

In Lesson 5, you will begin a new project that will teach you even more complex EQ5 skills. The name of this quilt is Antique Rose. You will use many of the basic skills that you learned in Part I of this tutorial and you will also learn to:

- *Create a fabric palette*
- *Search the Libraries*
- *Edit a design in EasyDraw*
- *Edit a design in PatchDraw*
- *Resize and rotate in PatchDraw*
- *Use a layout from the Library*
- *Flip and rotate blocks on Layer 1*
- *Set appliqué on Layer 2*
- *Rotate on Layers*
- *Add blocks to the User Libraries*
- *Add fabrics to the User Libraries*
- *Save your palette in the Palette Library*
- *Save the current palette as the default*

Antique Rose Quilt

Starting a New Project

Start a new project with the file name *Antique Rose*. If you need help with this procedure, see "Starting a New Project" in Lesson 1.

Tip

- **Remember to consult the EQ5 manuals and the Help file whenever necessary.**

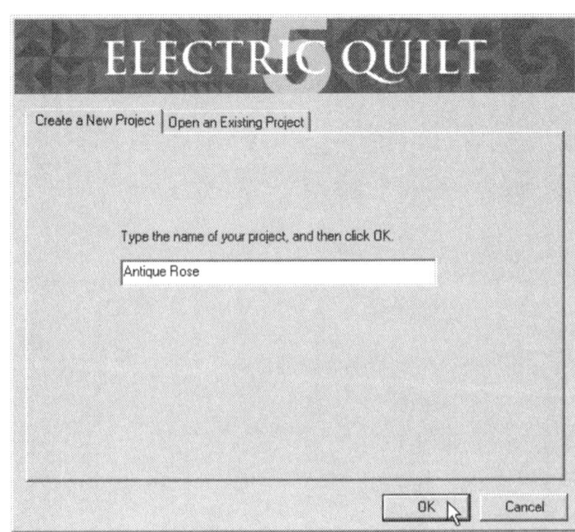

EQ5 Opening Screen

Creating a Fabric Palette

In EQ5 you can select a variety of fabrics from any of the Fabric Libraries and add them to your Sketchbook to create your own customized palette. The procedure is the same whether you are copying fabrics from a single collection or from several collections.

5 You will have easier access to the new fabrics if you clear the default fabrics from the Sketchbook first.

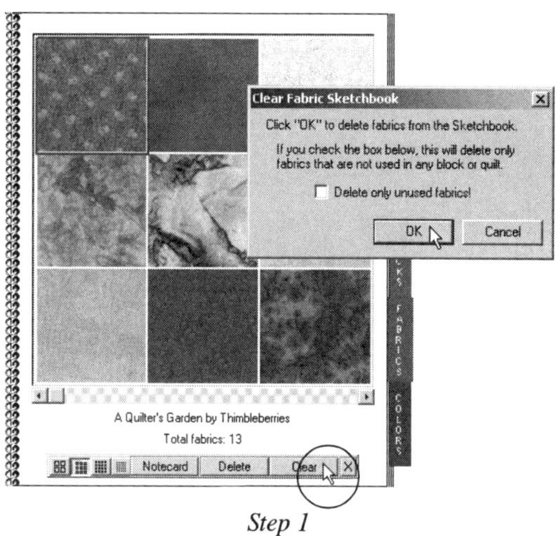

Step 1

1 Open the Sketchbook (F8) and then click on the Fabrics tab. Click on the Clear button at the bottom of the Sketchbook. The Clear Fabric Sketchbook box will open. Click on OK. All of the fabrics in the Sketchbook will be eliminated. Close the Sketchbook.

Tip

- **You will notice that in the Clear Fabric Sketchbook box you have the option to delete only fabrics that are not used in a block or quilt in the current project file. This feature is helpful when you want to clear unused fabrics from a Sketchbook that contains designs that you have already colored.**

Step 2

Step 2

2 Click on Libraries in the main menu then click on Fabric Library. The Fabric Libraries box will open. Click on EQ Libraries and then click on one of the libraries listed.

3 The fabric collections in this library will be listed in alphabetical order and you can click on one to open it. The fabric swatches in this collection will be displayed in the Fabric Libraries box. The first fabric swatch is framed automatically.

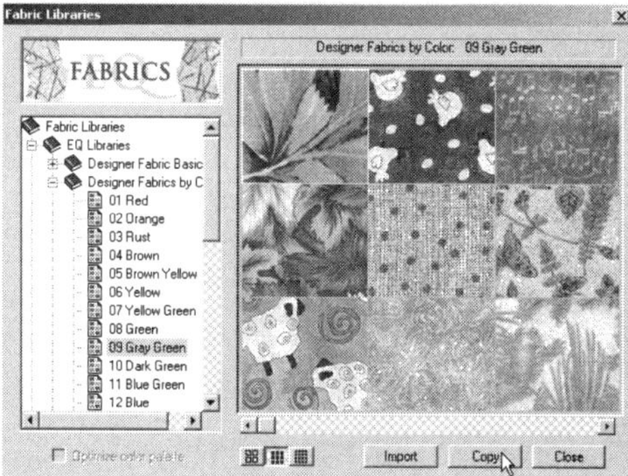

Step 3 & 4

4 Click on Copy to place the first sample in the Sketchbook. To quickly copy the remaining fabrics in the collection into the Sketchbook, hold down the Enter key on your keyboard.The fabrics will temporarily disappear from the library.

If you want to install fabrics from more than one collection, open each library individually and copy just the fabric samples that you want from that collection. Close the Fabric Libraries box.

Tip

- **Remember that you have several options for viewing the fabrics that are displayed in the Fabric Libraries box. The display buttons are located at the bottom of the Fabric Libraries box, to the left of the Import button. You can choose to display four, nine, or sixteen fabrics simultaneously on the screen.**

5 Open your Fabric Sketchbook (F8) and use the slider rectangle to view your new fabric palette. Close the Sketchbook.

EasyDraw Color

Tabs on EasyDraw™ Worktable

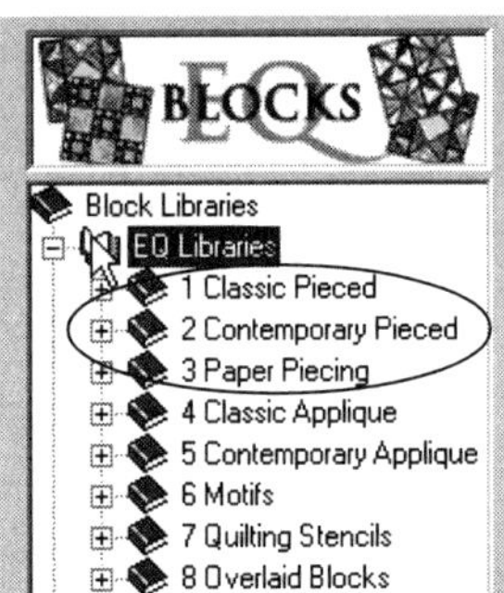

Pieced Block Libraries in EQ5

Drawing Distinctions in EQ5

In Part I of this tutorial, you drew several designs on the EasyDraw™ worktable. Here in Part II, you are ready to learn about all three of EQ5's drawing worktables: *EasyDraw™, PatchDraw,* and *Overlaid.*

EasyDraw™

EasyDraw™ is used for drawing pieced designs. Pieced designs are composed of lines, arcs, or a combination of lines and arcs. All lines and arcs in an EasyDraw™ design must connect to each other. There are two tabs on the EasyDraw™ worktable: *EasyDraw™* and *Color.*

There are three pieced block libraries in EQ5: *Classic Pieced, Contemporary Pieced,* and *Paper Piecing*. All of the designs in these libraries were created on the EasyDraw™ worktable.

PatchDraw

PatchDraw is used for drawing appliqué designs. Appliqué designs are composed of closed patches that are layered. There are two tabs on the PatchDraw worktable: *PatchDraw* and *Color.*

PatchDraw Color

Tabs on PatchDraw Worktable

If an appliqué design is on a background square, it is an appliqué block. You will recall that you used an appliqué block in the Star Gazing quilt in Lesson 4.

If an appliqué design is not on a background square, it is an appliqué motif.

There are three appliqué libraries in EQ5:
5 *Classic Appliqué, Contemporary Appliqué,* and *Motifs*. All of the designs in these libraries were created on the PatchDraw worktable.

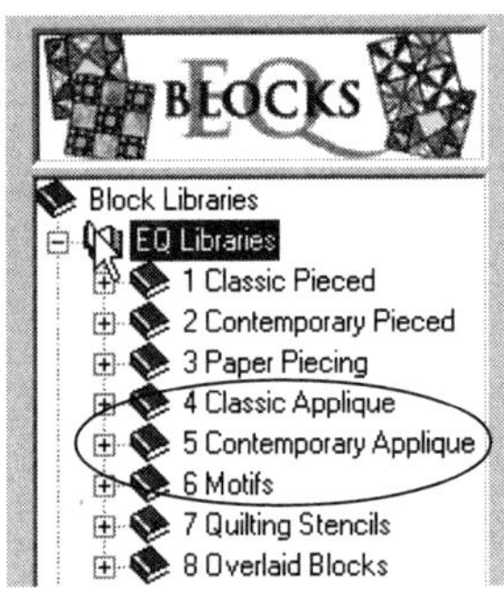

Appliqué Libraries in EQ5

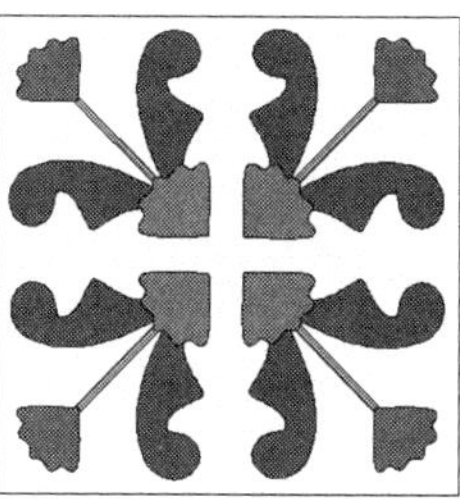

Appliqué Block

Appliqué Motif

Pieced Applique Color

Tabs on Overlaid Worktable

Overlaid Library in EQ5

The designs in the Classic Appliqué and Contemporary Appliqué libraries are appliqué blocks because they are on background squares. With the removal of their background squares, these blocks can also be used as appliqué motifs. You will learn how to remove a background square from an appliqué block later in this lesson.

The designs in the Motifs Library have no background squares. With the addition of background squares, these appliqué motifs can also be used as appliqué blocks. You will learn how to add a background square to an appliqué motif in the next lesson.

For any new PatchDraw design, the worktable opens with a background square that can be easily removed. In this lesson and in subsequent lessons in this tutorial, you will add background squares or remove them, depending on your use of the appliqué designs in that particular lesson.

Overlaid

The Overlaid worktable is used for combining EasyDraw™ and PatchDraw drawings into one block design. There are three tabs on the Overlaid worktable: *Pieced, Appliqué,* and *Color.*

There is one Overlaid Library in EQ5. Each design in this library was created in both EasyDraw™ and PatchDraw. You will experiment with Overlaid blocks later in this tutorial.

Tip

- **The Quilting Stencil Library contains designs that were drawn in either EasyDraw™ or PatchDraw. As you learned in Lesson 4, there are no colored versions of the designs in the 7Quilting Stencils Library.**

Searching the Libraries

Now you are going to gather the designs that you will need for your Antique Rose quilt.

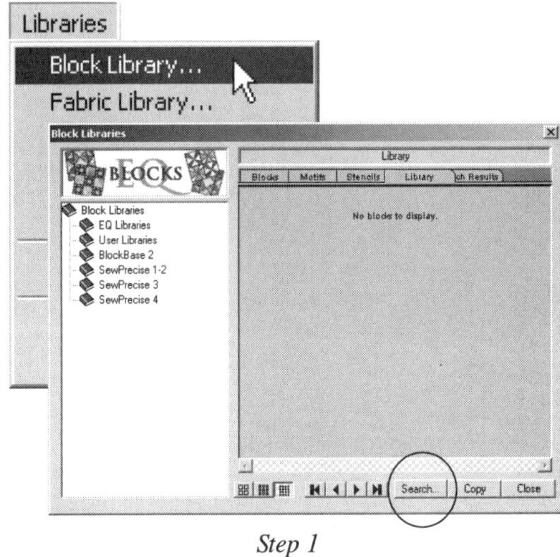

Step 1

1 Click on Libraries in the main menu and then click on Block Library. Click the Search button at the bottom of the Block Libraries box.

2 In the Search Block Notecard box, type in *Log Cabin*. Search Name is checked by default. Click on the Search button at the bottom of this Search Block Notecard box. EQ5 will tell you how many block names contain these words. Click on OK and the Search Results tab will open with these blocks displayed.

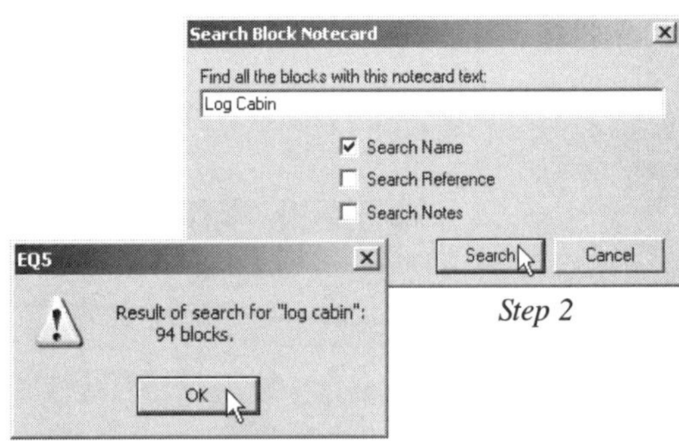

Step 2

The number of blocks in your search will differ depending on what EQ programs you have linked.

3 Click on the Log Cabin (2) block. This design is in the first vertical row on the Search Results tab. Remember that you can simply place the cursor over a design, without clicking, to display the name in a tooltip. Click on the Copy button at the bottom of the Block Libraries box.

Tip

- **If you select Search Reference and Search Notes in the Search Block Notecard box, EQ5 will check these categories for the keyword.**

4 Click on the Search button again and then type in *Corner 4B* in the Search Block Notecard box. Click on the Search button. When EQ5 tells you how many blocks were found in your search, click on OK. The Search Results tab will open with these blocks displayed.

5 Click on the Corner 4B block. Click Copy to place this design in your Sketchbook.

6 In the Search Block Notecard box, type in *Old Rose*. Click on the Search button. Click on OK and the Search Results tab will open with these blocks displayed.

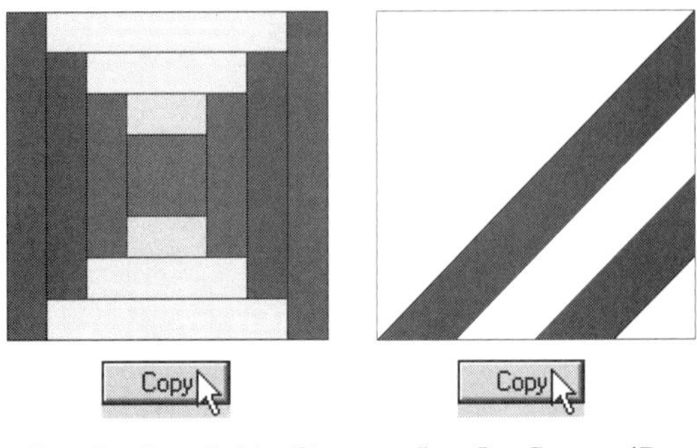

Step 3 – Log Cabin (2) *Step 5 – Corner 4B*

Step 7 – Old Rose of Sharon from Canada

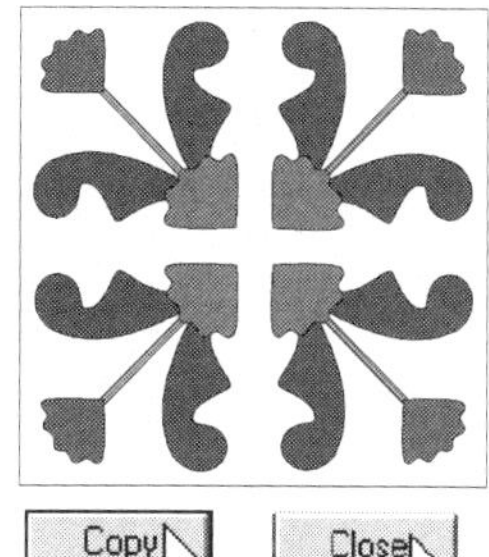

Step 9 – Tulips

7 Click on the Old Rose of Sharon from Canada block. Be careful to select the appliqué block, not the appliqué motif, when copying this design to your Sketchbook. Click Copy to place the design in your Sketchbook.

8 In the Search Block Notecard box, type in *Tulips*. Click on the Search button. Click on OK and the Search Results tab will open with these blocks displayed.

9 Click on the Tulips block. This design is in the first vertical row on the Search Results tab. Click on Copy and then click on Close.

Editing a Design in EasyDraw™

You will now modify the Log Cabin (2) block to create a new design, the Quartered Cabin.

Step 1

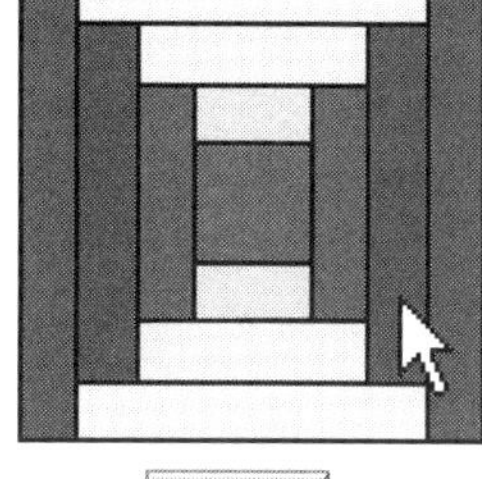

Step 2

Tip

- **When you edit a block from the Libraries, EQ5 will automatically select the appropriate worktable for the block. Since this Log Cabin (2) block was originally drawn in EasyDraw™, this worktable will open when you select the block for editing.**

1 Open the Block Sketchbook (F8) to view the blocks you copied from the Libraries.

2 Click on the Log Cabin (2) block to select it and then click on the Edit button at the bottom of the Sketchbook to place this block on the worktable.

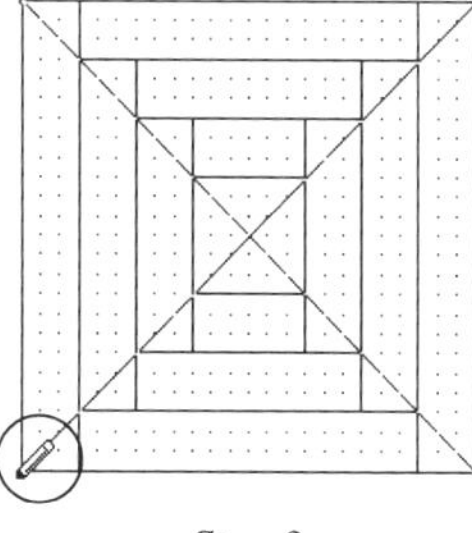

Step 3

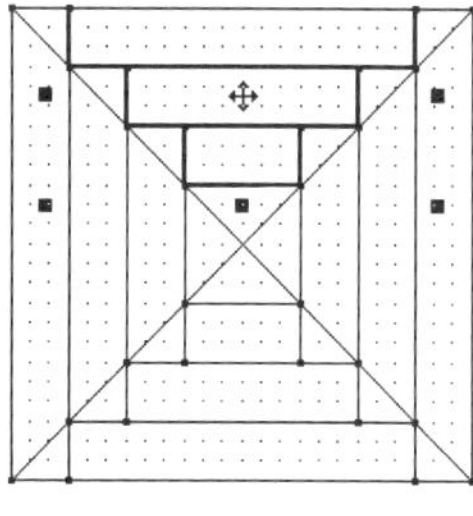

Step 4

3 The Line tool is automatically engaged. With the Log Cabin (2) block on the worktable, draw two diagonal lines across the block, as shown.

4 Click on the Select tool, hold down the Shift key, and click on each of the horizontal and vertical lines within the upper quarter of the block. These lines will darken.

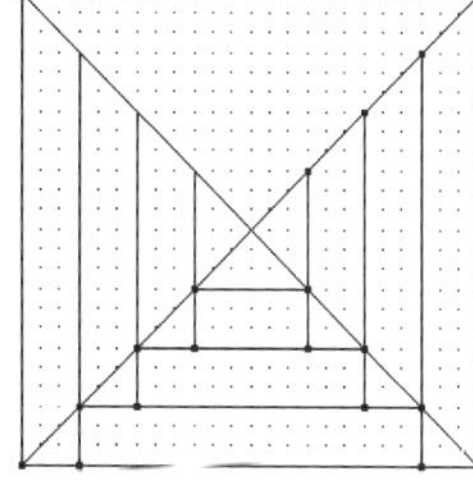

Step 5

Refresh Button

5 After all of the lines have been selected, press the Delete key on the keyboard to erase them. Click on the Refresh Screen button to clean the debris from your screen.

Tip

- **You can also remove each line individually by clicking on a line with the Select tool and then pressing the Delete key after each selection.**

6 You are now going to use a different method for deleting multiple lines in the block. This technique involves drawing a frame or "marquee" around the lines that you want to delete.

Click on the Select tool. Click on a spot slightly outside of the block outline on the left side and slightly above the horizontal center. Holding down the mouse button, draw a frame or marquee from this point to a point slightly outside the lower-right corner of the block outline. All of the lines that are *completely* encased in this frame will highlight. In this case, the selected lines are all within the bottom quarter of the block. Press the Delete key to eliminate them. This is a fast way to remove multiple lines in a drawing! Save in Sketchbook.

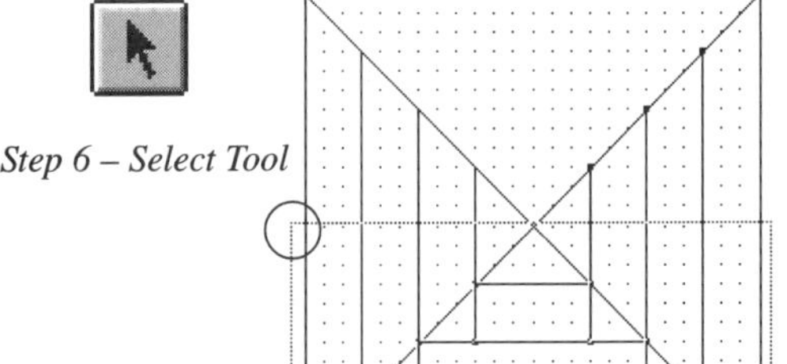

Step 6 – Select Tool

Step 6

**Tip**

- **If you have clicked on the Color tab before deleting the lines, use the technique described in Step 4 and 5 above to eliminate the lines. The marquee technique works only if the lines have not been sectioned by nodes. Lines will be sectioned where they cross other lines if you have clicked on the Color tab and then clicked back. If you then marquee and delete as directed, the diagonal lines on the bottom will be eliminated with the other lines.**

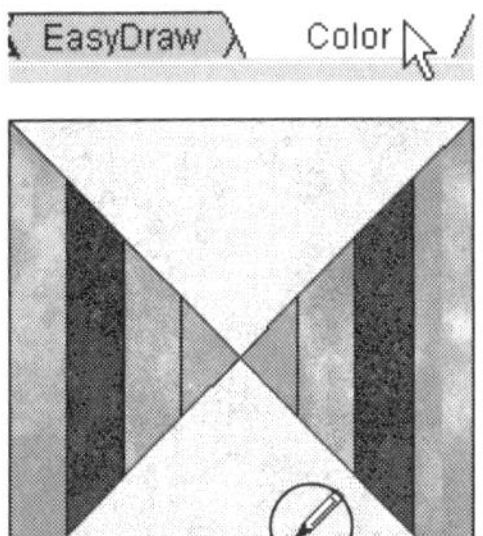

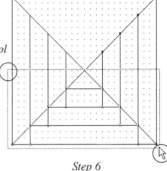

Step 7 – Color and Save in Sketchbook

7 Click on the Color tab and color the Quartered Cabin. Save in Sketchbook.

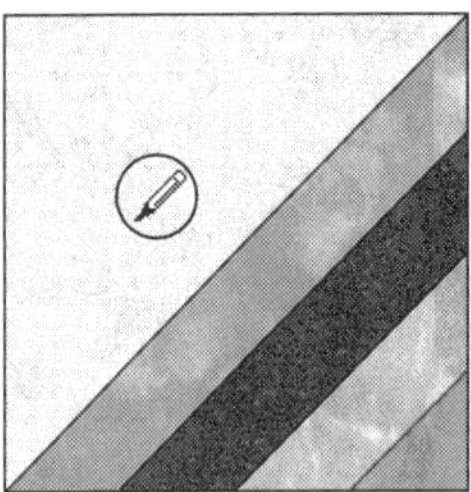

Step 8 – Color and Save in Sketchbook

8 Open the Sketchbook (F8) and select the Corner 4B design. Place it on the worktable and then click on the Color tab. Color the design with the same sequence of colors that you used in the Quartered Cabin. Save in Sketchbook.

5

9 Open the Sketchbook (F8) and select the Old Rose of Sharon design. Click on Edit to place it on the worktable. Click on the Color tab and color this design. Save in Sketchbook.

Step 9 – Color and Save in Sketchbook

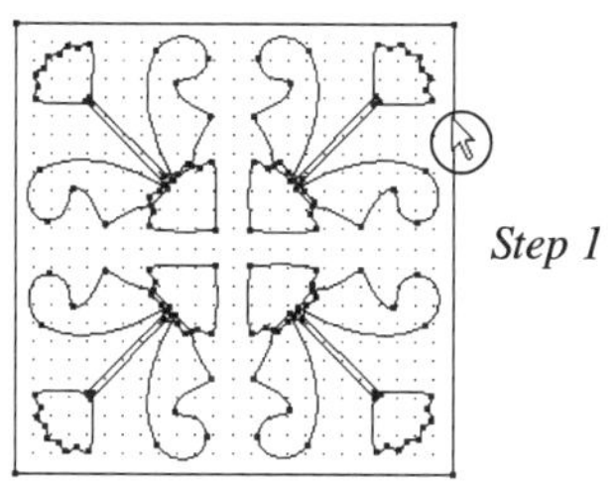

Step 1 & 2

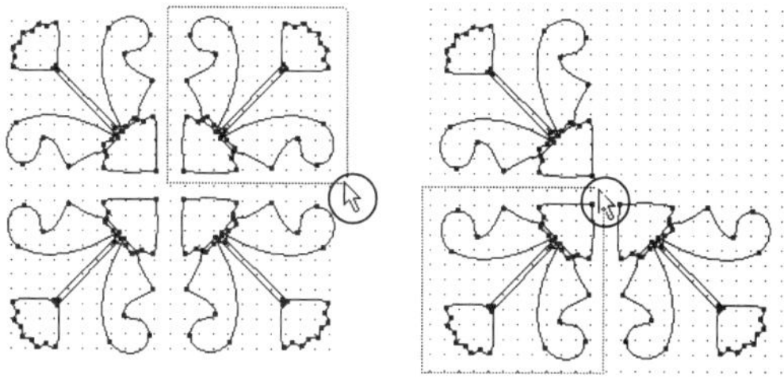

Step 3

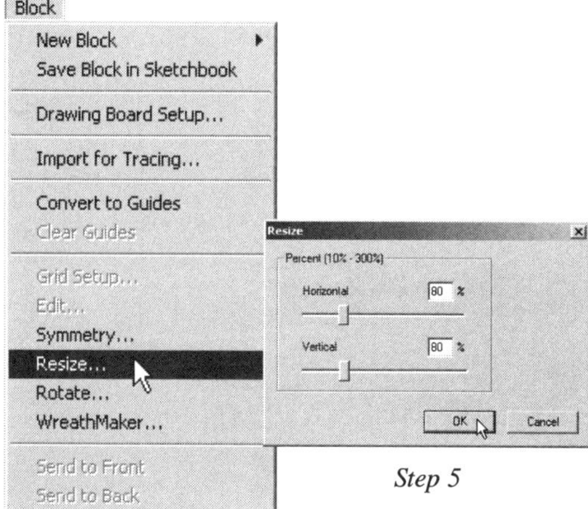

Step 5

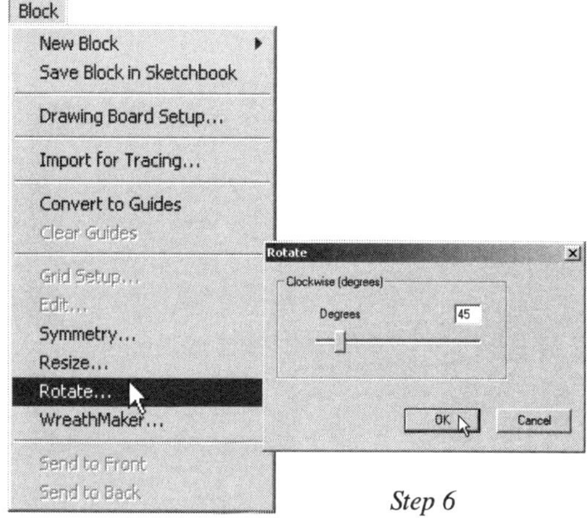

Step 6

Editing a Design in PatchDraw

Now you will edit a PatchDraw design to create two variations for your Antique Rose quilt.

1 Open the Block Sketchbook (F8) and place the Tulips appliqué block on the worktable for editing.

2 Click on the Select tool and then click on the block outline. Press the Delete button to eliminate the background square. This design is now an appliqué motif, that is, it has no background square.

3 With the Select tool, draw a frame or marquee around the tulip motif in the upper-right of the design. Be sure that this entire flower is within the selection box. Press the Delete key.

Draw a marquee around the tulip motif in the lower-left of the design. Be sure that this entire flower is within the selection box. Press the Delete key. Use the Refresh Screen button to clean the debris from your screen.

4 Click on Edit in the main menu and then click on Select All. You can also use the shortcut Ctrl+A to select all.

5 Click on Block in the main menu and then click on Resize. In the Resize box, type in 80 for the Horizontal and Vertical percentages. Click on OK. The size of the tulip motif will be reduced to 80% of its original size.

6 Click on Block in the Main Menu again and then click on Rotate. In the Rotate box, type in 45 for the degree of rotation. Click on OK. Click off of the design and then click the Refresh Screen button. Save in Sketchbook.

Tip

- **You can also access the Resize and Rotate options through the PatchDraw Worktable Context Menu. Select the parts of the design that you want to change and then secondary click on the worktable. The PatchDraw Worktable Context Menu will open and you can click on the option that you want to exercise.**

Twin Tulips Motif

Step 7 – Color & Save in Sketchbook

7 Click on the Color tab and color this Twin Tulips motif. Save in Sketchbook. This is the design that you will superimpose on Layer 2, over the Quartered Cabin blocks.

You will need another variation of this Tulip design to use in your quilt.

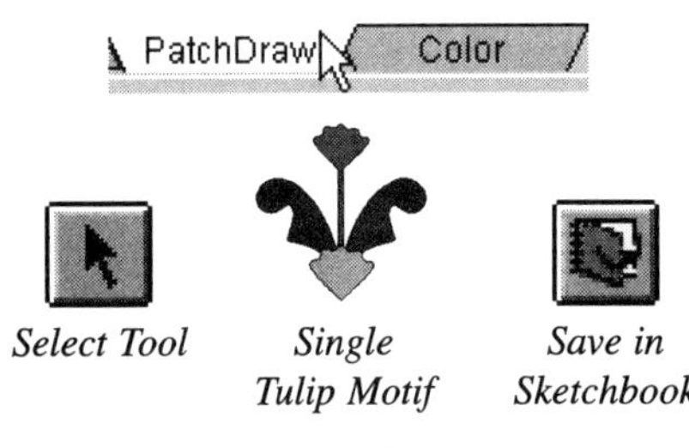

Select Tool *Single Tulip Motif* *Save in Sketchbook*

Step 8

8 Click on the PatchDraw tab, click on the Select tool, and then marquee the lower tulip motif in the design. Delete. Recolor this Single Tulip motif, if necessary. Save in Sketchbook. This is the design that you will superimpose on Layer 2 of the border triangles. You will also use this Single Tulip motif as a stencil.

Using a Layout from the Library

EQ5 contains a Layout Library that contains many standard quilt layouts, as well as a large selection of unusual layout styles. You can use these designs as they are or adapt them to your particular needs.

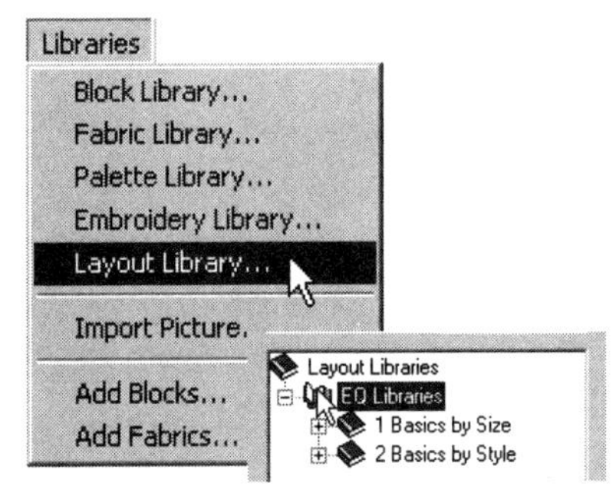

Step 1

1 Click on Libraries and then click on Layout Library. A Layout Libraries box will open. Click on EQ Libraries. You will see two style libraries in this list: *Basics by Size* and *Basics by Style*.

2 Click on Basics by Size and then click on 05Twin. Copy the layout that is "11.5" Blocks – 35 Total." Remember that you can identify a design by placing the cursor, without clicking, over the object to make the tooltip appear. Close the Libraries.

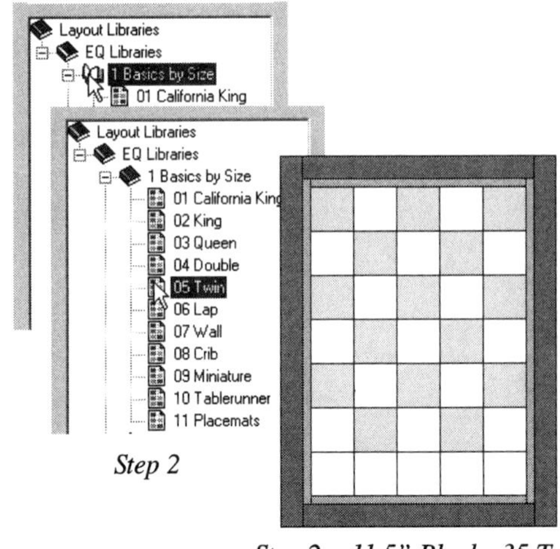

Step 2

Step 2 – 11.5" Blocks-35 Total

Tip

- **Notice the viewing option buttons below the slider bar in the Layout Libraries box. You can choose to display *two, four,* or *twelve* layouts simultaneously.**

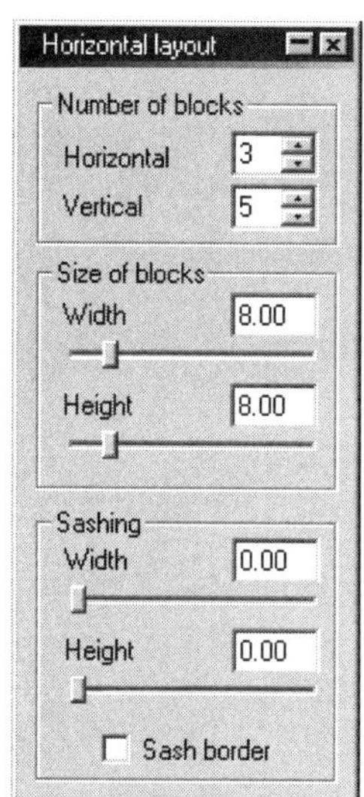

Step 4

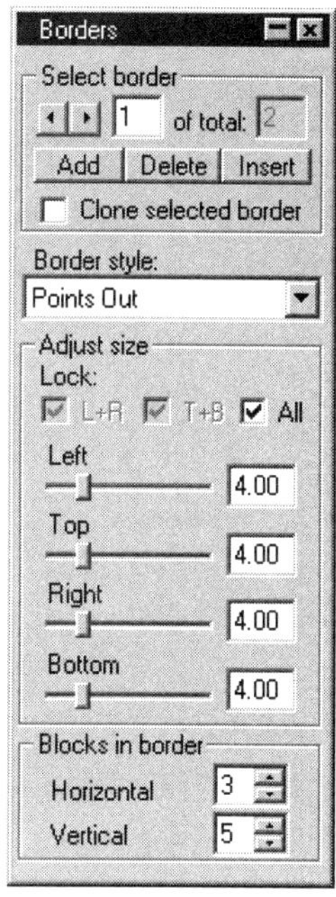

Step 5 – Border 1

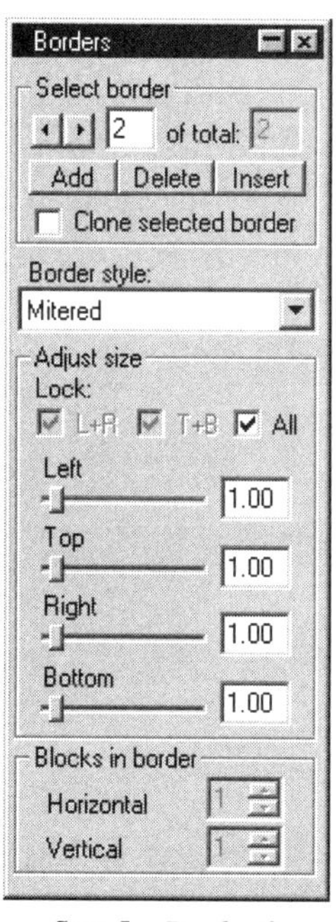

Step 5 – Border 2

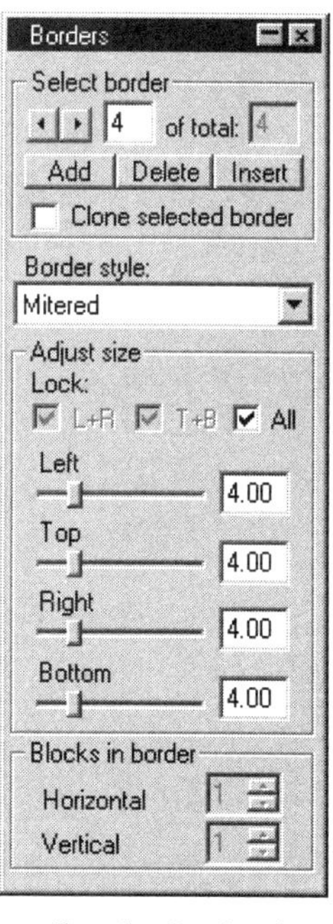

Step 5 – Border 4

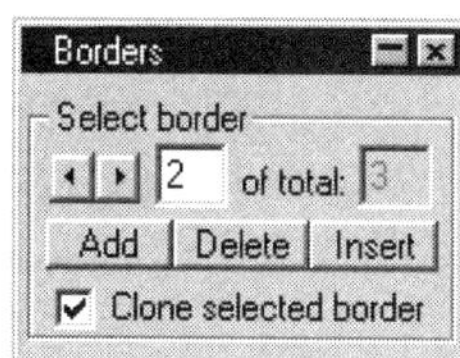

Step 5 – Create Border 3

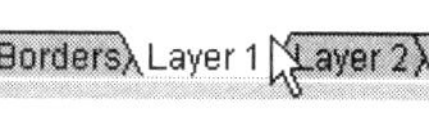

Step 6

3 Open the Quilts Sketchbook (F8) and select the layout you just copied. Click on the Edit button at the bottom of the Sketchbook to place the new layout on the worktable.

4 You will now modify this layout for your Antique Rose quilt. With the layout on the quilt worktable, click on the Layout tab. Set these values in the Layout palette:

Number of blocks:	Horizontal – 3 Vertical – 5
Size of blocks:	Width – 8.00 Height – 8.00
Sashing:	Width – 0.00 Height – 0.00
Sash border	unchecked

5 Click on the Borders tab and set these values:

Border 1

Border style:	Points Out
Adjust size:	4.00 (Lock: All)
Blocks in border:	Horizontal – 3 Vertical – 5

Border 2

Border style:	Mitered
Adjust size:	1.00 (Lock: All)

Border 3
Check Clone selected border in the Borders box. Click on Add. A third border will appear in the layout and it will be a clone of the selected (second) border.

Border 4
Click to deselect Clone selected border. Click on the Add button to add the fourth border. Adjust the size of this Mitered border to 4.00 for all sides.

6 Click on the Layer 1 tab and then click on Save in Sketchbook.

Setting Blocks into the Layout

1 Click on the Set tool and the Blocks palette will open. You are now ready to set the blocks into the quilt layout!

Step 1 – Set Tool

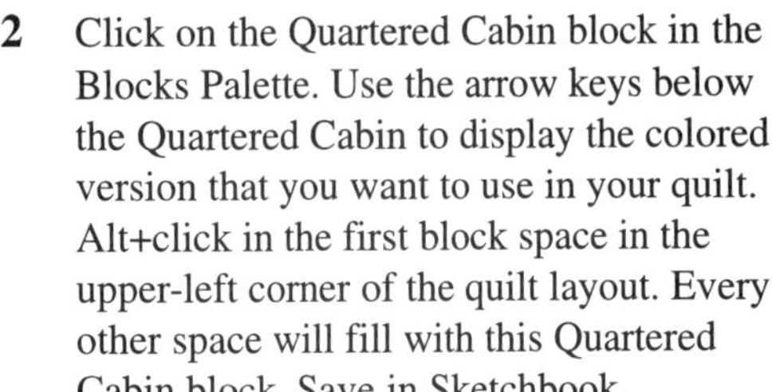

2 Click on the Quartered Cabin block in the Blocks Palette. Use the arrow keys below the Quartered Cabin to display the colored version that you want to use in your quilt. Alt+click in the first block space in the upper-left corner of the quilt layout. Every other space will fill with this Quartered Cabin block. Save in Sketchbook.

Step 2

Step 3

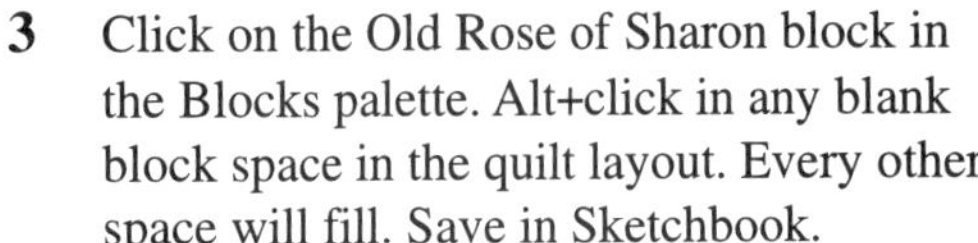

3 Click on the Old Rose of Sharon block in the Blocks palette. Alt+click in any blank block space in the quilt layout. Every other space will fill. Save in Sketchbook.

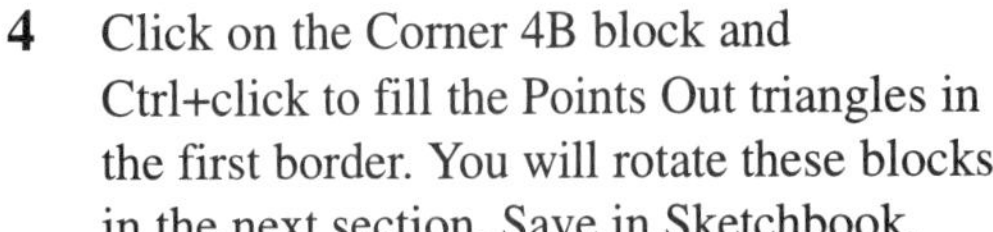

4 Click on the Corner 4B block and Ctrl+click to fill the Points Out triangles in the first border. You will rotate these blocks in the next section. Save in Sketchbook.

Step 4

5 Click on the Plain Block tool and then select a color in the Fabrics palette. Ctrl+click to color the Points In triangles in the first border. Ctrl+click to color the corner blocks in the first row with this same fabric. Save in Sketchbook.

Step 5 – Plain Block Tool

Step 5

6 Ctrl+click to color the remaining borders in the quilt layout. Save in Sketchbook.

Flipping and Rotating Blocks on Layer 1

1 Click on the Flip tool in the Quilt Tools. The cursor will change to a curved arrow over a straight line and the Fabrics palette will disappear from the worktable. Every click of the Flip tool will transform the design into a mirror image of itself.

Step 1 – Flip Tool & Cursor

2 Click once on the Old Rose of Sharon blocks in the second row to flip them. Flip the Old Rose of Sharon blocks in the fourth row. Save in Sketchbook.

Step 2

Step 3 – Rotate Tool & Cursor

Step 3 – Rotate the Corner 4B blocks in Border 1 until they appear like the image above.

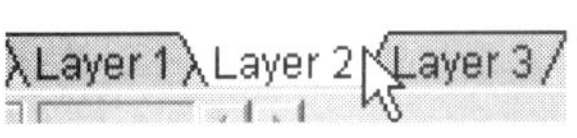

Step 2 – Set Tool

Twin Tulips Motif

Step 2

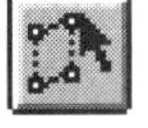

Adjust Tool

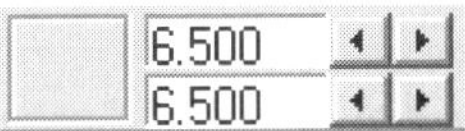

Size on Graph Pad

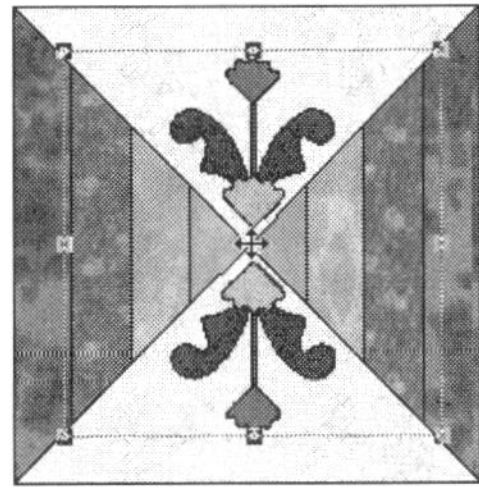

Step 3

3 Click on the Rotate tool in the Quilt Tools. The cursor will change to a curved arrow. Every click of the Rotate tool will turn a selected block by 90°. Click on each of the Corner 4B blocks in the first border to rotate, as shown. Save in Sketchbook.

Tip

- **Be sure to position the cursor so that the tip of the arrow is touching the design that you want to rotate.**

Setting Appliqué on Layer 2

The procedure for setting appliqué motifs on Layer 2 is very similar to the procedure that you used in Lesson 4 for setting quilt stencils on the Star Gazing quilt. Your primary tools will be the *Adjust tool,* the *Graph Pad,* and the *Zoom tools.*

1 If the Graph Pad is not on the worktable, click on View in the main menu and then click on Graph Pad so that it is checked. The Graph Pad will open on the worktable but will be activated only when you select a design on Layers with the Adjust tool.

2 With your Antique Rose quilt on the worktable, click on the Layer 2 tab. Click on the Set tool and then click on the Motif tab in the Blocks palette. Click on the Twin Tulips motif. Start in a corner of a Quartered Cabin block and, holding down the Shift key, click and drag the cursor diagonally to form the Twin Tulips motif in this space.

Tip

- **Remember to use the Zoom tools when working on Layers!**

3 Click on the Adjust tool and select the Twin Tulips Motif. Set the block size on the Graph Pad to 6.500 x 6.500. With the motif still selected, use the Adjust tool or the keyboard arrows to center the motif over the Quartered Cabin.

5

4 With the motif selected, Ctrl+C to copy and then Ctrl+V to paste another copy on the worktable. Move this copy to second Quartered Cabin block in the first row.

5 Click on the first motif as a reference and then, holding down the Shift key, click on the copy. Click on the Align Top tool. The second motif will align evenly with the first motif, along the upper edge. Click outside of the selection box. Click on the second motif and adjust its vertical position over the Quartered Cabin with the keyboard arrows, if necessary. One row of motifs is now correctly sized and positioned. You can use this row to create identical rows of motifs for the layout! Save in Sketchbook.

Align Top Tool

Save in Sketchbook

Step 5

6 Click on the Adjust tool and, holding down the Shift key, click on the two Twin Tulips motifs in the first row. Ctrl+C to copy and then Ctrl+V to paste another row of motifs on the worktable. Using the Adjust tool or the keyboard arrow keys, move this row of motifs over the third row in the layout. Copy and paste another row of motifs, placing it over the fifth row in the layout. Save in Sketchbook.

Step 6

Step 7 & 8

7 Click on the Adjust tool and then click on one of the Twin Tulips motifs in the first row. Copy and paste it on the Quartered Cabin in the second row. Center the design.

8 Copy and paste the motif on the fourth row. Position accurately. Save in Sketchbook.

9 Click on the Set tool and then click on the Single Tulip design on the Motifs tab of the Blocks palette. Zoom in to the bottom border of the quilt. Holding down the Shift key, click and drag to draw the Single Tulip motif over the center border triangle, as shown. Click on the Adjust tool and set the size on the Graph Pad to 6.50 x 6.50. Position the Single Tulip so that it is centered on the border triangle, as shown. Save in Sketchbook.

Set Tool

Single Tulip Motif

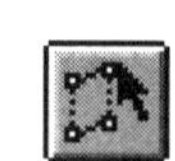

Adjust Tool

6.50
6.50

Step 9

5

Step 10

Step 11

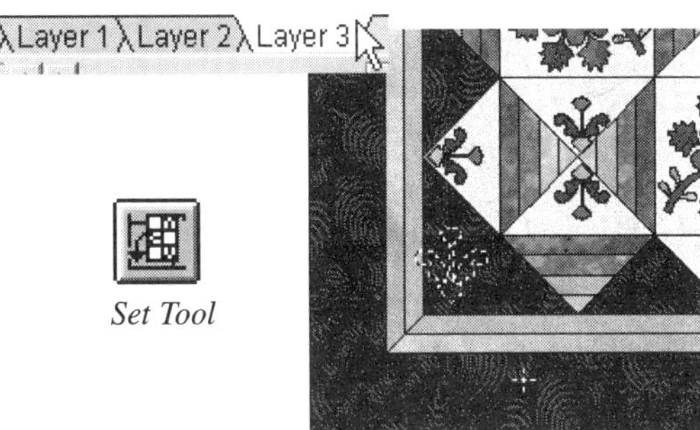

Set Tool

Step 1

Adjust Tool

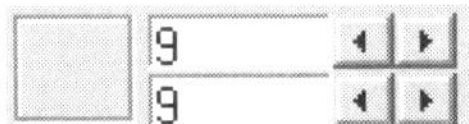

Thread Color Tool

Step 2

Step 3

Step 4 – Stencils correctly aligned

10 Copy and paste seven copies of this Single Tulip motif around the first border of the quilt, spacing them as shown.

11 Click on the Rotate tool in the Quilt tools. Click on each motif individually and rotate it to the correct orientation. Use the Adjust tool or the keyboard arrows to position each motif correctly over the blank triangle.

Setting Stencils on Layers

You will now add Single Tulip quilting stencils to the corners of the layout.

1 Click on Layer 3 and then click on the Set tool. Click on the Single Tulip on the Motif tab of the Blocks palette. Holding down the Shift key, click and drag to form a design on the worktable.

2 Click on the Adjust tool and then click on the Single Tulip stencil. Set the size of this stencil to 9.00 x 9.00 on the Graph Pad. If necessary, change the stencil color with the Thread Color tool. For detailed instructions on this procedure, see "Setting Block Stencils on Layers" in Lesson 4.

3 Move the stencil to the lower-right corner of the quilt layout. Use the left arrow on the Graph Pad Rotation tool to turn the design to - 45°, that is, minus 45°.

4 Copy and paste three more stencils on the worktable. Use the Adjust tool or keyboard arrows to position a stencil in each corner of the layout. Use the Rotate tool in the Quilt tools to turn each stencil to the correct orientation for its corner, as shown. Use the Align tools to align the motifs accurately. Save in Sketchbook.

Your Antique Rose quilt is now complete!

Completing Notecards

1 Open the Block Sketchbook and complete a Notecard for each design. Refer to "Completing Notecards" in Lesson 1 for full instructions.

2 Complete a Quilt Notecard for the Lesson 5 quilt and name the design Antique Rose. Remember to click on the Save button after adding information to the Notecard.

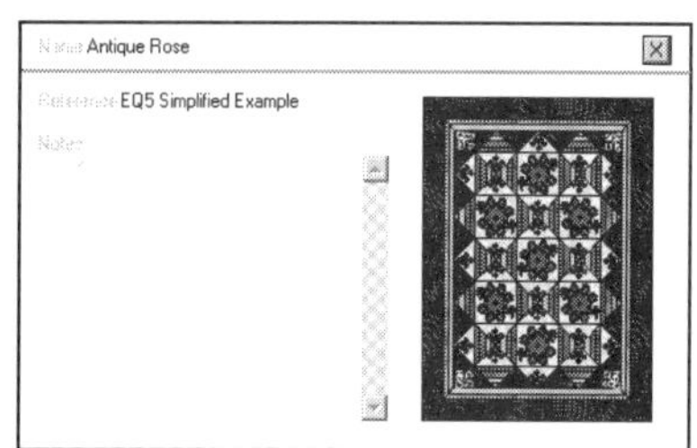

Step 2 – Complete Notecard and Save

Tip

- **You can rename a block, quilt, or fabric on its Notecard. When a design is stored in the User Library, the Notecard information will be stored with it.**

Adding Blocks to the User Libraries

Storing blocks in the User Libraries makes it easier to retrieve designs for use in a new project. Also, the User Libraries serve as a convenient and safe storage location in the event that a project file is corrupted or lost. If this happened, you would lose your quilt designs, but you would still have your block collection to rebuild the project. You will discover just how useful the User Libraries are in the following lessons when you retrieve blocks for use in new quilt designs!

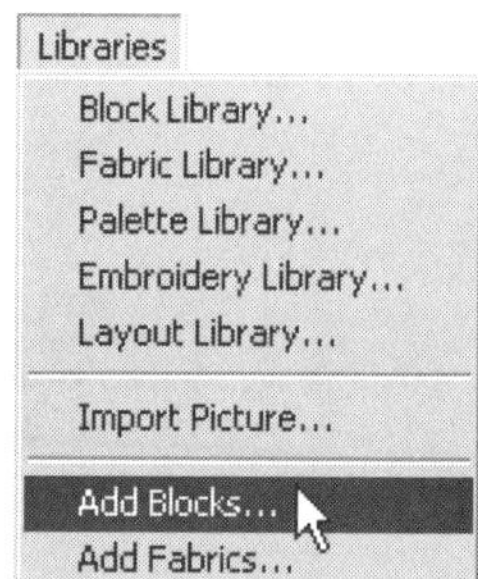

Step 1

1 Click on Libraries in the main menu and then click on Add Blocks. The Add Block to Library box will open and your blocks for this project will be displayed under Block Sketchbook. You will now create a new block style library for this tutorial that you will name Simplified Blocks.

2 The User Libraries are listed on the left in the Add Block to Library box. Click on the book icon next to User Libraries. Click on the small plus sign next to User Libraries to open the Library list. Click on the small plus sign next to the first Library or double click on the book icon next to the first Library.

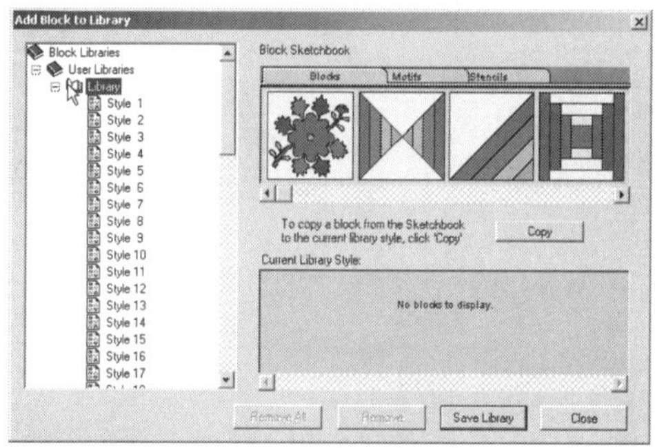

Step 2 – Open the Library List

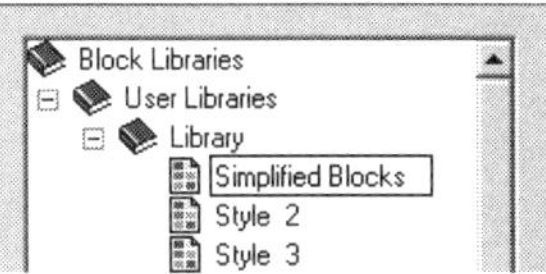

Step 3 – Rename Style

3 To rename a style library, click once on Style to select it. Wait a moment and then click again on Style. A rectangle will form around the word and you can now type inside the box to change the name of this style library. Type Simplified Blocks in this box. This box should remain selected for the next step.

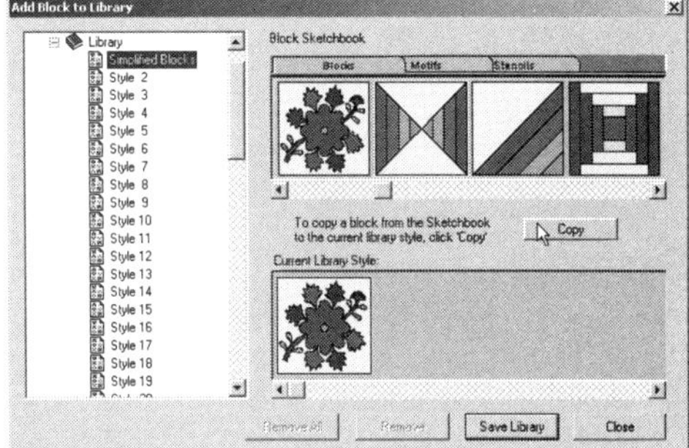
Step 4

4 The first design in your opened project is framed. Click on the Copy button beneath the Block Sketchbook. The copied design will appear in the Current Library Style box. The frame in the Block Sketchbook will move automatically to the next block. With the Copy button still selected, hold down the Enter key to copy all designs from the project Sketchbook to the User Library. Be sure that you also copy the designs on the Motif and Stencil tabs.

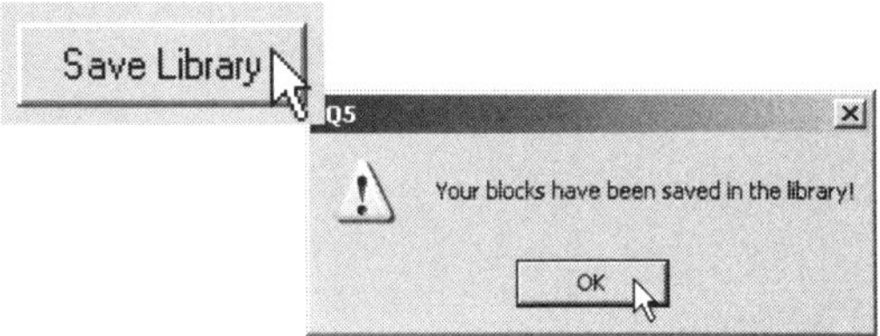

Step 5

5 Click on Save Library. A box will appear that tells you that your blocks have been saved in the style library that you selected. Click on OK.

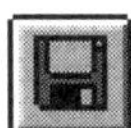
Step 6 – Close & Save

6 Close the Add Block to Library box by clicking on Close or on the X in the upper-right corner of the box and Save.

Your designs are now saved in the EQ5 Libraries, ready to be copied for use in other projects.

Adding Fabrics to the User Libraries

EQ5 also allows you to save fabrics in the User Libraries! The procedure is similar to the one for adding blocks to the Blocks User Libraries.

Step 1

1 Click on Libraries and then click on Add Fabrics. The Add Fabric to Library box will open and your palette for this project will be displayed under Fabric Sketchbook.

5

2 The User Libraries are listed on the left in the Add Fabric to Library box. Click on the book icon next to User Libraries. Click on the small plus sign next to the User Library to open the Library list. Click on the small plus sign next to the first Library or double click on the book icon next to the first Library. Click on Style 1 to select it. Wait a moment and then click on Style 1 again to enter the renaming mode. Type Simplified Fabrics in the box.

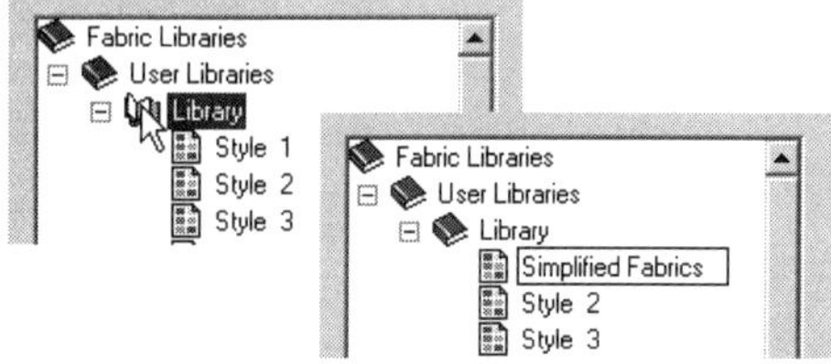

Step 2

3 Click on the Copy button beneath the Fabric Sketchbook to copy the first fabric sample. The copied fabric will appear in the Current Style box. The frame in the Fabric Sketchbook will move automatically to the next sample. With the Copy button still selected, hold down the Enter key to copy all fabrics from the project Sketchbook to the User Library.

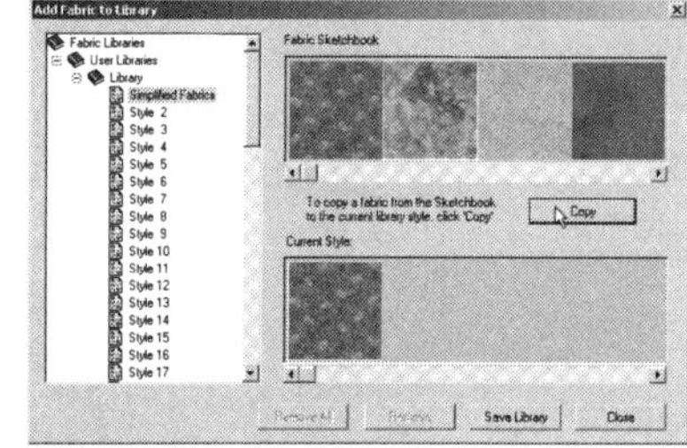

Step 3

4 Click on Save Library. A box will appear that tells you that your fabrics have been saved in the style library that you selected. Click on OK.

Step 4

5 Close the Add Fabric to Library box by clicking on Close or on the X in the upper-right corner of the box and Save.

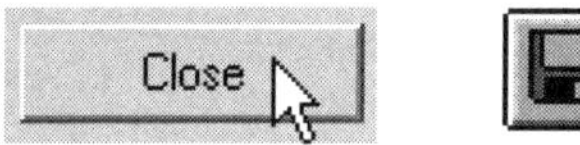

Step 5 – Close & Save

Saving Your Palette in the Palette Library

You can also save a customized fabric palette in the EQ5 Palette Library! This feature allows you to install an entire palette at once, rather than having to copy individual swatches.

1 Click on Libraries and then click on Palette Library. The Palette Library box will open with two tabs: *EQ5 Palettes* and *My Palettes*. On either tab, click on Show Sketchbook and the fabrics in this current project will be displayed in the Palette Library box.

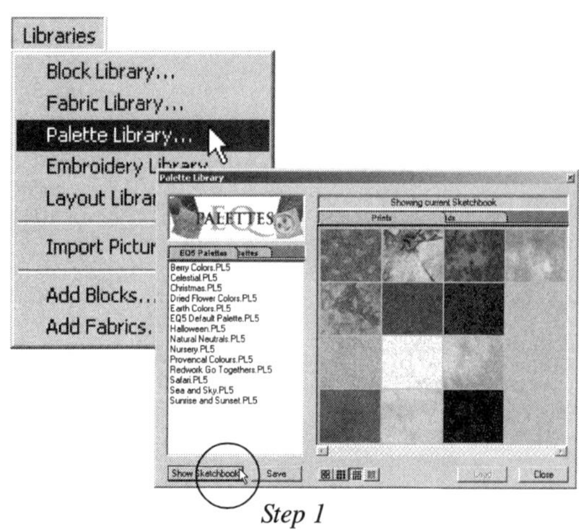

Step 1

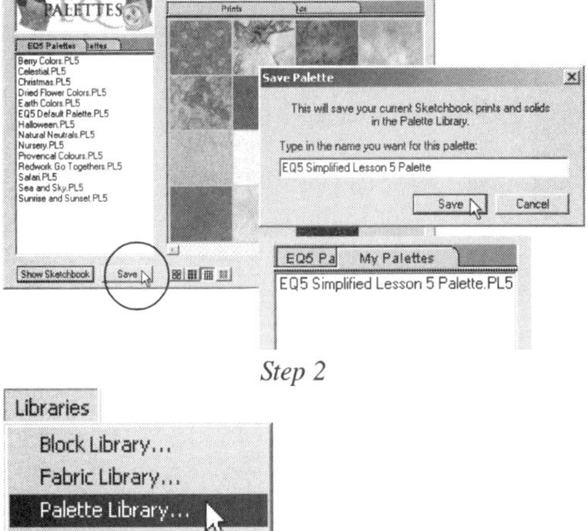

Step 2

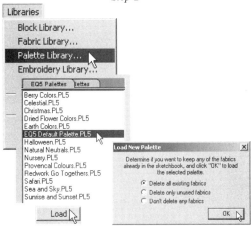

Change to EQ5's Default Palette

Here is the finished quilt!

2 Click on Save in the Palette Library box and a Save Palette box will open. EQ5 will ask you to type in the palette name under which you want to save the print and solid fabrics from this project. Type in any name that best describes your customized palette. Click on Save. Your palette is now saved under My Palettes in EQ5's Palette Library! Close Palette Library.

Saving the Current Palette as the Default

EQ5 also allows you to designate your current palette as the new default palette. Click on File and then click on Save Palette as Default. This project's palette is now the new default fabric palette for any project that you will subsequently create in EQ5. This can be easily changed at any point.

You have the option to change the palette back to EQ5's original default palette whenever you want. To do this, click on Libraries, click on Palette Library, and then click on EQ5 Default Palette on the EQ5 Palettes tab. Click on Load. The Load New Palette box will appear. Choose the option that you would like and click on OK. Click on Close. See the EQ5 manuals or the Help file for more information. You will explore the Palette Library in Lesson 7.

Exiting EQ5

Click on File and then click on Exit or use the shortcut Alt+F4 to close EQ5.

5

Combining EasyDraw™ and PatchDraw

Lesson 6

Lesson 6 – Combining EasyDraw™ & PatchDraw

6

In this lesson, you will combine the versatility of EasyDraw™ and PatchDraw to create a unique Overlaid block. You will also discover EQ5's amazing Symmetry tool that allows you to experiment easily with sixteen different block arrangements in a layout. The quilts that you will create for this lesson are a Symmetry Series.

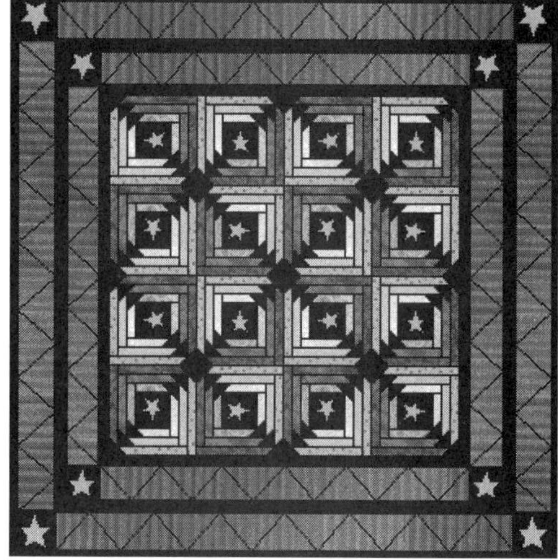

Symmetry 1

In addition to the design exercises, you will discover several effective techniques that will help you in actual quilt construction. You will:

- *Add a background square to an appliqué motif*
- *Create an Overlaid block*
- *Draw border stencils*
- *Rotate directional fabric*
- *Experiment with the Symmetry tool*
- *Maintain block rotation*
- *Print an Overlaid block*
- *Learn construction shortcuts*

Starting a New Project

Start a new project with the file name *Symmetry Series.*

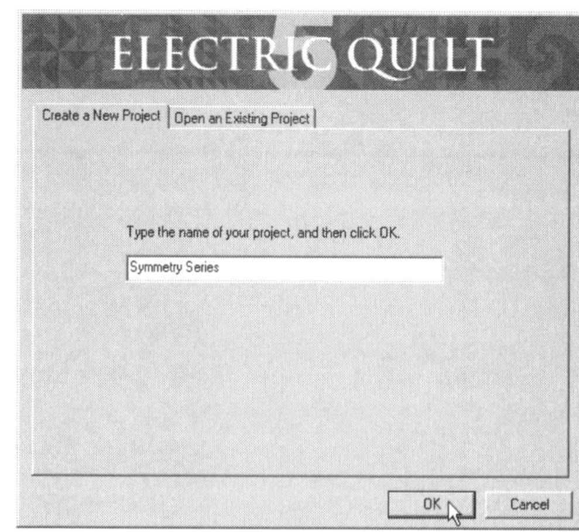

EQ5 Opening Screen

Selecting a Fabric Palette

At the end of Lesson 5, you set that project's palette as the default. This is the default palette for Lesson 6. You can keep all or part of this palette for this project or you can create a new palette from the Fabric Libraries, as I have done here. If you decide to select a new palette, follow the instructions in "Creating a Fabric Palette" in the beginning of Lesson 5.

You will learn how to rotate fabric designs later in this lesson, so be sure to select a directional fabric from the EQ5 Designer Fabric Basics Libraries or from STASH to use in the quilt borders. A striped fabric will work very well to illustrate this feature.

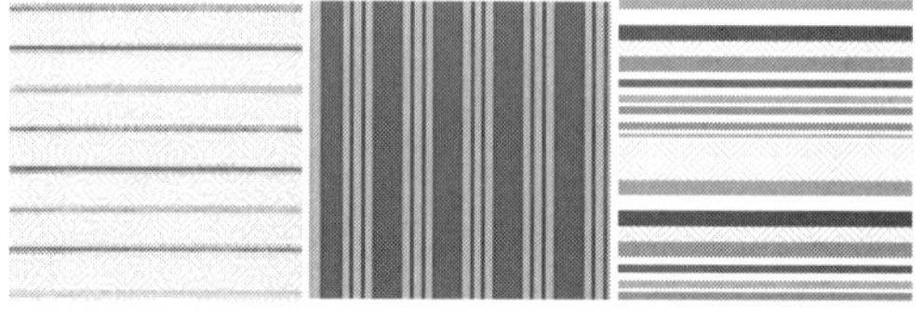

Examples of directional fabrics

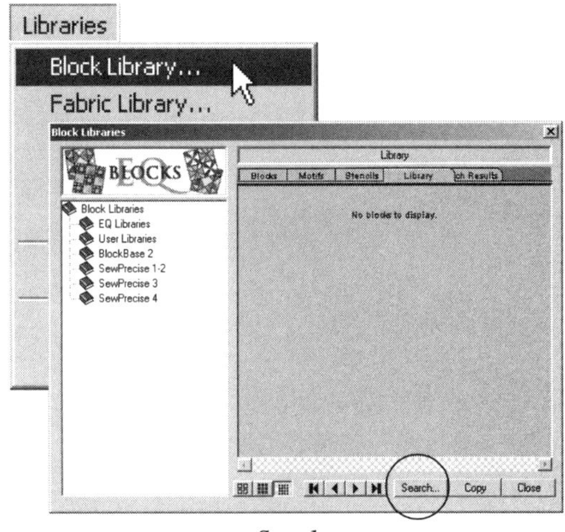

Step 1

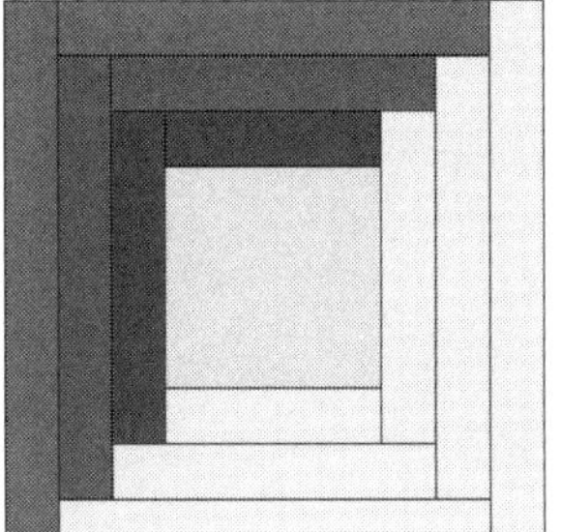

Large Center Log Cabin

Copy

Step 3

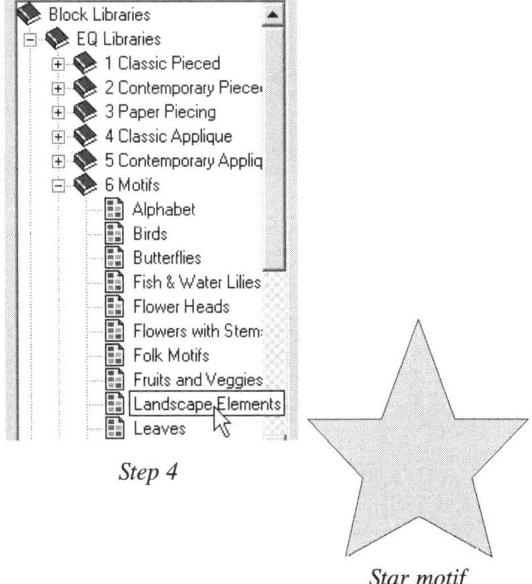

Step 4

Star motif

Selecting the Block

1 Click on Libraries in the main menu and then click on Block Library. Click on Search.

2 Type *Large Center Log Cabin* in the Search Block Notecard box. Be sure that Search name is checked. Click on the Search button at the bottom of this Search Block Notecard box or press the Enter key. Click on OK when EQ5 displays the results of the search.

3 Click on the Large Center Log Cabin block to select it and then click on Copy in the Block Libraries box.

4 Click on EQ Libraries on the left side of the Block Libraries box. Open the 6Motifs library and click on Landscape Elements. Click on the Star motif. Click on Copy to place this design in your Sketchbook. Click Close.

Tip

- **A search on the word "star" would have yielded hundreds of designs! A more practical approach to such a broad search would be to use more specific keywords, such as "variable star."**
- **You can also use the EQ5 Block Book to quickly and easily view all designs in the EQ5 Block Libraries. This can be very helpful when searching for designs of a particular type.**

You should now have two designs in your Sketchbook. The Large Center Log Cabin block will be on the Blocks tab and the Star will be on the Motifs tab.

Editing a Design in EasyDraw™

You will now make a few modifications to the Large Center Log Cabin before using it to create an Overlaid block. This new block is Geese in the Cabin.

1 Open the Block Sketchbook. Click on the Large Center Log Cabin block and click on Edit to place it on the worktable.

6

2 It will be helpful to have graph paper lines on the worktable when modifying this block. The Snap to Grid Points are set automatically because this design is from the EQ Libraries. Click on Block in the main menu and then click on Drawing Board Setup. Click on the Graph Paper tab and set these values:

Number of divisions:	Horizontal – 10 Vertical – 10
Style:	Graph paper lines

Click on OK.

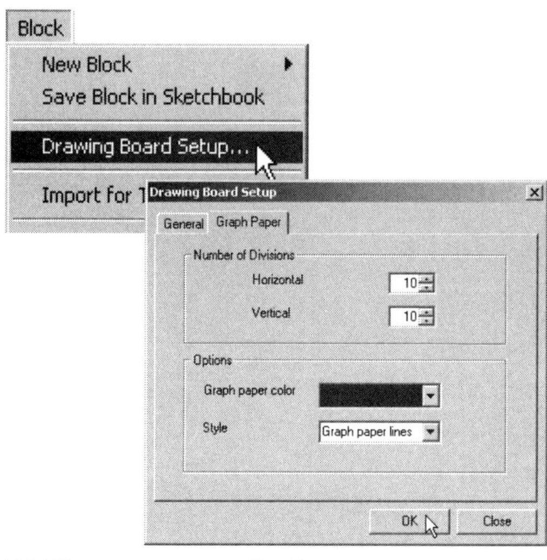

Step 2

3 Use the Line tool to draw six diagonal lines, as shown. These lines will form six geese across the block. Save in Sketchbook.

Line Tool

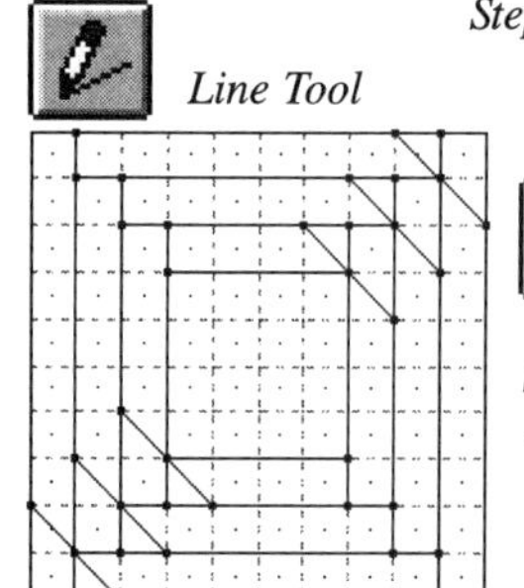

Step 3 – Create six lines of equal length in a diagonal pattern across the block and Save in Sketchbook.

4 Click on the Select tool and then, holding down the Shift key, select the extended vertical line within each of the geese. Press the Delete key to remove these lines. Save in Sketchbook.

5 Make a Notecard for this design and name it *Geese in the Cabin*. You will color this block later on the Overlaid worktable.

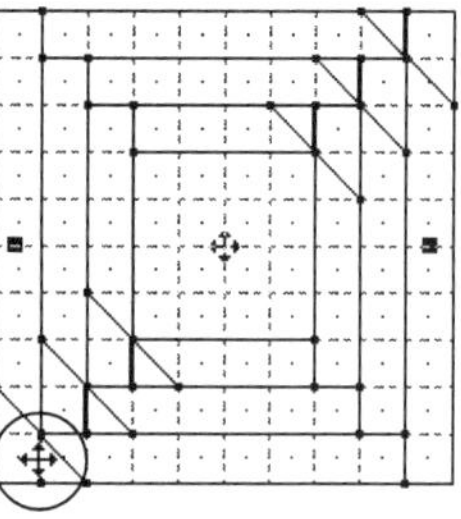

Step 4 – Delete vertical lines within geese.

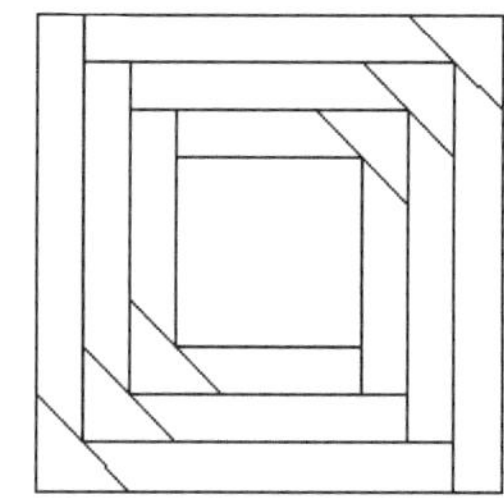

Step 4 – Geese in the Cabin (as seen on the color tab)

Adding a Background Square to an Appliqué Motif

As you learned in Lesson 5, an appliqué block has a background square and an appliqué motif does not. You can easily add a background square to an appliqué motif in EQ5, in order to use this design as an appliqué block in the quilt layout. You will now add a background square to the Star motif to create a Star block for the corners of the quilt borders.

1 Open the Sketchbook and select the Star motif for editing.

2 With the Star on the PatchDraw worktable, click on Edit and then click on Select All in the Edit menu. You can also use the shortcut Ctrl+A to select the entire design on the worktable. Ctrl+C to copy.

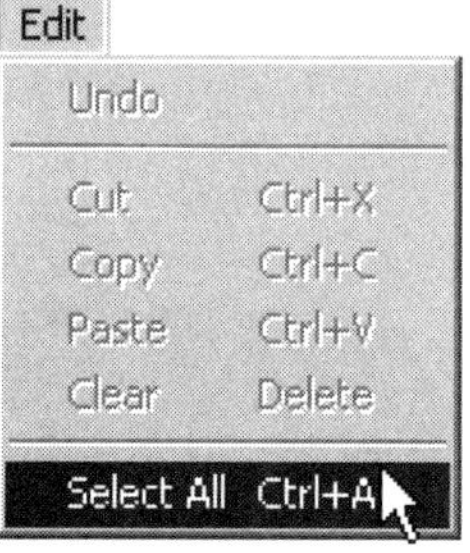

Step 2

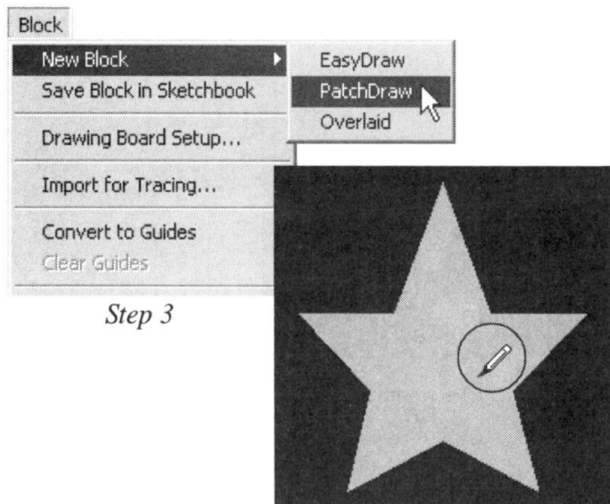

Step 3

Center Star, Color, and Save in Sketchbook

3 Click on Block in the main menu and then click on New Block. Click on PatchDraw in the extended menu. A new PatchDraw block will open with a background square in place. Ctrl+V to paste the Star design in the block. Center the Star and then color the design. Save in Sketchbook.

4 Make a Notecard for this Star block.

Resizing a Design in PatchDraw

You will resize the Star motif before using it to create a new Overlaid block design.

1 Open the Block Sketchbook and click on the Motifs tab. Place the Star on the worktable.

2 Ctrl+A to select all lines in the drawing. With the Star selected, secondary click on the worktable to open the PatchDraw Worktable Context Menu. Click on Resize.

3 In the Resize box, type in 30 for the Horizontal and Vertical percentages. Click on OK. The size of the Star motif will be reduced to 30% of its original size.

4 Save in Sketchbook. Make a Notecard for this Resized Star motif.

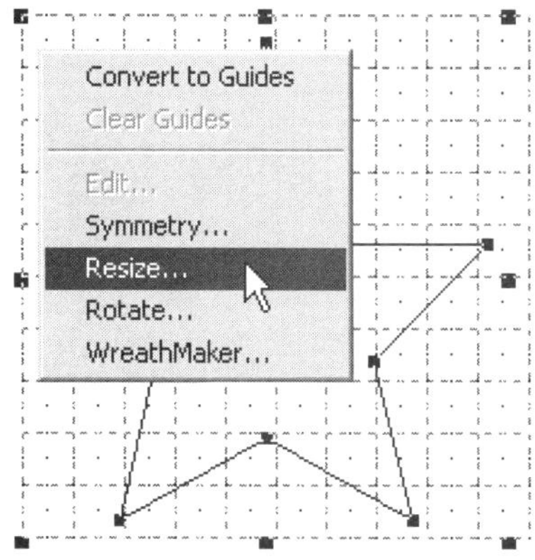

Step 1 & 2

Creating an Overlaid Block

The Overlaid block is the ideal way to combine pieced and appliqué designs into one block. There are a number of steps, but the process is not complicated. It is simply a matter of copying and pasting in the right order. You will now combine the Geese in the Cabin block with the Resized Star motif to form the Night Flight block.

First, you will copy the Geese in the Cabin block to the Pieced tab in the Overlaid worktable. Next, you will copy the Resized Star motif to the Appliqué tab in the Overlaid worktable. Last, you will color the new Night Flight Overlaid block design.

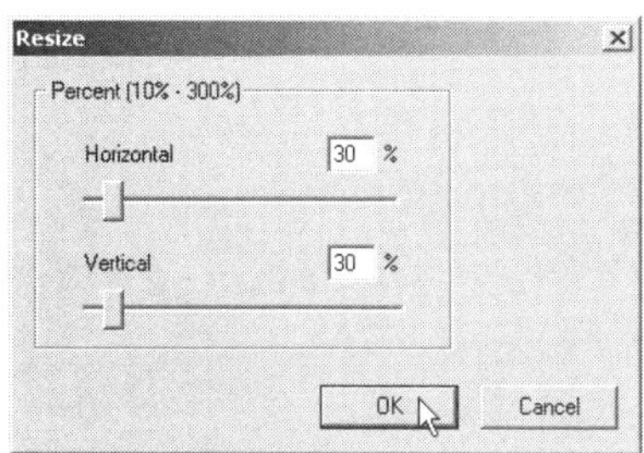

Step 3

Step 4

1 Open the block Sketchbook and select the Geese in the Cabin block for editing. Ctrl+A to select all. Ctrl+C to copy.

2 Click on Block in the main menu, click on New Block, and then click on Overlaid. The Overlaid worktable will open.

3 Click on the Pieced tab on the Overlaid worktable and Ctrl+V to paste. The Geese in the Cabin block will appear on the worktable. Position it carefully within the block outline while it is selected.

Click on the Color tab to be sure all the lines are there. If they are not, go back to the Pieced tab and draw the missing lines. Save in Sketchbook.

4 Open the Motifs Sketchbook and select the Resized Star for editing. On the worktable, drag a marquee around the image with the Select tool. Ctrl+C to copy.

5 Open the Sketchbook again and retrieve the Overlaid Geese in the Cabin block. When EQ5 asks if you want to keep the worktable block before editing this one, click on No.

6 Click on the Appliqué tab on the Overlaid worktable. Ctrl+V to paste. The Resized Star is now on the Overlaid worktable and you can adjust its position.

7 Click on the Color tab and Color the Night Flight block. Save in Sketchbook.

8 Create a Notecard for the Night Flight Overlaid block. Create a Notecard for the Overlaid Geese in the Cabin block. Save.

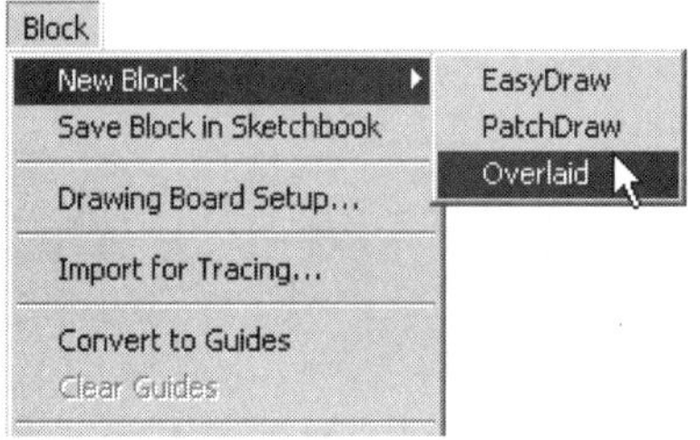

Step 2

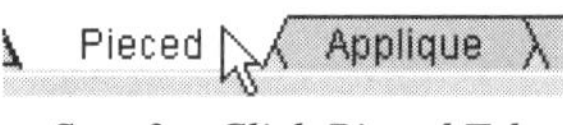

Step 3 – Click Pieced Tab

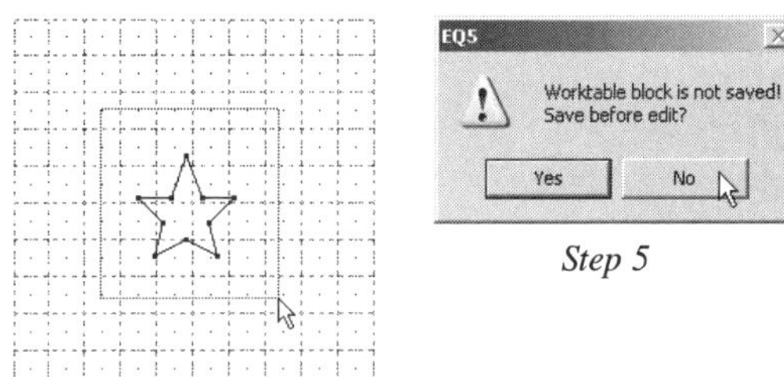

Step 4

Step 5

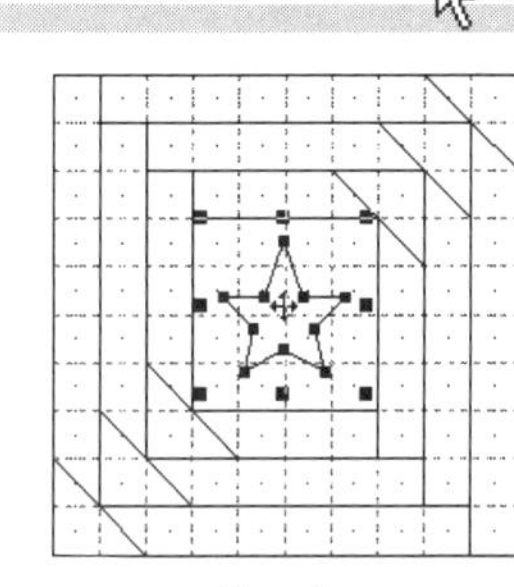

Step 6

Step 7 – Color Night Flight block & Save in Sketchbook

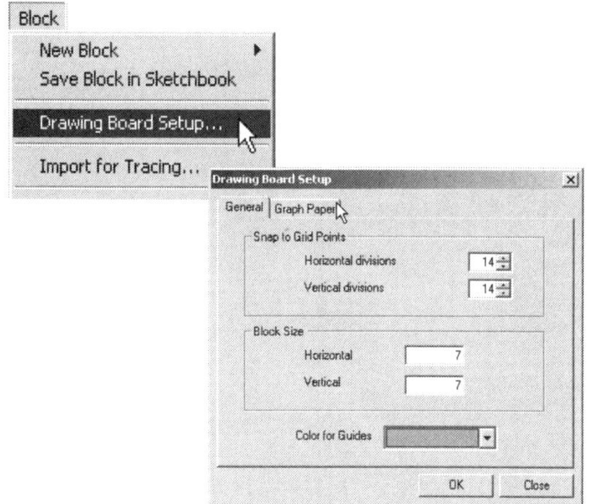

Step 1

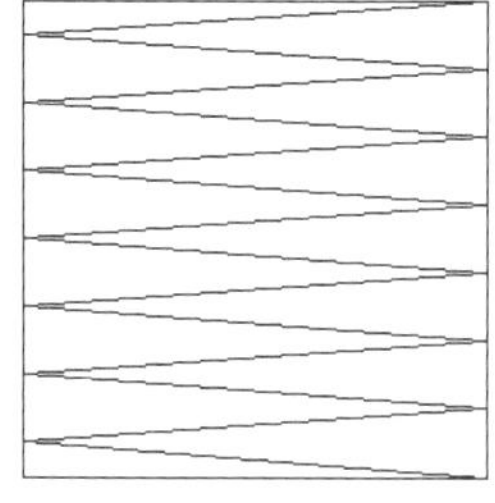

Step 2 – Seven Points Out & Save in Sketchbook

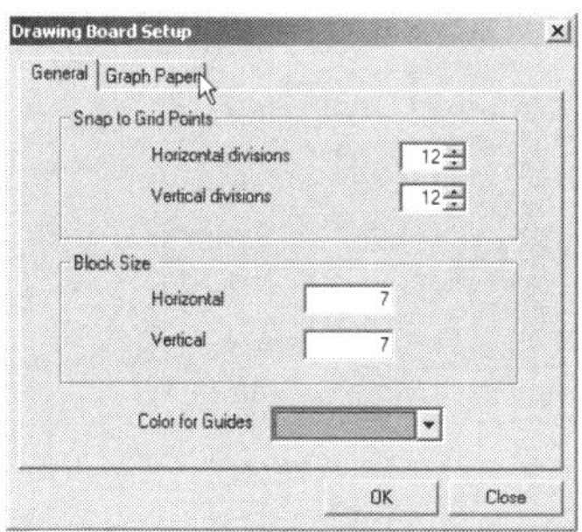

Step 3

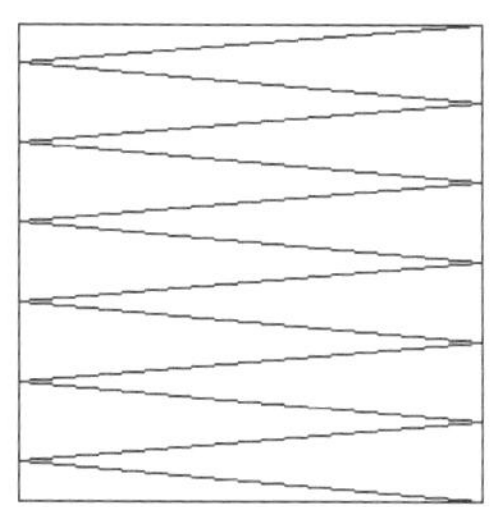

Step 4 – Six Points Out & Save in Sketchbook

Drawing Border Stencils

6

In this lesson, you will draw your own border stencils for the Symmetry Series! You will use a Seven Points Out block in Border 4 and a Six Points Out block in Border 2.

1 For the Seven Points Out block, click on Worktable and then click on Work on Block. Click on Block, click on New Block, and then click on EasyDraw™. Click on Block and then click on Drawing Board Setup. Set these values and then click OK:

General Tab

Snap to Grid Points:	Horizontal – 14
	Vertical – 14
Block Size:	define a square

Graph Paper Tab

Number of Divisions:	Horizontal – 14
	Vertical – 14
Options:	Graph Paper lines

2 Draw a block with seven points out, as shown. Save in Sketchbook.

3 For the Six Points Out block, click on Block, click on New Block, and then click on EasyDraw™. Set these values in the Drawing Board Setup and then click OK:

General Tab

Snap to Grid Points:	Horizontal – 12
	Vertical – 12
Block Size:	define a square

Graph Paper

Number of Divisions:	Horizontal – 12
	Vertical – 12
Options:	Graph Paper lines

4 Draw a block with six points out, as shown. Save in Sketchbook.

5 Create Notecards for the Seven Points Out and Six Points Out designs. Close Sketchbook and Save.

6

Planning a Layout and Borders

You have collected all of the designs that you will need for your Symmetry Series quilts. Now you will create the basic layout.

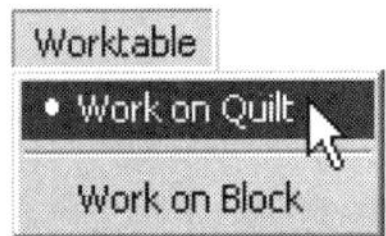

Step 1

1 Click on Worktable and then click on Work on Quilt. Click on Quilt in the main menu, click New Quilt, and click on Horizontal.

2 Click on the Layout tab and set these values:

Number of blocks:	Horizontal – 4 Vertical – 4
Size of blocks:	Width – 8.00 Height – 8.00
Sashing:	Width – 0.00 Height – 0.00
Sash border:	unchecked

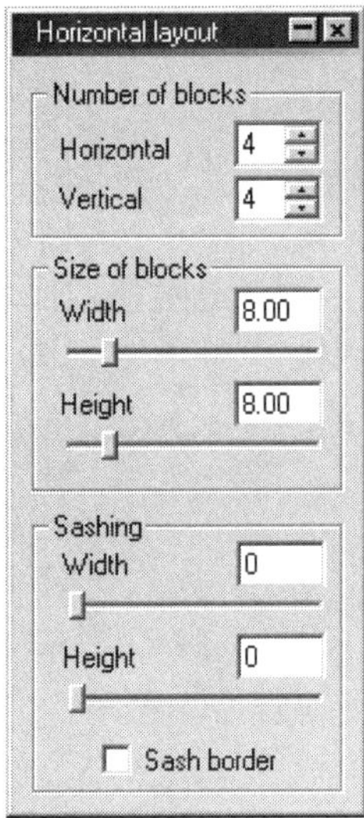

Step 2

3 Click on the Borders tab and establish these borders. Remember that to add a border, you must click the Add button in the Borders box. Border boxes 1-3 are illustrated here.

Border 1

Border Style:	Mitered
Adjust Size:	1.00 (Lock: All)

Border 2

Border Style:	Corner Blocks
Adjust Size:	3.00 (Lock: All)

Border 3

Border Style:	Mitered
Adjust Size:	1.00 (Lock: All)

Border 4

Border Style:	Corner Blocks
Adjust Size:	3.50 (Lock: All)

Border 5

Border Style:	Mitered
Adjust Size:	.50 (Lock: All)

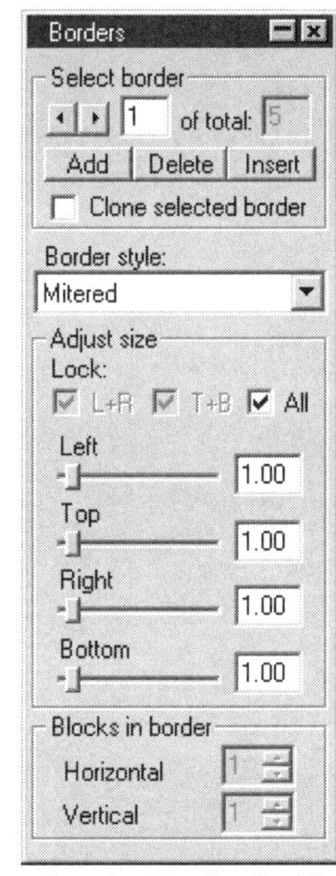

Step 3 – Border 1 of 5

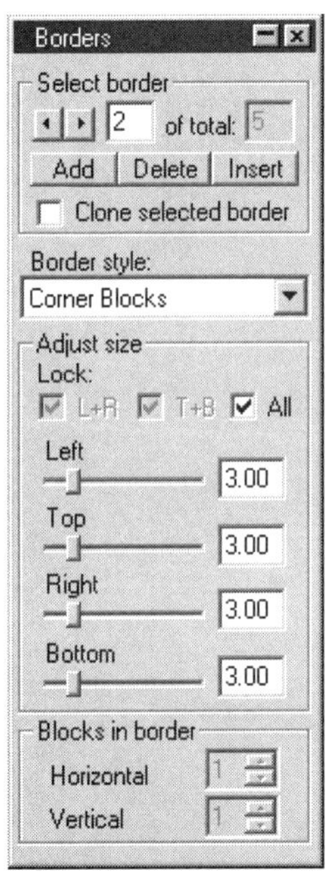

Step 3 – Border 2 of 5

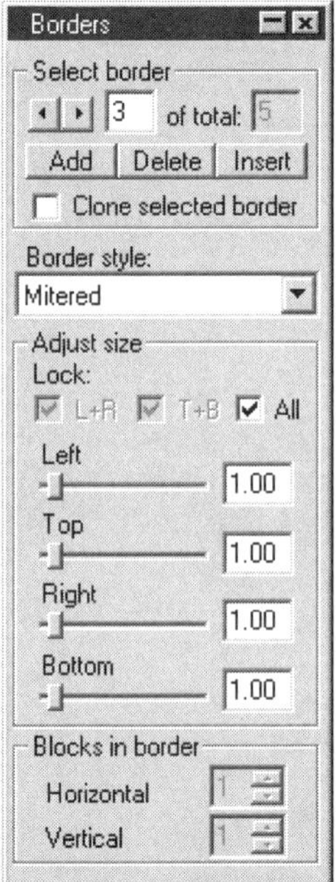

Step 3 – Border 3 of 5

Step 4

Step 1

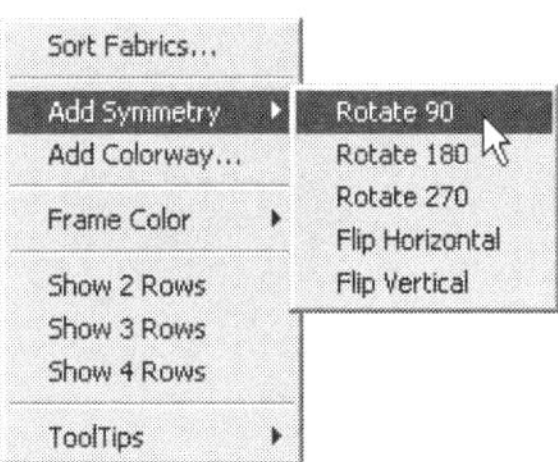

Step 2

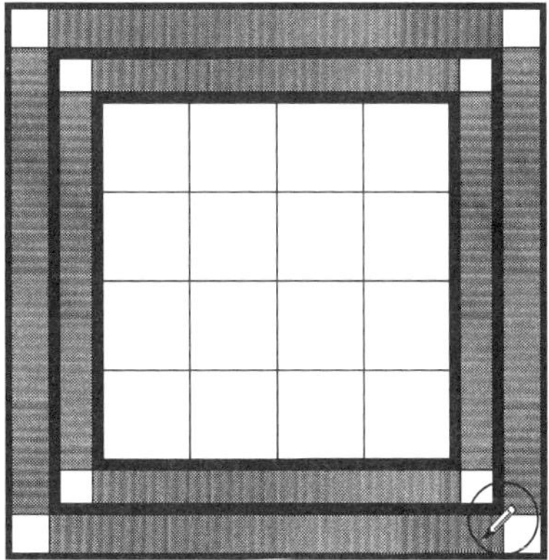

Quilt layout with directional fabric in borders

Tip

- **In this particular quilt, this last border is intended to be the binding, so it will not add to the size if you actually construct the quilt. It is being shown here because it will be a different color and will add to the impact of the design.**

4 Click on the Layer 1 tab. Save in Sketchbook.

Rotating Directional Fabric

EQ5 gives you the capability to rotate directional fabrics to a different orientation. This feature is available on the block worktables and on the quilt worktable.

1 With the quilt layout on the worktable, click on any color tool to open the Fabrics palette. Click on the directional fabric that you copied into the palette and then secondary click on the Prints palette. A Context Menu will open.

2 Click on Add Symmetry and then click on an appropriate rotation option for the directional fabric that you have selected. The new rotated fabric swatch will appear in the palette, directly after the original fabric. You can now use this fabric as you would any other fabric in the palette. Color the borders, using the original fabric and the new rotated fabric in at least one of the borders, as shown. Save in Sketchbook.

Tip

- **You must select a rotation option that will have a discernible effect on the particular directional fabric that you have selected. For example, if you rotate a vertically striped fabric by 180°, you might notice very little difference in the new swatch. If you rotate this same fabric by 90°, however, you will create a horizontal stripe that is noticeably different from the original swatch. Experiment to discover obvious rotations for the directional fabric in your palette.**
- **There are restrictions to this Add Symmetry function so be sure to check the EQ5 Help file for more information.**
- **After rotating directional fabric, you must save before exiting the program.**

Setting Quilt Stencils into the Borders

You will assemble the quilt for this lesson in a slightly different order than the quilts in previous lessons in this tutorial. Because you will be experimenting with a variety of block arrangements, you will finish the borders before placing the blocks in the layout. This will allow you to save your Symmetry Series quilts easily as you create them.

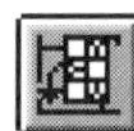

Step 1 – Set Tool & Rotate Tool

Step 1

1 Click the Set tool and Ctrl+click to set the Star block into the corner blocks of Borders 2 and 4. Use the Rotate tool to turn the Star blocks on the top of the quilt so that the top of the Star is pointing down. This will add balance to your quilt design when it is viewed from any angle. Save in Sketchbook.

Tip

- **As you learned in Lesson 4, you can set solid line stencils on Layer 2 or you can set dashed line stencils on Layer 3. If you set the stencils on Layer 2, remember to use the line drawing of the design.**

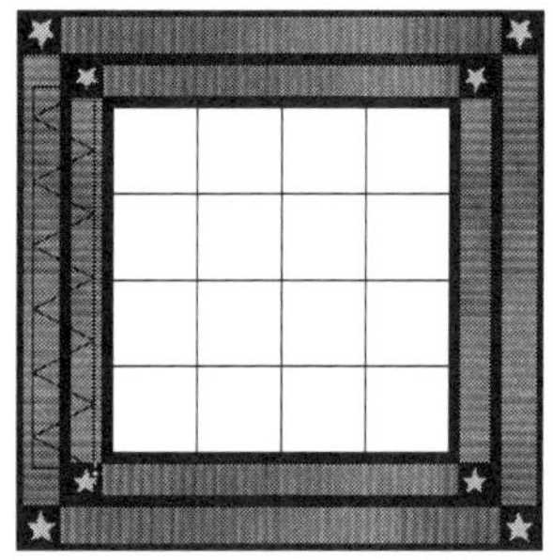

Step 2

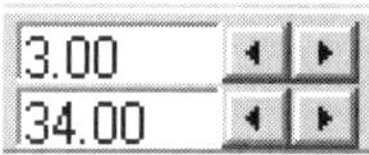

Step 3 – Stencil Size

2 Click on the Layer on which you want to set the stencils in Border 2 and then click on the Set tool. Select the Six Points Out design that you drew. Holding down the Shift key, click and drag the mouse to set the design on the worktable.

Tip

- **You can use the Tape Measure tool to measure between the two corner squares on one vertical segment of Border 2.**

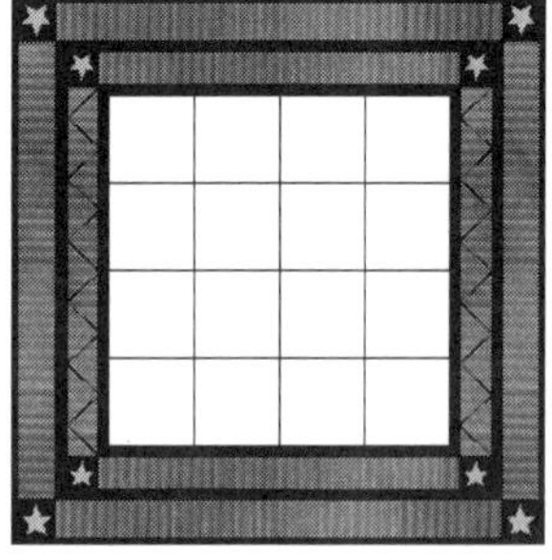

Step 4

Step 5 – Rotate

3 Click on the Adjust tool and then click on this stencil design. Set the size to 3.00 by 34.00 on the Graph Pad. Move it into position over one of the vertical segments of the second border.

4 With the stencil still selected, Ctrl+C to copy and Ctrl+V to paste another stencil on the worktable. Move this stencil over the remaining vertical segment of the second border.

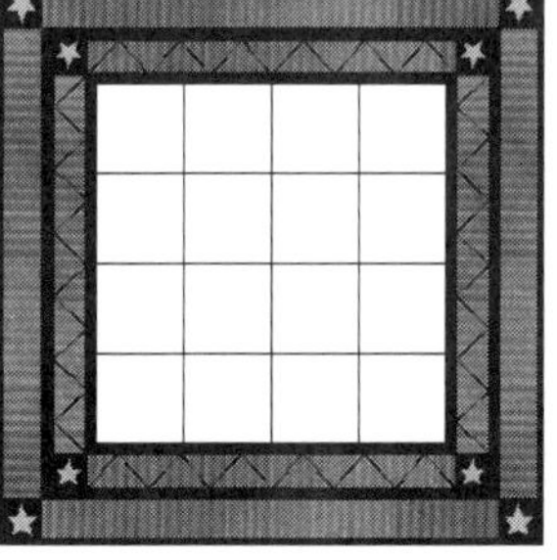

Step 6

Step 6 – Save in Sketchbook

Step 7 – Flip Tool

Step 7 – Border 2 stencils set & flipped

Step 8

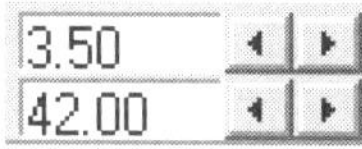

Step 8 – Stencil Size

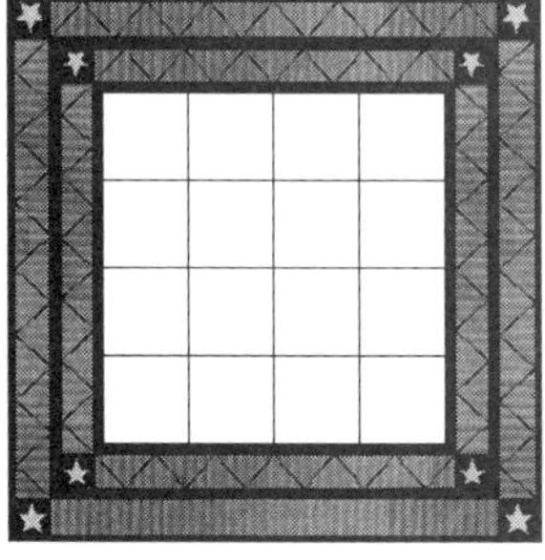

Step 10

Step 10 – Rotate

Step 12 – Flip Tool

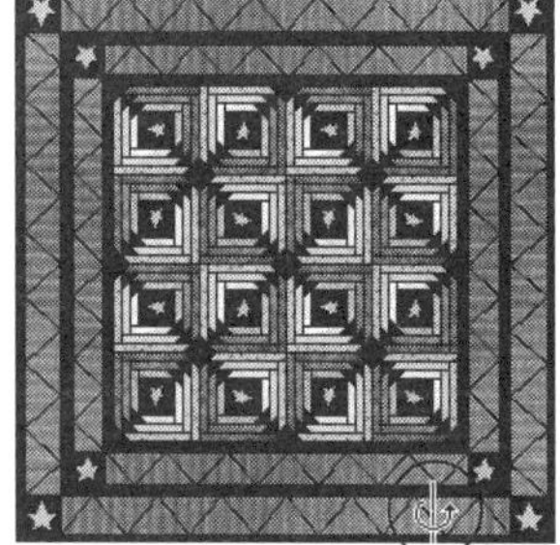

Step 12 – Border 4 stencils set & flipped

5 With the stencil still selected, Ctrl+C to copy and Ctrl+V to paste another copy of the border stencil on the worktable. Rotate this stencil by 90° on the Graph Pad. Move into position over one of the horizontal segments of the second border.

6 Copy and paste this stencil on the remaining horizontal segment of the second border. Save in Sketchbook.

7 Use the Flip tool to arrange the stencils in the correct orientation in the layout, as shown. Save in Sketchbook.

8 Click on the Set tool and then click on the Seven Points Out stencil in the palette. Holding down the Shift key, click and drag the mouse to set this stencil on the worktable. With the Adjust tool, set the size to 3.50 by 42.00 on the Graph Pad. Move this stencil into position over one of the vertical segments of the fourth border.

9 Copy and paste this stencil on the remaining vertical segment of the fourth border.

10 With the stencil still selected, Ctrl+C to copy and Ctrl+V to paste another copy of the worktable. Rotate this stencil by 90° on the Graph Pad. Move into position over one of the horizontal segments of the fourth border.

11 Copy and paste this stencil on the remaining horizontal segment of the fourth border. Save in Sketchbook.

12 Use the Flip tool to arrange the stencils in the correct orientation in the layout, as shown. Save in Sketchbook.

Experimenting with the Symmetry Tool

The Symmetry tool allows you to experiment quickly and easily with a sequence of block arrangements in a quilt layout! In order to see the effect of the Symmetry tool on the layout, you must set asymmetrical block designs in the quilt. This asymmetrical effect can be achieved by color or by design. You can use the same asymmetrical design throughout the quilt or use a combination of blocks. EQ5 will rotate and flip each set of four blocks within the quilt, starting in the upper-left corner, for a total variation of sixteen symmetrical layouts.

Step 1 – Set Night Flight Block

Step 1 – Save in Sketchbook

1 Click on Layer 1. Click on the Set tool and then click on the Night Flight block in the Blocks palette. Ctrl+click to set this block in all spaces in the layout. This is the basic quilt layout that you will use as a starting point for your symmetry experiment. Save in Sketchbook.

Step 2 – Symmetry Tool

Step 2 – First variation using Symmetry Tool

2 Click on the Symmetry tool in the Quilt tools and Ctrl+click on one of the Night Flight blocks in the quilt layout. This new layout is the first of the sixteen symmetrical layouts. With each successive Ctrl+click of the Symmetry tool, another symmetrical layout will be created. Save in Sketchbook for each design that you want to keep.

See the EQ5 manuals and the Help file for more information about the Symmetry tool.

Maintaining Block Rotation

EQ5 will allow you to maintain the specific rotation for a design in the quilt layout when you replace it with another design! The new design will be rotated to the same orientation as the previous design. This feature works on all Layers.

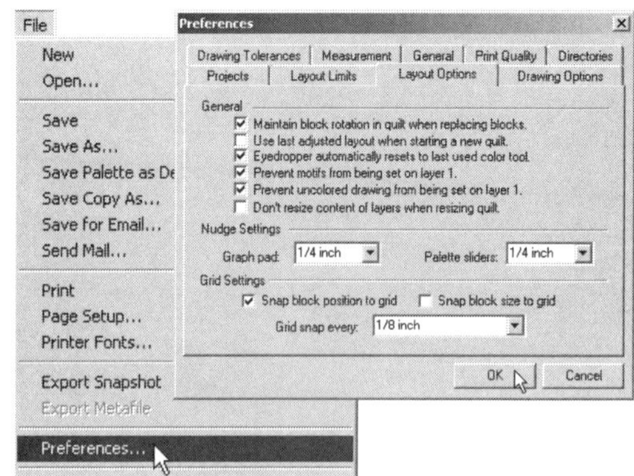

Step 1 – Maintain Block Rotation checked

1 Click on File, click on Preferences, and then click on Layout Options. The first item under General is *Maintain block rotation in quilt when replacing blocks.* Check to engage this function. Click OK.

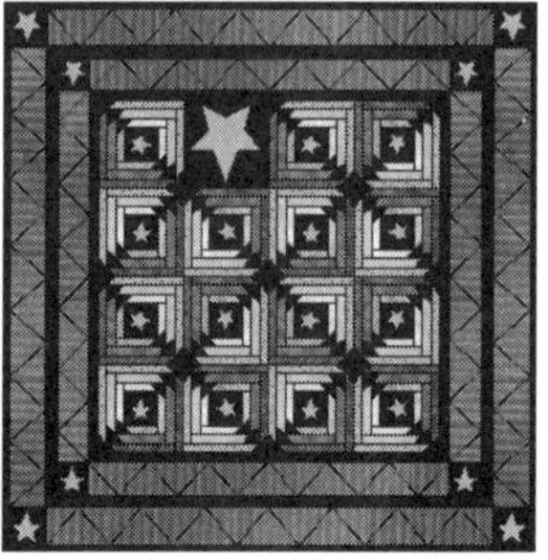

Step 2 – Star Block is Rotated 180°

Step 4 – Star Block is in the original orientation

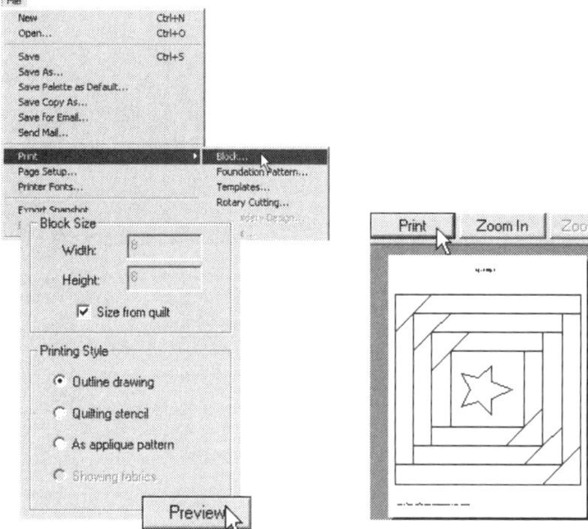

Print an Outline Drawing

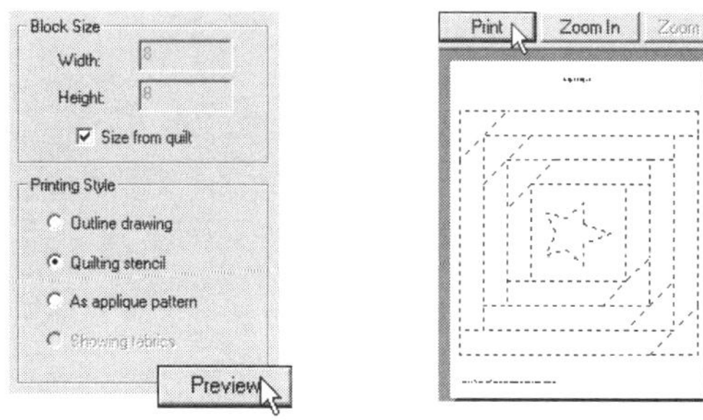

Print a Quilting Stencil

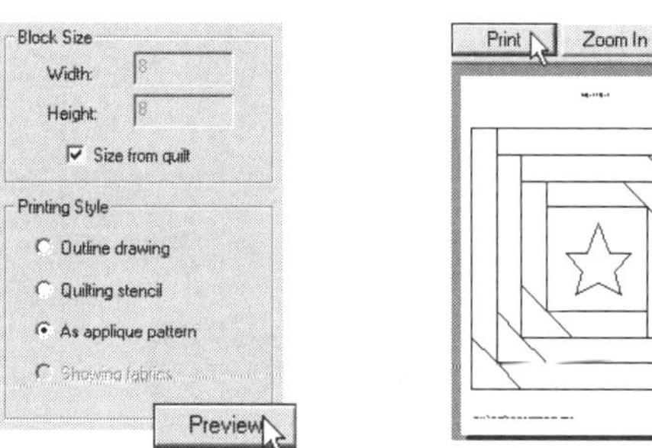

Print an Appliqué Pattern

2 Now, replace one of the rotated Night Flight blocks in the quilt layout with the Star block. You will notice that the Star block is in the same rotation as the Night Flight block that it replaced.

3 Click on File, click on Preferences, and then click on Layout Options. Uncheck *Maintain block rotation in quilt when replacing blocks*. Click on OK.

4 Using the Set tool, replace a rotated Night Flight block in the layout again with the Star block. You will notice that the replacement block is in the original orientation from the Sketchbook and not rotated like the block it replaced.

Printing an Overlaid Block

You can generate printouts of an Overlaid block just as easily as you can print EasyDraw™ and PatchDraw designs. Use the Night Flight block to experiment with these printing options.

To print an outline drawing:
Click on File, click on Print, and then click on Block. Under Block Size on the Block Size tab, set the desired width and height or Size from quilt (quilt worktable only). Click on Outline drawing. Preview and Print. All lines are visible in an outline drawing, including any overlapping appliqué patches.

To print a quilting stencil:
Click on File, click on Print, and then click on Block. Under Block Size on the Block Size tab, set the desired width and height or Size from quilt (quilt worktable only). Click Quilting stencil. Preview and Print. The design is displayed as quilting stitches in this printout.

To print an appliqué pattern:
Click on File, Print, and on Block. Under Block Size on the Block Size tab, set the desired width and height or Size from quilt (quilt worktable only). Click As appliqué pattern. Preview and Print. The design is realistically layered in this printout, so that you can see the effect of the overlapping appliqué patches.

6

To print showing fabrics:
Click on File, click on Print, and then click on Block. Under Block Size on the Block Size tab, set the desired width and height. Size from quilt (quilt worktable only) must be unchecked in order to print showing fabrics. Use the arrows under the block to display the colored version of the block that you want to print. Showing fabrics will now be available to you. Select this option. Preview and Print.

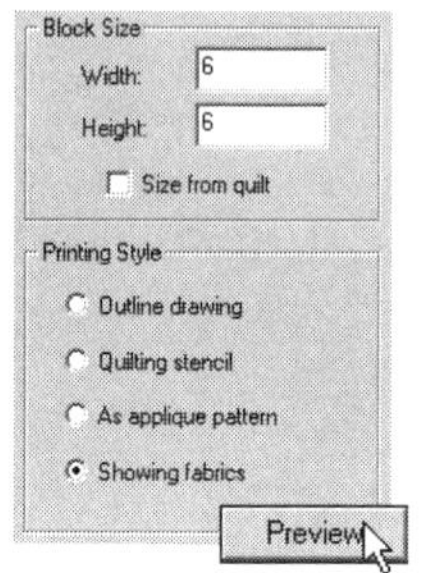

Print Showing Fabrics

To print a foundation pattern:
Print a foundation pattern for an Overlaid block from either the EasyDraw™ worktable or the Overlaid worktable.

If you *haven't* modified the designs from the EasyDraw™ worktable, you can simply use the original block on the EasyDraw™ worktable to generate the foundation pattern.

If you *have* modified the EasyDraw™ design after placing it on the Overlaid worktable, you must delete the contents on the Appliqué tab before generating the foundation pattern from the Pieced tab.

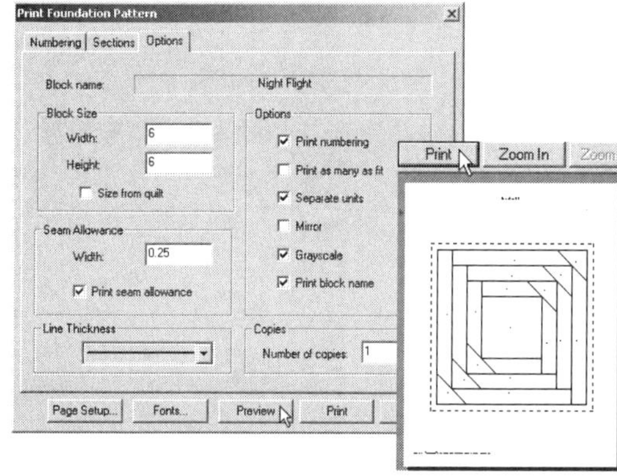

Print a Foundation Pattern

Click on the Appliqué tab and Ctrl+A to select all. Press the Delete key. Click on the Pieced tab. Click on File, click on Print, and then click on Foundation Pattern. Set the size of the block. Preview and Print.

To print templates:
Click on File, click on Print, and then click on Templates. Set the desired width and height or Size from quilt (quilt worktable only). Preview and Print.

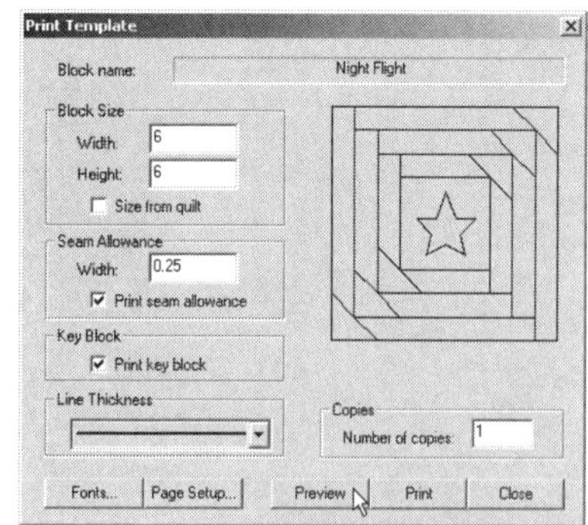

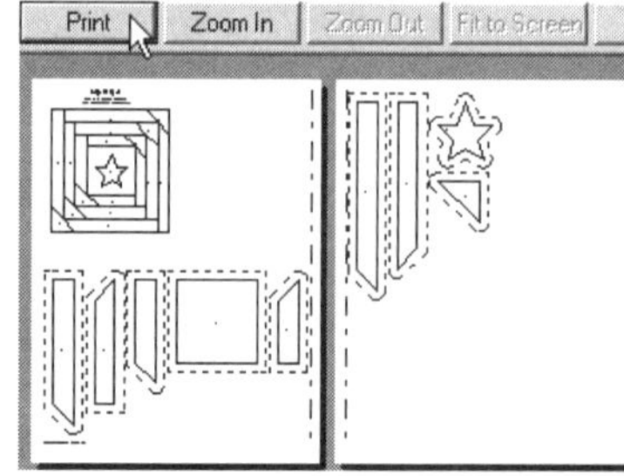

Print Templates

Learning Construction Shortcuts

With EQ5, you can simplify the construction of many elements in your quilt design by printing directly onto specialized products to create accurate templates, foundation patterns, and quilting stencils. There are many specialized materials available to quilters and they include a wide variety of fusibles, stabilizers, and tear away products. You can even use freezer paper and whole page adhesive labels to simplify quilt construction!

These techniques are intended for use with an ink jet printer only. Laser printers generate too much heat and can melt many of the materials mentioned here. This can cause extensive damage to a laser printer!

Tip

- **Be sure to print a test copy of the design on paper before printing it on the specialized material.**
- **Select a thick line for the printout so that the design is well defined.**
- **Remember to reverse an asymmetrical design before printing, if necessary.**
- **Remember to add or remove seam allowances, depending upon your particular construction method.**

Fusibles

From EQ5, you can print directly onto many fusible products. Cut the fusible to a standard paper size or define a custom size that your printer can handle. Be sure to print the patterns on the non-adhesive side of the product. Following the manufacturer's directions, press the printed patterns onto fabric, cut them out, and then fuse them to the background fabric or to other appliqué patches.

Stabilizers and Tear Away Products

You can print templates, foundation patterns, and quilting stencils on freezer paper, stabilizers, or tear away products. Cut the product to an acceptable size for your printer. If you have difficulty feeding the product through your printer, tape a narrow paper header on the leading edge.

If you are generating extra long or banner size patterns, be sure to guide the printout as it emerges. Be careful that it does not loop back into the paper feed tray!

Plastics

It is difficult, if not impossible, to print patterns directly onto template or stencil plastic. The plastic is too thick to feed through the printer and the surface will not absorb ink. The solution is to print template and stencil patterns onto whole page labels which can be applied to the plastic and then cut out!

Tip

- **Experiment with the various products to find the techniques and materials that work best for you, using the construction methods that you prefer. Be aware of your printer's capabilities as you explore these options.**

Adding Blocks to the User Libraries

You have created new designs in this lesson that can be added to the Block User Libraries.

1 Click on Libraries and then click on Add Blocks. The Add Block to Library box will open and your blocks for this project will be displayed under Block Sketchbook. Double-click on User Libraries in the Add Block to Library box and then double-click on the Library that contains the Simplified Blocks library. Click on this style library to open it.

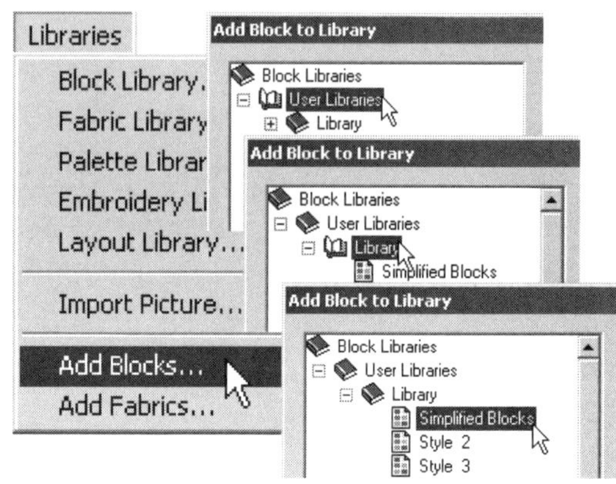

Step 1

2 Copy the blocks from this Symmetry Series project into this Simplified Blocks style library. Be sure to copy the designs on the Motif and Stencil tabs. EQ5 will tell you if you attempt to duplicate a design.

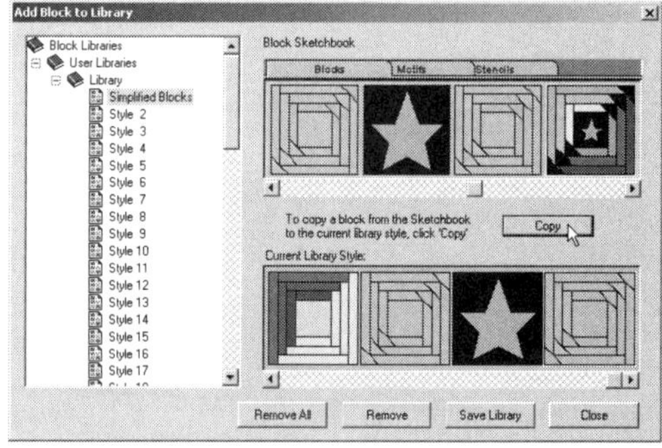

Step 2

3 Click on Save Library. A box will appear telling you that your blocks have been saved in the library. Click on OK and close the Add Block to Library box.

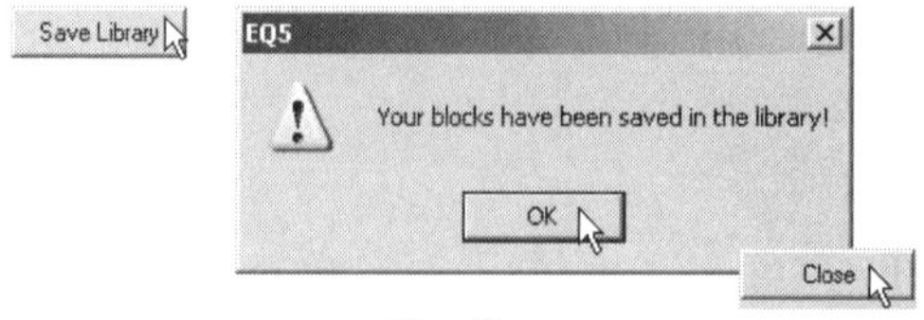

Step 3

Tip

- **Notice that you can also remove designs from the User Libraries through the Add Blocks feature. Please see the EQ5 manuals or the Help file for more information.**

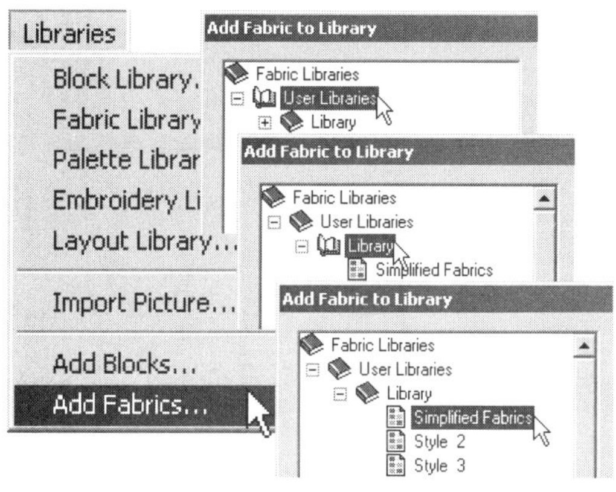

Step 1

Step 2

Step 3

Here is the finished quilt!

Adding Fabrics to the User Libraries

You can add any fabrics that you collected for this project to the Fabric User Libraries.

1 Click on Libraries and then click on Add Fabrics. The Add Fabric to Library box will open and your fabrics for this project will be displayed under Fabric Sketchbook. Double-click on User Libraries in the Add Fabric to Library box and then double-click on the Library that contains the Simplified Fabrics library. Click on this style library to open it.

2 Copy the fabrics from this Symmetry Series project into this Simplified Fabrics style library.

3 Click on Save Library. A box will appear telling you that your fabrics have been saved in the library. Click on OK and close the Add Fabrics to Library box.

Tip

- **Notice that you can also remove fabrics from the User Libraries through the Add Fabrics feature. Please see the EQ5 manuals or the Help file for more information.**

Exiting EQ5

Click on File and then click on Exit or use the shortcut Alt+F4 to close EQ5.

Discovering WreathMaker

Lesson 7

Lesson 7 – Discovering WreathMaker

In this lesson, you will discover WreathMaker, a unique EQ5 tool that enables you to create beautiful circular patterns from a single PatchDraw design. You will plan the Tic-Tac-Rose quilt as you learn to:

Tic-Tac-Rose Quilt

- *Install a palette from the Palette Library*
- *Design with WreathMaker*
- *Sort, move, and copy designs in the Blocks palette*
- *Experiment with EQ5 Color tools*
- *Sort the Fabrics palette*
- *Prepare the project for Emailing*
- *Print Foundation Patterns for triangular blocks*
- *Print Templates for triangular blocks*

Starting a New Project

Start a new project with the file name *Tic-Tac-Rose.*

Installing a Palette from the Palette Library

For this lesson, you are going to add a coordinated palette from the Palette Library to your Fabric Sketchbook.

1 Open the Fabric Sketchbook to view the current default palette in EQ5. When you load the new palette from the Palette Library, you will have the option to keep these default fabrics or remove them. Close the Sketchbook.

2 Click on Libraries in the main menu and then click on Palette Library. Click on the EQ5 Palettes tab and then click on one of the palettes in this library. The selected palette will display in the Palette Library box.

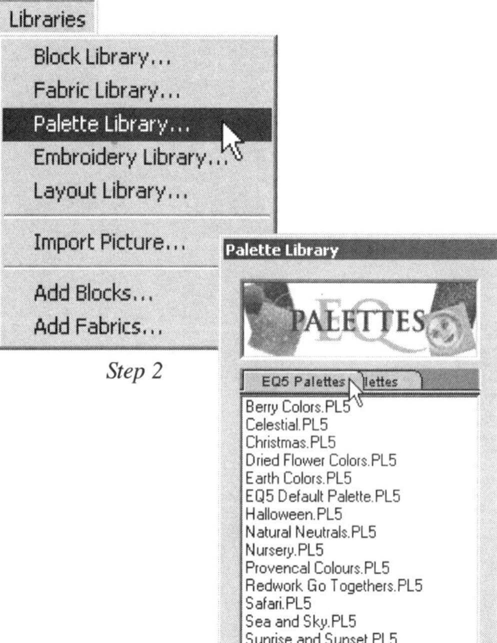

Step 2

Step 2

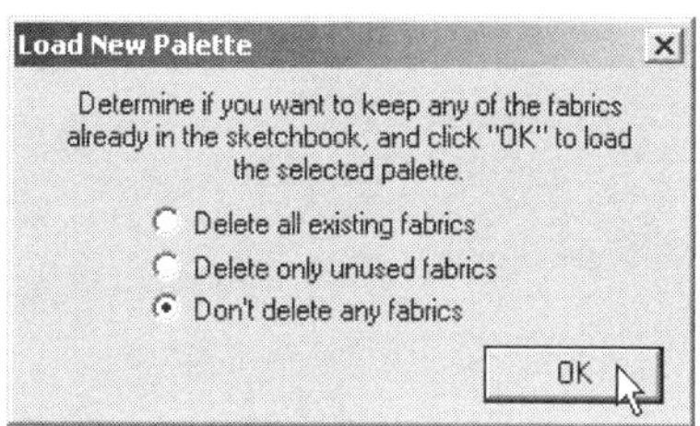

Step 3

3 Explore the palettes in this library, select the one that you want to install, and then click on Load. The Load New Palette box will open, offering you several options. Before adding the new palette, you can delete all existing fabrics from the current Fabric Sketchbook, delete only unused fabrics, or not delete any fabrics. Make your selection and then click on OK. The new palette will be added to the Fabric Sketchbook.

You can add more than one palette to the Sketchbook and you can also add individual fabrics from the EQ5 Libraries, the User Libraries, and STASH.

Tip

- **Palettes from the Palette Library are loaded in their entirety. You cannot load selected, individual swatches from these palettes.**

Copying Designs from the Libraries

As usual, your first task will be to gather the blocks that you will be using in the quilt design.

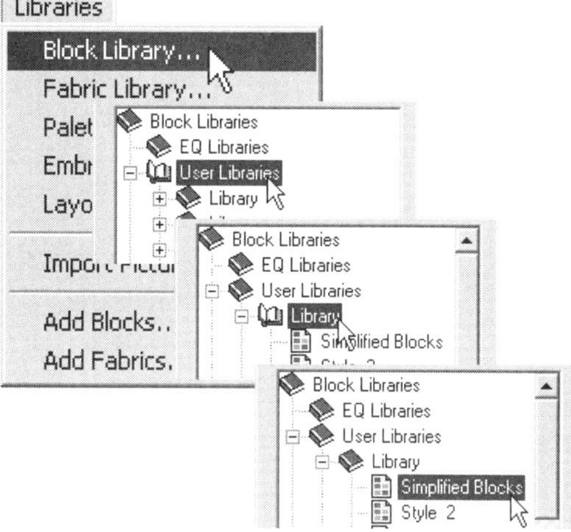

Step 1

1 Click on Libraries in the main menu and then click on Block Library. Click on User Libraries, click on the particular library that contains the Simplified Blocks style library, and then click on Simplified Blocks. Copy the Old Rose of Sharon block.

Old Rose of Sharon block colored

Christmas Cactus

2 Click on Search in the Block Libraries box and type in *Christmas Cactus*. Copy this block into the Sketchbook from the Search Results tab.

3 Click on Search again and then type in *Pineapple*. Copy the first block design on the Search Results tab. Close.

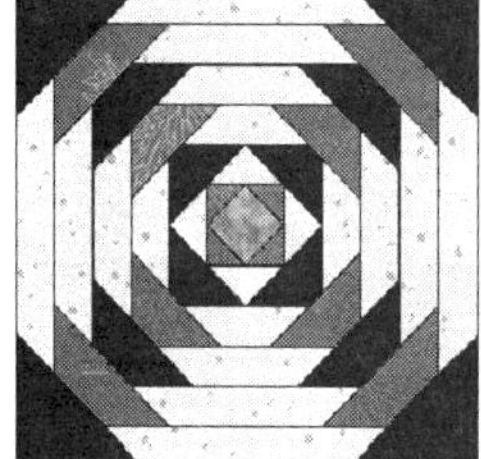

Pineapple block colored

Step 4 – Paintbrush Tool

4 Open the Block Sketchbook, place the Old Rose of Sharon design on the worktable, and color it. Save in Sketchbook. You are going to edit the Christmas Cactus, so don't color it yet. Color the Pineapple block with the dark values in the diagonal patches, as shown. Save in Sketchbook.

7

Editing a PatchDraw Design

You will now create several new PatchDraw designs by editing an appliqué block from the EQ Libraries. You will use one of these designs as the basic unit for WreathMaker.

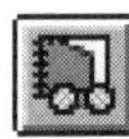

Step 1 – View Sketchbook

1 Open the Block Sketchbook and place the Christmas Cactus block on the worktable for editing.

Step 2 – Select Tool

Refresh Screen Button

2 Click on the Select tool and, holding down the Shift key, click on the two patches that form one flower in the design. Press the Delete key. Only the bow will remain in this quarter of the design. In the same manner, remove the three remaining flowering cacti from the block. Click on the Refresh Screen button.

Christmas Cactus with one flower removed

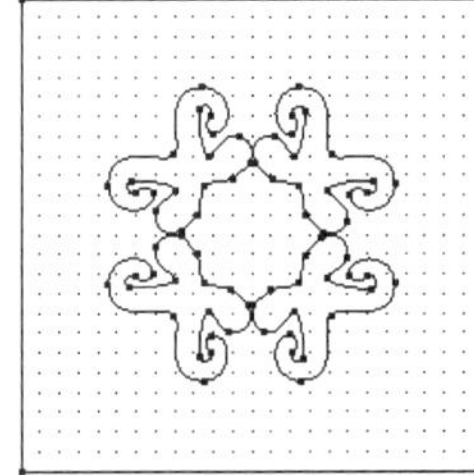

Christmas Cactus with only bows remaining

Tip

- **You can also delete these patches by clicking on each patch individually with the Select tool and then pressing the Delete key.**

3 With the Select tool, draw a marquee around all of the bows. Click on Block and then click on Resize in the Block menu. Type in 150 for the Horizontal and Vertical percentages. Click on OK. Click on Refresh Screen. Save in Sketchbook. Here is the Cactus Bow appliqué block.

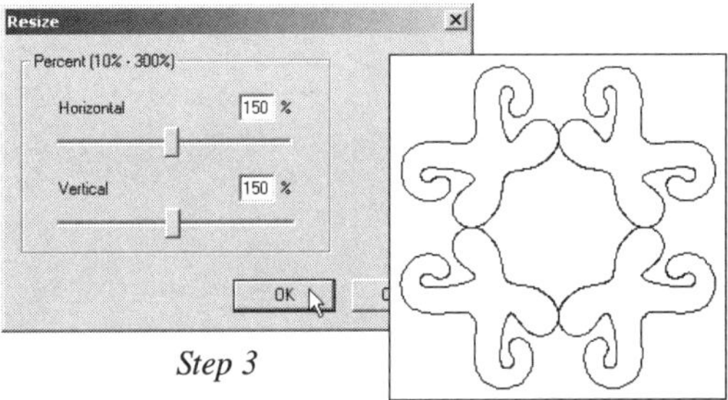

Step 3

Cactus Bow block

4 With the Select tool still engaged, remove the block outline. This is the Cactus Bow motif that you will use as a quilting stencil in the layout. Save in Sketchbook.

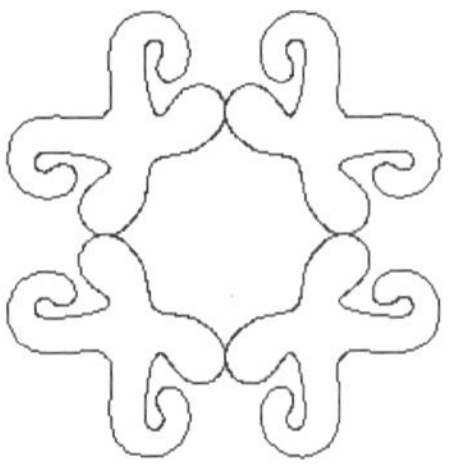

Step 4 – Cactus Bow motif and Save in Sketchbook

Now you are going to combine two PatchDraw designs together to make a new appliqué block.

5 Open the Sketchbook and select the Old Rose of Sharon block for editing. Click on the Select tool and, holding down the Shift key, click on the center circle and the rose. Ctrl+C to copy.

Step 5 – Select Tool

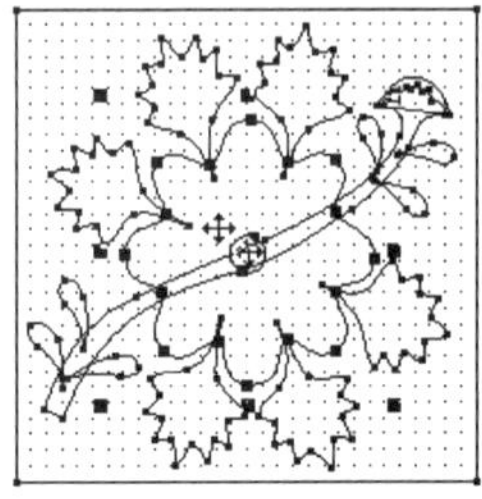

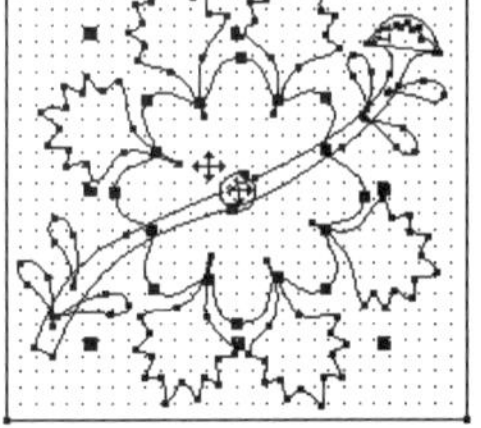

Step 5

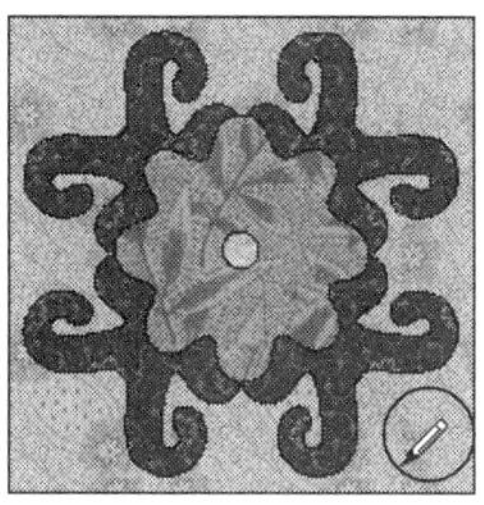

Step 6 – Color Ribbons & Rose block and Save in Sketchbook

Step 7 – Ribbons & Rose motif

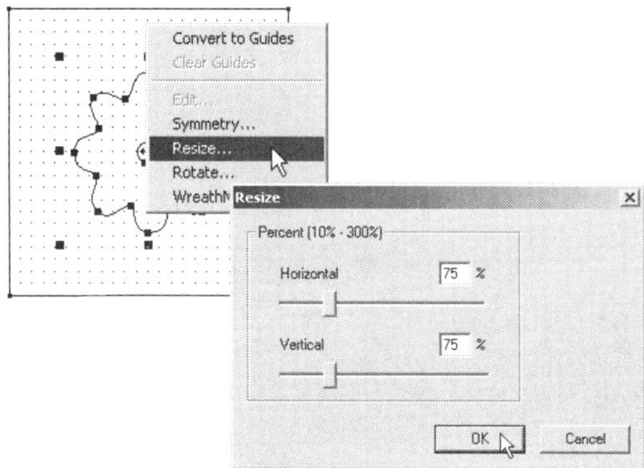

Step 8

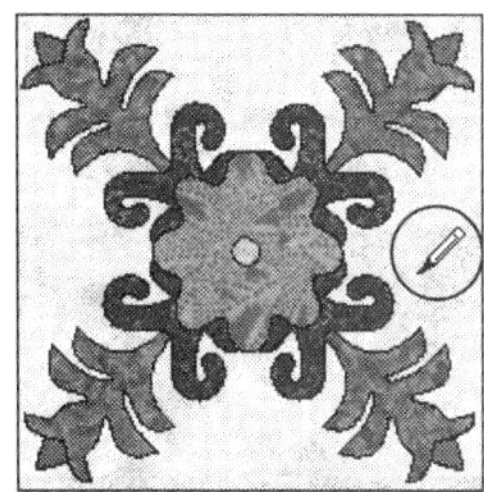

Step 9 – Color Cactus Rose block and Save in Sketchbook

Step 10 – Save

Tip

- **It can be difficult to select a small patch within a PatchDraw design, especially if there are other overlapping patches nearby. Use the Zoom In tool to make the selection easier.**

6 Open the Sketchbook and select the Cactus Bow block, not the motif. Click on Edit to place this design on the worktable. The Rose that you copied in Step 5 is still on your clipboard, so Ctrl+V to paste the Rose on the worktable. Center the flower on the Cactus Bow block and color the design. Save in Sketchbook. Here is the Ribbons & Rose appliqué block that you will set into the corners of Border 1.

7 Remove the background square. Save in Sketchbook. This is the Ribbons & Rose appliqué motif that you will use as the basic unit for experimenting with WreathMaker.

8 You are going to create a new block by adding one more element to the Christmas Cactus block. Click on Block, click on New Block, and then click on PatchDraw. The rose and its center are still on your clipboard from the previous steps, so you can use Ctrl+V to paste another copy of this design on the worktable. With the design still selected, secondary click on the worktable and then click on Resize. Type in 75 as the reduction percentage. Click on OK.

9 With the rose and center still selected, Ctrl+C to copy. Open the Block Sketchbook, click on the Christmas Cactus, click Edit, and Ctrl+V to paste the design in the center of the appliqué block. Color this new Cactus Rose design. Save in Sketchbook.

10 Name your new designs in the Block Sketchbook. Close Sketchbook and Save.

7

Designing with WreathMaker

There are many innovative ways to use the WreathMaker tool in EQ5. In this lesson, you will use the Ribbons & Rose motif you created to generate a unique appliqué wreath design.

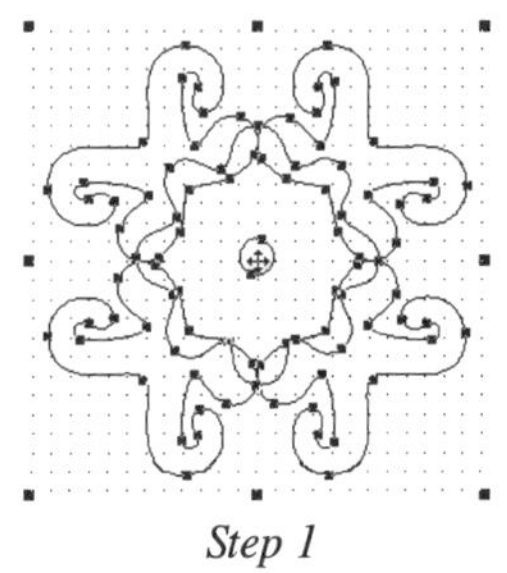

Step 1

1 Open the Blocks Sketchbook and then click on the Motif tab. Select the Ribbons & Rose motif and place it on the worktable for editing. Click on Edit in the main menu and then click on Select All in the Edit menu or use the Ctrl+A shortcut to select all patches in this design.

2 Click on Block in the main menu and then click on WreathMaker.

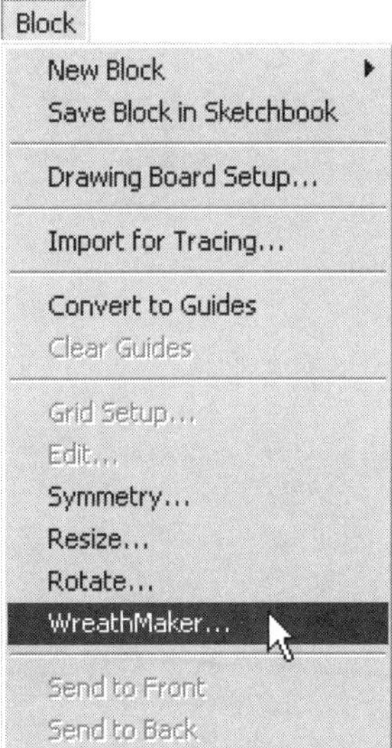

Step 2

Tip

- **There is a shortcut to the Block menu options. Select the object(s) in your drawing and then secondary click on the worktable. The PatchDraw Worktable Context Menu will open and you will find most of the Block menu options there, including WreathMaker.**
- **The WreathMaker box contains three settings: Number of clusters, Cluster spacing, and Resize cluster.**
- **Number of clusters – This is the number of times the selected image is repeated as a cluster in the wreath. The cluster can be composed of one or more patches. Acceptable values are 3 to 20.**
- **Cluster spacing – This percentage represents the position of the lower center point of each cluster selection box in relation to the center of the design area.**
- **Resize clusters – This is the percentage that the cluster size will change, based on its original size.**
- **See the EQ5 manuals and the Help file for more information about WreathMaker settings.**

3 Use the slider rectangles to set these WreathMaker values and then click OK:

Number of clusters:	6
Cluster spacing:	60
Resize clusters:	30

Your simple appliqué will be transformed into an unusual Rose Wreath motif! Save in Sketchbook.

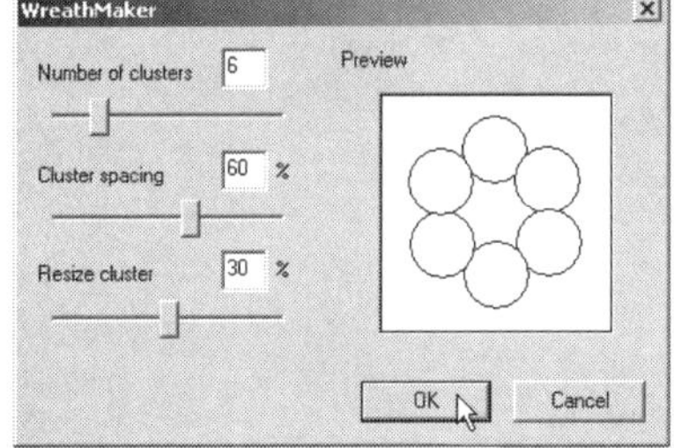

Step 3 – Set values and Save in Sketchbook

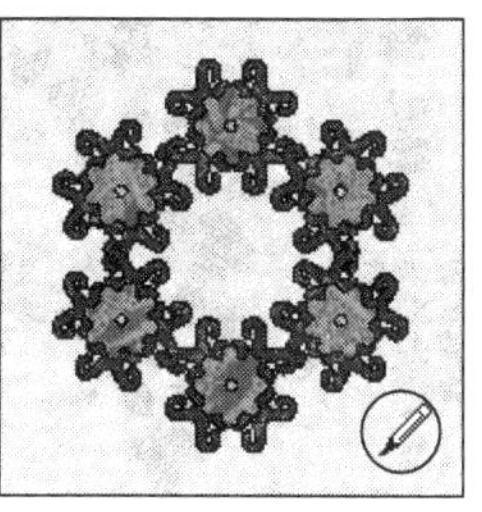

Step 5 – Color Rose Wreath block, Save in Sketchbook, and Save

4 Now you must add a background square to this Rose Wreath motif. Use Ctrl+A to select the design and then use Ctrl+C to copy to the clipboard. Click on Block, Click on New Block, and then click on PatchDraw. Use Ctrl+V to paste the Rose Wreath on the worktable. Center the design within the block outline while it is still selected and then click off to deselect.

5 Color your new Rose Wreath block. Save in Sketchbook. Record the block name and the WreathMaker settings on the Notcard for this design. Close the Notecard. Save.

Tip

- **Record the WreathMaker settings on the Notecard for any wreath that you create in EQ5.**

Selecting the Layout and Borders

For your Tic-Tac-Rose quilt, you will adapt one of the prepared layouts in EQ5's Layout Library.

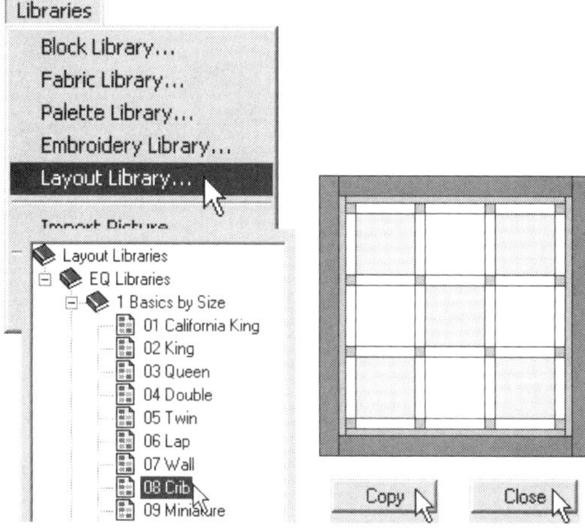

Step 1

1 Click on Libraries, click on Layout Library, and then click on EQ Libraries. Click to open 1Basics by Size and then click on 8Crib. Click on the layout that is "9" Blocks – 9 Total – 1.5" Sashing." Remember to place the cursor over a design to see the tooltip. Click on Copy. Close.

Step 2 – View Sketchbook

2 Open the Quilt Sketchbook and select this layout for editing.

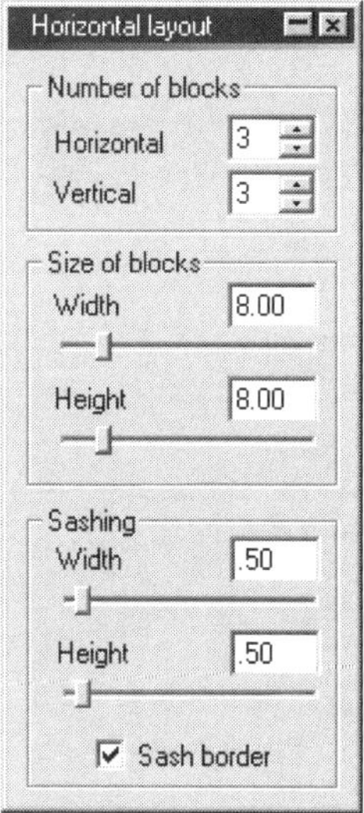

Step 3

3 With the layout on the worktable, click on the Layout tab and modify the settings to these:

Number of blocks:	Horizontal – 3 Vertical – 3
Size of blocks:	Width – 8.00 Height – 8.00
Sashing:	Width – 0.50 Height – 0.50
Sashing border:	checked

4 Click on the Border tab and establish these borders.

Border 1
Border style: Points Out

Adjust size: 4.00 (Lock: All)

Blocks in border: Horizontal – 3
Vertical – 3

Tip

- **The sash border option is on the Layout tab and is not considered to be part of the regular border sequence.**

Border 2
Border style: Mitered

Adjust size: 1.00 (Lock: All)

Border 3
Border style: Big & Little Points Out

Adjust size: 6.00 (Lock: All)

Blocks in border: Horizontal – 1
Vertical – 1

Border 4
Border style: Mitered

Adjust size: .50 (Lock: All)

This last border is intended to be the binding. It will not add to the quilt dimensions if you actually construct the quilt.

5 Click on Layer 1 to return to the quilt worktable. Save in Sketchbook.

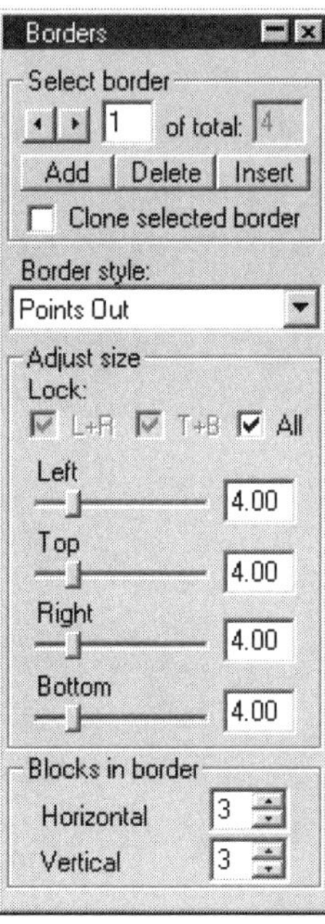

Step 4 – Border 1

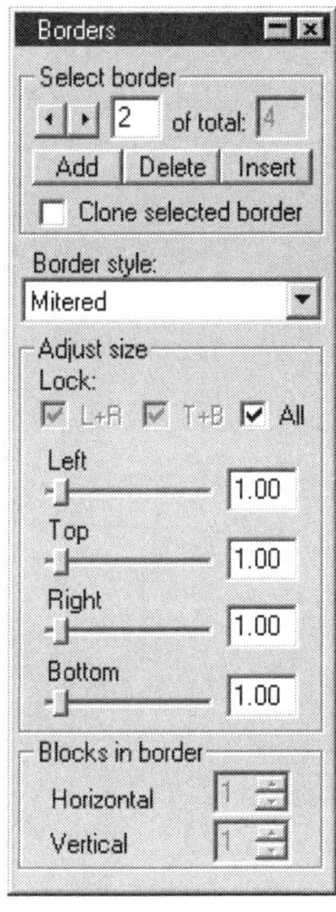

Step 4 – Border 2

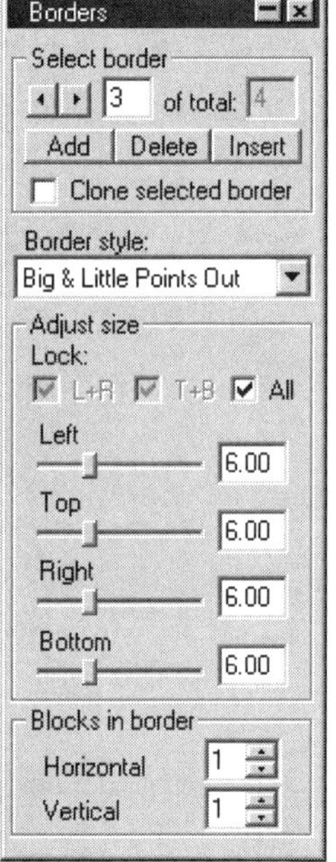

Step 4 – Border 3

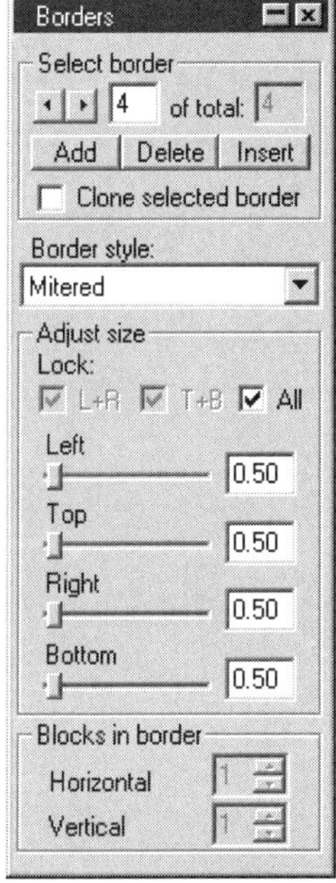

Step 4 – Border 4

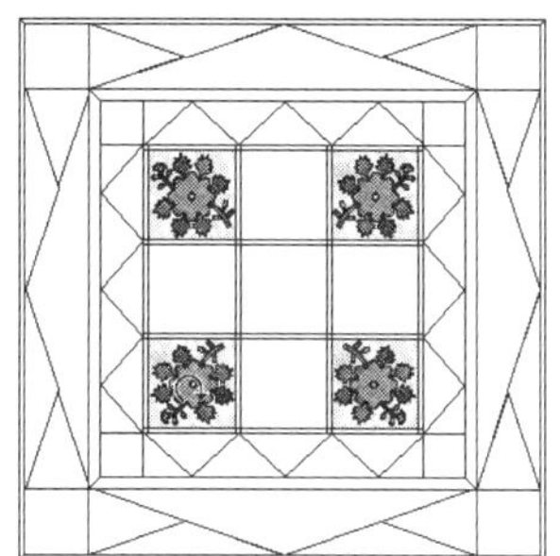

Step 1 & 2 – Old Rose of Sharon blocks flipped & rotated

Set & Flip Tools

Rotate & Plain Block Tools

Setting the Blocks into the Layout

1 Click the Set Tool and click on the Old Rose of Sharon block and set it into the four corners of the block area. Click on the Flip tool and click on the upper-left and lower-left blocks.

2 Click on the Rotate tool and then click once on the lower-right block to rotate it one quarter turn or 90° to the right. Click on the lower-left block three times to rotate it three quarter turns or 270°.

3 Set the Cactus Rose block in the center of the quilt layout.

4 Click on the Rose Wreath block and set it into the remaining blank spaces in the layout. Save in Sketchbook.

5 Click on the Plain Block tool, select a fabric in the palette, and then use Ctrl+click to color the sashings, the sashing squares, and the sashing border. Save in Sketchbook.

6 Click on the Pineapple block and Ctrl+click to set it into the Points Out triangles of the first border, as shown. Click on the Plain Block tool and color the remaining Points In triangles with fabric. Save in Sketchbook.

7 Click on the Ribbons & Rose appliqué block and Ctrl+click to set it into the corner blocks of the first border. Save in Sketchbook.

8 Click on the Plain Block tool, select a fabric, and Ctrl+click to color the second border.

9 Click on the Pineapple block and Ctrl+click to set it into the large Points Out triangles in the third border. Click on the Plain Block tool and color the remaining segments in this border. Color Border 4 and Save in Sketchbook.

7

Step 3 – Cactus Rose block

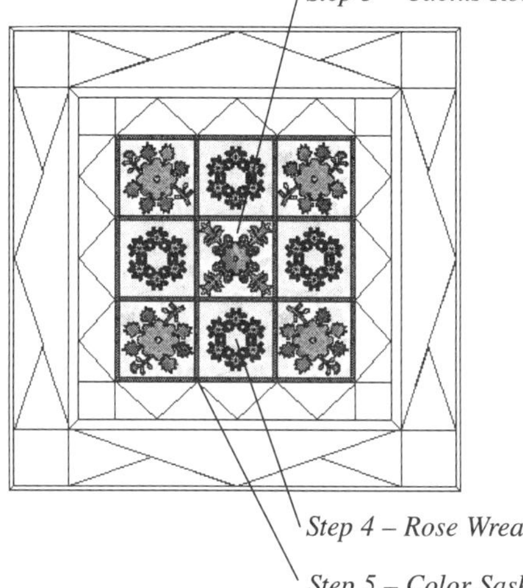

Step 4 – Rose Wreath block

Step 5 – Color Sashing

Step 6 – Pineapple block and Points In Triangles

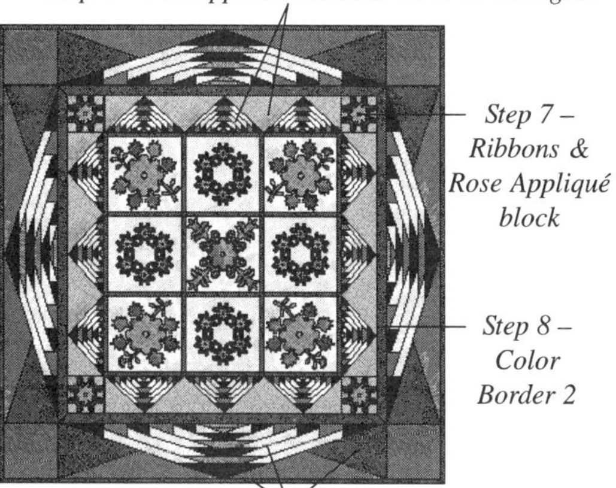

Step 7 – Ribbons & Rose Appliqué block

Step 8 – Color Border 2

Step 9 – Pineapple block, Border 3, and Border 4

Sorting, Moving, and Copying Designs in the Blocks Palette

EQ5 allows you to sort designs in the Blocks palette, as well as move or copy a design from one tab to another.

1. With your Tic-Tac-Rose quilt on the worktable, click on the Set tool to open the Blocks palette. Secondary click anywhere on the Blocks palette to open the Blocks Palette Context Menu.

2. Click on Sort Blocks. In the Sort Blocks box, click on the designs in the order in which you want them to appear in the palette. It is not necessary to select all of the designs on a tab. Click on Close when you are finished selecting the blocks that you want to sort to the front of the palette. The remaining blocks will automatically follow the sorted designs.

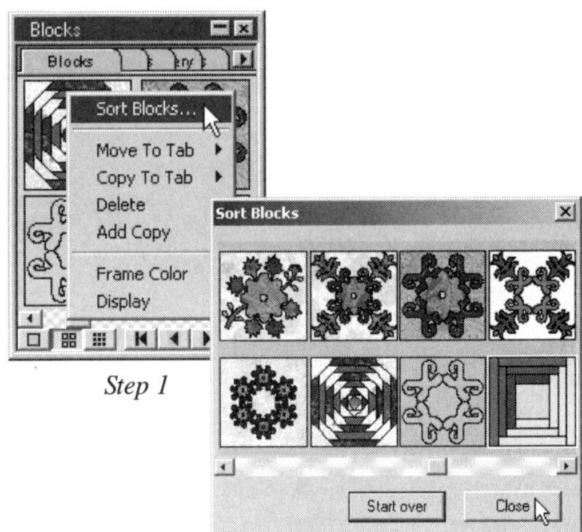

Step 1

Step 2

3. When you saved the Cactus Bow appliqué motif, EQ5 stored it on the Motif tab of the Block Sketchbook. Since you want to use it as a quilting stencil on Layer 3, it is better to store it on the Stencil tab. Click on the Motif tab and then click on the Cactus Bow appliqué to select it. Secondary click on the Blocks palette. The Blocks Palette Context Menu box will open.

4. Click on Move to Tab and then click on Stencil tab in the extended menu. The Cactus Bow appliqué is now stored on the Stencil tab. You will notice that, in addition to being able to move a design from tab to tab, you can also copy a design to another tab.

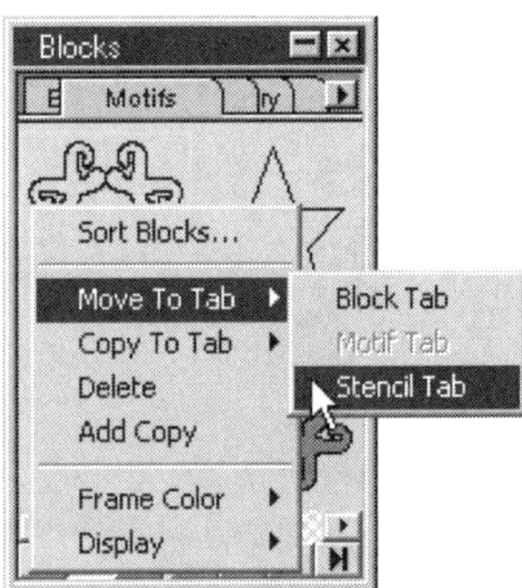

Step 3 & 4

Setting Stencils on Layer 3

You will now set a Cactus Bow quilting stencil in each corner of this quilt layout.

1. Click on Layer 3, click on the Set tool, and then click on the Cactus Bow motif.

2. Click and drag, holding down the Shift key, to set a stencil on each corner of the layout.

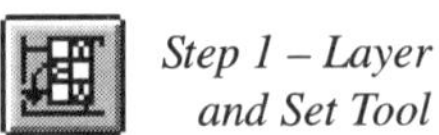

Step 1 – Layer 3 and Set Tool

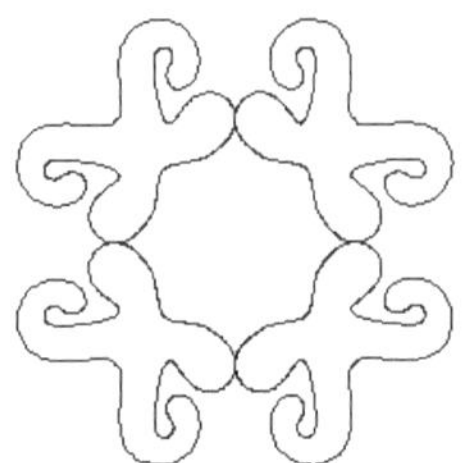

Cactus Bow Motif

Step 2

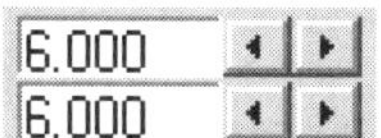

Step 3 – Set Size on the Graph Pad and Save in Sketchbook

Step 3

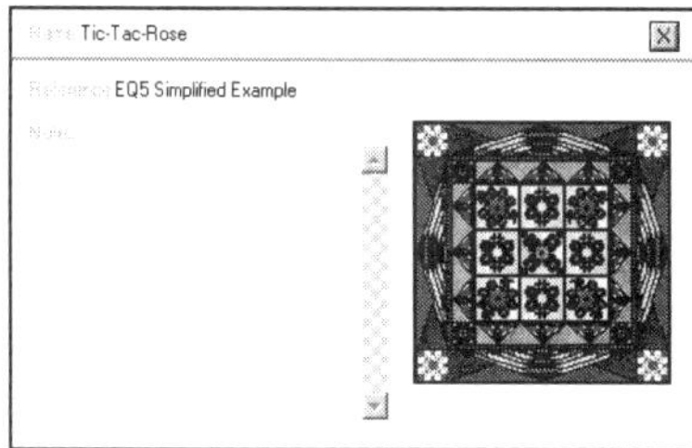

Step 4

 *Paintbrush Tool*

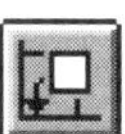 *Plain Block Tool*

 *Spraycan Tool*

 *Swap Tool*

 *Eyedropper Tool*

 *Thread Color Tool*

 *Fussy Cut Tool*

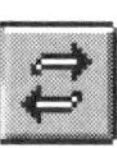 *EQ4 Swap Tool*

 *EQ4 Spraycan Tool*

3 Click on the Adjust tool and set the size of this stencil to 6.00 x 6.00 on the Graph Pad. Use the Same Size tools and the Align tools to adjust the size and position of each stencil on the layout. Use the Thread Color tool, if necessary to make the stencils more visible. Save in Sketchbook.

4 Create a quilt Notecard for your Tic-Tac-Rose quilt design. Save.

Tip

- **When on Layers, you may find it easier to set multiple designs on a blank area of the worktable instead of on the quilt layout. You can resize the designs there and then move them into position with the Adjust tool or the keyboard arrows.**

Remember that if you "lose" a design on Layers, you can find it by selecting all of the designs on that Layer. To select all designs on a Layer, click on the Adjust tool, hold down the Ctrl key, and click on any design on that Layer. All of the designs on that Layer will highlight. Click off of the selection area to deselect.

Experimenting with EQ5 Color Tools

EQ5's coloring tools are very powerful and flexible features that provide a full range of coloring functions on the block and quilt worktables.

These coloring tools are available to you on the drawing worktables: *Paintbrush, Spraycan, Eyedropper,* and *Fussy Cut tools*. The *EQ4 Spraycan* is also on these worktables.

These coloring tools are available to you on the quilt worktable: *Plain Block, Paintbrush, Spraycan, Swap, Thread Color, Eyedropper,* and *Fussy Cut tools*. The *EQ4 Spraycan* and *Swap tools* are also on the worktable.

Tip

- **The EQ4 Spraycan and Swap tools function differently than the EQ5 Spraycan and Swap tools. The EQ4 coloring tools are used for auditioning fabrics in a block or quilt before recoloring. See the EQ5 Help file for information about all of these coloring tools.**

You have used the Paintbrush tool throughout this tutorial to color single patches in a block. You have used the Plain Block and Paintbrush tools to color whole blocks, borders, and sashing. You have used the Eyedropper tool to locate previously-used fabrics in blocks and quilts. You have used the Thread Color tool to recolor designs on Layers 2 and 3.

There are three EQ5 coloring tools that you have not yet used in these lessons: *Spraycan, Swap,* and *Fussy Cut.*

7

EQ5 Spraycan Tool

The Spraycan tool is used for recoloring multiple patches within a block. With the colored design on the worktable, click on the Spraycan tool. Click on a swatch in the palette and then click on the colored patch that you want to recolor. All of the similarly-colored patches in the block will recolor. This tool works on the block worktables and on Layers 1 and 2 of the quilt worktable.

Tip

- **There are Ctrl+click and Alt+click combinations that you can use with the Paintbrush and Spraycan tools to create even more coloring functions on the quilt worktable. See the EQ manuals and the Help file for more information.**

EQ5 Swap Tool

The Swap tool is used for recoloring all patches of a selected color within the quilt layout, including borders. With the quilt on the worktable, click on Layer 1 and then click on the Swap tool. Select a new color in the Fabrics palette. Click on a fabric in the quilt layout. All of the patches colored with this fabric will recolor with the new fabric. This tool also works on Layer 2. Be sure to save your project before experimenting with fabric changes!

Tip

- **Block colorings created on the quilt worktable are saved automatically in the Block Sketchbook when the quilt is saved.**

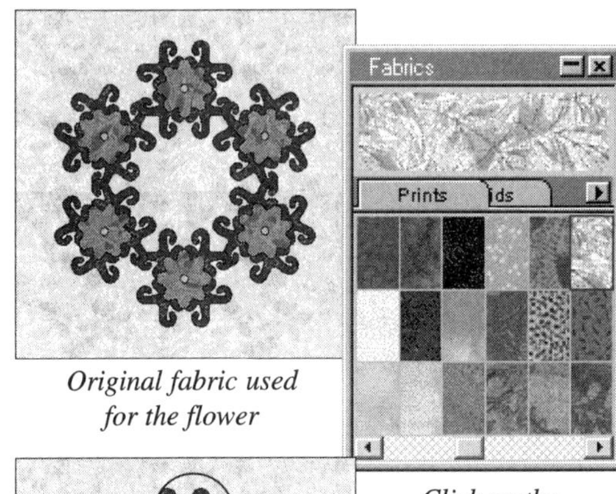

Original fabric used for the flower

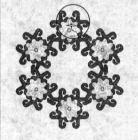

New fabric used for the flower

Click on the Spraycan tool and select a new fabric

Spraycan Tool

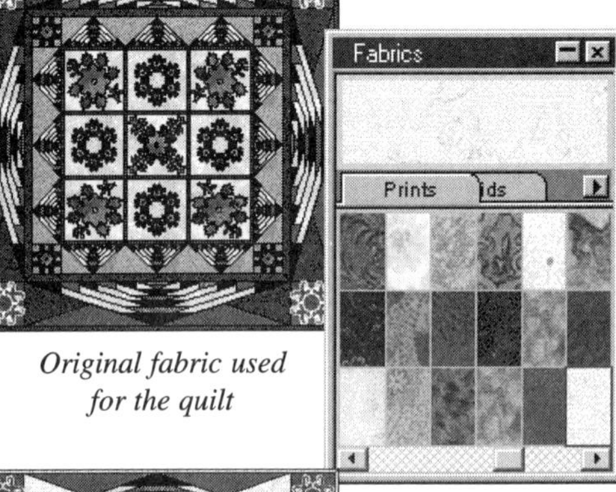

Original fabric used for the quilt

Click on the Swap tool and select a new fabric

Swap Tool

New fabric used for the qult

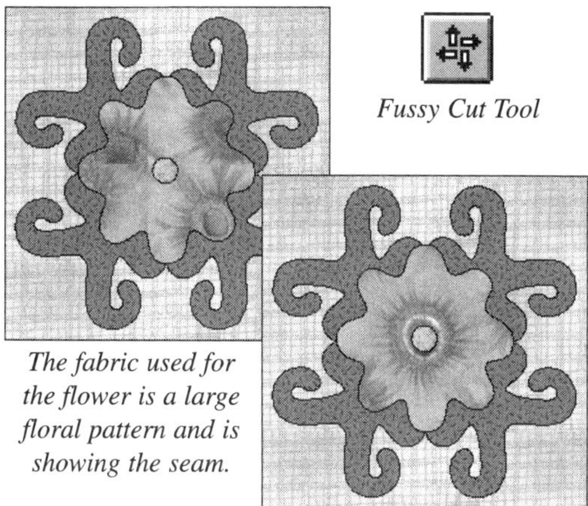

Fussy Cut Tool

The fabric used for the flower is a large floral pattern and is showing the seam.

The fabric has been adjusted to show one large centered flower and to hide the seam.

Fussy Cut Tool

The Fussy Cut tool is available to you on the block and quilt worktables. With this tool, you can shift a printed fabric within a patch in order to display an image in the fabric. This function is especially helpful when you are using a fabric that contains a "picture" such as a large floral print. This feature works on the block worktables and on Layers 1 and 2 of the quilt worktable.

With the colored design on the worktable, click on the Fussy Cut tool and then click on the printed fabric patch. Holding down the mouse button, drag the print until the image within the fabric is displayed to your satisfaction.

The effect of the Fussy Cut tool is only temporary, however, since the placement of the print image within the fabric cannot be printed or saved. You can use the Export Snapshot feature to generate a bitmap file or a printout of the design with this arrangement.

Sorting the Fabrics Palette

EQ5 allows you to sort fabrics in the Fabrics palette, just as you sorted blocks in the Blocks palette. Sorting can be done on the Color tab of any drawing worktable or on the quilt worktable.

1 Open the Color tab of a drawing worktable or open the quilt worktable. Click on the Paintbrush tool to open the Fabrics palette.

2 Secondary click anywhere on the Prints palette. The Fabrics Palette Context Menu will open. Click on Sort Fabrics. In the Sort Fabrics box, click on the swatches in the order in which you want them displayed in the Sketchbook. It isn't necessary to select all of the swatches, just choose the ones you want in the front of the palette and then click on Close. The remaining fabrics will align themselves after the selected fabrics. Click on Start Over to rearrange the palette.

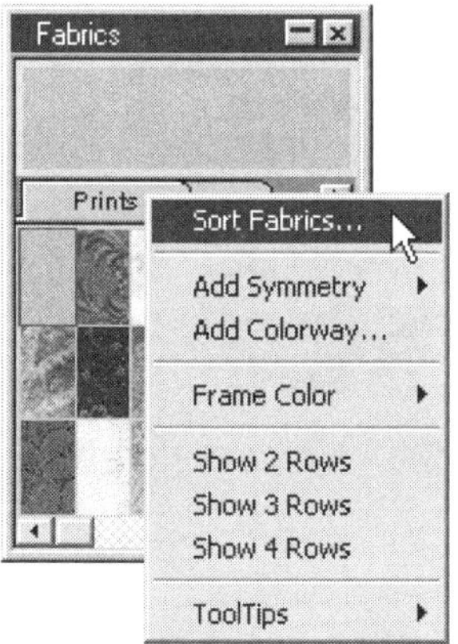

Step 2

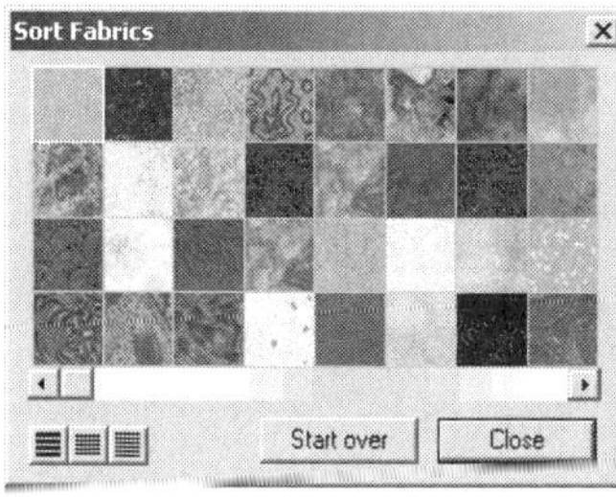

Step 2

3 Secondary click anywhere on the Solids palette. A Solid Fabric Palette Context Menu will open. Click on Sort Colors and then click on Manual in the extended menu. In the Sort Colors box, click on the swatches in the order in which you want them displayed in the Sketchbook. Again, just choose the swatches that you want in the front of the palette and then click on Close. The remaining colors will follow.

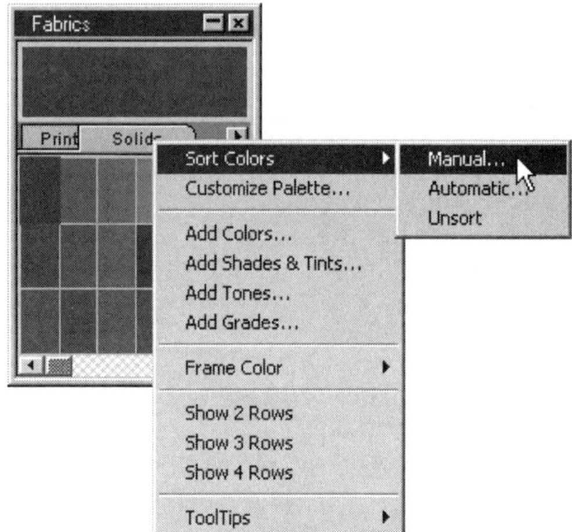

Step 3

Adding Blocks to the User Libraries

1 Click on Libraries and then click on Add Blocks. Open the Simplified Blocks library.

2 Copy the blocks from this Tic-Tac-Rose quilt into the Simplified Blocks style library. Be sure to also copy the designs on the Motif and Stencil tabs.

3 Click on Save Library, and then click on OK when EQ5 tells you that your designs have been saved. Close the Add Block to Library box.

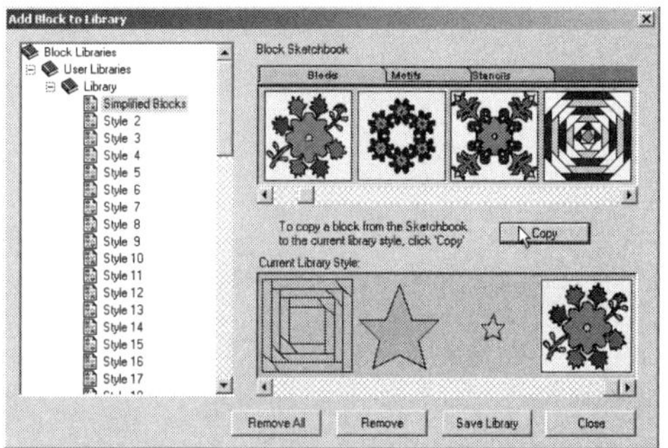

Add Blocks to Simplified Blocks Library

Adding Fabrics to the User Libraries

You can add the fabrics that you collected for Tic-Tac-Rose to the Fabric User Libraries.

1 Click on Libraries and then click on Add Fabrics. Open the Simplified Fabrics library.

2 Copy the fabrics from this quilt into the Simplified Fabrics style library.

3 Click on Save Library, and then click on OK when EQ5 tells you that your designs have been saved. Close the Add Fabrics to Library box.

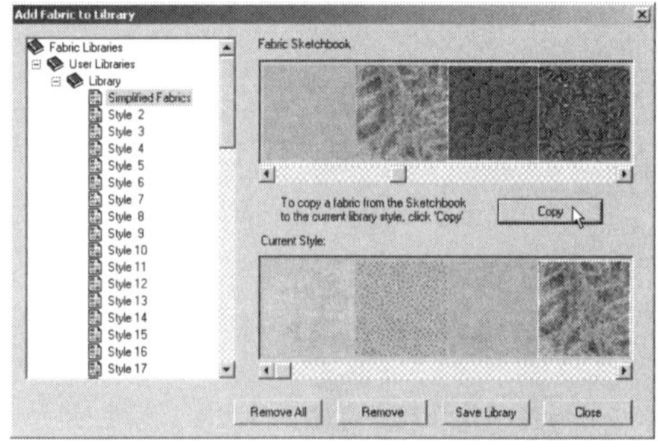

Add Fabrics to Simplified Fabrics Library

Preparing a Project for Emailing

EQ5 will streamline your project in preparation for emailing the file to another user! With this feature, you can reduce the size of the file by removing all unused block designs and fabrics from the project. You will also find this feature helpful for simply cleaning up a finished project!

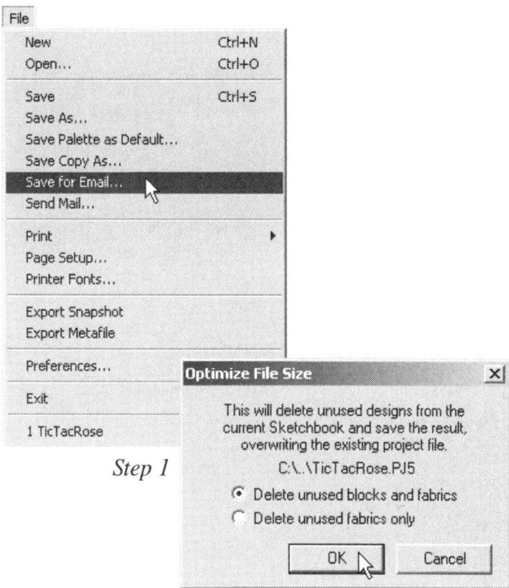

Step 1

Step 2

Tip

- **Be sure to backup your project file with Save As or Save Copy As before using the Save for Email function! If you Save As, you will be working with a copy of the original project file. If you Save Copy As, you will still be working with the original project file.**

1 Click on File and then click on Save for Email. An Optimize File Size box will open.

2 You have the option to delete unused blocks and fabrics or to delete only unused fabrics. Make your selection and then click on OK.

3 Check the Sketchbook before Emailing the file. Fabrics that remain in the Sketchbook are those that you used in the project. If you chose to keep any unused designs, they will remain in the Block Sketchbook.

Tip

- **The Save for Email function will not delete unused colorings of block designs that are in the quilt layout. You must remove these unwanted colorings manually from the Block Sketchbook.**
- **EQ5 will give you a warning if you attempt to delete a coloring that is in a saved quilt design.**
- **See the EQ manuals and the Help file for more information.**

Printing Foundation Patterns for Triangular Blocks

Printing foundation patterns for triangular designs requires a slightly different approach than generating square or rectangular printouts. The triangular blocks in this Tic-Tac-Rose quilt are the Pineapple blocks in the first and third borders.

Step 1

1 With your Tic-Tac-Rose quilt on the worktable, click on the Select tool and then click on one of the Pineapple triangle blocks in the first border.

2 Click on File, click on Print, and then click on Foundation Pattern. On the Options tab, click on Size from quilt and then click on Preview. You will see the entire block on the Preview screen even though only half of it is actually visible in the quilt layout. Close the Print Foundation Pattern box.

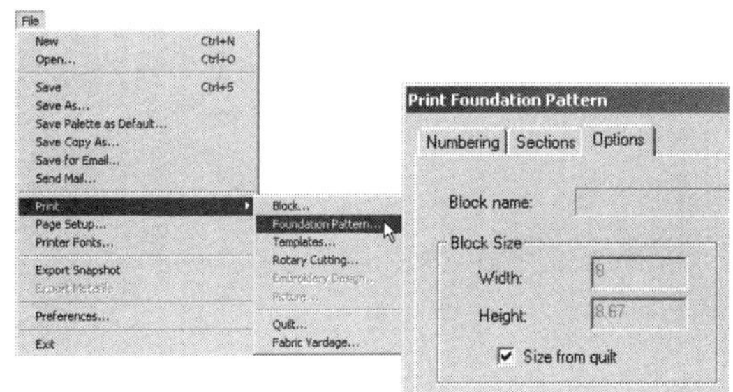

Step 2

Now, to generate a triangular printout of this block, you must first divide the drawing on the block worktable.

3 Open the Block Sketchbook and select the Pineapple block for editing. With the Line tool, draw a diagonal line through the drawing. Here is your Split Pineapple block. Recolor only half of this design. You will arrange this half of the block so that it is visible in the quilt layout. Save in Sketchbook.

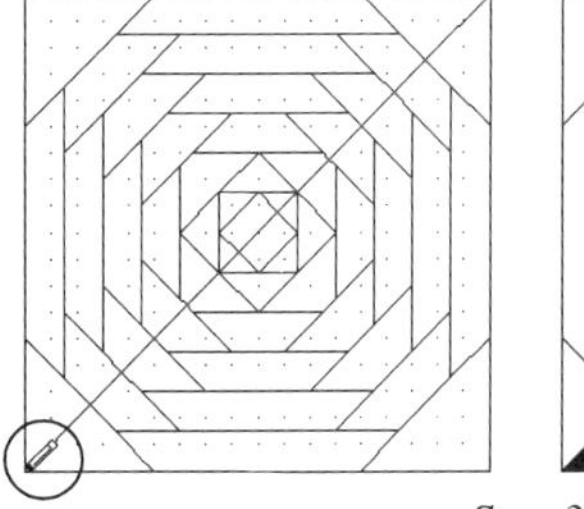

Step 3

4 On the Quilt Worktable set the Split Pineapple block into the first border with Ctrl+click. Rotate each border separately with an Alt+click so that the colored half of the block is displayed in the layout. Save in Sketchbook.

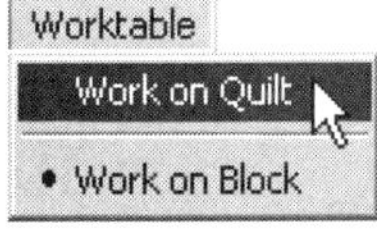

Step 4

Step 4 – Set Split Pineapple Block

5 Ctrl+click to set the Split Pineapple in the large triangles of the third border. Rotate each border separately so that the colored half of the block is visible. Save in Sketchbook.

6 Click on the Select tool and click on one of the Split Pineapple blocks in the first border. Click on File, click on Print, and click on Foundation Pattern. Click on the Options tab and then click on the Size from quilt so that it is checked. Be sure that these options are also checked: *Print numbering* and *Separate units*. Preview.

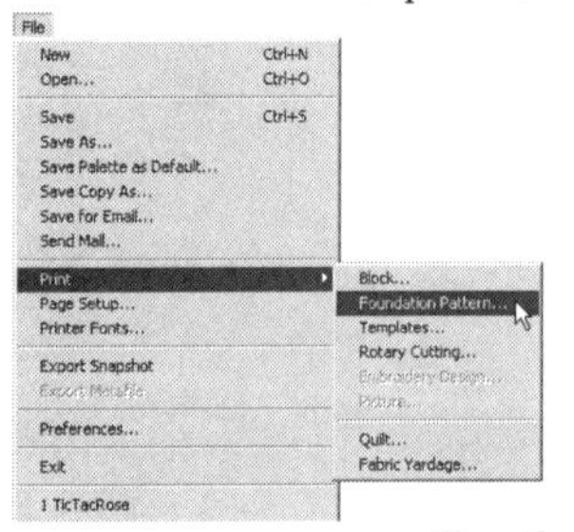

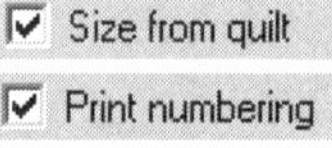

Step 6

7 On the Preview screen, click on the Delete button and then click on one of diagonal halves of the Split Pineapple block. Press the Delete key. This half of the block will be eliminated from the printout. Print.

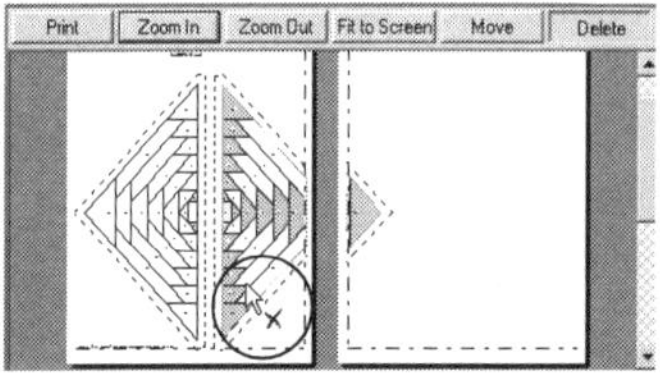

Step 7

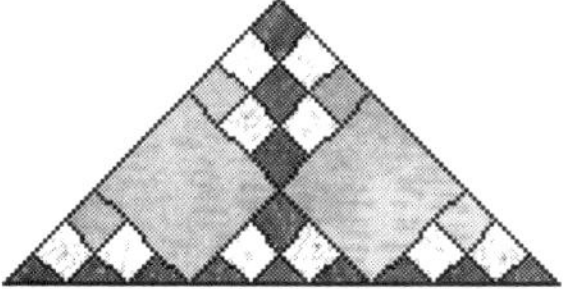

Tip – Halved Double Nine Patch and Quartered Double Nine Patch (taken from Lessons 2 & 3)

Step 1

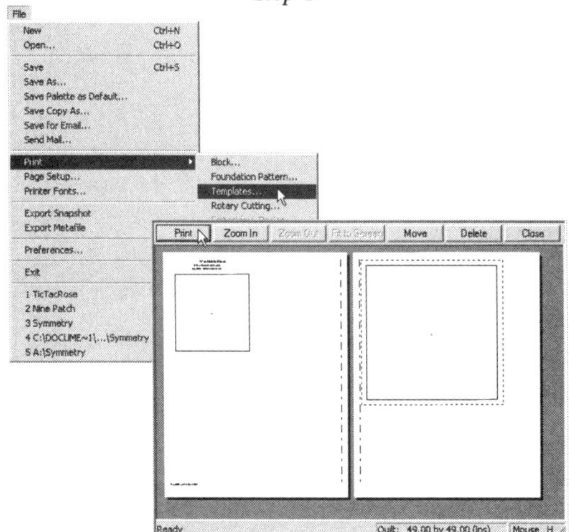

Step 2

Step 3

You have just generated an accurate printout of a triangular Foundation Pattern in the quilt layout!

Tip

- **You can also use this procedure to print triangular pieced blocks in an on-point quilt layout, such as the halved Double Nine Patch blocks in the Stars Squared quilt (Lesson 2) and in the Two-Stepping Stars quilt (Lesson 3).**
- **For the corner triangles in an on-point layout, divide the pieced design into quarters diagonally. Examples of an on-point quarter design are the Double Nine Patch corner blocks in the Stars Squared quilt (Lesson 2) and the Two-Stepping Stars quilt (Lesson 3).**

Printing Templates for Triangular Blocks

Printing triangular templates is similar to printing triangular foundation patterns.

1. With your Tic-Tac-Rose quilt on the worktable, click on the Select tool and then click on one of the plain triangular patches in the first border.

2. Click on File, click on Print, and then click on Templates. Click on Size from quilt and then click on Preview. You will see the entire block on the Preview screen even though only half of it is actually visible in the quilt layout. Click on Close.

3. Now, look at the smaller triangles in this border that are adjacent to the corner blocks. This triangle is actually one quarter of the full square or one half the size of the plain triangle in this border.

   To generate accurate triangular printouts of these blocks, you must first divide the drawings on the block worktable, just as you did with the triangular foundation pattern.

4 Click on Worktable and then click on Work on Block. Click on Block and then click on New Block. Click on EasyDraw™ in the extended menu. With the Line tool, draw one diagonal line across the block to form a Half Square Triangle block. Recolor only half of this design. You will arrange this half of the block so that it is visible in the quilt layout. Save in Sketchbook.

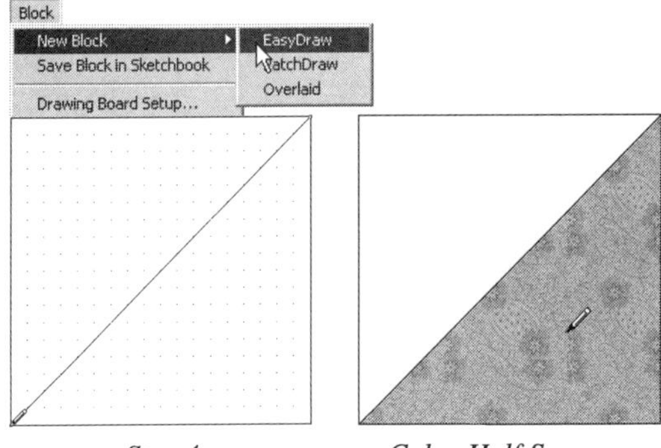

Step 4

Color Half Square Triangle block

5 With the Half Square Triangle on the worktable, draw another diagonal line in the opposite direction, forming a Quarter Square Triangle block. Recolor only one quarter of this design. Remember to save these new blocks in your Simplified Block Library as well. You will arrange this quarter of the block so that it is visible in the quilt layout. Save in Sketchbook.

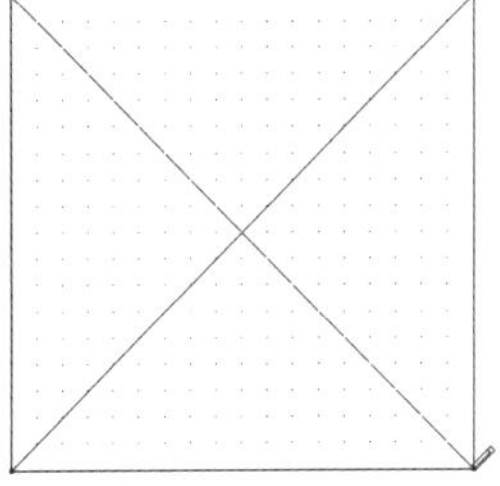

Step 5

Color Quarter Square Triangle block

6 Click on Work on Quilt to return to your Tic-Tac-Rose design on the worktable. Set the Half Square Triangle block into the eight spaces in the first border with Ctrl+click. Rotate each border separately with an Alt+click so that the colored half of the block is displayed in the layout. Save in Sketchbook.

Set & Rotate Half Square Triangle blocks in eight spaces in first border.

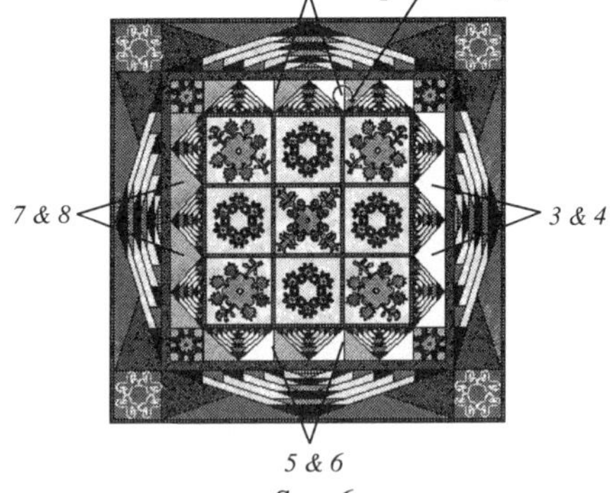

Step 6

7 In the first border, set the Quarter Square Triangle block into the eight spaces that are adjacent to the corner blocks. Rotate each triangle separately so that the colored quarter of the block is displayed. Save in Sketchbook.

Set and Rotate Quarter Square Triangle blocks adjacent to the corner blocks.

Step 7 – Upper Right Segment of Quilt

8 Click on the Select tool and click on one of the new Half Square Triangle blocks. Click on File, click on Print, and click on Templates. Be sure that the Size from quilt is checked. Preview and Print.

Tip

- **If you uncheck Print key block, you can fit this template on one page.**

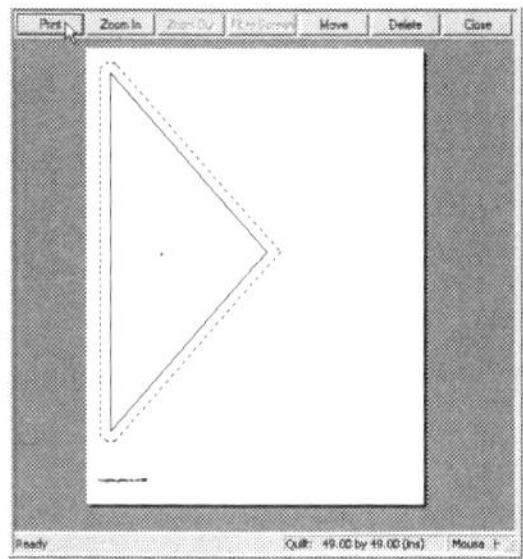

Step 8 – Preview of Half Square Triangle block

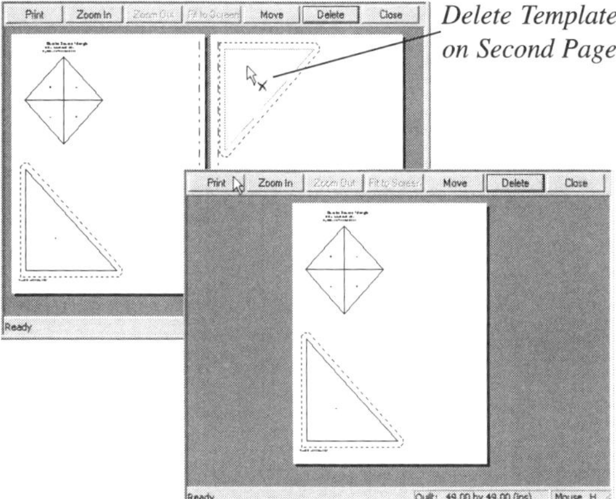

Step 9 – Preview of Quarter Square Triangle block

Here is the finished quilt!

9 Click on the Select tool and click on one of the new Quarter Square Triangle blocks. Click on File, click on Print, and click on Templates. Be sure that the Size from quilt is checked. Check Print key block. Preview. Delete the template on the second page. Print.

You have just generated accurate templates of the plain triangular blocks in this quilt layout!

Tip

- **You can also use this procedure to print plain setting triangle templates for an on-point quilt layout.**
- **Be sure that you cut the fabric for these plain triangles so that the straight-of-grain is on the outer edges. EQ5 arranges the templates on the page in the same orientation that they occur in the quilt, so it is easy to recognize the outer edges of the block. Draw arrows on the templates so that you don't forget!**

Exiting EQ5

Click on File and then click on Exit.

Exploring PatchDraw

Lesson 8

Lesson 8 – Exploring PatchDraw

You are ready to discover another versatile PatchDraw feature, the Shape tools: *Simple Shape, Polygon,* and *Simple Oval*. These convenient tools offer endless possibilities for creating unique appliqué designs for your quilts. In designing the Sparklers quilt in this lesson, you will learn to:

- *Import a fabric bitmap file*
- *Set up the drawing board for a rectangular block*
- *Draw with the Arc tool*
- *Draw with the Shape tools*
- *Use a Medallion layout*
- *Set a Tile On Point Corners border*
- *Plan uneven borders*
- *Create Prairie Points*
- *Clip designs on Layers*

Sparklers Quilt

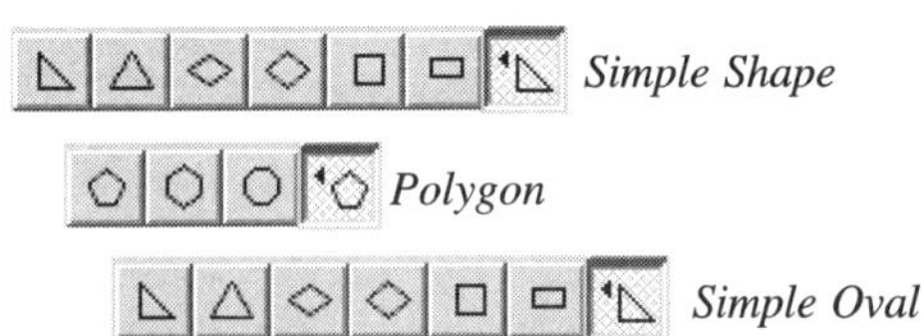

8

Starting a New Project

Start a new project with the file name *Sparklers*. You can use the default palette for this project, copy new fabrics from the Libraries, load new palettes from the Palette Library, or use any of these features in combination.

Importing a Fabric Bitmap File

In Lesson 5, you created a customized fabric palette, saved it in the EQ5 Palette Library and in the User Library, and then set it as the default palette. In Lesson 7, you added an EQ5 palette to this collection, sorted it, and saved it in the User Libraries. In this lesson, you will learn to import fabrics into EQ5!

EQ5 allows you to import fabric bitmap (.bmp) files into your current project Sketchbook and then save them in the Libraries. Bitmaps are a type of graphic file that can be generated in a variety of sources. This includes images that you select or develop in other graphic programs, images that you generate through a scanner, and images that you collect from the Internet.

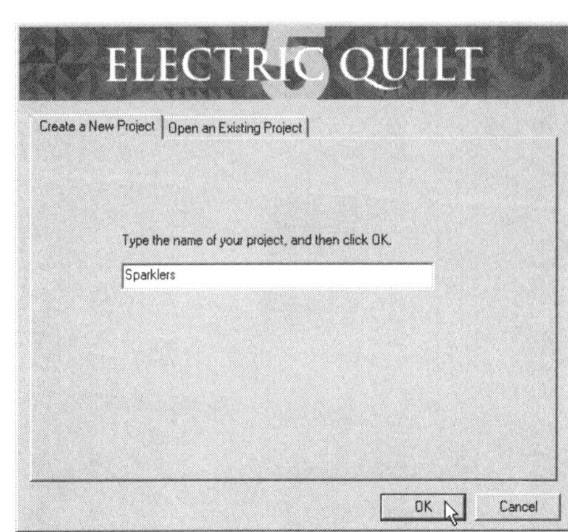

EQ5 Opening Page

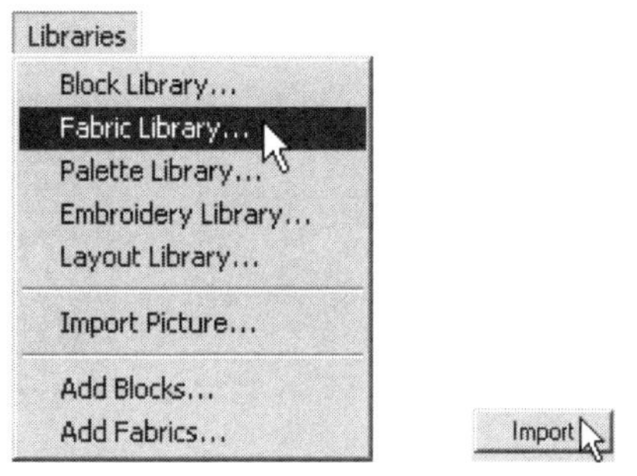

Step 1

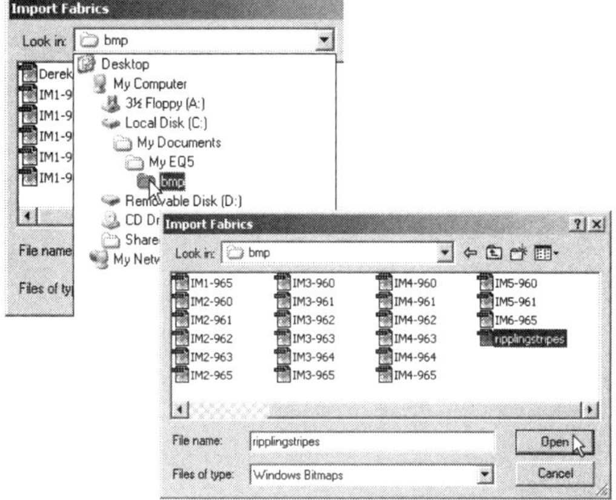

Step 2

Step 3

Rippling Stripes fabric by Moda

Using this file format, you can import fabric swatches into EQ5 and use them in the Fabrics palette. You will find specific instructions on how to scan fabrics for use in EQ5 on pages *158-159* of the *EQ5 Design Cookbook*. If you don't have a bitmap file to import or a way to generate one, you can safely skip this section and proceed to "Copying Designs from the Libraries."

1 To import fabric swatches into your current Fabric Sketchbook, click on Libraries and then click on Fabric Library. Click on the Import button at the bottom of the Fabric Libraries box.

2 An Import Fabrics box will open. Navigate to the directory where you stored the fabric .bmp file, click on the file, and then click on Open. The box will close automatically and you will return to the Fabric Libraries.

3 The fabric swatch will appear in the Fabric Libraries directory window. Click on Copy. The fabric will disappear. It has been placed in the Fabric Sketchbook of your Sparklers project file. Click on Close.

4 Open the Fabric Sketchbook and use the slider rectangle to find the new fabric swatch. You can now use this fabric as you would use any other fabric in EQ5!

Tip

- **See Lesson 5, "Adding fabrics to the User Libraries" for instructions on adding this imported fabric to the EQ5 Libraries.**

The fabric imported in this lesson is "Rippling Stripes" by Moda.

Copying Designs from the Libraries

You will now copy three designs from the EQ5 Libraries to use in your Sparklers quilt. You will use Corner 4 in the center star blocks and borders of the quilt. You will use the Half Square Triangle as Prairie Points, and you will use the Star to create a series of appliqué and stencil designs for your quilt.

1 Do a search in the EQ5 Block Libraries for the Corner 4 block design and copy it into the Sketchbook.

2 Open the Simplified Blocks style library in the User Library. Copy the Half Square Triangle, the Star block, and the Star motif.

3 Color the designs. Save in Sketchbook.

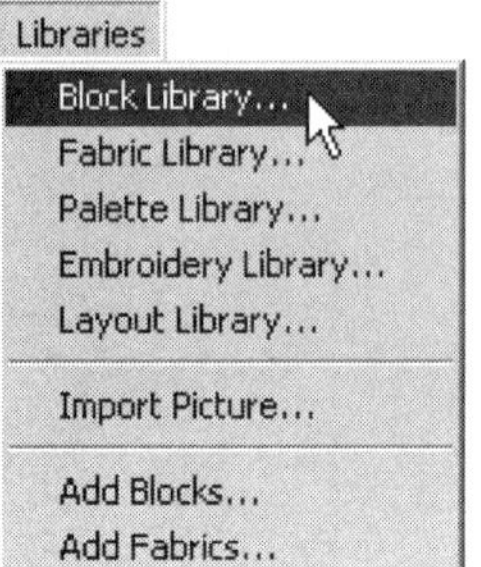

Step 1

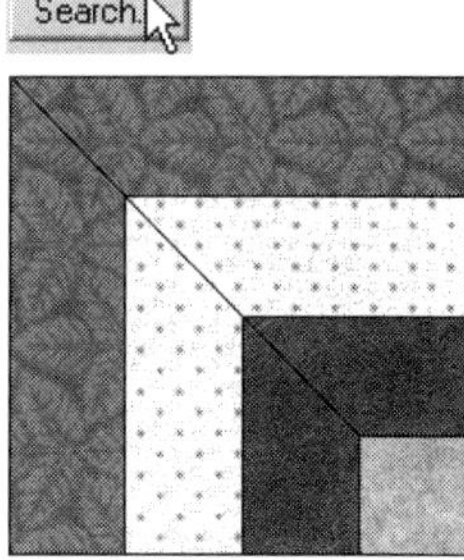

Step 1 – Corner 4 Block after coloring

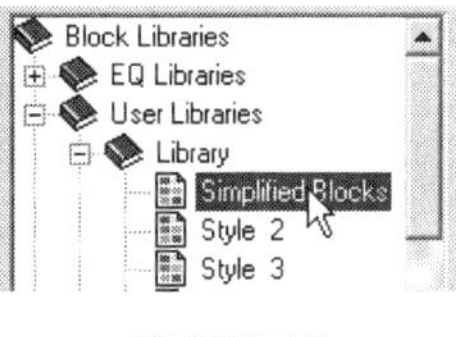

Step 2

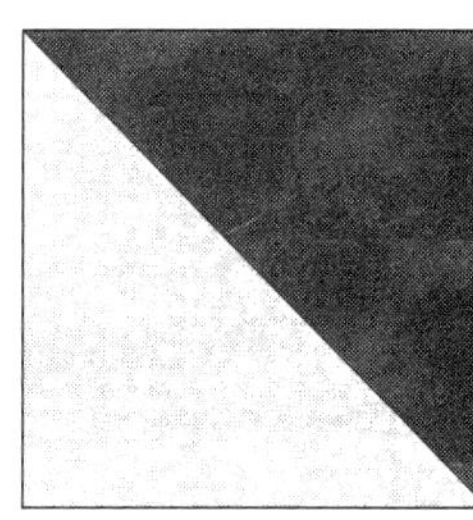

Step 2 – Half Square Triangle after coloring

Step 2 – Star Block and Star Motif after coloring

Drawing with the Arc Tool

You are going to draw a Triple Swag block to use in your Sparklers quilt. In order to achieve a deep arc on this design, you will draw it as a rectangle, but you will use it as a square in the quilt layout.

1 Click on Worktable in the main menu and then click on Work on Block. Click on Block in the main menu, click on New Block, and then click on EasyDraw™.

2 Click on Block and then click on Drawing Board Setup. Set the following values:

General Tab
Snap to Grid Points: Horizontal – 24
Vertical – 24

Block Size: Horizontal – 8
Vertical – 4

Graph Paper Tab
Number of Divisions: Horizontal – 16
Vertical – 8

Options: Graph Paper lines

Click on OK.

3 Click on the Arc tool and draw four arcs, as shown. Save in Sketchbook.

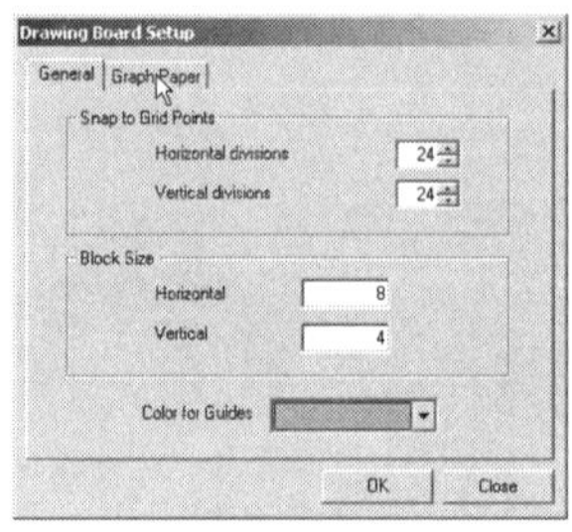

Step 2 – Drawing Board Setup

Arc Tool

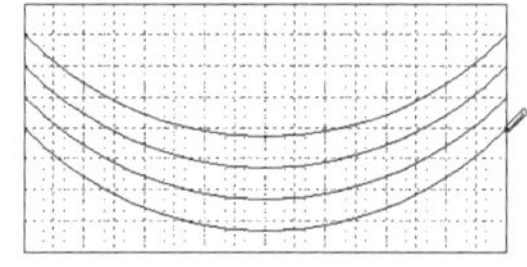

Step 3 – Triple Swag block on EasyDraw™ Worktable

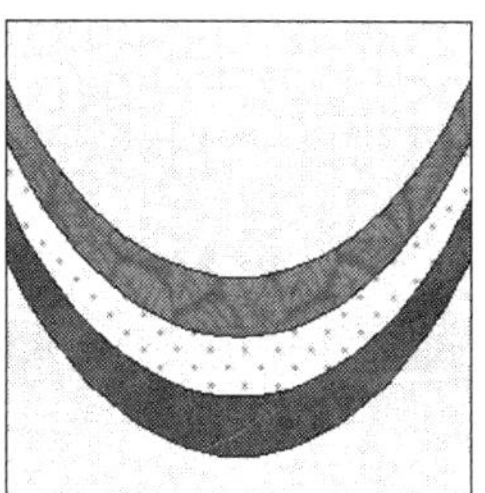

Step 4 – Triple Swag block

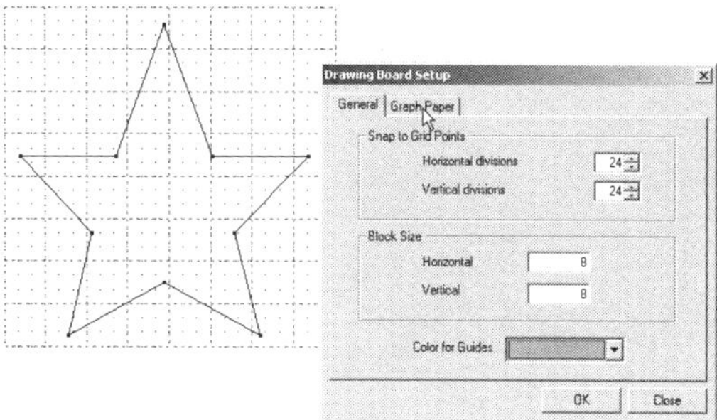

Step 1

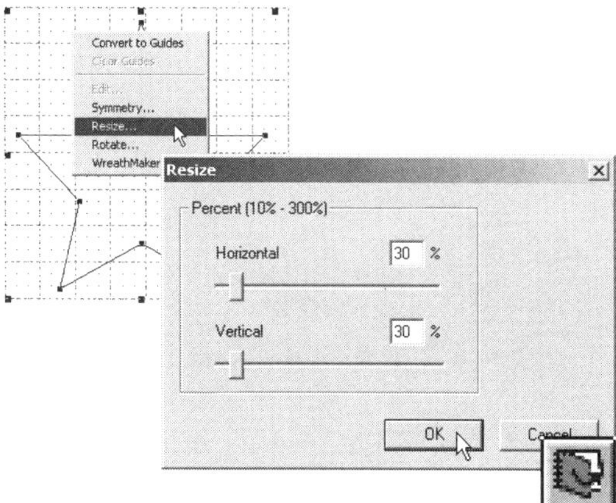

Step 2 – Resize Star motif and Save in Sketchbook

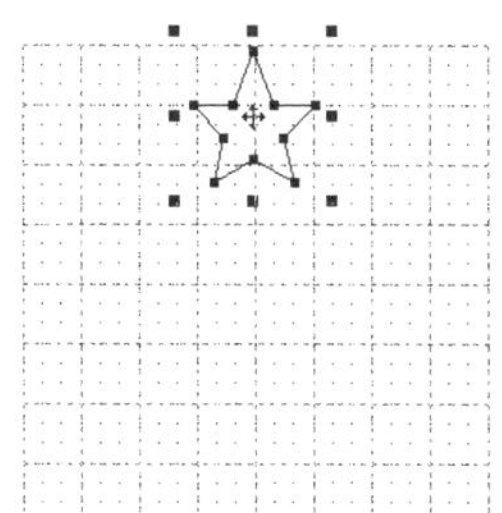

Step 3 – Reduced Star Motif centered at the top of graph paper

Tip

- **To flip the curve of an arc, press the Space bar before releasing the mouse button.**

4 Color the Triple Swag block and create a Notecard for it. Save in Sketchbook.

Drawing with the Shape Tools

EQ5 makes drawing appliqué designs very easy by providing basic shapes for you to use in the Simple Shape, Polygon, and Simple Oval tools. You will use these Shape tools, together with WreathMaker, to create two quilting stencils, an appliqué block, and an appliqué motif.

1 Open the Block Sketchbook and select the Star motif for editing. With the Star on the worktable, click on Block and then click on Drawing Board Setup. Set these values:

General Tab

Snap to Grid Points:	Horizontal – 24
	Vertical – 24
Block Size:	Horizontal – 8
	Vertical – 8

Graph Paper Tab

Number of Divisions:	Horizontal – 8
	Vertical – 8
Options:	Graph Paper lines

Click on OK. These settings will make it easier for you to position the patches in your appliqué design.

2 Ctrl+A to select all lines in the Star and then click with the secondary mouse button on the worktable to open the PatchDraw Worktable Context Menu. Click on Resize. In the Resize box, type in 30 for the reduction percentage. Click on OK. The Star is now resized to 30% of its original size. This is the Reduced Star. Save in Sketchbook.

3 With the Star still selected, hold down the mouse button and move the Reduced Star motif to the top of the graph paper, centering it as shown.

4 Click on the small arrow on the Simple Shape tool button and then click on the rectangle in the extended bar. Starting under the center of the Reduced Star, click and drag to draw a narrow vertical rectangle that is three graph paper units long, as shown. To move the rectangle, click on it with the Select tool and drag. Save in Sketchbook. You will use this Star1 unit to create the quilting stencils and the appliqué block for this quilt.

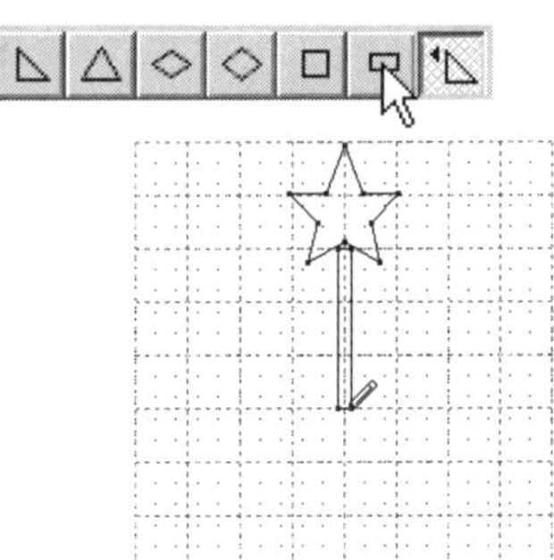

Step 4 – Draw Rectangle to form Star1 unit and Save in Sketchbook

Tip

- **Once you have clicked on the arrow on one of the Shape tool buttons, you must select a tool in the extended bar. The bar does not retract until you have made this selection, and you cannot activate any other function on the worktable until you do this. Note that the shape that you selected is now displayed on that Shape tool button in the PatchDraw toolbar.**

8

5 Now you will create a wreath design from this Star1 unit. Ctrl+A to select all, and then secondary click to open the PatchDraw Worktable Context Menu. Click on WreathMaker.

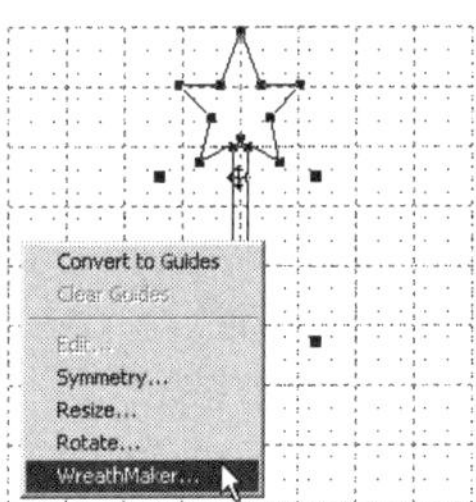

Step 5

6 Type in these values in the WreathMaker box:

Number of clusters – 8

Cluster spacing – 80

Resize cluster – 40

Click on OK. Save in Sketchbook. Be sure to record these settings on the Notecard for this design. You will use this Star1 Wreath design as a quilting stencil in the layout.

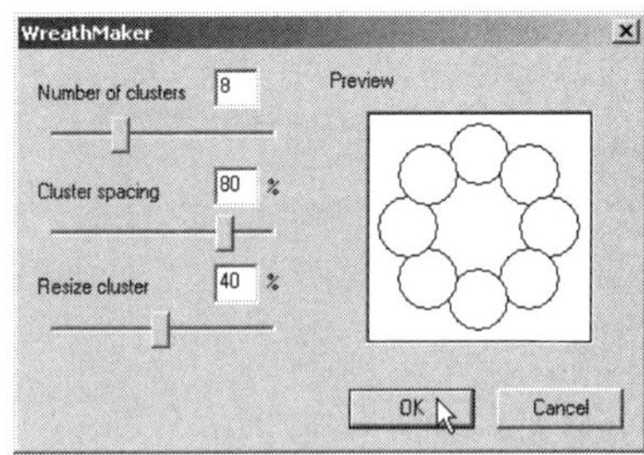

Step 6

Tip

- **Experiment with the WreathMaker settings. You can restore your original wreath design by retrieving it from the Sketchbook.**

You will now modify this Star1 Wreath by pasting another star in the center.

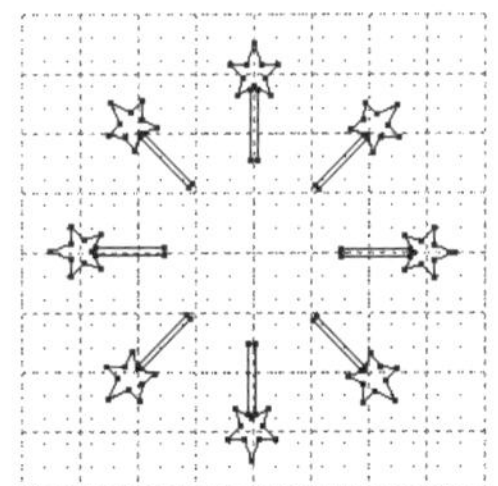

Step 6 – Star1 Wreath and Save in Sketchbook

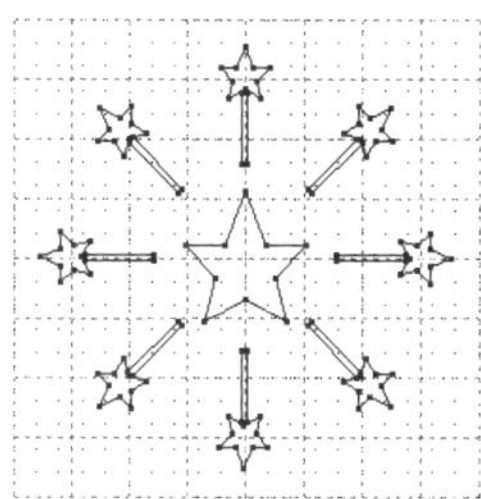

Step 7 – Star Wreath Star motif

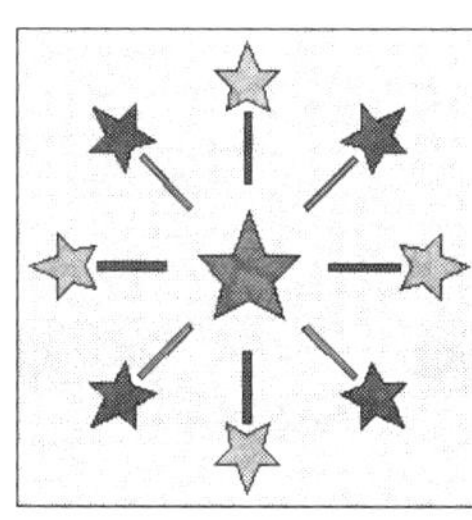

Step 8 – Color Star Wreath Star block and Save in Sketchbook

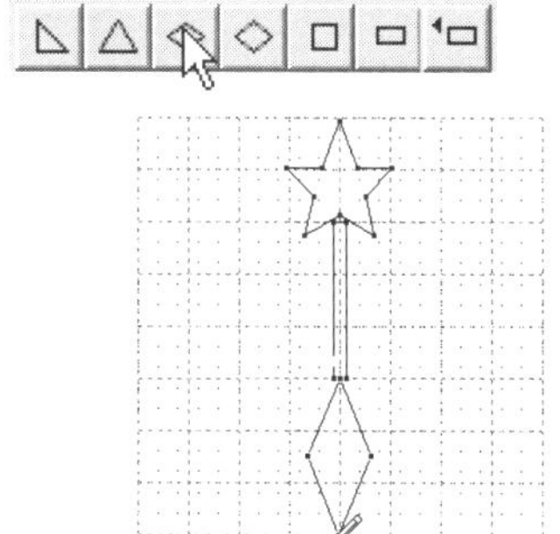

Step 9 – Draw diamond to form Sparkler unit and Save in Sketchbook

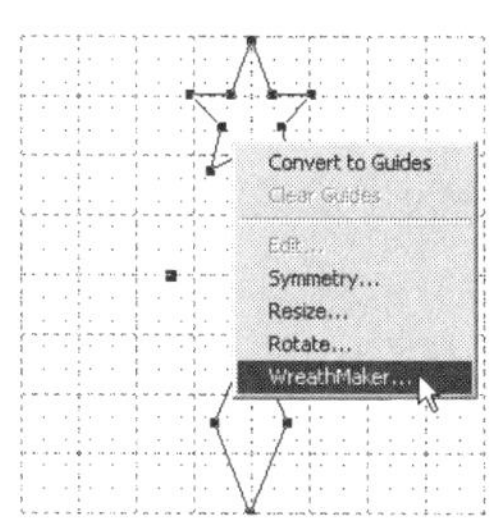

Step 10

7 Open the Block Sketchbook and select the Reduced Star motif for editing. Ctrl+A to select the Star and then Ctrl+C to copy. Open the Block Sketchbook and select the new Star1 Wreath motif that you just created. Ctrl+V to paste the Reduced Star and move the star to the center of the wreath. Save in Sketchbook. This is the Star Wreath Star motif that you will use for the quilting stencil in the center patch of the four star medallion.

8 To create an appliqué block from this Star Wreath Star, Ctrl+A to select all and then Ctrl+C to copy. Click on Block and then click on New Block. Click on PatchDraw in the extended menu. Ctrl+V to paste the design and center the design in the block. Color and Save in Sketchbook. You will use this Star Wreath Star block in Border 7.

Tip

- **Patches are layered in the order in which they are drawn. You will learn how to change the appliqué layering order in the next lesson.**

8

Now you will create the basic unit for the Sparkler Wreath by modifying the Star1 unit. You should still have the 8 x 8 graph paper on the PatchDraw worktable.

9 Open the Sketchbook, click on the Motif tab, and place the Star1 unit on the worktable for editing. Click on the small arrow on the Simple Shape tool and then select the smaller diamond shape on the extended toolbar. This shape is third from the left on the extended bar. Draw a diamond three graph paper units long at the base of the narrow rectangle. Save in Sketchbook. This is the Sparkler unit.

Tip

- **You will find it easier to draw this diamond and center it directly under the rectangle if you zoom in on the lower worktable.**

10 Ctrl+A to select all of the Sparkler unit. Secondary click on the worktable and then click on WreathMaker.

11 Type in these values in the WreathMaker box:

Number of clusters – 8

Cluster spacing – 80

Resize cluster – 40

Click on OK.

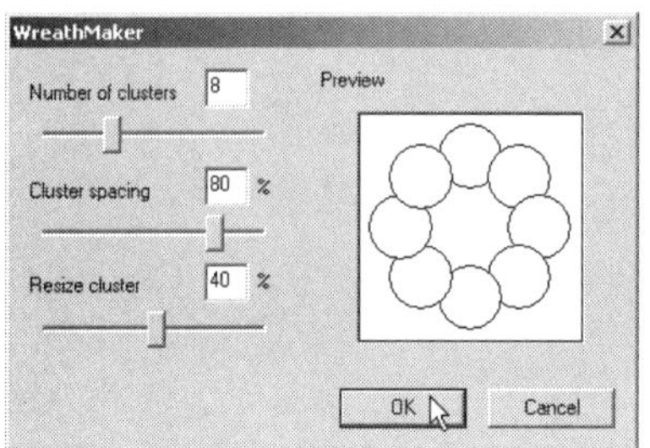

Step 11

12 Zoom in to the center of the wreath design and click on the smaller diamond shape in the Simple Shape toolbar. Starting in the center of the wreath, draw eight diamond shapes, as shown. Color and Save in Sketchbook. You will place a Sparkler Wreath over each of the four stars in the center medallion of the quilt.

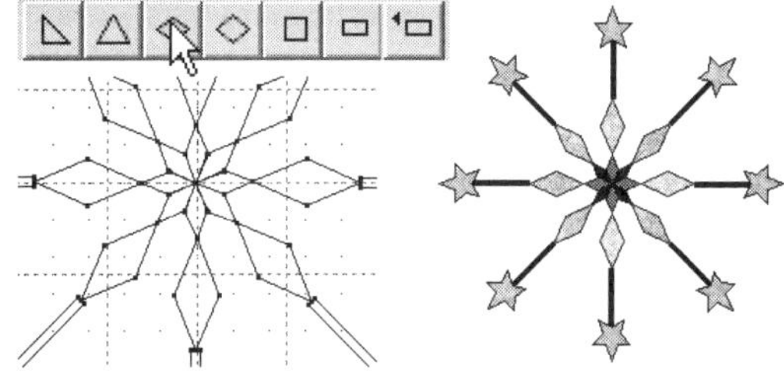
Step 12 – Zoomed in view of eight diamonds and colored Sparkler Wreath

13 Name your new designs on their Notecards. Save.

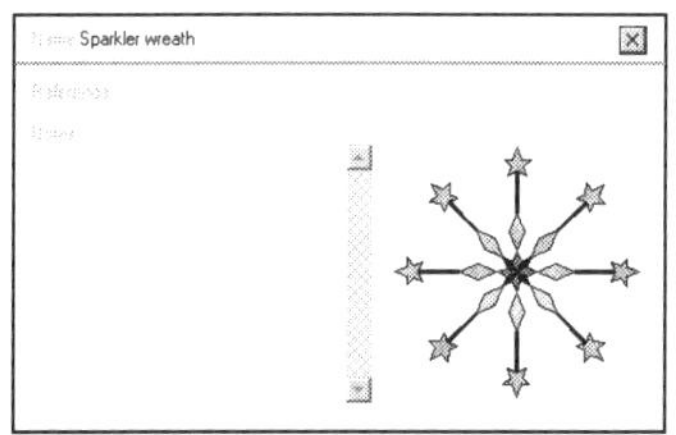

Step 13 – Name designs on Notecards and Save

**Tip**

- **Remember to use the convenient Edit/Undo or Ctrl+Z shortcut when you are designing in PatchDraw.**

Selecting the Layout and Borders

A medallion quilt layout is one in which a center block or panel of blocks is framed by a series of borders. In this lesson, you will use a medallion layout from the EQ5 Layout Libraries, modify it, and add several borders, including an uneven border. Having the capability to specify uneven borders is important when you want to create a rectangular quilt layout from a square block arrangement.

1 Click on Libraries and then click on Layout Library. The Layout Libraries box will open. Click on EQ Libraries. Click on 2Basics by Style. Click on Stars, click on Stars 44, and then click copy. Close the Libraries.

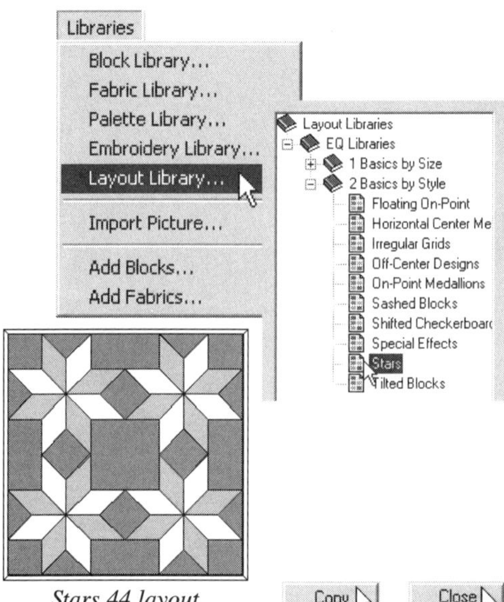

Stars 44 layout

Step 1

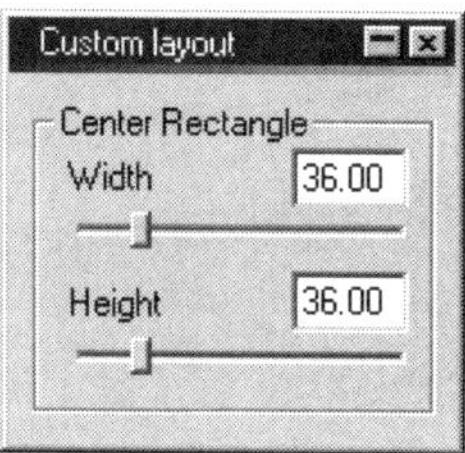

Step 2

2 Open the Quilt Sketchbook and select the new layout for editing. Click on the Layout tab and the Custom layout box will open. Set the following values:

Center Rectangle:	Width – 36.00 Height – 36.00

3 Click on the Borders tab and establish these borders. Border boxes 1, 3, 5, and 8 are illustrated here.

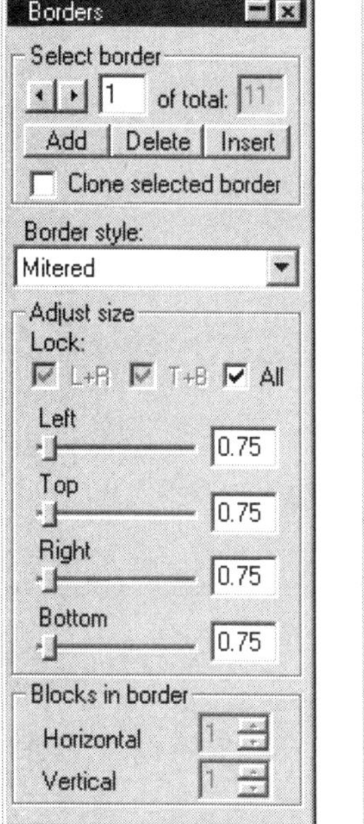

Step 3 – Border 1

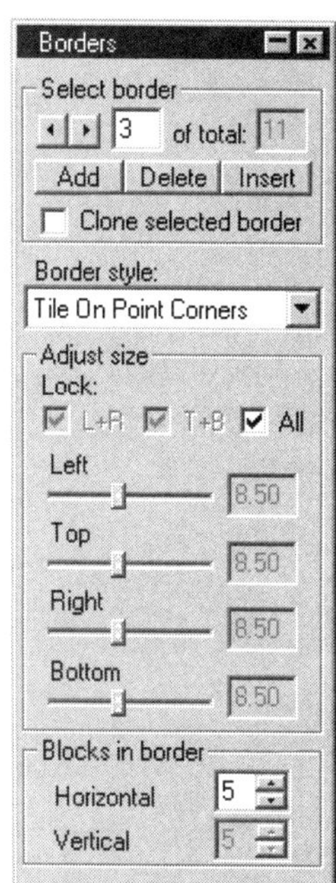

Step 3 – Border 3

Border 1

Border style:	Mitered
Size:	.75 (Lock: All)

Border 2

Border style:	Mitered
Size:	.75 (Lock: All)

Border 3

Border style:	Tile On Point Corners
Blocks in border:	Horizontal – 5

Notice that EQ5 has added a spacer to accommodate the number of Horizontal blocks in border that you specified.

Tip

- **For a Tile border such as Border 3, you will designate how many squares you want in the horizontal border. EQ5 then calculates the number of blocks that are required to construct the vertical border from the same size blocks. A spacer may be added to make the blocks fit evenly. Experiment with the Tile size by changing the number of horizontal blocks. Notice that as you change the number of horizontal blocks, the Tile size changes. Please see the EQ5 manuals or the Help file for more information.**

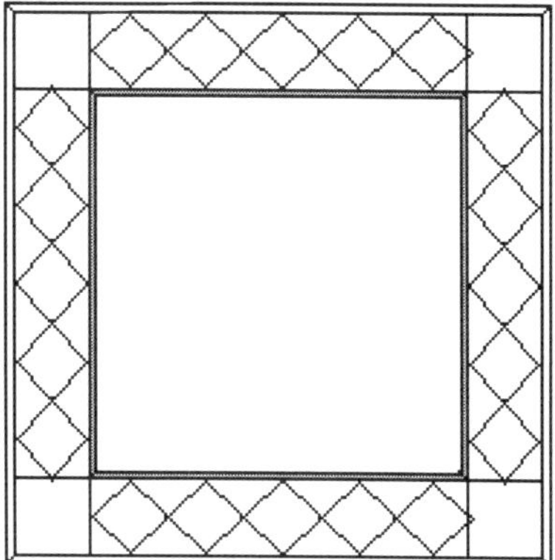

Border 3 – Spacer is illustrated by the area filled with gray

Border 4

Border style:	Mitered
Size:	1.00 (Lock: All)

Border 5

Border style:	Blocks
Size:	L+R – 0.00 T+B – 6.00
Blocks in border:	Horizontal – 10 Vertical – 1

Border 6

Border style:	Mitered
Size:	1.00 (Lock: All)

Border 7

Border style:	Corner Blocks
Size:	8.00 (Lock: All)

Border 8

Border style:	Long Horizontal
Size:	L+R – 0.00 T+B – 1.00

Border 9

Border style:	Blocks
Size:	L+R – 0.00 T+B – 4.00
Blocks in border:	Horizontal – 19 Vertical – 1

Border 10

Border style:	Long Horizontal
Size:	L+R – 0.00 T+B – 1.00

Border 11 (Prairie Points)

Border style:	Points Out
Size:	L+R – 0.00 T+B – 3.00
Blocks in border:	Horizontal – 19 Vertical – 1

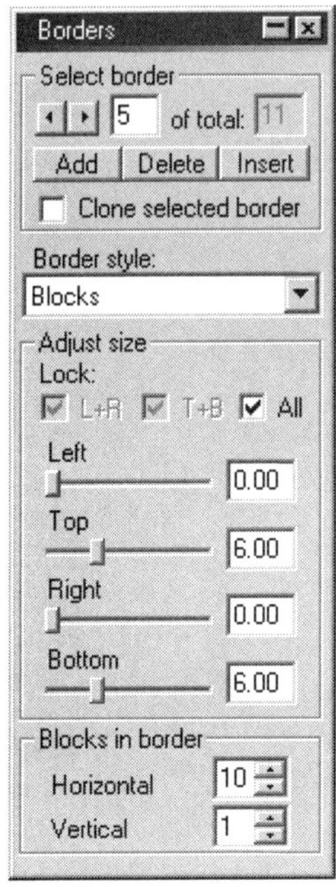

Step 3 – Border 5

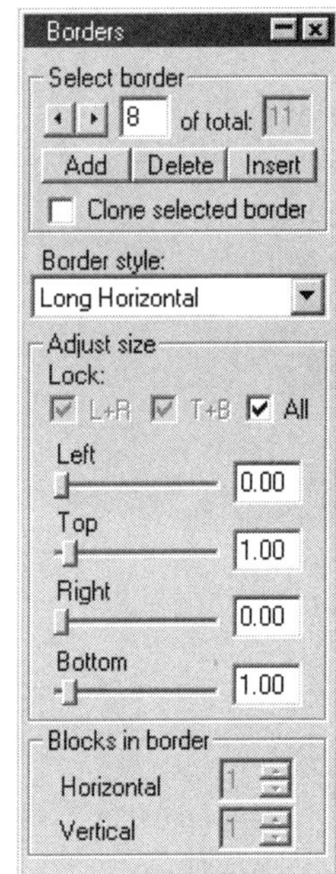

Step 3 – Border 8

Quilt as it is seen on Layer 1 Tab

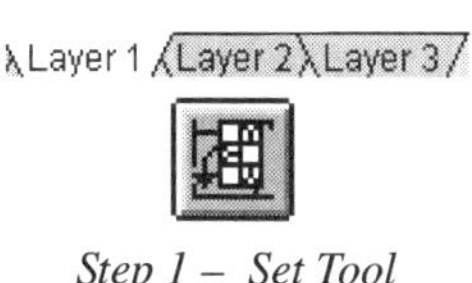

Step 1 – Set Tool

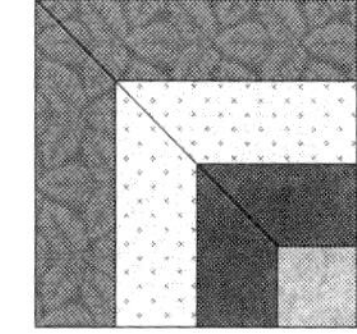

Step 1 – Corner 4 block

Step 1 – Quilt with Corner 4 block set and rotated

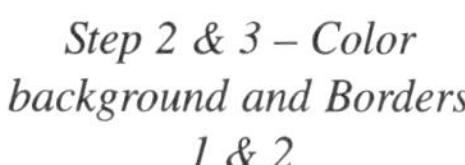

Step 2 & 3 – Color background and Borders 1 & 2

Step 4 – Border 3

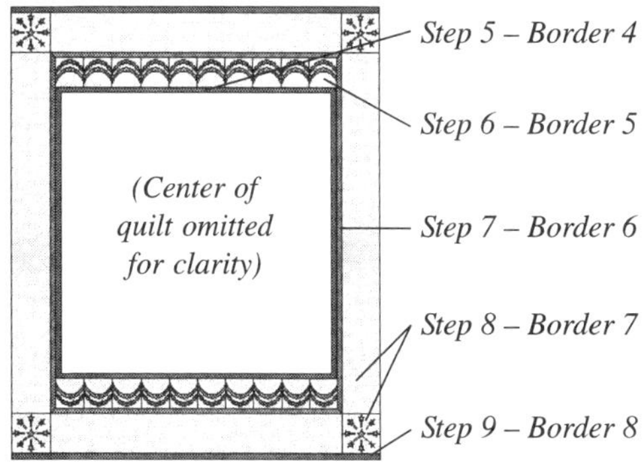

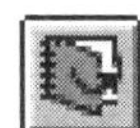

Step 9 – Save in Sketchbook

Setting Designs into the Layout

1. Click on the Layer 1 tab and Save in Sketchbook to save your layout. Click on the Set tool and then select the Corner 4 block in the Blocks palette. Click to set this block in each star point in the quilt center. Rotate each block to the correct orientation with the Rotate tool. Save in Sketchbook.

2. Click on the Paintbrush tool and Ctrl+click to color the background in the center medallion of the quilt. Save in Sketchbook.

3. Color Borders 1 and 2. Save in Sketchbook.

4. Click on the Set tool and Ctrl+click to set the Corner 4 block in the corners of Border 3. Rotate to the correct orientation. Ctrl+click to set this block in the border. Alt+click with the Rotate tool to turn the blocks on each side of the border to the correct orientation. Color the background triangles in this border with the Paintbrush or the Plain Block tool. Color the spacer that EQ5 has added for this Tile On Point Corner border. Save in Sketchbook.

5. Color Border 4. Save in Sketchbook.

6. Ctrl+click to set the Triple Swag block in Border 5. Alt+click with the Rotate tool to turn the Triple Swag blocks on the top of the quilt. Save in Sketchbook. You will add the appliqué Stars in the next section.

7. Color Border 6. Save in Sketchbook.

8. Color Border 7. Using the Set tool, Ctrl+click to set the Star Wreath Star block in the corners. Save in Sketchbook.

9. Color Border 8. Save in Sketchbook.

10 Ctrl+click to set the Star block in Border 9. Alt+click with the Rotate tool on the top border to turn these Star blocks so that the top of the Star points down to the center of the quilt. This will balance your quilt when viewed from any side. Click on the Plain Block tool and recolor alternate blocks in this border, as shown. Save in Sketchbook.

11 Color Border 10. Save in Sketchbook.

12 Ctrl+click to set the Half Square Triangle into Border 11. Alt+click with the Rotate tool to turn the Half Square Triangles to the correct orientation. Save in Sketchbook.

Tip

- **Setting Half Square Triangles into Prairie Point borders will enable you to generate a template of the finished Points.**

Be sure that you use your imported fabric in the quilt design! Moda's Rippling Stripes is used here in the alternating plain blocks in Border 9.

Setting Appliqué on Layer 2

1 Click on Layer 2. Click on the Set tool and then click on the Sparkler Wreath motif in the Blocks palette. Holding down the Shift key, click and drag to set this appliqué on the worktable. Use the Adjust tool and the Graph Pad to set the size at 18.000 x 18.000. Center the Sparkler Wreath over one of the four medallion stars.

Tip

- **Remember that you can move a palette on the worktable by clicking on the blue bar at the top of the palette and dragging the box to another location.**

2 With the Sparkler Wreath still selected, Ctrl+C to copy and Ctrl+V to paste another motif on the worktable. Center the new Sparkler Wreath over a medallion star in the layout. Zoom in and align this second motif, using the first motif as a reference.

3 Create two more motifs for the remaining medallion stars in the center. Align these wreaths. Save in Sketchbook.

Step 10 – Set Star block in bottom section of the quilt

Step 10 – Rotate Star block in top section of the quilt

Step 10 – Recolor alternate blocks in bottom section of the quilt

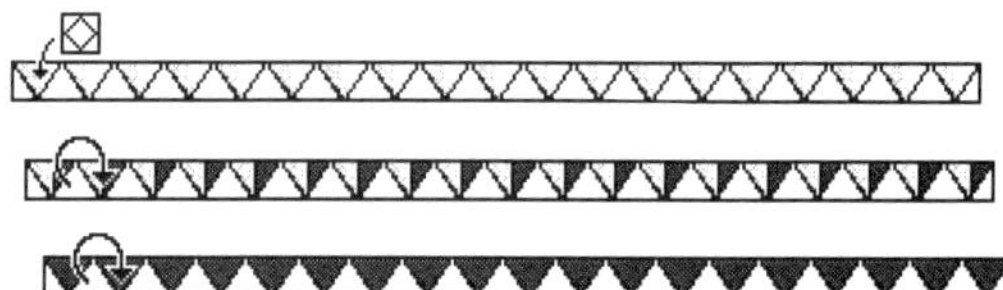

Step 12 – Set Half Square Triangle and Rotate so that Border 11 looks alike on the bottom and top (Bottom shown being rotated here)

Quillt with borders completed

Sparkler Wreath Motif

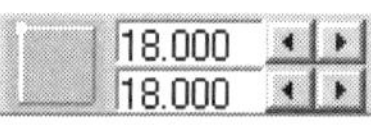

Step 1

Step 3 – Four Sparkler Wreath's positioned over medallion stars

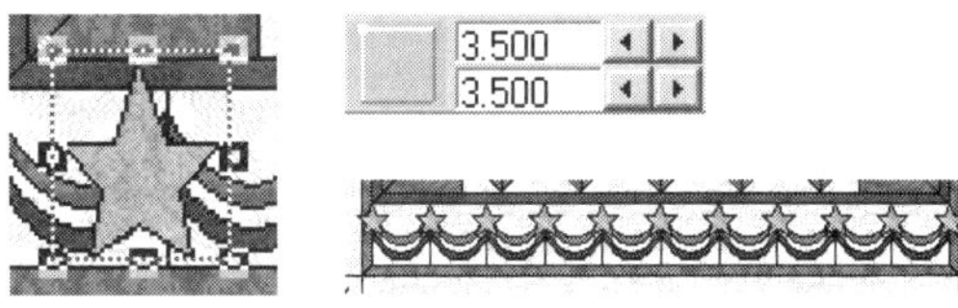

Step 4 – Place stars on bottom segment

4 Set a Star motif between two Triple Swag blocks on the bottom segment of Border 5. Set the block size to 3.500 x 3.500 on the Graph Pad. Adjust the motif so that it is centered. Copy and paste Star motifs between the Triple Swag blocks and on the ends of this border. Save in Sketchbook.

Step 5 – Place stars on top segment and Save in Sketchbook

5 Using the first Star as reference, align the motifs on this side of Border 5. Holding down the Shift key, select each Star motif in this row, and then copy and paste this row of motifs to the top segment of Border 5. Rotate each Star motif on the opposite side so that the top of the Star points in to the center of the quilt. Save in Sketchbook.

Tip

- **Be sure to use the Zoom tools when setting designs on Layers!**

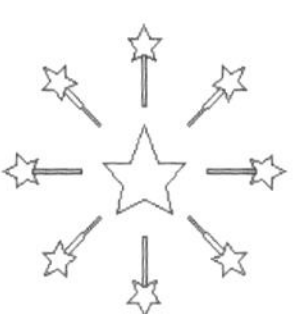
Star Wreath Star motif

Step 1

Setting Stencils on Layer 3

1 Click on Layer 3 and then click on the Set tool. Select the Star Wreath Star motif and set this design in the center patch of the quilt layout. Set the size to 9.000 x 9.000 on the Graph Pad. Center the Star Wreath Star over the space. Save in Sketchbook.

8

Tip

- **Remember to use the Thread Color tool, if necessary, to make your quilting stencils more visible on the layout.**

Same Width Same Height tool

Clip tools

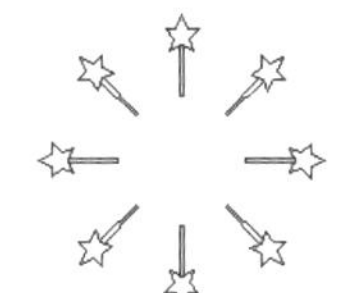
Star1 Wreath motif

2 Click on the Set tool and then click on the Star1 Wreath motif. Set this design over one of the side rectangles in the medallion. Using the center Star Wreath Star as a reference, set the size with the Same Width and Height tool. Align the design with the top of the Star Wreath Star stencil. Adjust the position of the design so that only three Star units in the wreath are visible on the side rectangle. Click on the last Clip tool in the Graph Pad. This is the Clip to Center Rectangle tool and it will trim the design at the edge of the center area. Save in Sketchbook.

Step 2

Step 2 – Save in Sketchbook

3 Ctrl+C and Ctrl+V to create three more Star1 Wreath stencils for the remaining side rectangles in the medallion center. Position them as shown and Save in Sketchbook.

4 Set a Star1 Wreath in one of the corner squares. Set the size and align with one of the stencils in a side rectangle. Move the stencil until only one Star unit in the wreath is visible in the corner. Click on the Clip to Center Rectangle tool.

5 Ctrl+C and Ctrl+V to create three more Star1 Wreath stencils for the remaining corners in the medallion center. Set the size and align, just as you did for the first corner stencil. Move each stencil until only one Star unit is visible. Click on the Clip to Center Rectangle tool. Save in Sketchbook.

6 Open the Sketchbook and create a Notecard for your Sparkler quilt.

Step 3

Step 4

Step 5

Step 5 – Save in Sketchbook

Tip

- **When constructing this design, consider using metallic thread for the appliqué and quilting stencils. This will add even more sparkle to your Sparkler quilt!**

Adding Blocks to the User Libraries

1 Click on Libraries and then click on Add Blocks. Open the Simplified Blocks library.

2 Copy the blocks from this Sparklers quilt into the Simplified Blocks style library. Be sure to also copy the designs on the Motif and Stencil tabs.

3 Click on Save Library, click on OK when EQ5 tells you that your designs have been saved. Close the Add Block to Library box.

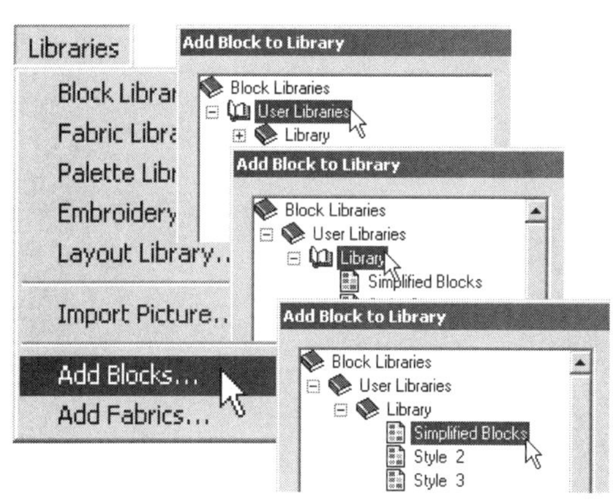

Step 1

Step 2

Close

Step 3

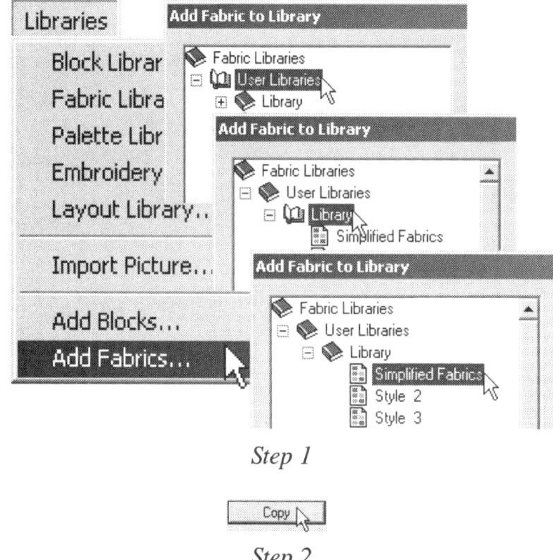

Step 1

Step 2

Save Library

EQ5

Your fabrics have been saved in the library!

OK

Close

Step 3

Here is the finished quilt!

You can add the fabrics that you collected for Sparklers to the Fabric User Libraries.

1 Click on Libraries and then click on Add Fabrics. Open the Simplified Fabrics library.

2 Copy the fabrics from this quilt into the Simplified Fabrics style library.

3 Click on Save Library, click on OK when EQ5 tells you that your fabrics have been saved. Close the Add Fabric to Library box.

Adding Blocks from a Previous Project to the User Libraries

At any point, you can open another project file and copy designs into the User Libraries. In preparation for Lesson 9, you will now copy the Eight-Pointed Star block that you used in your Nine Patch project into the User Libraries.

1 Use Ctrl+O to display EQ5's opening screen and click on the Open an Existing Project tab.

2 Click on the Nine Patch project in the list or, if necessary, click on the small folder icon at the bottom of this tab and navigate to the Nine Patch project in the PJ5 directory. Open the Nine Patch project and add the Eight-Pointed Star block to the Simplified Blocks library. Save Library. Close the Add Block to Library box.

Exiting EQ5

Click on File and then click on Exit.

Drawing With PatchDraw

Lesson 9

Lesson 9 – Drawing with PatchDraw

In this lesson, you will experiment with EQ5's new Strip quilt layout feature as you design An EQ View. In addition to practicing many of the skills you have learned so far in this tutorial, you will:

- *Draw a new design in EasyDraw™*
- *Draw new designs in PatchDraw*
- *Layer patches in PatchDraw*
- *Edit arcs in PatchDraw*
- *Rotate a patch manually in PatchDraw*
- *Plan a Horizontal Strip layout*
- *Clone a strip*
- *Create a quilt label*

An EQ View Quilt

Starting a New Project

Start a new project with the file name *An EQ View*.

This project is intended to be "scrappy," which means it will look best if you use a wide variety of fabrics. The easiest way to achieve a scrappy look is to begin with the default palette, adding fabrics and changing colors on the layout as you put the quilt together.

Copying Designs from the Libraries

9

1 Open the Block Library and copy these fourteen designs. You can use the Search feature in the Library, or you can go directly to the libraries in this list and copy the designs into your project file.

1Classic Pieced / Classics
  Log Cabin
  Friendship Star

1Classic Pieced / Diamond in Square
  Snail's Trail

1Classic Pieced / Old Favorites
  The Palm
  Meadow Flower
  Friendship Bouquet

1Classic Pieced / Pictures
  Proud Pine

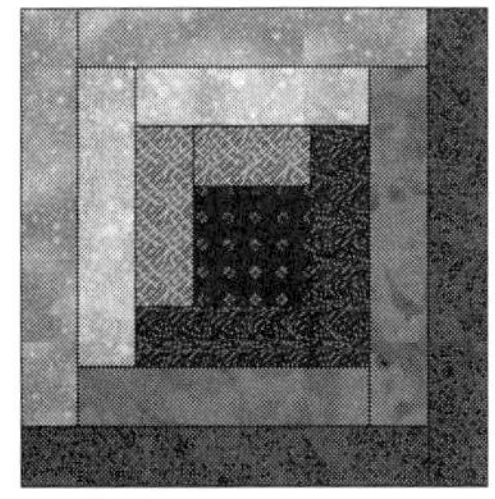

Log Cabin

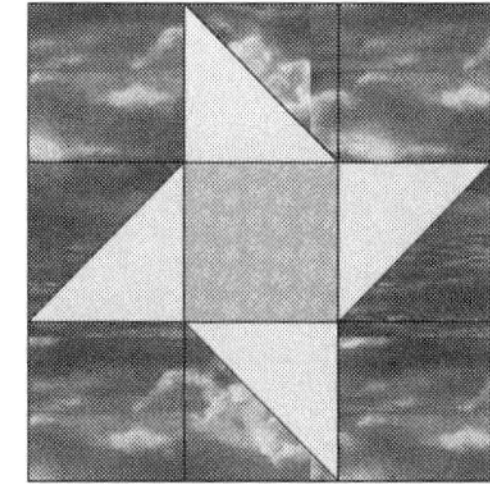

Friendship Star

Snail's Trail

The Palm

Meadow Flower

Friendship Bouquet

Proud Pine

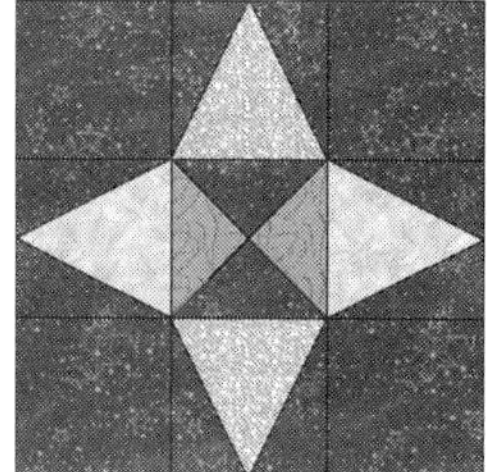
Arkansas Snowflake

Dizzy Spinner

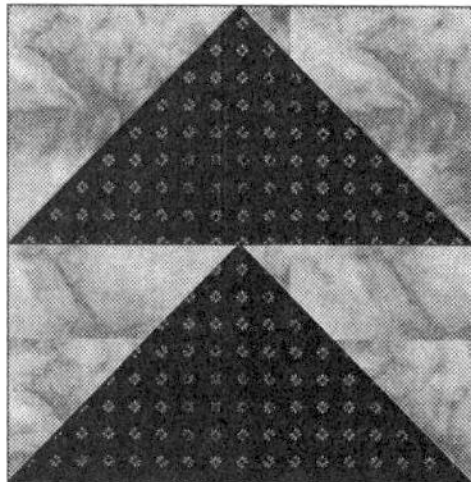
Flying Geese I

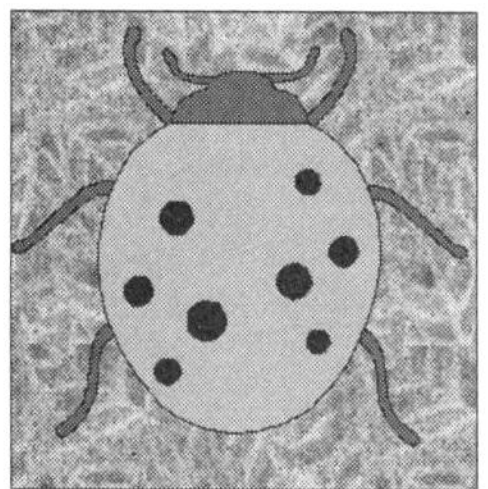
Ladybug

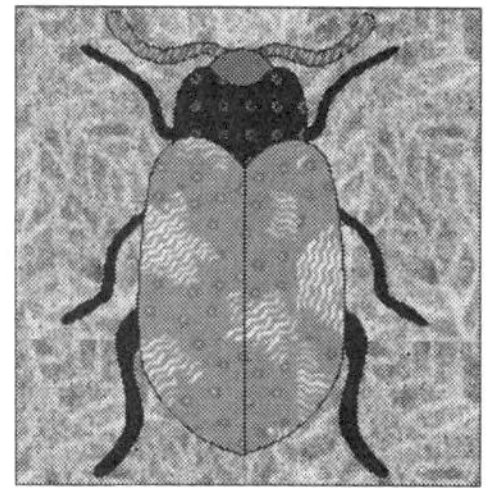
Beetle

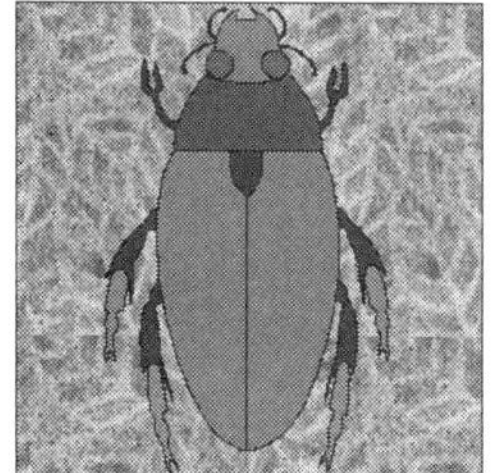
Beetle

Eight-Pointed Star

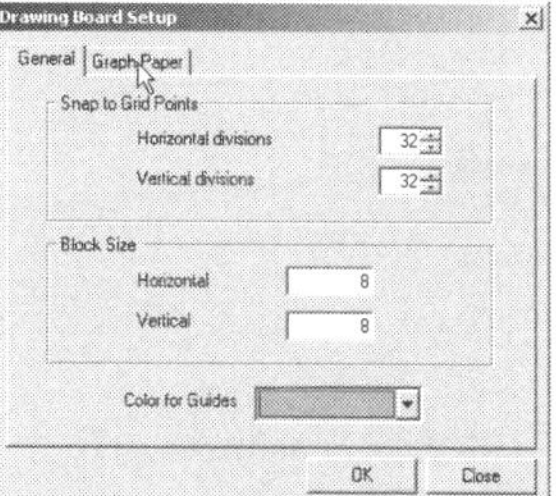

Step 1

1Classic Pieced / Simple Blocks
    Arkansas Snowflake

2Contemporary Pieced / Spinning Suns
    Pick one to use as a centipede. I selected the Dizzy Spinner.

3Paper Piecing / Flying Geese
    Flying Geese I

5Contemporary Appliqué / Bugs
    Pick three bugs that appeal to you. I used the Ladybug and two different Beetles.

User Libraries / Simplified Blocks
    Eight-Pointed Star

2 Color the blocks. You can easily recolor them later on the quilt layout. Save in Sketchbook.

Drawing a New Design in EasyDraw™

You will need a Picket Fence block for this quilt design. If you have BlockBase and have linked it to EQ5, you can use the Search function in the EQ Libraries to find Picket Fence with Mid Rib. Otherwise, you can draw this block from the following instructions.

1 Click on Worktable and then click on Work on Block. Click on Block, click on New Block, and then click on EasyDraw™. Click on Block and then click on Drawing Board Setup. Make these selections:

General Tab

Snap to Grid Points:	Horizontal – 32 Vertical – 32
Block Size:	define a square

Graph Paper:

Number of divisions:	Horizontal – 8 Vertical – 8
Options:	Graph Paper lines

Click on OK.

2 Draw the Picket Fence block, as shown. Color and Save in Sketchbook.

Tip

- **When drawing the horizontal brace for the fence, extend the lines over and slightly past each vertical line. EQ5 will trim these lines automatically to the intersecting points when you click over to the Color tab.**

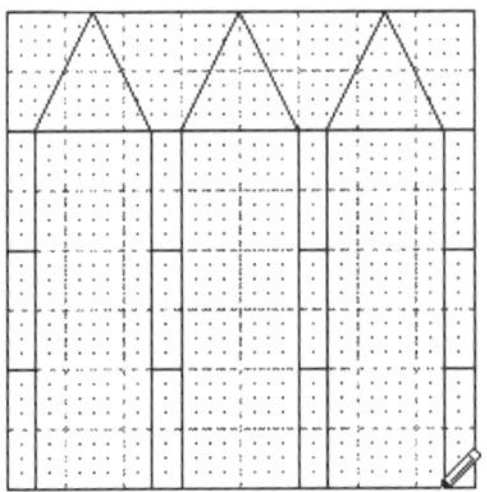

Draw Picket Fence with Mid Rib

Color Picket Fence with Mid Rib

Drawing New Designs in PatchDraw

You will now draw two very simple appliqué designs for your new quilt. The first is a stylized bird that is composed of several connected arcs. The second is a butterfly that is composed of pre-drawn shapes from the Shape tools.

Bezier Tool

Bezier Edit Tool

Before you begin to draw these designs, practice with the Bezier and the Bezier Edit tools, drawing arcs and editing them until you become accustomed to working with these tools. For information on editing arcs, see the following section, *Editing Arcs in PatchDraw.*

1 Click on Block, click on New Block, and then click on PatchDraw. In the Drawing Board Setup, establish 8 x 8 graph paper. This will make it easier for you to draw balanced designs.

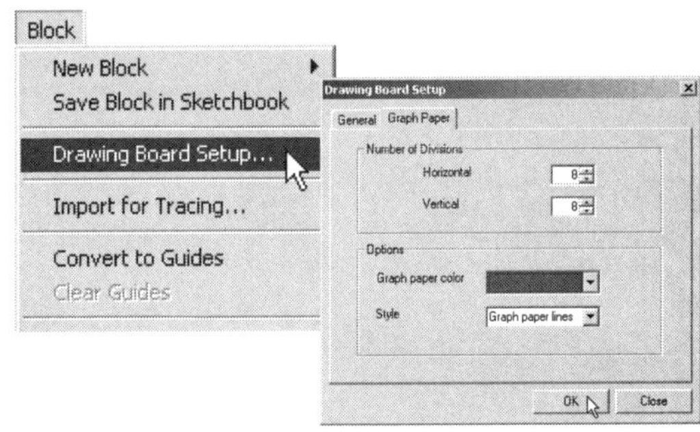

Step 1

2 This first design is simply four arcs, drawn in sequence to form a bird in flight. You probably drew birds like this when you were a child!

9

Click on the Bezier tool and, starting in the center of the graph paper, draw one arc to the left edge of the block outline. Release the mouse button at the end of this arc. Starting at this same point, draw another arc that returns to the beginning node, forming a wing that is a closed shape. Starting at this center point again, draw an arc on the right side of the graph paper. Starting at the end point of this arc, draw another arc that returns to the center point, forming a second wing that is a closed shape.

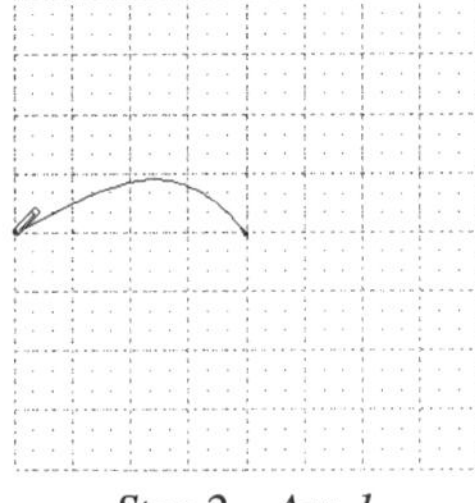

Step 2 – Arc 1

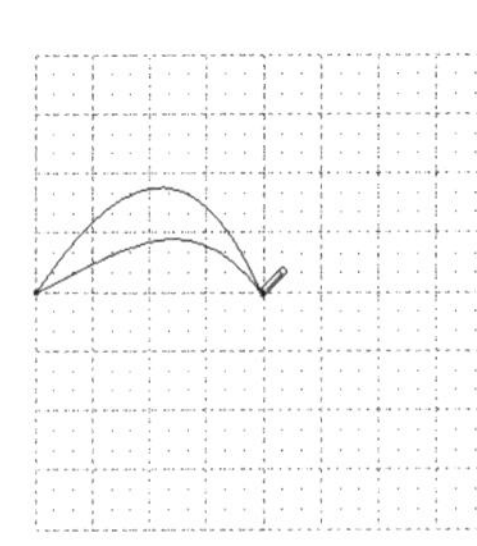

Step 2 – Arc 2

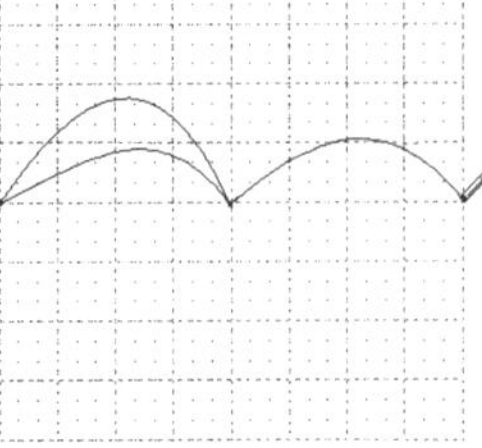

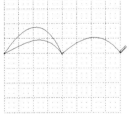

Step 2 – Arc 3

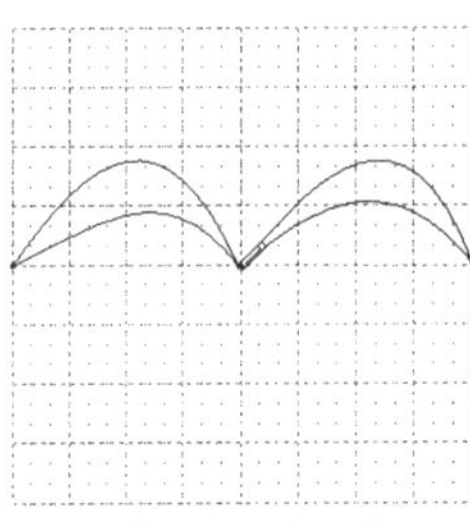

Step 2 – Arc 4

Step 2 – Draw Bird in Flight

Bezier Edit Tool

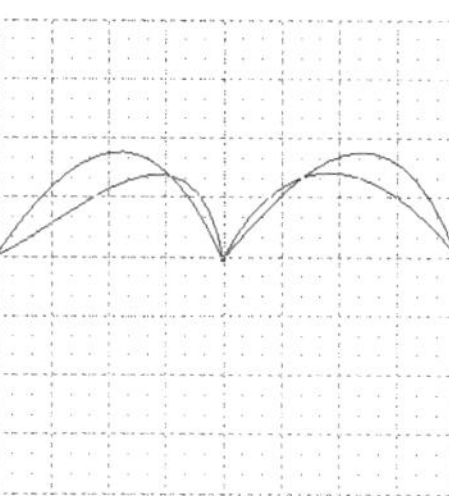

Step 3 – An example of the arcs overlapped. Your bird should NOT have the arcs overlapping.

Step 4 – Color Bird and Save in Sketchbook

Simple Oval Tools

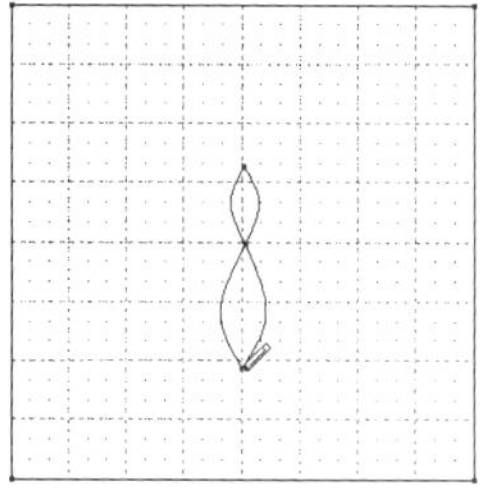

Step 5

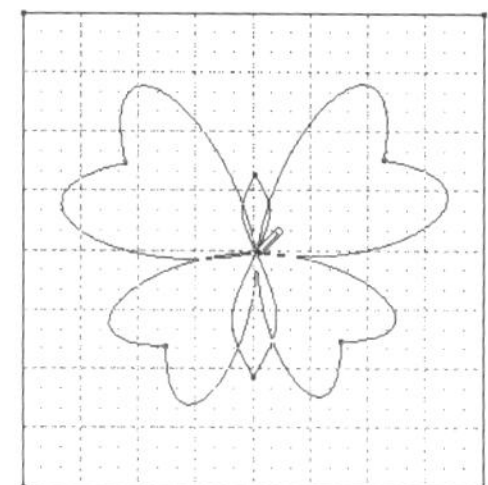

Step 6

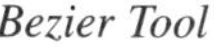

Bezier Tool

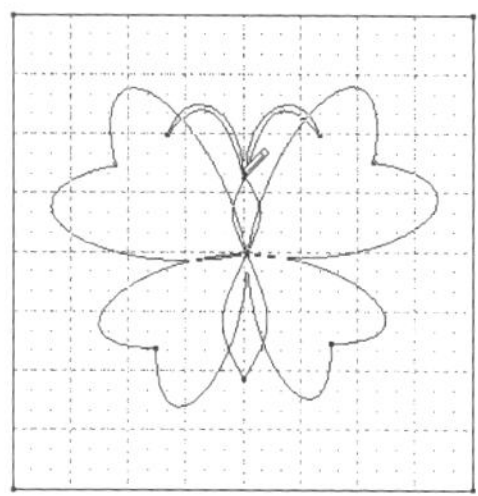

Step 7

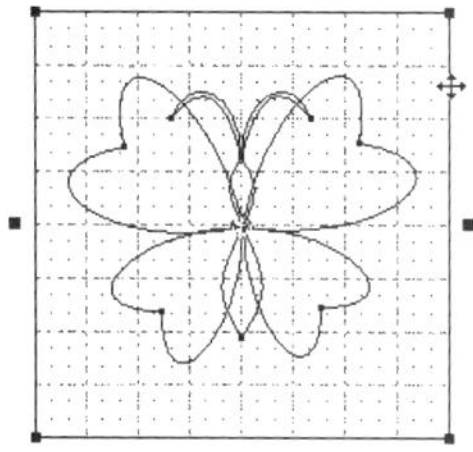

Step 8

3 Click on the Bezier Edit tool to edit these arcs to your satisfaction. For details on editing arcs, look ahead to *Editing Arcs in PatchDraw* on pages 168 and 169. The arcs should not overlap each other as in the shape of a figure eight (8).

4 Click on the Select tool, click on the block outline, and then press the Delete key to eliminate the background square. Color the Bird. Save in Sketchbook.

Tip

- **Remember to use the Edit/Undo feature and the Zoom tools while you are learning to draw in PatchDraw.**

5 Click on Block, click on New Block, and then click on PatchDraw. Click on the Simple Oval tool and then click on the fourth oval shape from the left. Draw two of these shapes, as shown.

6 Click on the Simple Oval tool and then click on the heart shape. Draw four hearts, as shown. Save in Sketchbook.

7 Click on the Bezier tool and draw antennae for the Butterfly. Remember that in PatchDraw you must create a closed shape for each object. The antennae structure should resemble the two shapes that you drew for the Bird, that is, two closed curves. Use the Bezier Edit tool to curve and adjust the arcs. Save in Sketchbook.

8 Delete the block outline with the Select tool to make the Butterfly an appliqué motif. Save in Sketchbook.

To move or delete a patch:
Click on the patch with the Select tool. Click on the directional arrows in the middle of the patch and drag it to a new location. Use the Delete key to remove the selected patch.

To adjust the size of a patch:
Click on the patch with the Select tool. Click on one of the surrounding nodes and drag to resize the patch.

Tip

- **To rotate a patch manually on the worktable, marquee or click on the patch with the Select tool, and then hold down the Ctrl key while you click on the directional arrows in the center of the patch. The patch will be surrounded by arrows. Click and drag one of the curved corner arrows in a clockwise or counter-clockwise direction to turn the patch. Click and drag one of the straight arrows to skew the patch. Click off the patch to disengage.**

9 Patches are layered in the order in which they are drawn. You can change the layering order of patches with the Send to Front and Send to Back features on the Color tab.

Click on the Color tab and then click on the Select tool. Click on the oval that forms the lower part of the Butterfly's body. This patch will highlight. Click on Block in the main menu and then click on Send to Front. The lower oval is now layered on top of the two lower hearts. Color the design and Save in Sketchbook.

**Tip**

- **You can also re-layer patches through the Color Worktable Context Menu. With the patch selected, secondary click on the worktable. The menu will open with Send to Front and Send to Back as options.**

Editing Arcs in PatchDraw

To move or delete an arc that is not joined to another arc or line:
On the PatchDraw worktable click on the Select tool and then click on the arc. The arc will be surrounded by nodes. Drag the arc by the directional arrows in the center or press the Delete key on your keyboard.

To adjust the size of an arc that is not joined to another arc or line:
Click on the Select tool and then click on the arc. The arc will be surrounded by nodes. Position the cursor on one of the nodes surrounding the arc. An arrow will appear that indicates the direction of adjustment. Pull the node in this direction to adjust the arc to your satisfaction.

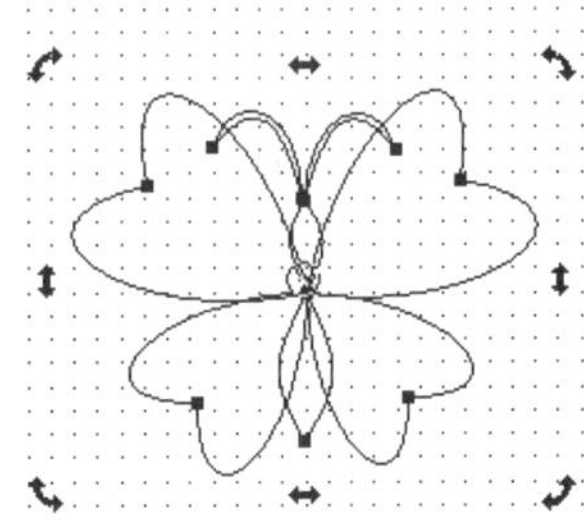

Tip – Butterfly motif in manual rotation mode

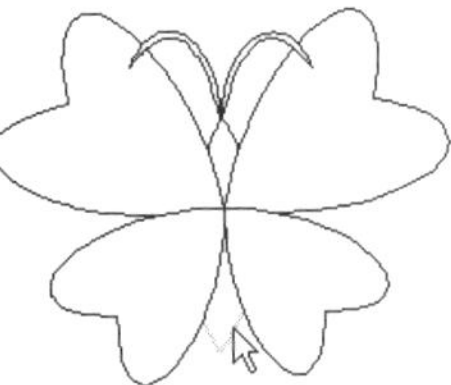

Select the lower oval

Send to Front

Step 9

Select Tool

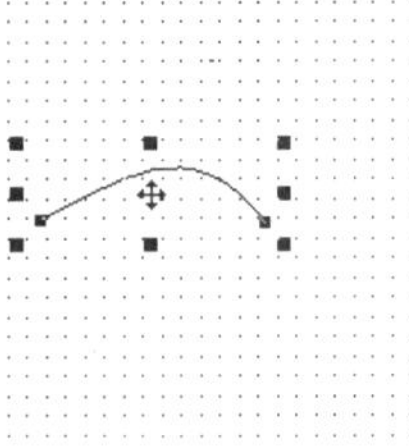

Select the arc

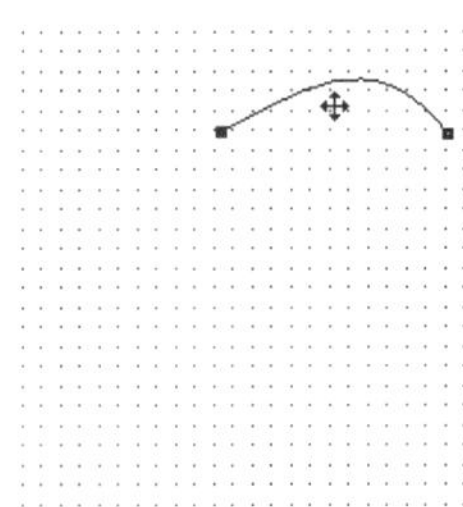

Drag to move the arc

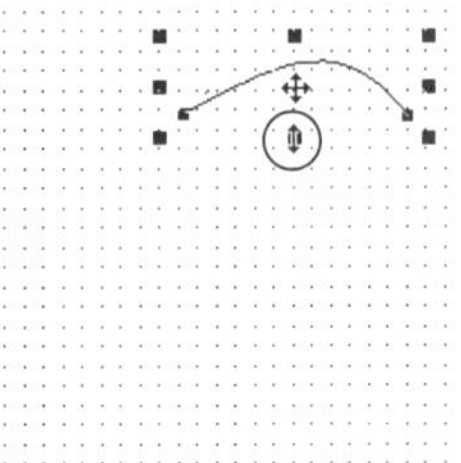

Select arc and position cursor over node

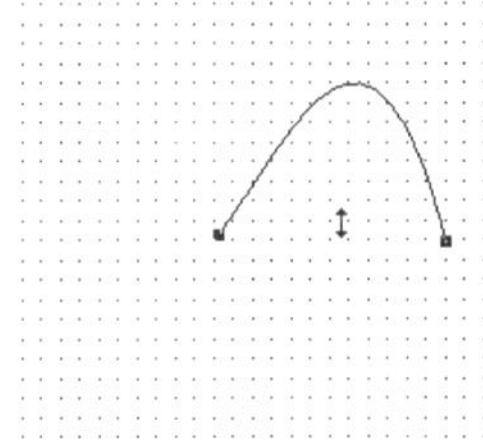

Drag to resize arc

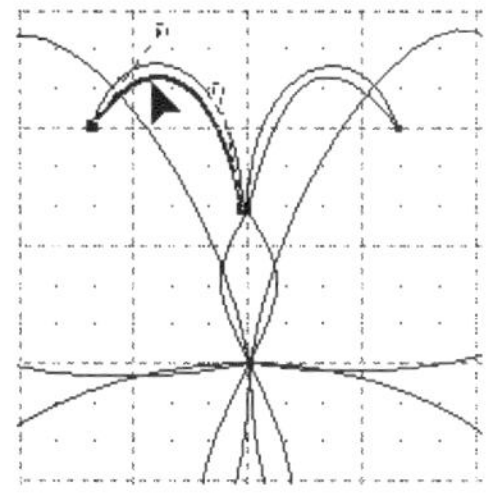

Click on the arc

Click and drag node

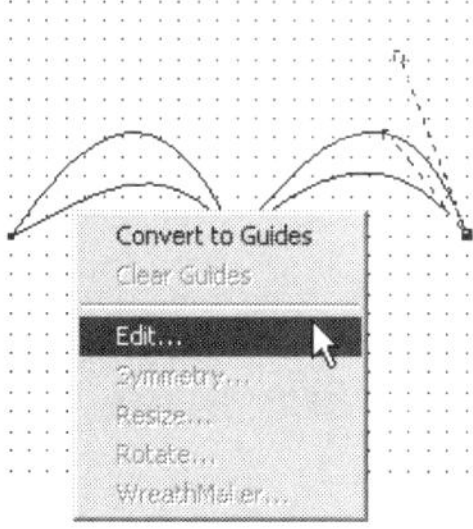

Click end node of right arcs and select edit

Bezier Edit Tool

Click Break to separate the arcs

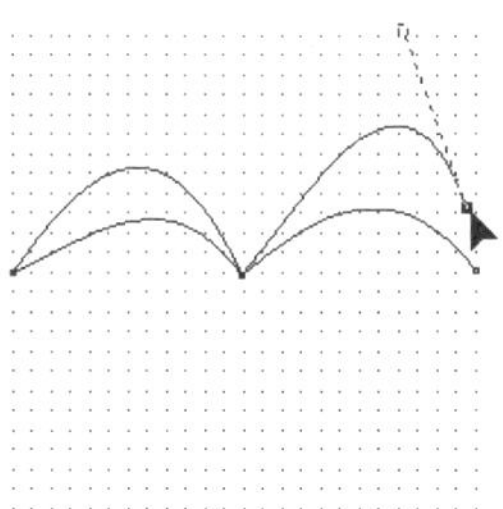

End of arc can now be moved separately

To edit the curve of an arc:
Click on the Bezier Edit tool and then click on the arc. Two handles will appear on the nodes, which will allow you to adjust the curvature of the arc. To move the end node of an arc, click on the node and drag.

To move or delete an arc that is joined to another arc or line:
You must first separate the arc from the connected lines or arcs. Click on the Bezier Edit tool and then click on one of the end nodes of the arc that you want to move or remove. Two handles will appear on the arc. It would be helpful to use the Zoom tools at this point so that you are able to see the nodes clearly. Secondary click on the nodes and a pop-up menu will open. Click on Edit and an Edit Node box will open.

Click on Break in the Edit Node box. This will separate the nodes so that the arc is no longer connected to form a closed curve. Break the nodes at the other end of the arc in the same manner. Click on the arc with the Select tool and it will be framed with nodes and the directional arrows will appear. Move the arc by dragging or press Delete to eliminate the arc.

For more information on editing arcs, be sure to check the EQ5 manuals and the Help file.

Planning a Horizontal Strip Layout and Borders

The new Strip Layout feature in EQ5 allows you great flexibility in planning quilts that are composed of multiple horizontal or vertical strips. These layouts can include any combination of strip styles and widths. You can even create Bargello designs!

**Tip**

- **See the EQ5 Design Cookbook or the Help file for illustrations and descriptions of the strip styles available to you with these layouts.**

1 Click on Worktable and then click on Work on Quilt. Click on Quilt and then click on New Quilt. Click on Horizontal Strip Quilt.

2 Click on the Layout tab and the first strip will be automatically selected. Use the Add button in the Horizontal Strip Quilt box to add strips to the layout. Select each strip and establish the following settings:

Strip 1

Strip style:	Diamonds
Size of strip:	Width – 8.00 Length – 36.00
Number of blocks:	Along length – 5

Strip 2

Strip style:	Half Drop
Size of strip:	Width – 2.00 Length – 36.00
Number of blocks:	Along length – 18

Strip 3

Strip style:	Half Drop Diamonds
Size of strip:	Width – 12.00 Length – 36.00
Number of blocks:	Along length – 3

Strip 4

Strip style:	Pieced Blocks

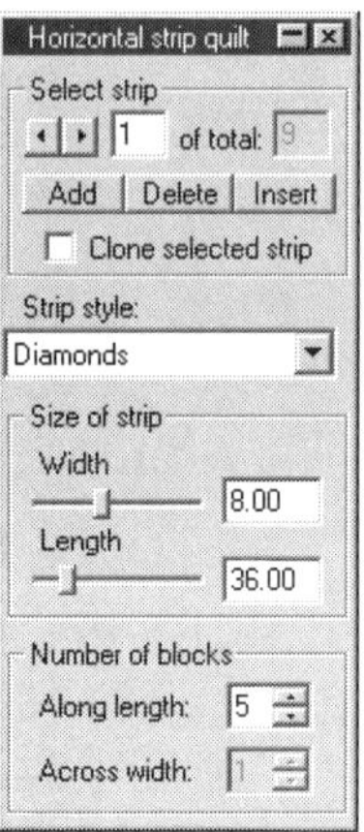

Step 2 – Strip 1

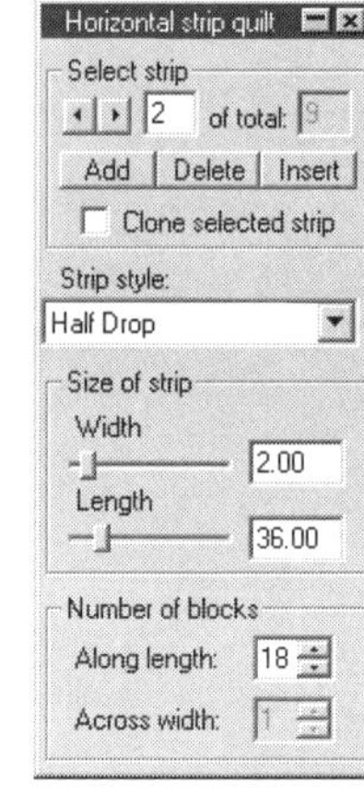

Step 2 – Strip 2

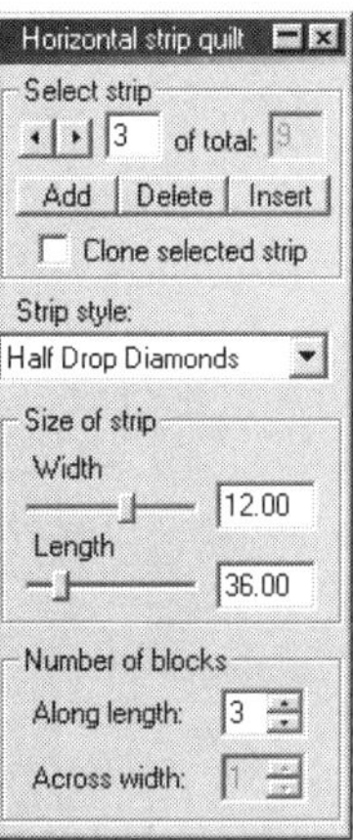

Step 2 – Strip 3

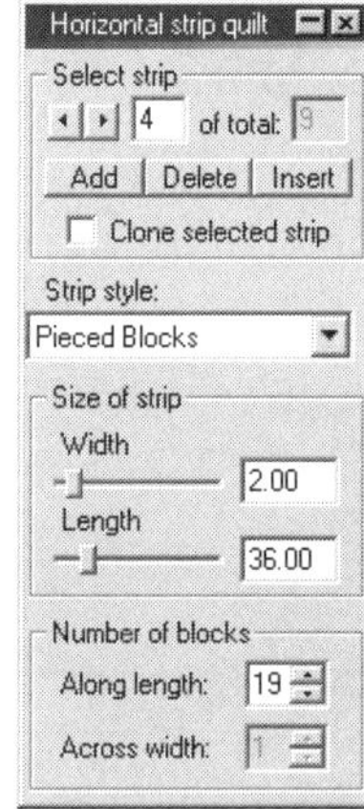

Step 2 – Strip 4

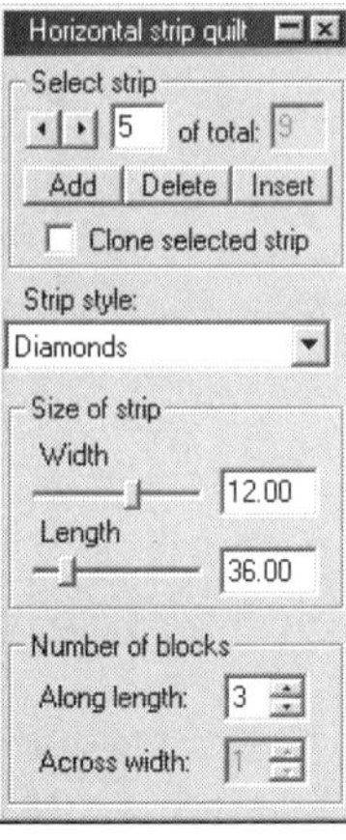

Step 2 – Strip 5

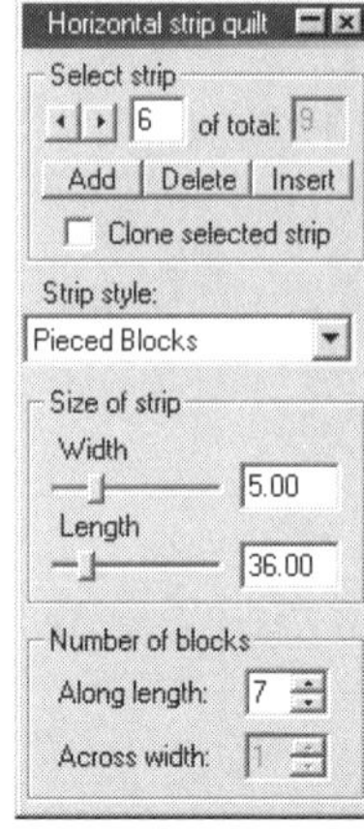

Step 2 – Strip 6

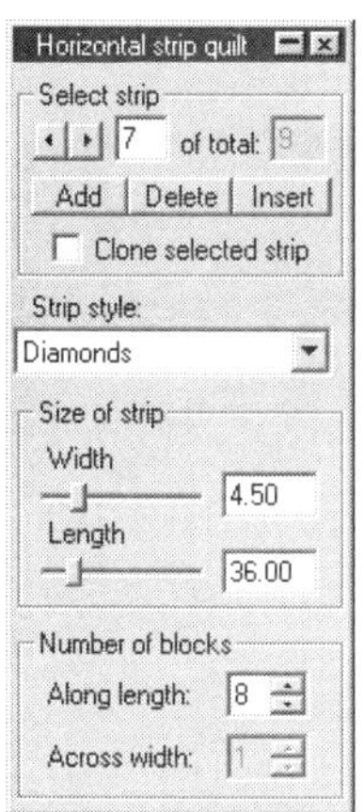

Step 2 – Strip 7

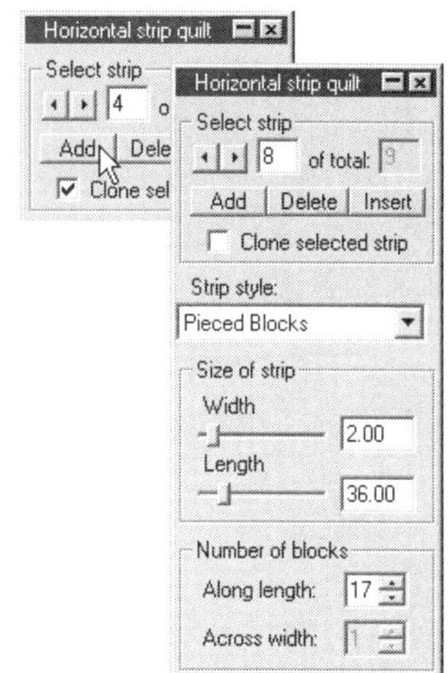

Step 2 – Strip 8

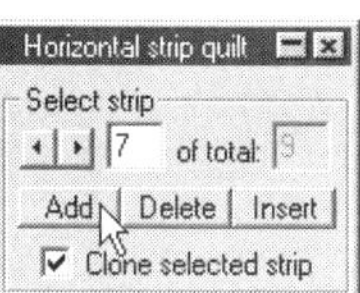

Step 2 –Create Strip 9

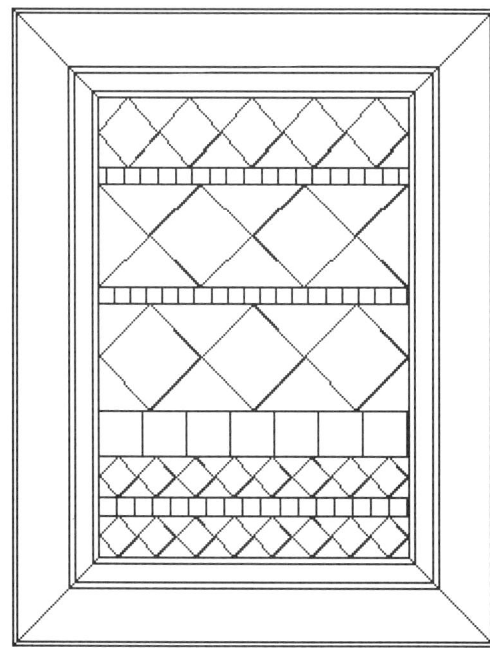

View of all nine strips

Size of strip: Width – 2.00
Length – 36.00

Number of blocks: Along length – 19

Strip 5

Strip style: Diamonds

Size of strip: Width – 12.00
Length – 36.00

Number of blocks: Along length – 3

Strip 6

Strip style: Pieced Blocks

Size of strip: Width – 5.00
Length – 36.00

Number of blocks: Along length – 7

Strip 7

Strip style: Diamonds

Size of strip: Width – 4.50
Length – 36.00

Number of blocks: Along length – 8

Strip 8

Move the cursor to Strip 4, check Clone selected strip in the Horizontal strip quilt box, and then click on Add. This action will add a new strip to the bottom of the layout that is identical to Strip 4. The only change that you need to make in this strip is in the Number of blocks: Along length.

Strip style: Pieced Blocks

Size of strip: Width – 2.00
Length – 36.00

Number of blocks: Along length – 17

Strip 9

Move the cursor to Strip 7, check Clone selected strip in the Horizontal strip quilt box, and then click on Add. A new strip will be added to the bottom of the layout that is identical to Strip 7. No modifications are necessary.

3 Click on the Borders tab and establish these borders. Border boxes 1-4 are illustrated here.

Border 1
Border style: Mitered

Size: .75 (Lock: All)

Border 2
Border style: Mitered

Size: 2.00 (Lock: All)

Border 3
Border style: Mitered

Size: .75 (Lock: All)

Border 4
Border style: Mitered

Size: 6.00 (Lock: All)

Border 5
Border style: Mitered

Size: .50 (Lock: All)

This border is intended to be the binding and will not add to the actual quilt dimensions.

4 Click on Layer 1 and Save in Sketchbook.

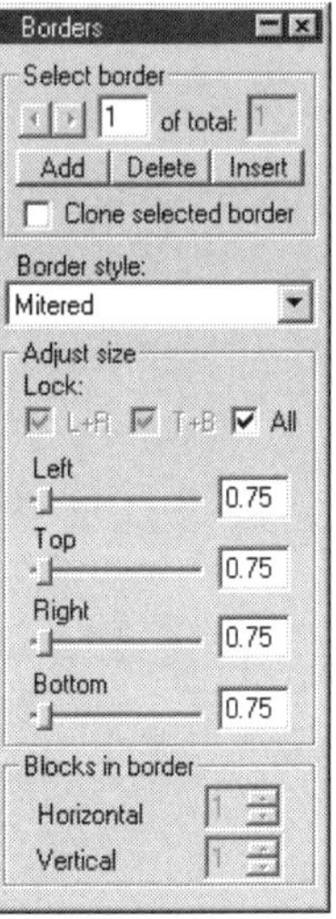

Step 3 – Border 1

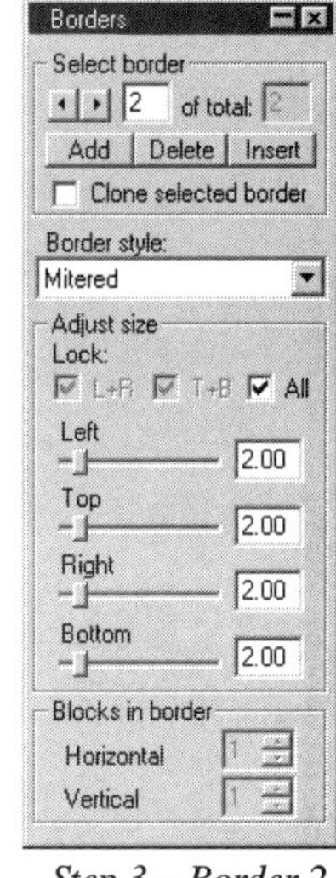

Step 3 – Border 2

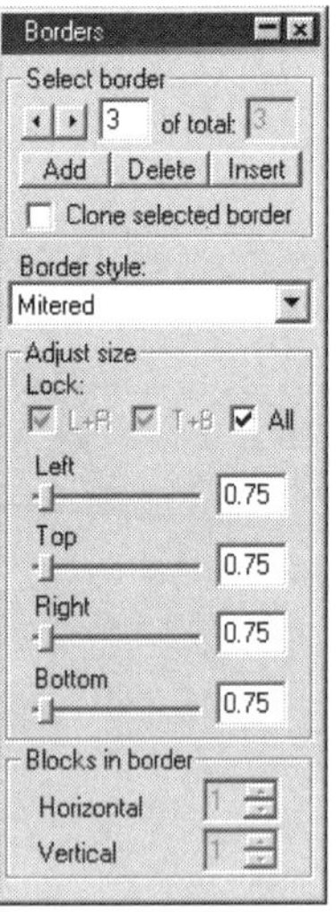

Step 3 – Border 3

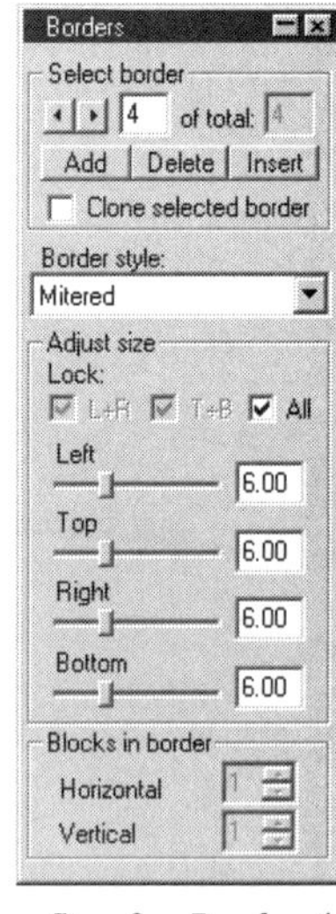

Step 3 – Border 4

Borders Layer 1 Layer 2

Step 4 – Layer 1 and Save in Sketchbook

Setting Designs into the Layout

You are going to set blocks into this quilt layout, starting at the bottom strip.

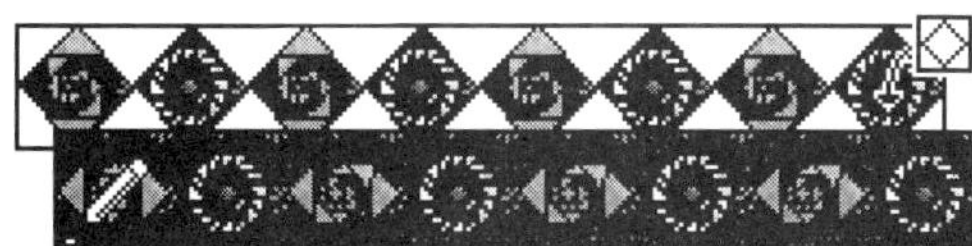

Step 1 – Set Ninth Strip

1 Click on the Set tool and then click on the Snail's Trail block. Click on alternate spaces in the ninth strip to set this design in the layout. In the remaining spaces in this strip, set the Dizzy Spinner or the equivalent block that you selected for a centipede. Rotate blocks and then Ctrl+click with the Paintbrush tool to color the empty spaces in this strip. Save in Sketchbook.

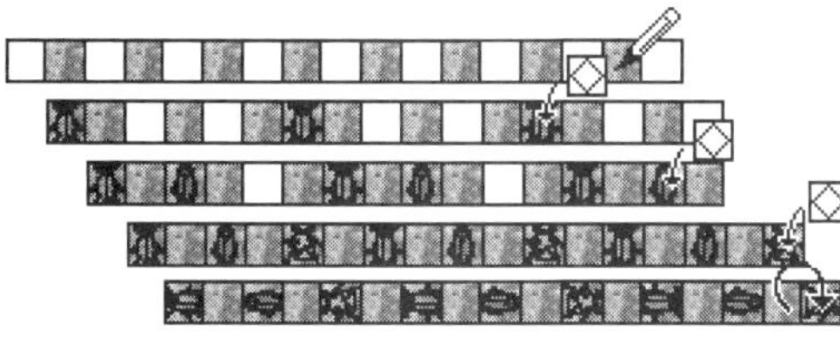

Step 2 – Set Eighth Strip

2 In the eighth strip, color alternate spaces with the Plain Block or Paintbrush tools. Set one of the three bug designs in your Sketchbook in each of the remaining spaces in this strip. Use the Rotate tool to turn the bugs in any direction. Save in Sketchbook.

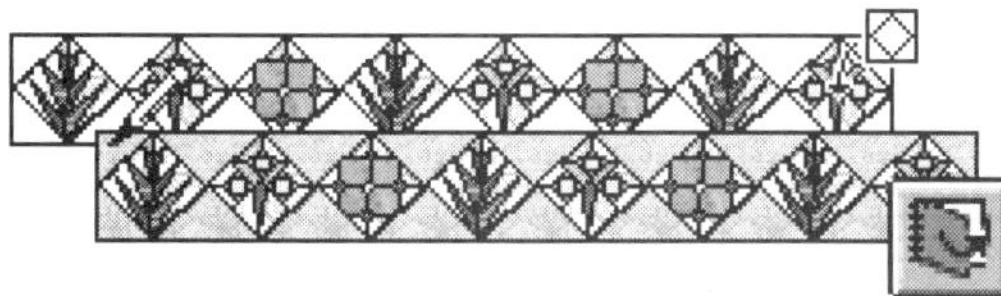

Step 3 – Set Seventh Strip and Save in Sketchbook

3 Set The Palm, Meadow Flower, and the Friendship Bouquet into the on-point spaces of the seventh strip. Ctrl+click with the Paintbrush tool to color all the setting triangles in this strip simultaneously. Save in Sketchbook.

Tip

- **When setting designs into any quilt layout, it is a good idea to save the layout in its various stages in your Sketchbook. This makes it easier to edit your design at any point, or to return to an earlier version if you are dissatisfied with how the design is developing.**

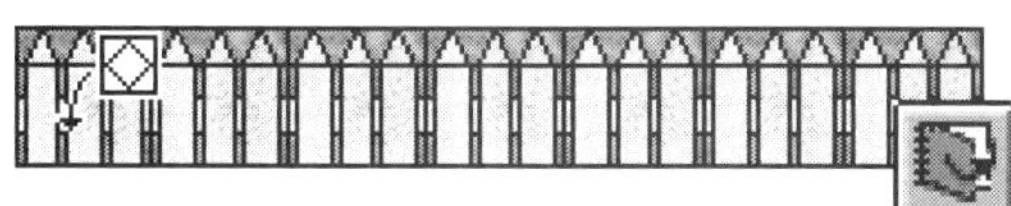

Step 4 – Set Sixth Strip and Save in Sketchbook

4 Ctrl+click to set the Picket Fence in the sixth strip. Save in Sketchbook.

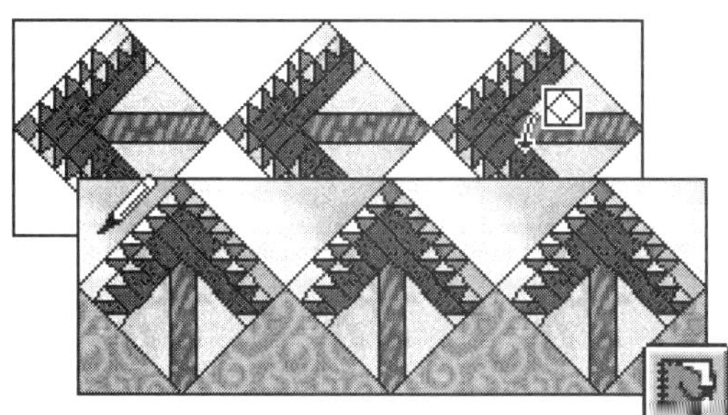

Step 5 – Set Fifth Strip and Save in Sketchbook

5 Use the Set tool to place the Proud Pine in the fifth strip. Rotate the blocks and then use the Paintbrush tool to color the setting triangles in this strip individually. Save in Sketchbook.

9

6 In the fourth strip, color alternate spaces with the Plain Block or Paintbrush tools. Set a Flying Geese I block in each of the remaining empty spaces in this strip. Use the Rotate tool to turn the geese in one direction. Save in Sketchbook.

Step 6 – Set Fourth Strip and Save in Sketchbook

7 The third strip is intended to portray wooded mountains and a high mountain range with a lake. To achieve this effect, color one Log Cabin block in shades of green. Set this Wooded Mountain design in the triangles at the bottom of the third strip.

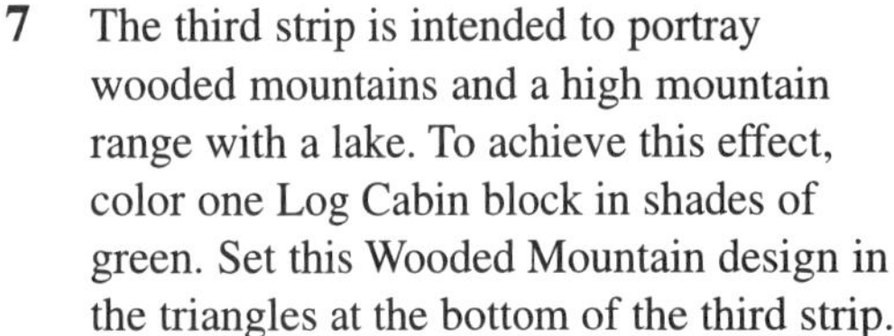

Create another coloring of the Log Cabin using shades of purple on the top half and shades of blue on the bottom half. Set this Mountain/Mountain Lake design in the whole block spaces in the third strip. Rotate all Log Cabins to the correct orientation. Save in Sketchbook. Use the Paintbrush or Plain Block tool to color the plain triangles at the top of this strip. Save in Sketchbook.

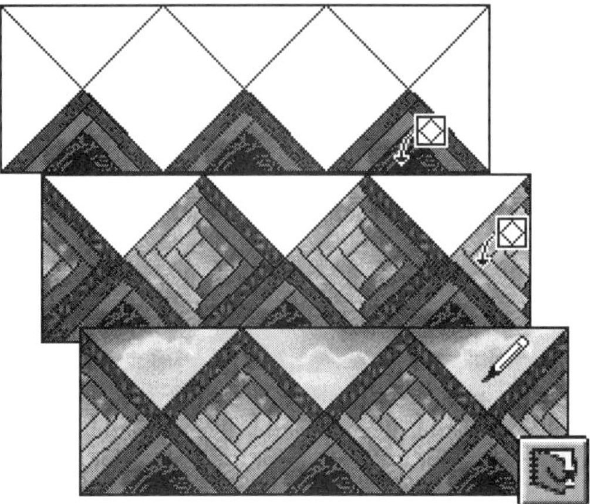

Step 7 – Set Third Strip and Save in Sketchbook

8 In the second strip, color alternate spaces with the Plain Block or Paintbrush tools. Set a Friendship Star block in each of the remaining empty spaces in this strip. Use the Flip tool to mirror image alternate stars. Save in Sketchbook.

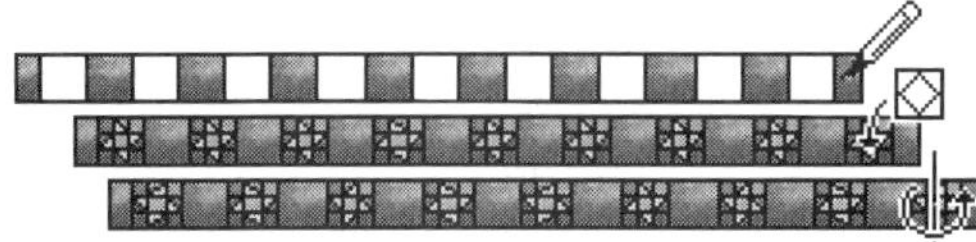

Step 8 – Set Second Strip and Save in Sketchbook

9 Set the Arkansas Snowflake block in the first strip, as shown. Set the Eight-Pointed Star in alternate spaces. Color the setting triangles in this strip. Save in Sketchbook.

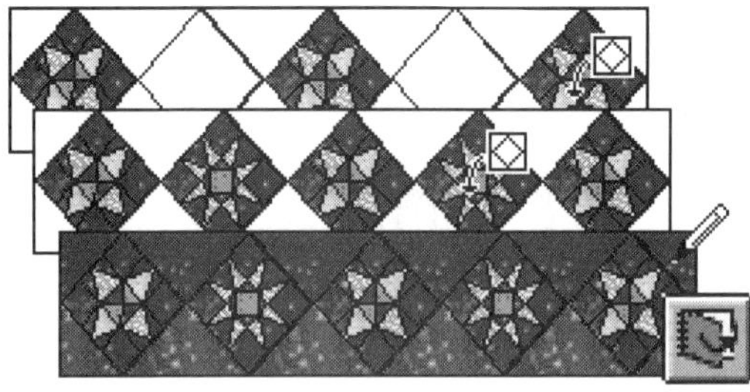

Step 9 – Set First Strip and Save in Sketchbook

10 Click on Layer 2 and use the Set tool to place two Butterfly motifs on the layout. With the Adjust tool and the Graph Pad, size the larger Butterfly motif to 4.000 x 4.000. Use the Rotation tool on the Graph pad to turn this Butterfly to a -45° angle. Position this design on the quilt layout, as shown.

Size the smaller Butterfly to 2.500 x 2.500. Rotate this motif to 45° and position this design on the quilt layout, as shown. Save in Sketchbook.

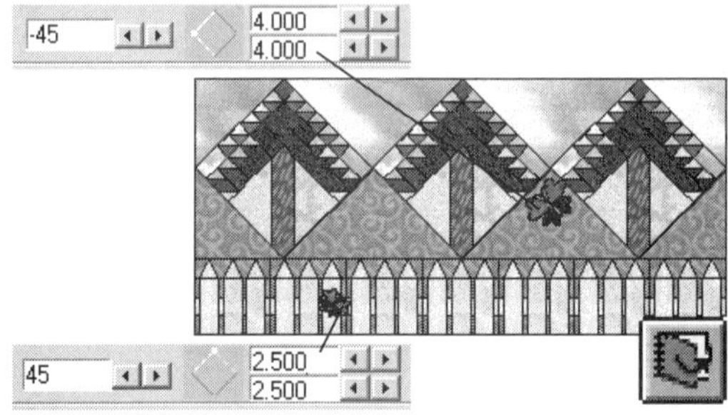

Step 10 – Place two Butterfly Motifs on the layout

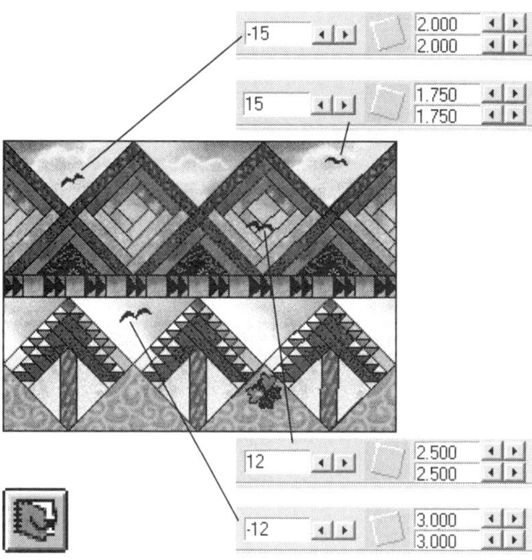

Step 11 – Place four Bird Motifs on the layout

11 Set four Bird motifs on the worktable. Size the first Bird motif to 2.000 x 2.000. Rotate the design to -15° and position it on the left side of the mountain range, as shown.

Size the second Bird motif to 1.750 x 1.750. Rotate the design to 15° and position it on the right side of the mountain range, as shown.

Size the third Bird motif to 2.500 x 2.500 set the rotation to 12°. Position this third Bird motif in the middle of the mountain range, as shown.

Set the fourth Bird motif to 3.000 x 3.000 and set the rotation to -12°. Position this Bird between the two pine trees on the left, as shown. Save in Sketchbook.

Tip

- **Remember that you can generate accurate printouts for the triangular blocks in a quilt layout. See "Printing Foundation Patterns for Triangular Blocks" and "Printing Templates for Triangular Blocks" in Lesson 7.**

Color Borders

Finishing the Quilt Design

Color the borders. Create Notecards for the block and quilt designs in the Sketchbook. Save.

Adding Designs and Fabrics to the User Libraries

1 Add your new designs to the Simplified Blocks library. Be sure to also copy the designs on the Motif and Stencil tabs.

2 Add any fabrics that you collected for this project to the Simplified Fabrics library.

Creating a Quilt Label

With EQ5, you can create a unique label for each of your quilt designs! You will design a simple label in this lesson, but feel free to experiment with more complex designs.

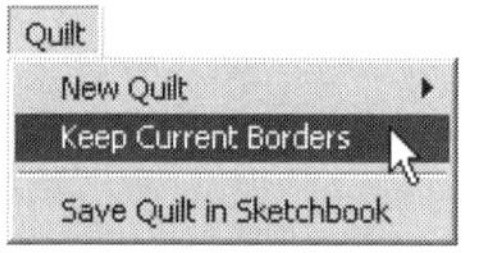

Step 1 – Uncheck Keep Current Borders

1 Click on Worktable and then click on Work on Quilt. Click on Quilt and uncheck Keep current borders. Click on Quilt, click on New Quilt, and then click on Horizontal.

2 Click on the Layout tab and set these values:

Number of blocks:	Horizontal – 1 Vertical – 1
Size of blocks:	Width – 6 Height – 6
Sashing:	Width – 0 Height – 0
Sashing border:	unchecked

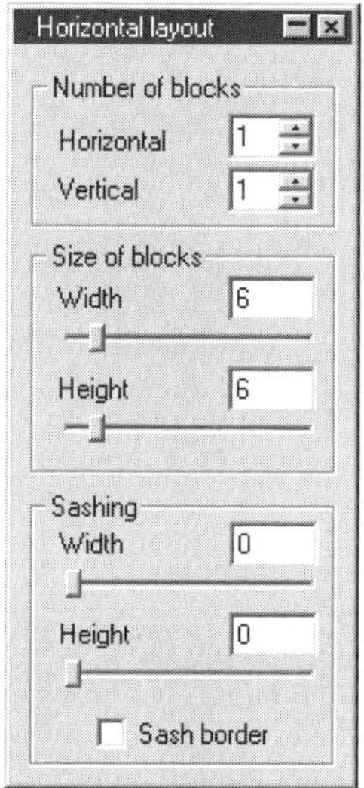

Step 2 – Layout Tab

3 Click on the Borders tab and set these values:

Border 1

Border style:	Tile Squares
Blocks in border:	Horizontal – 6

Border 2

Border style:	Mitered
Adjust size:	0.25 (Lock: All)

9

Step 4 – Layer 1 & Set Tool

4 Click on the Layer 1 tab and then click on the Set tool. Select a block or several blocks in the Blocks palette and set them into the Border.

5 Color the second border. Save in Sketchbook.

Here is a customized label for your new quilt!

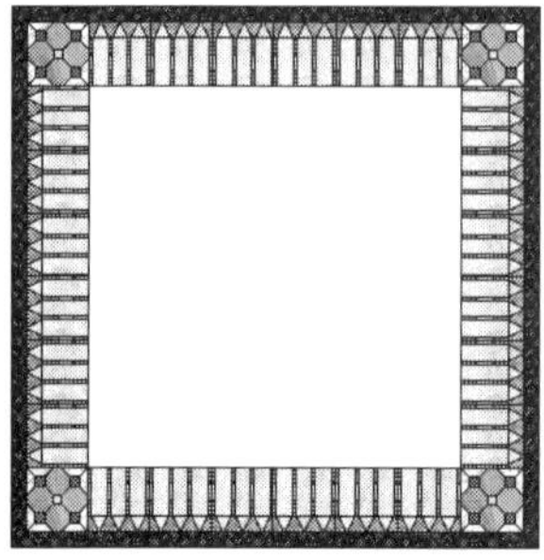

Step 5 – Color & Save in Sketchbook

Here is the finished quilt!

There are a variety of ways to finish this label. You can export this design and add text with a graphics or word processing program. You can export this label for digitizing with your embroidery software. You can print the label on fabric that has been specially treated with a fixative and add text with permanent pens. You can even print your label on T-shirt transfer paper. Any text you add to a design that will be printed on T-shirt transfer paper, however, must be mirror-imaged so that it is in the correct orientation in the final printout. Many printers now offer you this mirror-imaging option when you select transfer paper in the printer's Page Setup.

Experiment with the many options that are available for creating your own quilt label designs!

Tip

- **For information on exporting from EQ5, see "Exporting A Snapshot: Quilts and Blocks" in Lesson 3 or the EQ5 manuals and the Help file.**

Exiting EQ5

Click on File and then click on Exit.

Customizing a Layout

Lesson 10

Lesson 10 – Customizing a Layout

In addition to the wide range of layout choices that you have already discovered in EQ5, you also have the freedom and flexibility of Custom Set! This is a special layout that allows you to combine any arrangement of block styles and sizes to fill the central area of your quilt. In designing the quilt for this lesson, Patchwork Patio, you will learn to:

- *Establish a Custom Set layout*
- *Use the Selected Block coordinates*
- *Rotate on Layers*
- *Design a quilt backing*

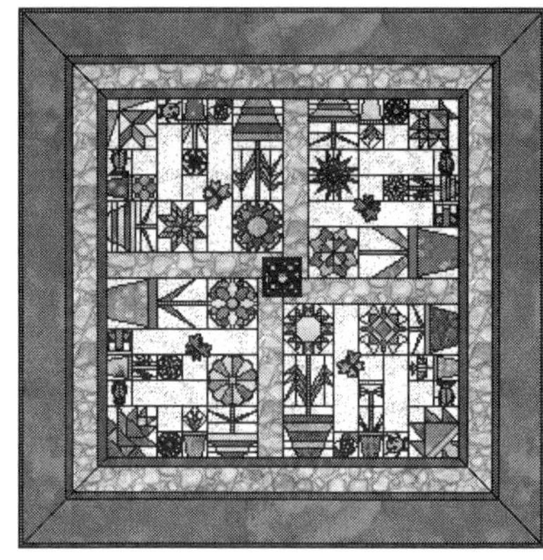

Patchwork Patio

Starting a New Project

Start a new project with the file name *Patchwork Patio*. This quilt is intended to be "scrappy" so begin the project with any palette, adding fabrics as you work. Remember that you can recolor the designs directly on the quilt layout.

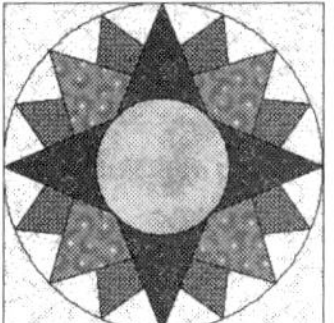

Circle Star

Courtyard

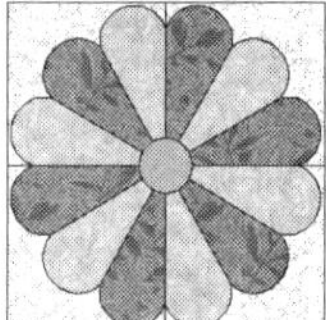

3 Petal Small Center Dresden Plate

Copying Designs from the Libraries

This quilt design is particularly flexible, so feel free to experiment by exploring the EQ5 Libraries and selecting different block designs than those listed here. Your goal is to create a pretty garden of your favorite patchwork blocks!

Blazing Star

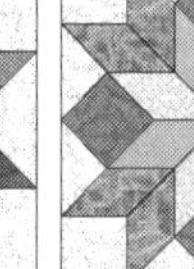

Love in a Mist

Wheel of Fortune

1 Use the Search feature in the EQ Libraries, or go directly to the libraries in this list to copy these designs.

1Classic Pieced / Compass & Wheels
   Circle Star
   Courtyard

10

1Classic Pieced / Dresden Plate
   3 Petal Small Center Dresden Plate

1Classic Pieced / Eight-Pointed Stars
   Blazing Star
   Love in a Mist

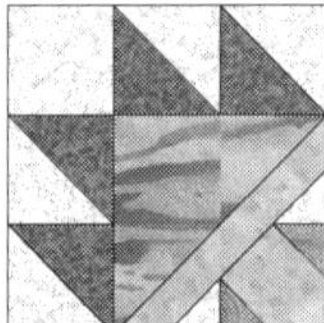

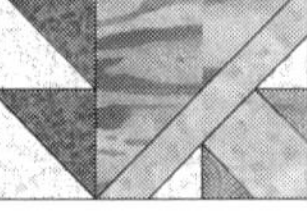

Texas Flower

Star of North Carolina

Grape Basket

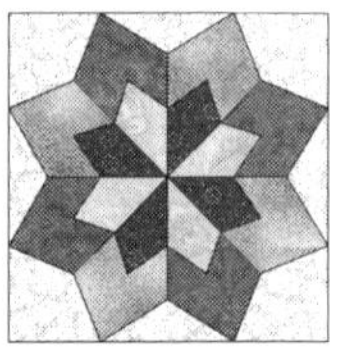

Double Star

Split 12 Point Star

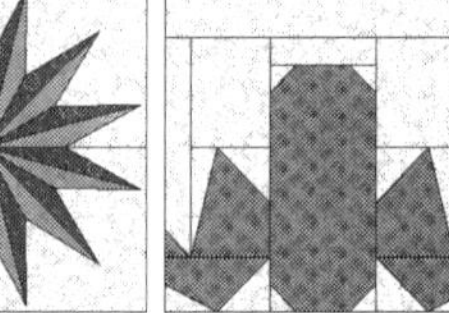

Frog Went A Courtin'

Lily Block

Amaryllis Bulb

Peony

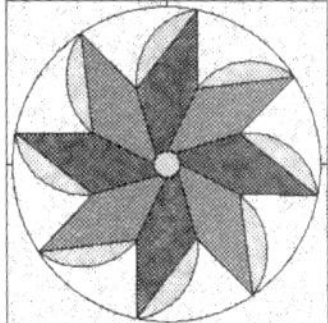

Star Dahlia

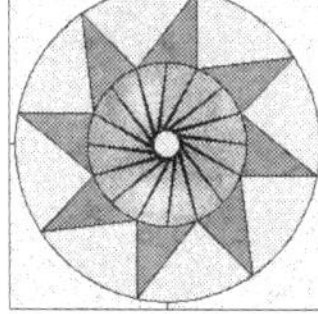

Kirsten's Star

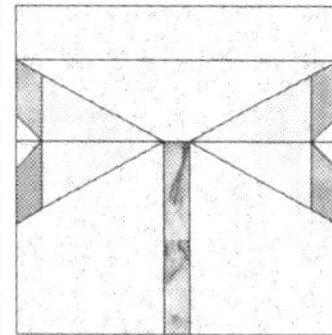

Lilies

Tulip Leaves

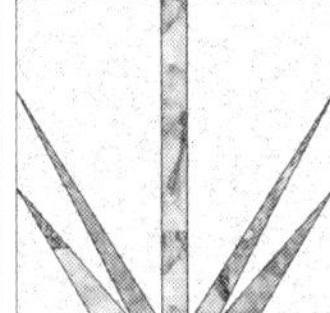

Daffodil Leaves

Iris Leaves

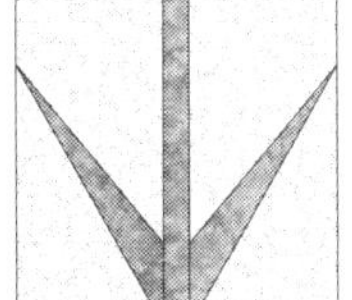

Stem and Leaves

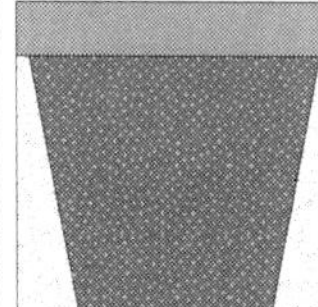

Flower Pot

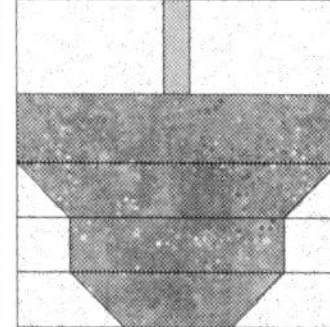

Ceramic Planter

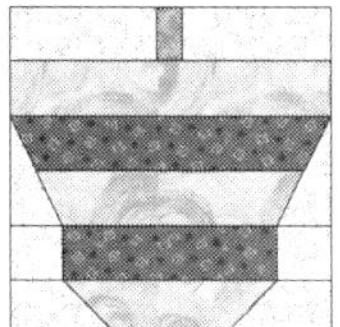

Striped Vase

Crocus

Snowdrop

Celtic Patch 4

See Lesson 9 for an illustration of these blocks:

- *Meadow Flower*
- *Snail's Trail*
- *Dizzy Spinner*
- *Beetle 1*
- *Beetle 2*
- *Ladybug*
- *Butterfly*

1Classic Pieced / Ladies Art Company
- Wheel of Fortune
- Texas Flower
- Star of North Carolina

1Classic Pieced / Pictures
- Grape Basket

1Classic Pieced / Stars
- Double Star
- Split 12 Point Star

2Contemporary Pieced / Fauna
- Frog Went A Courtin'

2Contemporary Pieced / Flora
- Lily Block
- Amaryllis Bulb
- Peony

2Contemporary Pieced / Spinning Suns
- Star Dahlia
- Kirsten's Star

3Paper Piecing / Flowerbed Foundations
- Lilies
- Tulip Leaves
- Daffodil Leaves
- Iris Leaves
- Stem and Leaves
- Flower Pot
- Ceramic Planter
- Striped Vase
- Crocus
- Snowdrop

5Contemporary Appliqué / Tile & Celtic designs
- Celtic Patch 4

User Libraries / Simplified Blocks
- Meadow Flower
- Snail's Trail
- Dizzy Spinner (or the design you used as a centipede in Lesson 9)
- Bugs (choose 3)
- Butterfly (motif)

2 Color (or recolor) the designs. Save in Sketchbook.

Drawing a Block in EasyDraw™

You will need a plain block for your quilt layout. Click on Block, click on New Block, and then click on EasyDraw™. Color this block with a neutral background. Save in Sketchbook. Create another coloring to use for the patio path. You can recolor these blocks later on the quilt layout, if necessary. Save in Sketchbook.

Plain block – Neutral Background

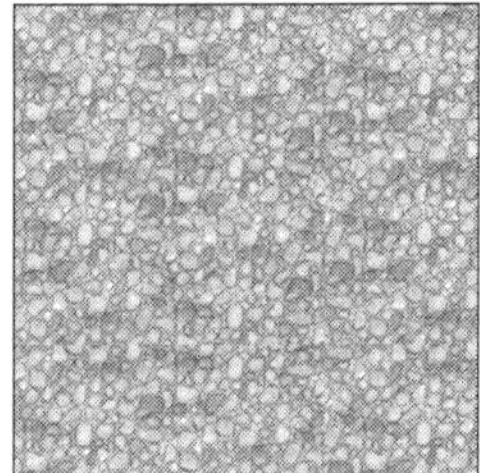

Plain block – Patio Path

Establishing a Custom Set Layout

You will notice that Custom Set is different from any other layout in EQ5 because the center design area is completely empty. You have total creative freedom to fill this space!

Quilt
New Quilt
Keep Current Borders
Save Quilt in Sketchbook
Horizontal
On-point
Variable Point
Baby Blocks
Variable Blocks
Horizontal Strip Quilt
Vertical Strip Quilt
One Patch Quilt
Custom Set

Step 1

Custom layout
Center Rectangle
Width 42
Height 42

Step 2

1 Click on Worktable and then click on Work on Quilt. Click on Quilt, click on New Quilt, and then click on Custom Set.

2 Click on the Layout tab. The Custom Set dialog box will open. Set these values.

Center Rectangle:	Width – 42
	Height – 42

3 Click on the Border tab and establish these borders. Border boxes 1 and 2 are illustrated here.

Border 1

Border style:	Mitered
Size:	1.00 (Lock: All)

Border 2

Border style:	Mitered
Size:	3.00 (Lock: All)

Border 3

Border style:	Mitered
Size:	1.00 (Lock: All)

Border 4

Border style:	Mitered
Size:	5.00 (Lock: All)

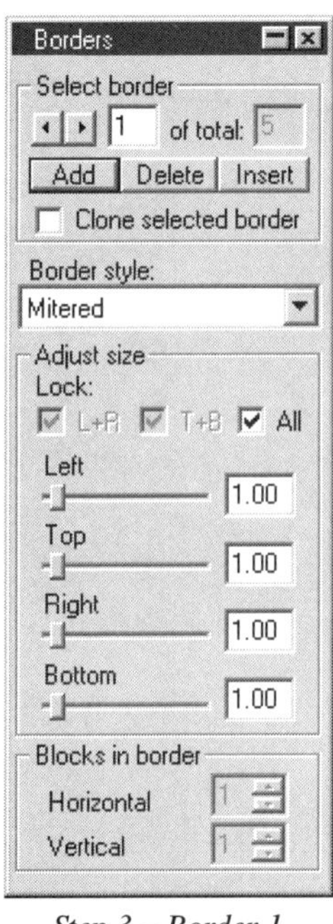

Step 3 – Border 1

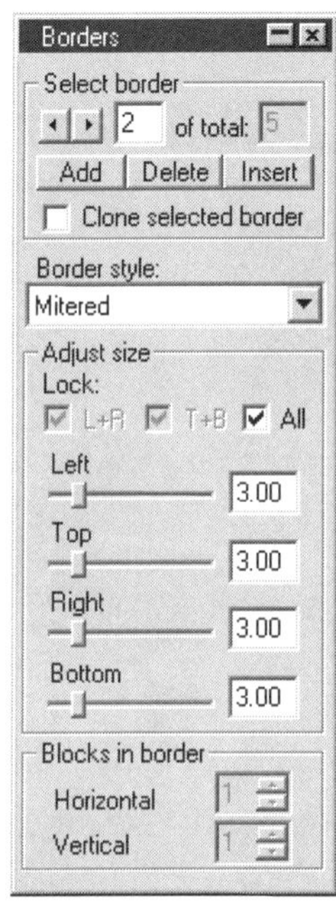

Step 3 – Border 2

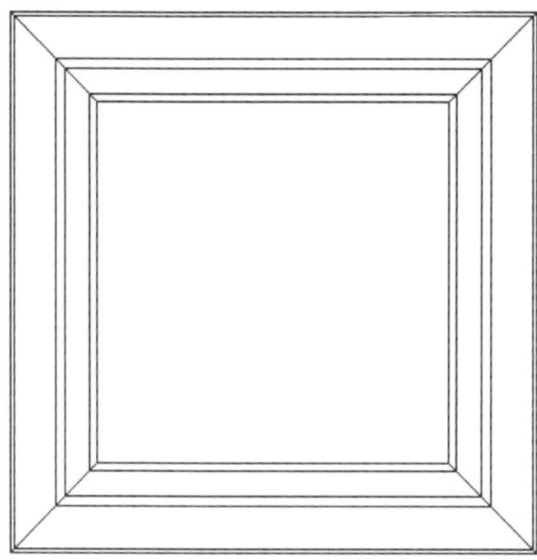

Quilt with all five borders set

Border 5

Border style:	Mitered
Size:	.50 (Lock: All)

This last border is intended to be the binding and will not add to the actual quilt dimensions.

4 Click on Layer 1 and Save in Sketchbook.

Step 4 – Layer 1 and Save in Sketchbook

Setting Blocks into the Layout

Throughout this tutorial you have used a variety of tools in combination with the Graph Pad to set appliqué and quilting stencils on Layers 2 and 3. You will use the same tools and techniques in this lesson as you set designs on Layer 1 in the Custom Set layout.

You will also discover how to use the Selected Block coordinates to ensure precise placement for designs on all Layers: Layer 1 (Custom Set), Layer 2 (appliqué), and Layer 3 (quilting stencils).

The Patchwork Patio quilt is easy to create! This design is composed of four sections or quadrants. You will create one quadrant and then copy the blocks in this section, pasting them into the remaining three quadrants. You will rotate the designs as necessary and then substitute different designs for variety. You will find that filling a Custom Set layout is as easy as piecing a puzzle!

Here is the Block Layout Diagram for the upper-left quadrant. Each of the other three quadrants is identical to this upper-left quadrant, but each is rotated to a different 90° orientation.

Block Layout Diagram for upper-left quadrant

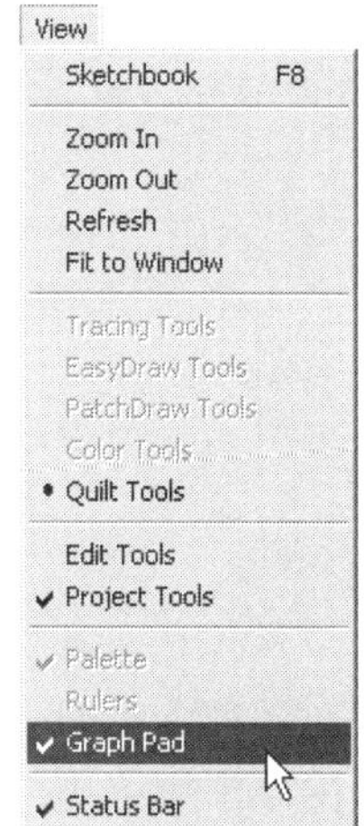

Step 1

1 Click on View in the main menu and then click on Graph Pad so that it is checked. The Graph Pad will open on the worktable but it will not be activated until you select a design with the Adjust tool.

2 Click on the Layer 1 tab and then click on the Set tool. Select the Peony block in the Blocks palette and set this block in the upper-left corner of the quilt layout. You will adjust the size and position of this block in the next steps.

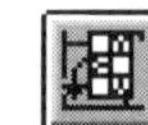

Step 2 – Set Tool

Step 2 – Peony block

Tip

- **Remember that to set designs on Layers, you must hold down the Shift key with the Set tool and drag the cursor diagonally to form the design on the worktable.**
- **Remember to use the zoom tools when necessary!**

3 Click on the Adjust tool, click on the Peony block, and set the size to 6" x 6" on the Graph Pad.

Step 3 – Adjust Tool

Reference Point for X & Y values

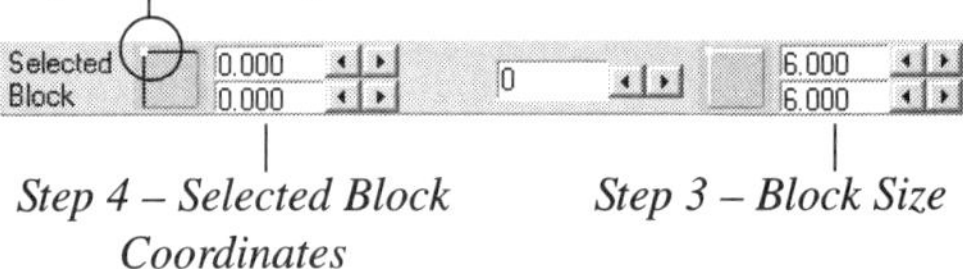

Step 4 – Selected Block Coordinates

Step 3 – Block Size

4 The first Graph Pad tool on the left is the Selected Block coordinates. The two numbers in this display (X and Y) show the location of the upper-left corner of the selected block in relation to the upper-left corner of the quilt's center design area. The white dot that you see on the small block diagram next to the coordinates is the reference point for these X and Y values.

The upper-left corner of the center design area of the quilt layout is the Zero Point, or 0, 0. This is 0 at the left edge (X) and 0 at the top edge (Y) of the center design area. All designs placed in a Custom Set layout are measured in relation to this point.

With the Peony still selected, click on the arrows in the Selected Block coordinates and set these values to 0, 0. The upper-left corner of the Peony block will now be perfectly aligned at the Zero Point! Click on the Rotate tool in the Quilt tools and rotate the Peony to the correct orientation. Save in Sketchbook.

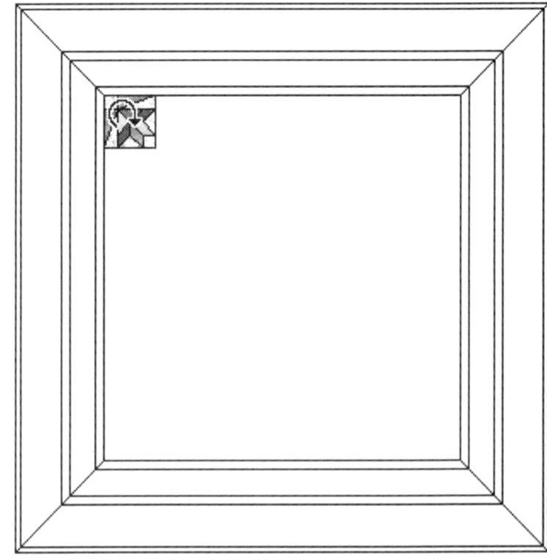

Step 4 – Rotate Peony Block

Step 4 – Save in Sketchbook

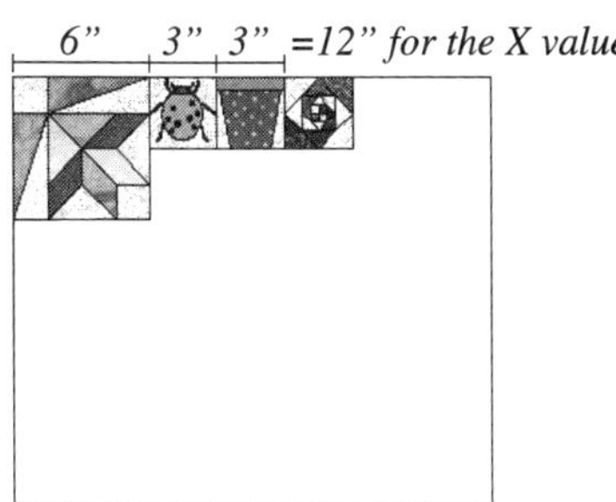

Tip – Snail Trail block has the coordinates (12,0)

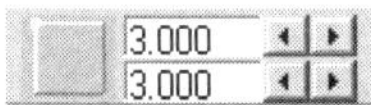

Step 5 – Block Size

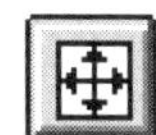

Same Width Same Height Tool

Align Top Tool

Step 6 & 7 – Same Width Same Height and Top Align

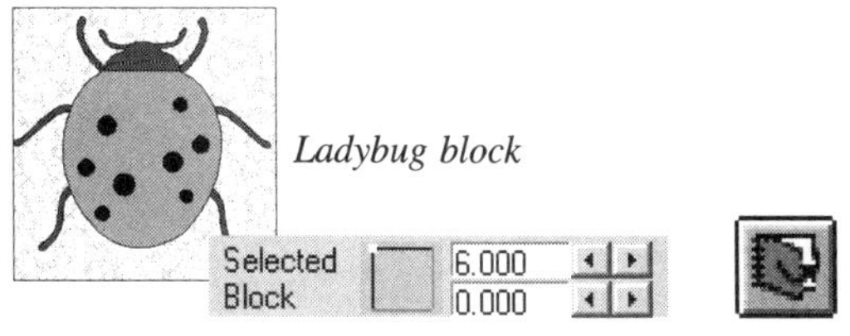

Ladybug block

Step 8 – Set Coordinates for Bug block and Save in Sketchbook

Tip

- **Block coordinates in the Custom Set layout reflect the location of the upper-left corner of the selected block, relative to the Zero Point (0, 0). Measuring from this Zero Point, you can easily calculate the correct X and Y coordinates for each new block that you add to the layout. Simply total the sizes of the blocks that are between the Zero Point and the upper-left corner of the new block.**

All blocks along the left edge of the center design area have 0 as the X coordinate. X indicates a point on the horizontal axis. All blocks along the top edge of the center design area have 0 as the Y coordinate. Y indicates a point on the vertical axis. You will now set several blocks along the top horizontal edge of the quilt layout and place them precisely using X and Y coordinates.

5 Click on the Set tool, select one of the bug blocks in the Blocks palette, and set it on the worktable, to the right of the Peony block. Size this block to 3" x 3" on the Graph Pad. Don't worry about correct placement and orientation at this point.

6 Set the Flower Pot block and the Snail's Trail block on the worktable. Using the bug block as a reference, size these blocks to 3" x 3" with the Same Width Same Height tool. Click off of the selection box to deselect.

7 Now, using the Peony block as a reference, select the three small blocks and align to the top. Since these blocks are now aligned along the top edge of the Peony block, which is also the top edge of the center design area, the Y coordinate for all three blocks is 0. Click off of the selection box.

8 Click on the bug block with the Adjust tool. Since the Peony block is 6" x 6", the upper-left corner of the bug block should be 6" from the Zero Point. Set the X coordinate of the bug block to 6. Save in Sketchbook

9 Select the Flower Pot block. Since the Peony block and the bug block total 9" in width, the upper-left corner of this block should be 9" from the Zero Point. Set the X coordinate of this Flower Pot block to 9. Save in Sketchbook.

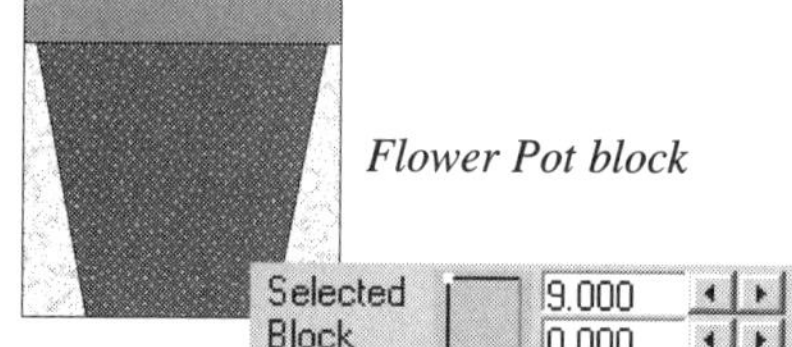

Step 9 – Set Coordinates for Flower Pot block and Save in Sketchbook

10 Select the Snail's Trail block. Since the Peony block, the bug block, and the Flower Pot total 12" in width, the X coordinate for the Snail's Trail should be 12. Save in Sketchbook.

Step 10 – Set Coordinates for Snail's Trail block and Save in Sketchbook

11 Set the Striped Vase block on the worktable and use the Peony block to size it to 6" x 6" and align it to the top. Since the distance from the Zero Point is 15", set the X coordinate to 15.

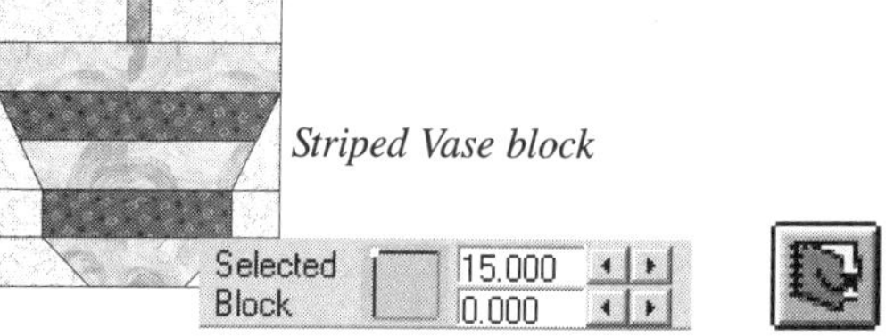

Step 11 – Set Coordinates for Striped Vase block and Save in Sketchbook

12 Rotate the blocks in this section to the correct orientation, using the Rotate tool in the Quilt tools. Save in Sketchbook.

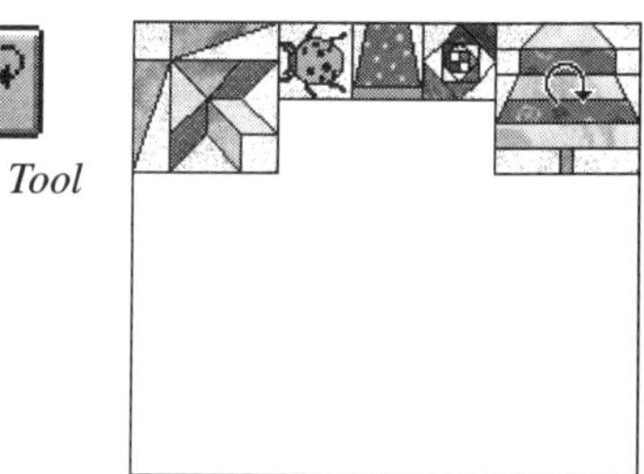

Rotate Tool

Step 12 – Rotate Blocks as shown

Tip

- **Occasionally a design will disappear when you switch tools, change screens, or use the Zoom tools. The easiest way to find a "lost" block on Layers is to highlight all of the designs on that Layer. Click on the Adjust tool and, holding down the Ctrl key, click on any design on the Layer. All of the designs on that Layer will highlight, including the "lost" design. Click off of the selected area to deselect.**

Now you will set several blocks along the left vertical edge of the quilt layout.

13 Set a second bug block under the Peony block and use the first bug block to size it to 3" x 3". Use the Peony block to align it to the left. This bug block is 6" down from the Zero Point, which is the width of the Peony block. With the X coordinate at 0, set the Y coordinate to 6. Save in Sketchbook.

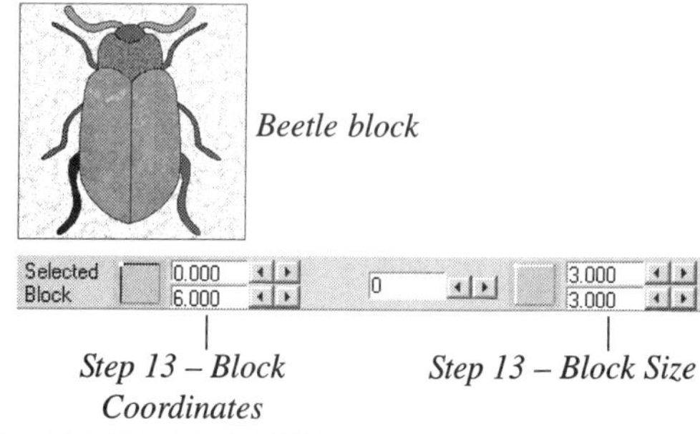

Step 13 – Block Coordinates

Step 13 – Block Size

10

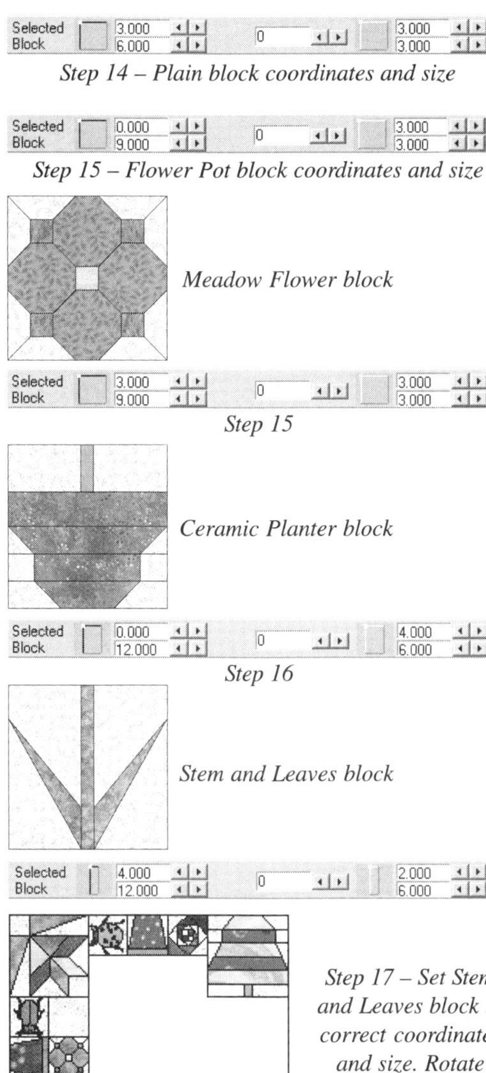

Step 14 – Plain block coordinates and size

Step 15 – Flower Pot block coordinates and size

Meadow Flower block

Step 15

Ceramic Planter block

Step 16

Stem and Leaves block

Step 17 – Set Stem and Leaves block to correct coordinates and size. Rotate blocks as shown.

Step 18 – Plain block coordinates and size

Blazing Star block

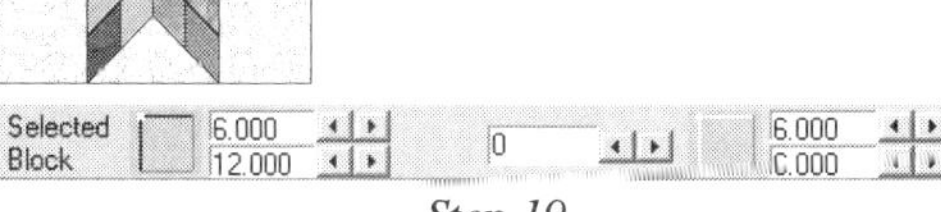

Step 19

14 Set a plain block to the right of this bug block. Use the bug block as a reference for the size and the top alignment. Set the coordinates for this plain block to 3, 6. These coordinates reflect the block's horizontal and vertical distance from the Zero Point. Save in Sketchbook.

15 Set a Flower Pot and a Meadow Flower on the worktable. Use the second bug block to size these designs. Use the second bug block to align the Flower Pot to the left. Use the plain block to align the Meadow Flower to the left. Set the Y coordinate for the Flower Pot at 9. Set the Y coordinate for the Meadow Flower at 9. Save in Sketchbook.

16 Set the Ceramic Planter on the worktable. Set the size to 4" x 6". Set the Selected Block coordinates to 0, 12. Save in Sketchbook.

17 Set a Stem and Leaves block on the worktable. Set the size to 2" x 6". Set the Selected Block coordinates to 4, 12. Use the Rotate tool in the Quilt tools to turn the blocks in this section of the layout to the correct orientation. Save in Sketchbook.

18 Set a plain block on the worktable and set the size to 3" x 9". Move the block to coordinates 6, 3. Save in Sketchbook.

19 Set the Blazing Star on the worktable and size to 6" x 6". Move the block to coordinates 6, 12. Save in Sketchbook.

Tip

- **With a little practice, you will be able to position designs visually and then simply adjust their locations until the coordinates are correct. You won't have to continually add and subtract to find the coordinates for the selected block. You can plan your Custom Set layouts in such a way as to simplify the placement process. For example, the fact that all of the blocks in this Patchwork Patio quilt are whole sizes means that the Selected Block coordinates for all designs on Layer 1 are whole numbers and will end in .000! This makes it significantly easier to check design placement in this layout.**

20 Set the Tulip Leaves, Kirsten's Star, and a plain block on the worktable. Use the Flower Pot block at the top of the layout to size these blocks and align them to the left. Adjust their coordinates to the following:

Tulip Leaves:	9, 3
Kirsten's Star:	9, 6
Plain block:	9, 9

Rotate the Tulip Leaves block to the correct orientation. Save in Sketchbook.

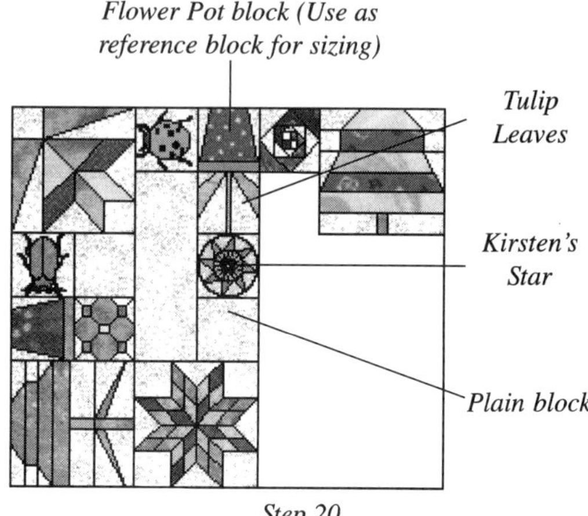

Step 20

21 Set a plain block on the worktable. Size to 3" x 15" and set the coordinates to 12, 3. Save in Sketchbook.

Step 21 – Plain block coordinates and size

22 Set the Iris Leaves and Circle Star on the worktable and use the Striped Vase block to size the blocks and align them to the left. Set to these coordinates:

Iris Leaves:	15, 6
Circle Star:	15, 12

Rotate the Iris Leaves block to the correct orientation. Save in Sketchbook.

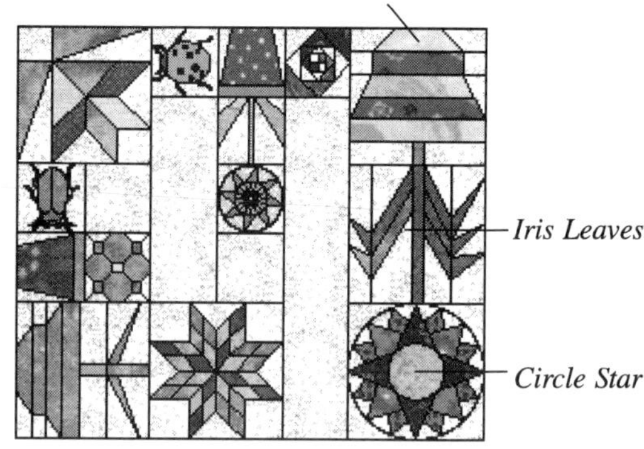

Step 22

23 Set a plain block on the worktable using the coloring you made for the patio path and size to 21" x 3". The coordinates for this block are 0, 18. Save in Sketchbook.

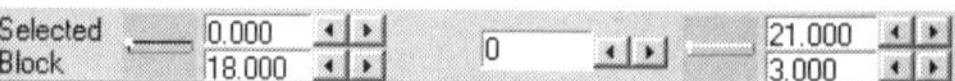

Step 23 – Plain block coordinates and size

Step 23 – Save in Sketchbook

Tip

- **In File / Preferences there are nudge settings and snap options for the Graph Pad. See the EQ5 manuals and the Help file for more information.**

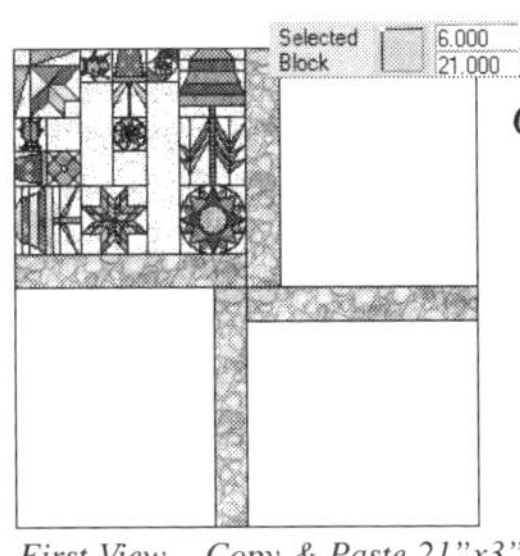

Graph Pad Rotation Tool

First View – Copy & Paste 21"x3" rectangle for garden path

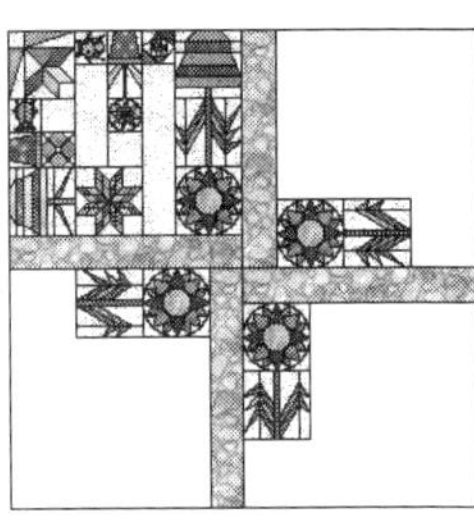

Second View

Third View

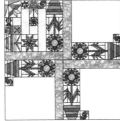

Fourth View

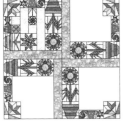

Fifth View

Sixth View

Seventh View

EighthView

Step 24

Substitute different designs for variety (see the color quilt for a larger view)

You have finished one quadrant in the quilt layout and you can now use this section to complete the remaining quadrants! The easiest way to do this is to copy and paste the individual blocks in this first quadrant into the other quadrants, working from the center of the quilt layout. You can replace the original designs with different blocks after you have completed the layout.

24 Copy and paste another 21" x 3" rectangle on the worktable. Rotate this block 90° with the Graph Pad Rotation tool and position it on the right side of the completed quadrant. Copy and paste another horizontal rectangle and another vertical rectangle, forming the garden path. Position them as shown. Save in Sketchbook.

Continue to fill the quilt layout with copied designs, working out from the center of the layout.

Use the Adjust tool, the Align tools, keyboard keys, and the Selected Block coordinates to position the blocks in the layout. Remember to save often!

After you have filled the entire design area on Layer 1, you can replace the designs with those in your Sketchbook or others that you have chosen from the Libraries.

Tip

- **To replace a design on Layers, click on the Set tool and then click on the replacement design on the Blocks palette. Click in the center of the design that you want to replace. The new design will replace the previous design.**
- **If you have checked Maintain block rotation under Layout Options in Preferences, the new design will be in the same orientation as the design it replaces. See the EQ5 manuals and the Help file for more information on this feature.**

Now you are ready to set the designs on Layer 2! There are five designs on this Layer: four Butterfly designs and one Patio Grate.

25 Click on Layer 2 and set four Butterfly motifs on the worktable. Size one to 4" x 4". Use this design as a reference for sizing the other three Butterfly motifs. Rotate each Butterfly, experimenting with the three rotation methods described in the Tip below. Save in Sketchbook.

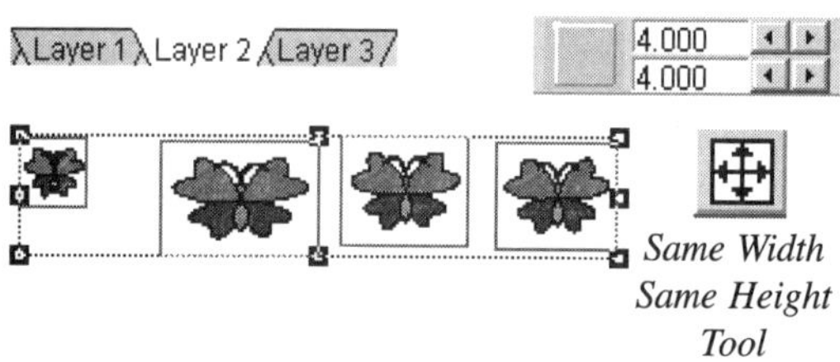

Same Width Same Height Tool

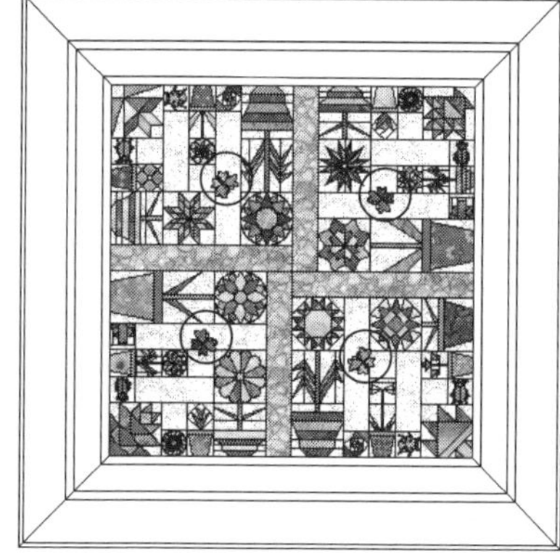

Step 25

Tip

- **There are three tools for rotating a design on Layers:**
- **The Rotate tool in the Quilt tools rotates a design clockwise by 90 degrees with each click. The pivot point is the center of the design.**
- **The Graph Pad Rotation tool rotates the block by one degree increments, up to 180 degrees in either direction. The pivot point is the upper left corner of the design.**
- **The Adjust tool rotates a design manually. The pivot point is the center of the design. Select a block with the Adjust tool. Hold down the Ctrl key and click on the directional arrows in the center of the design. A curved arrow will appear with the directional arrow cursor. Move the cursor over one of the corner nodes until only the rotation arrow remains. Drag the corner of the block clockwise or counter-clockwise to the desired orientation. Use the straight arrows to skew the design.**

Celtic Patch 4 (Patio Grate) block

Step 26

26 Set the Patio Grate block, size to 4.5" x 4.5", and position at 18.75, 18.75. Save in Sketchbook.

Finishing the Quilt Design

Color the borders and create a Notecard for the Patchwork Patio quilt design. Save.

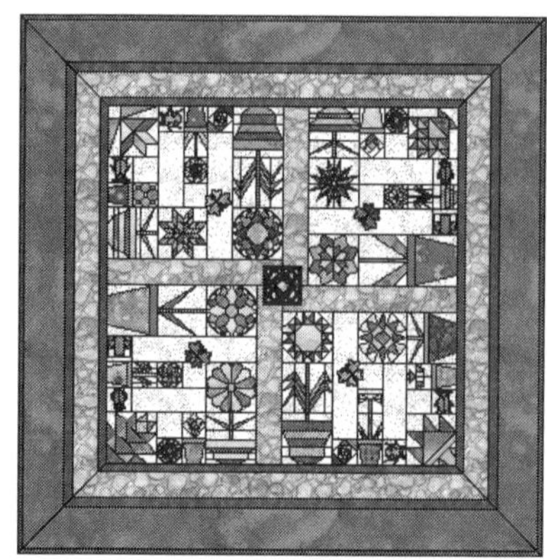

Color Borders

Adding Designs and Fabrics to the User Libraries

10

1 Add your new designs to the Simplified Blocks library.

2 Add any fabrics that you collected for this project to the Simplified Fabrics library.

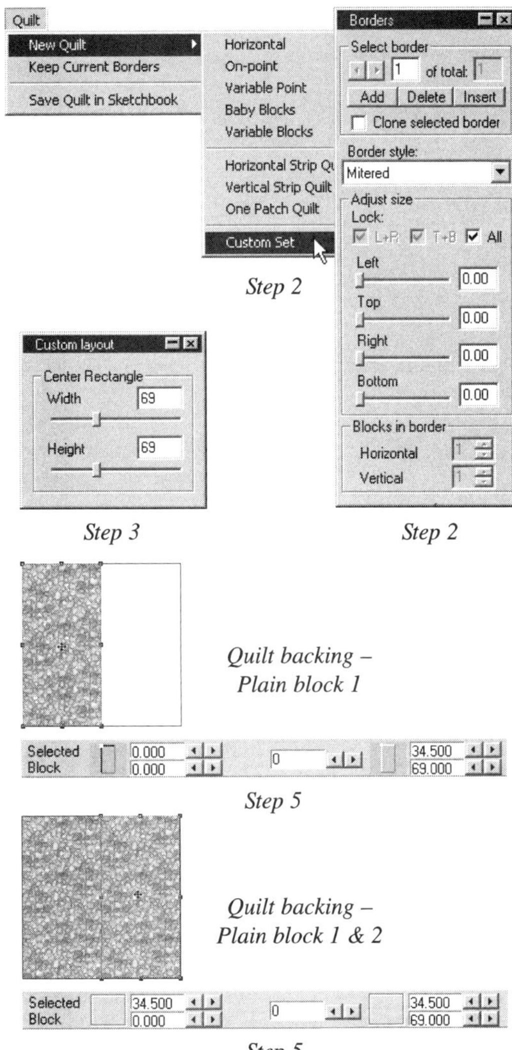

Step 1 – Quilt Size

Step 2

Step 3

Step 2

Quilt backing – Plain block 1

Step 5

Quilt backing – Plain block 1 & 2

Step 5

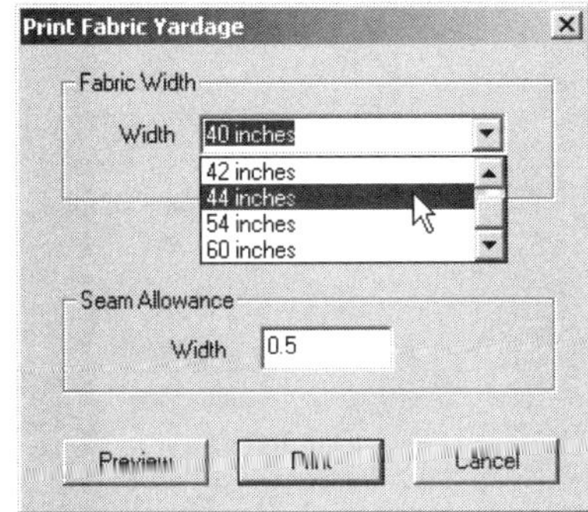

Step 6

Designing a Quilt Backing

Not only can you use EQ5 to design your quilt tops, but you can also use the program to piece your quilt backings! You can make these quilt backings as simple or as complicated as you would like because EQ5 makes it easy to experiment. The following instructions are for a basic quilt backing. Feel free to develop more advanced backing layouts, using leftover blocks and fabrics from your quilt tops.

1. Place the quilt on the worktable and note the finished size on the right side of the bottom bar. This Patchwork Patio quilt measures 63" x 63".

2. Click on Quilt, click on New Quilt, and then click on Custom Set. Click on the Borders tab and set the default border to "0.00".

3. Click on the Layout tab. Since the quilt backing should be no less than 6" wider and 6" longer than the finished quilt, set the Center Rectangle for the Patchwork Patio to 69" x 69".

4. You will need two panels to construct the backing for this 69" x 69" quilt, each measuring 34.5" x 69". Since this quilt is square, it doesn't matter if these panels are set horizontally or vertically. Experiment when designing a quilt backing for a rectangular quilt to determine which layout would provide more efficient coverage.

5. On Layer 1 set a plain block on the worktable and set the size to 34.5" x 69". Copy and paste another plain block on the worktable and use the Selected Block coordinates to align it accurately next to the first panel. Save in Sketchbook.

6. Click on File, click on Print, and click on Fabric Yardage. Select the appropriate fabric width and .5" seam allowances. Preview and Print. Be sure to create a Notecard for this backing layout.

10

Exiting EQ5

Exit EQ5.

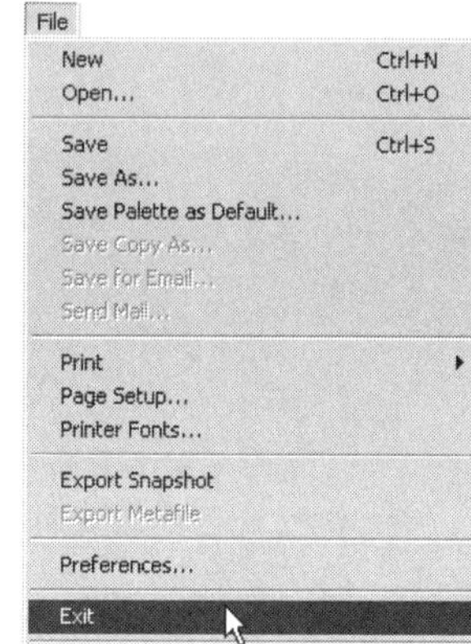

Exiting EQ5

CONGRATULATIONS! You have completed this tutorial and are well on your way to becoming an EQ5 expert! Here are your accomplishments:

You explored EQ5's vast Block and Fabric Libraries and incorporated a wide selection of these designs into the quilts that you developed here. You created your own customized fabric palettes and block collections and saved them in your personal libraries. You imported a fabric bitmap file into EQ5, used it in your project, and then added it to your personal fabric libraries. You sorted the Blocks and Fabrics palettes and rotated a directional fabric.

You discovered EQ5's sophisticated drawing tools and used them to create pieced, appliqué, and overlaid blocks. You drew block and border stencils. You edited, resized, deleted, flipped, rotated, and colored pieced and appliqué designs. You applied WreathMaker to make unique circular designs. You colored your designs and changed the color selections in your blocks and quilts with EQ5's versatile Color tools.

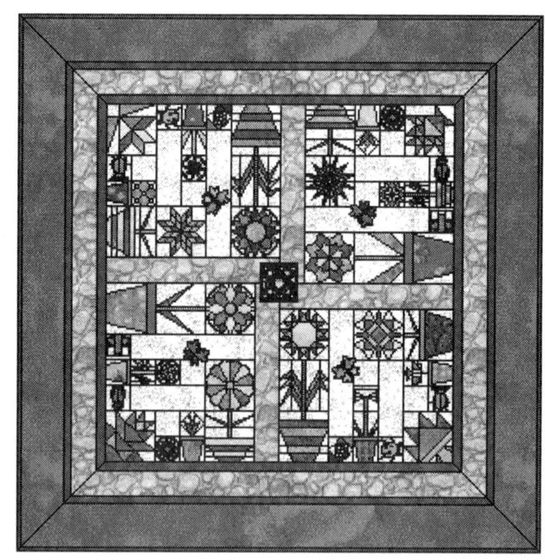

Here is the finished quilt!

You planned a variety of quilt layouts using EQ5's broad range of border styles and manipulated these layouts easily. You added sashing and Prairie Points, cloned borders and layout strips, and experimented with the Symmetry tool.

You superimposed appliqué and stenciling on your quilts. You generated fabric yardage requirements as well as rotary cutting instructions. You learned construction shortcuts, prepared a project for emailing, created a quilt label, and designed a quilt backing.

You generated a variety of printouts with the many printing options that EQ5 offers. You printed blocks, templates, foundation patterns, appliqué, stencils, and quilts. You created accurate patterns for triangular blocks. You exported your block and quilt designs as bitmap files, to the Windows clipboard, and to the printer.

You documented your individual EQ5 projects by creating Notecards for the Sketchbook designs. You saved your work and then retrieved these project files to create new designs. With this new EQ5 knowledge and experience, you can now approach quilt designing with total confidence, creativity, and control.

GOOD LUCK!

Index

Index

E

F

G

H

I

K

L

M

N

O

P

Q

R

S

T

Tools *Quick Reference*

EQ5 Tools *Quick Reference*

Project Tools

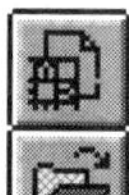 Create a New Project

 Open a Project

 Save

 Print

 Export Snapshot 

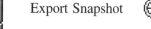

Export Metafile

 View Sketchbook

 Save in Sketchbook

 Zoom In 

 Zoom Out

 Refresh Screen

 Fit to Window

Edit Tools

 Cut

 Copy

 Paste

Quilt Tools

 Select tool 

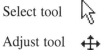

Adjust tool

 Tape Measure tool 

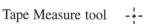

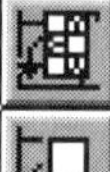 Set tool 

Plain Block tool

 Rotate tool 

Flip tool

Symmetry tool 

Color Tools

 Paintbrush tool 

Spraycan tool

 Swap tool 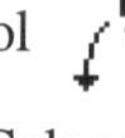

Thread Color tool

Eyedropper tool 

Fussy Cut tool 

 EQ4 Spraycan tool

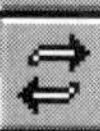 EQ4 Swap tool 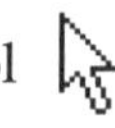

EasyDraw™/ Pieced Tools

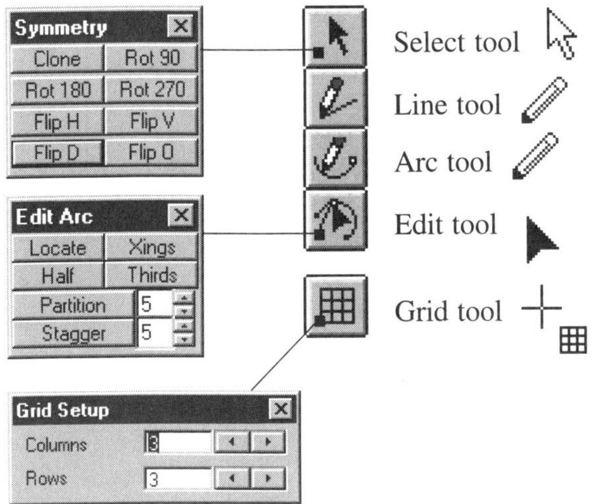

PatchDraw / Appliqué Tools

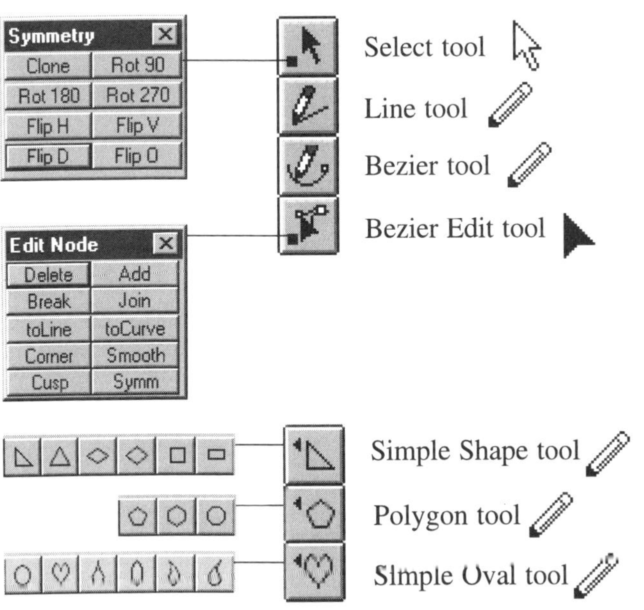

Graph Pad Tools

 Do not clip

 Clip to border of quilt

Clip to center rectangle of quilt

 Align left

 Align right

 Align top

 Align bottom

 Same width

 Same height

 Same width and height

To see these Graph Pad tools on your screen, see page 62 in Lesson 4.

About the Author

Fran Iverson Gonzalez, professional quilt designer and teacher, is the author of the widely acclaimed ***EQ Simplified*** tutorial series for the Electric Quilt program. She also designed EQ's two popular, instructive Internet Mystery quilts, ***Sky Lights*** and ***EQuinox***, and was a regular contributor to the Japanese quilt magazine **Patchwork Quilt Tsushin** in 2000-2001**.** She has quilted for over 25 years and has taught for 12 of those years. Fran has conducted hands-on EQ classes at the International Quilt Festival in Houston, TX and has taught at several major quilt shows. She also teaches a series of Electric Quilt classes online at **Quilt University** (www.quiltuniversity.com). Visit her website at: http://www.flash.net/~qltcnfig/

Fran lives in Edmond, Oklahoma with her husband Larry, a neuroscientist and college professor. They have a bright and talented daughter, Karen, and an ancient family cat, Bobbie Sox.